# PC Troubleshooting Pocket Book

Michael Tooley

NEWNES

Newnes
An imprint of Butterworth-Heinemann Ltd
Linacre House, Jordan Hill, Oxford OX2 8DP

℞ A member of the Reed Elsevier plc group

OXFORD   LONDON   BOSTON
MUNICH   NEW DELHI   SINGAPORE   SYDNEY
TOKYO   TORONTO   WELLINGTON

First published 1994
Reprinted 1995

**British Library Cataloguing in Publication Data**
A catalogue record for this book is
available from the British Library
ISBN 0 7506 1727 6


Typeset by 🅰 Tek-Art, Croydon, Surrey
Printed and bound in Great Britain by Clays Ltd, St Ives plc

# Preface

Sooner or later, most PC users find themselves confronted with hardware or software failure or the need to upgrade or optimise a system for some new application. The 'PC Troubleshooting Pocket Book' provides a concise and compact reference which describes in a clear and straightforward manner the principles and practice of fault finding and upgrading IBM PCs and compatible systems.

The book is aimed at anyone who is involved with the installation, configuration, maintenance, upgrading, repair or support of PC systems. It also provides non-technical users with sufficient background information to diagnose basic faults and carry out simple modifications and repairs.

In computer troubleshooting, as with any field of endeavour, there are a number of short-cuts which can be instrumental in helping to avoid hours of frustration and costly effort. I have thus included a number of 'tips' which will help you avoid many of these pitfalls. These snippets of information are the culmination of twenty years of practical computing experience, the past twelve of which has been with IBM and compatible systems.

The book also includes the commented source code for five diagnostic utilities. These programs have been written in Microsoft's immensely popular QuickBASIC and will help you to check and modify the configuration of your system as well as carry out routine tests and adjustments of such items as disk drives, printers and monitors. Microsoft's QuickBASIC is currently 'bundled' with MS-DOS 5.0 and 6.0 and it is eminently suitable for the complete beginner to programming. If you don't have access to Microsoft QuickBASIC, or if you would prefer not to type in the programs, a disk with fully compiled versions of the program listings is available (for further details please see Chapter 17). Finally, the programs may be freely adapted, copied and modified and you are encouraged to use them as the basis for your own personalised diagnostic routines.

Happy troubleshooting!

**Michael Tooley**

# Contents

# 1
# Introduction

PC troubleshooting covers a very wide variety of activities including diagnosing and correcting hardware faults and ensuring that systems are correctly configured for the applications which run on them. This chapter sets the scene for the rest of the book and explains the underlying principles of troubleshooting and fault finding.

## A word about you

This book makes very few assumptions about your previous experience and the level of underpinning knowledge which you might (or might not) have. You should at least be familiar with the basic constituents of a PC system; system unit, display, keyboard and mouse. In addition, you have probably had some experience of using DOS and/or Windows. That's all!

Don't panic if you are a complete beginner to fault finding and repair. You can begin by tackling simple faults and slowly gain experience by moving on to progressively more difficult (and more challenging) faults. With very little experience you should be able to diagnose and rectify simple hardware problems, install a wide variety of upgrades, and optimise your system by making changes to the CONFIG.SYS and AUTOEXEC.BAT files.

With more experience you will be able to tackle fault finding to 'replaceable unit' level. Examples of this could be diagnosing and replacing a faulty I/O card, a power supply, or disk drive.

Fault finding to component level requires the greatest skill. It also requires an investment in specialised diagnostic equipment and tools. Nowadays, however, component level fault finding is often either impractical or uneconomic; you may require equipment available only to the specialist and it may be cheaper to replace a card or disk drive rather than spend several hours attempting to repair it.

## Approach to troubleshooting

Whatever your background it is important to develop a systematic approach to troubleshooting right from the start. This will help you to cope with obscure as well as routine faults.
The following stages are typical:

(a) Perform functional tests and observations. If the fault has been reported by someone else, it is important to obtain all relevant information and not make any assumptions which may lead you along a blind alley.

(b) Eliminate functional parts of the system from your investigation.

(c) Isolate the problem to a particular area of the system. This will often involve associating the fault with one or more of the following:
    (i)    power supply (including mains cable and fuse)

(ii)    system motherboard (includes CPU, ROM and RAM)
(iii)   graphics adapter (includes video RAM)
(iv)   disk adapter (includes disk controller)
(v)    other I/O adapter cards (e.g., serial communications cards, modem cards, etc.)
(vi)   floppy disk drive (including disk drive cables and connectors)
(viii)  hard disk drive (including disk drive cables and connectors)
(ix)   keyboard and mouse
(x)    display
(xi)   software (including configuration programs such as CONFIG.SYS and AUTOEXEC.BAT)
(xii)  external hardware (such as a printer sharer or external drive)
(xii)  communications or network problems.

(d) Disassemble (as necessary) and investigate individual components and sub-systems (e.g., carry out RAM diagnostics, gain access to system board, remove suspect SIMM).

(e) Identify and replace faulty components (e.g., check SIMM and replace with functional component).

(f) Perform appropriate functional tests (e.g., re-run RAM diagnostics, check memory is fully operational).

(g) Re-assemble system and, if appropriate, 'burn-in'.

## TIP

If you have more than one system available, items such as the system unit, display, keyboard, and external cables can all be checked (and eliminated from further investigation) without having to remove or dismantle anything. Simply disconnect the suspect part and substitute the equivalent part from an identical or compatible system which is known to be functional

## Where to start

It is, perhaps, worth saying that a system which appears to be totally dead can be a much easier prospect than one which displays an intermittent fault.

Start at the beginning and move progressively towards the end. This sounds obvious but many would-be troubleshooters ignore this advice and jump in at a later stage. By so doing, they often make erroneous assumptions and all too often ignore some crucial piece of information.

## What to ask

If you are troubleshooting someone else's system you may be presented with a box and no information other than that 'it doesn't work'. It has to be said that the average user is remarkably inadequate when it comes to describing faults on items of technical equipment. Furthermore he/she rarely connects the circumstances which lead up to equipment failure with the actual appearance of the fault. For example, a PC which has been relocated to a shelf over a radiator is bound to be a candidate for a very early death...

If you do have to deal with non-technical users it is well worth producing your own checklist of questions. To help you, the questions that I regularly use are as follows:

1. Has the fault just appeared or has it got progressively worse?
2. Is the fault present all the time?
3. If the fault is intermittent, under what circumstances does the fault appear?
4. Did the system work satisfactorily before? If not, in what way were you dissatisfied with its performance?
5. Has the configuration of the system changed in any way? If so, how has it changed?
6. What action (if any) have you taken to rectify the fault?
7. How did you first become aware of the fault?
8. Did you hear, see, or smell anything when the system failed?
9. What was actually happening when the system crashed?

In addition, you may wish to ask supplementary questions or make a few simple suggestions such as:

10. Have you checked the power to the system?
11. Is the printer on-line and is it loaded with paper?
12. Is the network 'up and running'?

In judging what reliance to place on the user's responses, it usually helps to make some assessment of the level of the user's technical expertise. You can do this by asking a few simple (but non-technical) questions and noting what comes back. Try something along the following lines:

13. How long have you been using the system?
14. Is this the first PC that you have used/owned?
15. How confident do you feel when you use the system?

In any event, it is important to have some empathy with the user and ensure that they do not feel insulted by your questions. A user who feels ignorant or threatened may often consciously or subconsciously withold information. After all, the secretary who spills a cup of coffee over a keyboard is unlikely to admit to it within the boss's hearing...

# Categorising faults

It helps to divide faults into the following categories; hardware faults, software faults, and configuration problems. This book is organised on this basis.

## Hardware faults

Hardware faults are generally attributable to component malfunction or component failure. Electronic components do not generally wear out with age but they become less reliable at the end of their normal service life. It is very important to realise that component reliability is greatly reduced when components are operated at, or near, their maximum ratings. As an example, a capacitor rated at 25V and operated at 10V at a temperature of 20 deg.C will exhibit a mean-time-to-failure (MTTF) of around 200,000 hours. When operated at 40 deg.C with 20V applied, its MTTF will be reduced by a factor of 10 to about 20,000 hours.

## Software faults

Software faults can arise from a number of causes including defective coding, corrupted data, viruses, 'software bombs' and 'trojan horses'. Software faults attributable to defective coding can be minimised by comprehensive software testing before a product is released. Unfortunately, this doesn't always happen. Furthermore, modern software can be extremely complex and 'bugs' can often appear in 'finished' products due to quite unforeseen circumstances (such as

**TIP**

The mean-time-to-failure (MTTF) of a system can be greatly extended by simply keeping it cool. Always ensure that your PC is kept out of direct sunlight and away from other heat producing sources (such as radiators). Always ensure that ventilation slots are kept clear and there is adequate air flow around the system enclosure. Avoid placing tower systems under desks, in corners, or sandwiched between shelves.

changes in operating system code). Most reputable software houses respond favourably to reports from users and offer software upgrades, 'bug fixes' and 'work arounds' which can be instrumental in overcoming most problems. The moral to this is that if you don't get satisfactory service from your software distributor/supplier you should tell all your friends and take your business elsewhere...

In recent years, computer viruses have become an increasing nuisance. A persistent virus can be extremely problematic and, in severe cases, can result in total loss of your precious data. You can avoid this trauma by adhering to a strict code of practice and by investing in a proprietary anti-virus package.

### Configuration problems

Configuration problems exist when both hardware and software are operating correctly but neither has been optimised for use with the other. Incorrectly configured systems may operate slower or provide significantly reduced functionality when compared with their fully optimised counterparts. Unfortunately, there is a 'grey' area in which it is hard to decide upon whether a system has been correctly optimised as different software packages may require quite different configurations.

## A brief history of the PC

The original IBM PC was announced in 1981 and made its first appearance in 1982. The PC had an 8088 central processing unit and a mere 64K bytes of system board RAM. The basic RAM was, however, expandable to an almost unheard of total of 640K bytes. The original PC supported two 360K byte floppy disk drives, an 80 column x 25 line text display and up to 16 colours using a Colour Graphics Adapter (CGA).

The XT (eXtended Technology) version of the PC appeared in 1983. This machine provided users with a single 360K byte floppy drive and a 10M byte hard disk. This was later followed by AT (Advanced Technology) specification machines which were based on an 80286 microprocessor (rather than the 8088 used in its predecessors) together with 256K bytes of RAM fitted to the system board. The standard AT provided 1.2M bytes of floppy disk storage together with a 20M byte hard disk.

Not surprisingly, the standards set by IBM attracted much interest from other manufacturers, notable amongst whom were Compaq and Olivetti. These companies were not merely content to produce machines with an identical specification but went on to make their own significant improvements to IBM's basic specifications. Other manufacturers were happy to 'clone' the PC; indeed, one could be forgiven for thinking that the highest accolade that could be offered by the computer press was that a machine was 'IBM compatible'.

Since those early days, the IBM PC has become the 'de facto' standard for personal computing. Other manufacturers (such as Apple, Commodore and Atari) have produced systems with quite different specifications but none has been as phenomenally successful as IBM.

'386, '486 and Pentium-based systems now provide performance specifications which would have been quite unheard of a decade ago and which have allowed software developers to produce an increasingly sophisticated range of products which will support multi-users on networked systems as well as single-users running multiple tasks on stand-alone machines.

IBM compatible systems are now produced by a very large number of well known manufacturers including Viglen, Dell, Elonex, Dan Technology, Amstrad, and Research Machines. Machines are invariably produced to exacting specifications and you can be reasonably certain that the company will provide a good standard of after-sales service. Indeed, most reputable manufacturers will support their equipment for a number of years after it ceases to be part of a 'current product range'.

Finally, many small companies have begun assembling PC-compatible systems in recent years using individual components and boards imported from Far-East manufacturers. In many cases these systems offer performance specifications which rival those of well known brands, however the constituent parts may be of uncertain pedigree.

### Burn-in

Any reputable manufacturer or distributor will check and 'burn-in' (or 'soak test') a system prior to despatching it to the end-user. This means running the system for several hours in an environment which simulates the range of operational conditions in which the system in question is likely to encounter.

'Burn-in' can be instrumental in detecting components that may quickly fail either due to defective manufacture or to incorrect specification. In the case of a PC, 'burn-in' should continuously exercise *all* parts of the system, including floppy and hard disk drives.

---

**TIP**

It is always wise to 'soak test' a system following any troubleshooting activity (particularly if it involves the replacement of an item of hardware). Chapter 17 includes a program which you can use.

---

## Conventions used in this book

The following conventions have been used in this book:
1. Special keys and combinations of special keys are enclosed within angled braces and the simultaneous depression of two (or more keys) is indicated using a hyphen. Hence <SHIFT-F1> means 'press the shift key down and, whilst keeping it held down, press the F1 key'.
2. In addition, many of the special function keys (such as Control, Alternate, etc) have been abbreviated. Thus <CTRL> refers to the Control key, <ALT> refers to the Alternate key and <DEL> refers to the Delete key. <CTRL-ALT-DEL> refers to the *simultaneous* depression of all three keys.
3. DOS commands and optional switches and parameters have

all been shown in upper case. In practice, DOS will invariably accept entries made in either upper or lower case. Thus, as far as DOS is concerned, **dir a:** is the same as **DIR A:**. For consistency we have used upper case but you may make entries in either upper or lower case, as desired.

4. Where several complete lines of text are to be entered (such as those required to create a batch file) each line should be terminated with the <ENTER> key.

5. Unless otherwise stated, addresses and data values are given in hexadecimal (base 16).

# 2
# PC Fundamentals

An understanding of the basic operation of a microcomputer system is an essential first step to getting the best out of your PC. This chapter provides the basic under-pinning knowledge required to carry out successful upgrading and troubleshooting.

The chapter begins by describing the basic components of a microcomputer and how data is represented within it. The chapter includes a quick tour of a system with particular reference to the central processing unit (CPU), memory (ROM and RAM), and the means of input and output. The chapter concludes with a brief introduction to some of the facilities provided by an operating system.

## Microcomputer basics

The basic components of a microcomputer system are:

(a) a central processing unit (CPU);

(b) a memory, comprising both 'read/write' and 'read only' devices (commonly called RAM and ROM respectively); and

(c) a mass storage device for programs and/or data (e.g., a floppy and/or hard disk drive); and

(d) a means of providing user input and output (via a keyboard and display interface); and

(e) interface circuits for external input and output (I/O). These circuits (commonly called 'ports') simplify the connection of peripheral devices such as printers, modems, mice, and joysticks.

In a *microcomputer* (as distinct from a mini or mainframe machine) the functions of the CPU are provided by a single VLSI microprocessor chip (e.g., an Intel 8086, 8088, 80286, 80386, 80486, or Pentium). The microprocessor is crucial to the overall performance of the system. Indeed, successive generations of PC are normally categorised by reference to the type of chip used. The 'original' PC used an 8088, AT systems are based on an 80286, '386 machines use an 80386, and so on.

Semiconductor devices are also used for the fast read/write and read-only memory. Strictly speaking, both types of memory permit 'random access' since any item of data can be retrieved with equal ease regardless of its actual location within the memory. Despite this, the term 'RAM' has become synonymous with semiconductor read/write memory.

The semiconductor ROM provides non-volatile storage for part of the operating system code (this 'BIOS' code remains intact when the power supply is disconnected). The semiconductor RAM provides storage for the remainder of the operating system code (the 'DOS'), applications programs and transient data (including that which corresponds to the screen display).

It is important to note that any program or data stored in RAM will be lost when the power supply is switched off or disconnected. The only exception to this is a small amount of 'CMOS memory' kept alive by means of a battery. This 'battery-backed' memory (used on AT and later machines) is used to retain important configuration data, such as the type of hard and floppy disk fitted to the system and the amount of RAM present.

### TIP

It is well worth noting down the contents of the CMOS memory to avoid the frustration of having to puzzle out the settings for your own particular system when the backup battery eventually fails and has to be replaced. To view the current CMOS configuration settings press the 'Del' key during the boot-up sequence and enter the 'Setup' routine.

## Catching the bus

The basic components of the system (CPU, RAM, ROM and I/O) are linked together using a multiple-wire connecting system known as a 'bus' (see Figure 2.1). Three different buses are present (together with any specialised 'local' buses used for high-speed data transfer). The three main buses are:

(a) an 'address bus', used to specify memory locations;
(b) a 'data bus', on which data is transferred between devices; and
(c) a 'control bus', which provides timing and control signals throughout the system.

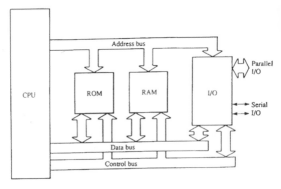

*Figure 2.1  Basic components of a microcomputer system*

## Expanding the system

In the generalised system shown in Figure 2.1, we have included the keyboard, display and disk interface within the block marked 'I/O'. The IBM PC provides the user with somewhat greater flexibility by making the bus and power connections available at a number of 'expansion connectors'. The connectors permit the use of 'adapter cards' (see Figure 2.2). These adapters allow the system to be configured for different types of display, mass storage device, etc. Commonly available expansion cards include: floppy and hard disk adapters, expansion memory cards, games (joystick) adapters, sound and video cards, internal modems, CD-ROM cards, and additional serial/parallel ports.

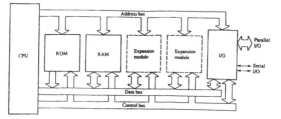

*Figure 2.2 System expansion using adapter cards*

## Clocks and timing

To distinguish valid data from the transient and indeterminate states
that occur when data is changing, all bus data transfers must occur
at known times within a regular cycle of 'reading' and 'writing'. Therefore the movement of data around a microcomputer system is syn-
chronised using a master 'system clock'. This signal is the basic heartbeat of the system; the faster the clock frequency the smaller the
time taken to execute a single machine instruction.

Some microprocessors have internal clock circuitry but the Intel
processor family requires the services of an external clock generator. The PC's clock signal is thus generated using external logic, the
basic timing element of which is a quartz crystal. This device ensures that the clock signal is both highly accurate and extremely
stable. The 'system clock' signal is then obtained by dividing this
fundamental output frequency by a factor of 4.

## Interrupting the system

Another control signal of particular note is the 'interrupt'. Interrupts
provide an efficient means of responding to the needs of external
hardware, such as a keyboard or a modem connected to the serial
port. The Intel family of processors provides interrupts which are
both 'maskable' and 'non-maskable'.

When a non-maskable interrupt input is asserted, the processor
must suspend execution of the current instruction and respond immediately to the interrupt. In the case of a maskable interrupt, the
processor's response will depend upon whether interrupts are currently enabled or disabled (when enabled, the CPU will suspend its
current task and carry out the requisite interrupt service routine).
The response to interrupts can be enabled or disabled by means of
program instructions (EI and DI respectively).

In practice, interrupt signals may be generated from a number of
sources and since each will require its own customised response a
mechanism must be provided for identifying the source of the interrupt and vectoring to the appropriate interrupt service routine. In
order to assist in this task, the PC uses a programmable interrupt
controller chip (based on an 8239A, or its equivalent).

A further type of interrupt is generated by software. These 'software interrupts' provide an efficient means of accessing the BIOS
and DOS services (see page 184 for an example of this).

## Data representation

The number of individual lines present within the address bus and
data bus depends upon the particular microprocessor employed (see

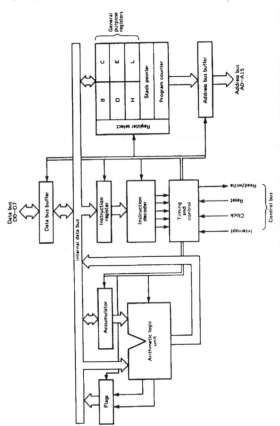

Figure 2.3  Simplified internal architecture of a CPU

Table 2.1). Some processors (notably the 80386SX, 80486SX, etc) only have a 16-bit external data bus to permit the use of a lower-cost motherboard whilst still retaining software compatibility with their full bus width processors (such as the 80386DX, 80486DX, etc).

Signals on all lines, no matter whether they are used for address, data, or control, can exist in only two basic states: logic 0 ('low') or logic 1 ('high'). Data and addresses are represented by binary numbers (a sequence of 1s and 0s) that appear respectively on the data and address bus.

The largest binary number that can appear on a 16-bit data bus corresponds to the condition when all sixteen of the lines are at logic 1. Therefore the largest value of data that can be present on the bus *at any instant of time* is equivalent to the binary number 1111111111111111 (or 65535). Similarly, the highest address that can appear on a 20-bit address bus is 11111111111111111111 (or 1,048,575).

*Table 2.1  CPU specifications*

| Processor | Register size (bits) | Data bus size (bits) | Address bus size (bits) | Addressing range | Clock speed | Year of introduction (approx) |
|---|---|---|---|---|---|---|
| 8086 | 16 | 16 | 20 | 1Mb | 5, 8 | 1978 |
| 8088 | 16 | 8 | 20 | 1Mb | 5, 8 | 1979 |
| 80286 | 16 | 16 | 24 | 16Mb | 12, 16, 20 | 1982 |
| 80386DX | 32 | 32 | 32 | 4Gb | 16, 20, 25, 33, 40 | 1985 |
| 80386SX | 32 | 16 | 24 | 16Mb | 16, 20, 25 | 1988 |
| 80486DX | 32 | 32 | 32 | 4Gb | 25, 33, 50 | 1989 |
| 80486SX | 32 | 32 | 32 | 4Gb | 20, 25 | 1991 |
| Pentium | 32 | 32 | 32 | 4Gb | 25, 33, 50, 66 | 1992 |

## Binary and hexadecimal

For convenience, the binary data present within a system is often converted to hexadecimal (base 16). This format is easier for mere humans to comprehend and offers the advantage over denary (base 10) in that it can be converted to and from binary with ease. The first sixteen numbers in binary, denary, and hexadecimal are shown in Table 2.2. A single hexadecimal character (in the range zero to F) is used to represent a group of four binary digits (bits). This group of four bits (or single hex. character) is sometimes called a 'nibble'.

A 'byte' of data comprises a group of eight bits. Thus a byte can be represented by just two hex. characters. A group of sixteen bits (a 'word') can be represented by four hex. characters, thirty-two bits (a 'double word') by eight hex. characters, and so on.

### TIP

The value of a byte expressed in binary can be easily converted to hexadecimal by arranging the bits in groups of four and converting each nibble into hexadecimal using Table 2.2. Taking 10100011 as an example; 1010=A and 0011=3 thus 10100011 can be represented by hex. A3.

*Table 2.2   Binary, denary and hexadecimal numbers*

| Binary (base 2) | Denary (base 10) | Hexadecimal (base 16) |
|---|---|---|
| 0000 | 0 | 0 |
| 0001 | 1 | 1 |
| 0010 | 2 | 2 |
| 0011 | 3 | 3 |
| 0100 | 4 | 4 |
| 0101 | 5 | 5 |
| 0110 | 6 | 6 |
| 0111 | 7 | 7 |
| 1000 | 8 | 8 |
| 1001 | 9 | 9 |
| 1010 | 10 | A |
| 1011 | 11 | B |
| 1100 | 12 | C |
| 1101 | 13 | D |
| 1110 | 14 | E |
| 1111 | 15 | F |

## Data in memory

A byte of data can be stored at each address within the total memory space of a computer. Hence one byte can be stored at each of the 1,048,576 memory locations within a machine offering 1Mbyte of RAM. In the case of words and double words, the least significant data byte is stored at the lowest memory address (a word will require two bytes of memory storage whilst a long word will require four bytes). To illustrate this, a byte of 3F, a word of 2C3E, and a double word of F0A29E41 are shown as they would appear stored in memory in Figure 2.4.

| Byte data | | Word data | | Double word data | |
|-----------|----|-----------|----|-----------------|----|
| | | | | Address + 3 | F0 |
| | | | | Address + 2 | A2 |
| | | Address + 1 | 2C | Address + 1 | 9E |
| Address | 3F | Address | 3E | Address | 41 |

*Figure 2.4  Comparison of byte, word, and double word data*

Individual bits within a word are numbered from 0 (least significant bit) to 15 (most significant bit). In the case of double words, the bits are numbered from 0 (least significant bit) to 31 (most significant bit). Negative (or 'signed') numbers can be represented using 'two's complement' notation where the leading (most significant) bit indicates the sign of the number (1 = negative, 0 = positive).

The range of integer data values that can be represented as bytes, words and long words are shown in the Table 2.3.

### Table 2.3  Data types

| | | |
|---|---|---|
| Unsigned byte | 8 | 0 to 255 |
| Signed byte | 8 | −128 to +127 |
| Unsigned word | 16 | 0 to 65535 |
| Signed word | 16 | −32768 to +32767 |
| Unsigned double word | 32 | 0 to 4294836225 |
| Signed double word | 32 | −1073741824.0 to 1073676289 |

## A quick tour of the system

To explain the operation of the microcomputer system shown in the Figure 2.1 in greater detail, we shall examine each major system component individually. We shall start with the single most important component of the system, the CPU.

### The CPU

The CPU forms the heart of any microcomputer and, consequently, its operation is crucial to the entire system. The primary function of the microprocessor is that of fetching, decoding, and executing instructions resident in memory. As such, it must be able to transfer data from external memory into its own internal registers and vice versa. Furthermore, it must operate predictably, distinguishing, for example, between an operation contained within an instruction and any accompanying addresses of read/write memory locations. In addition, various system housekeeping tasks need to be performed including responding to interrupts from external devices.

The main parts of a microprocessor are:

(a) registers for temporary storage of addresses and data;

(b) an 'arithmetic logic unit' (ALU) that performs arithmetic and logic operations; and

(c) a means of controlling and timing operations within the system.

The majority of operations performed by a microprocessor involve the movement of data. Indeed, the program code (a set of instructions stored in ROM or RAM) must itself be fetched from memory prior to execution. The microprocessor thus performs a continuous sequence of instruction fetch and execute cycles. The act of fetching an instruction code (or operand or data value) from memory involves a read operation whilst the act of moving data from the microprocessor to a memory location involves a write operation.

Microprocessors determine the source of data (when it is being read) and the destination of data (when it is being written) by placing a unique address on the address bus. The address at which the data is to be placed (during a write operation) or from which it is to be fetched (during a read operation) can either constitute part of the memory of the system (in which case it may be within ROM or RAM) or it can be considered to be associated with input/output (I/O).

Since the data bus is connected to a number of VLSI devices, an essential requirement of such chips (e.g. ROM or RAM) is that their data outputs should be capable of being isolated from the bus whenever necessary. These VLSI devices are fitted with select or enable inputs which are driven by address decoding logic (not shown in Figures 2.1 and 2.3). This logic ensures that ROM, RAM and I/O devices never simultaneously attempt to place data on the bus!

The inputs of the address decoding logic are derived from one, or more, of the address bus lines. The address decoder effectively divides the available memory into blocks corresponding to a particular function (ROM, RAM, I/O, etc). Hence, where the processor is reading and writing to RAM, for example, the address decoding logic will ensure that only the RAM is selected whilst the ROM and I/O remain isolated from the data bus.

Within the CPU, data is stored in several 'registers'. Registers themselves can be thought of as a simple pigeon-hole arrangement that can store as many bits as there are holes available. Generally, these devices are can store groups of sixteen or thirty-two bits. Additionally, some registers may be configured as either one register of sixteen bits or two registers of thirty-two bits.

Some microprocessor registers are accessible to the programmer whereas others are used by the microprocessor itself. Registers may be classified as either 'general purpose' or 'dedicated'. In the latter case a particular function is associated with the register, such as holding the result of an operation or signalling the result of a comparison.

The ALU can perform arithmetic operations (addition and subtraction) and logic (complementation, logical AND, logical OR, etc). The ALU operates on two inputs (sixteen or thirty-two bits in length depending upon the CPU type) and it provides one output (again of sixteen or thirty-two bits). In addition, the ALU status is preserved in the 'flag register' so that, for example, an overflow, zero or negative result can be detected.

The control unit is reponsible for the movement of data within the CPU and the management of control signals, both internal and external. The control unit asserts the requisite signals to read or write data as appropriate to the current instruction.

## Parallel input and output

The transfer of data within a microprocessor system involves moving groups of 8, 16 or 32-bits using the bus architecture described earlier. Consequently it is a relatively simple matter to transfer data into and out of the system in parallel form. This process is further simplified by using a Programmable Parallel I/O device (8255, or equivalent). This device provides registers for the temporary storage of data that not only "buffer" the data but also provide a degree of electrical isolation from the system data bus.

## Serial input and output

Parallel data transfer is primarily suited to high-speed operation over relatively short distances, a typical example being the linking of a microcomputer to an adjacent dot matrix printer. There are, however, some applications in which parallel data transfer is inappropriate, the most common example being data communication by means of telephone lines. In such cases data must be sent serially (one bit after another) rather than in parallel form.

To transmit data in serial form, the parallel data from the microprocessor must be reorganised into a stream of bits. This task is greatly simplified by using an LSI interface device that contains a shift register which is loaded with parallel data from the data bus. This data is then read out as a serial bit stream by successive shifting. The reverse process, serial-to-parallel conversion, also uses a shift register. Here data is loaded in serial form, each bit shifting further into the register until it becomes full. Data is then placed simultaneously on the parallel output lines. The basic principles of parallel-to-serial and serial-to-parallel data conversion are illustrated in Figures 2.5(a) and 2.5(b) respectively.

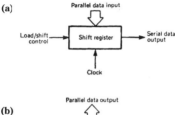

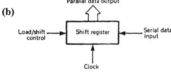

*Figure 2.5  Basic principles of parallel-to-serial and serial-to-paralel data conversion*

## Operating systems

Many of the functions of an operating system (like those associated with disk filing) are obvious. Others, however, are so closely related to the machine's hardware that the average user remains blissfully unaware of them. This, of course, is as it should be. As far as most end-users of computer systems are concerned, the operating system provides an environment from which it is possible to launch and run applications programs and to carry out elementary maintenance of disk files. Here, the operating system is perhaps better described as a 'microcomputer resource manager'.

The operating system provides an essential bridge between the user's application programs and the system hardware. In order to provide a standardised environment (which will cater for a variety of different hardware configurations) and ensure a high degree of software portability, part of the operating system (the 'DOS') is hardware independent. The hardware dependent remainder (the 'BIOS') provides the individual low-level routines required by the machine in question.

A well-behaved applications program will interact with the hardware independent (DOS) routines. These, in turn, will interact with the lower-level hardware dependent (BIOS) routines. Figure 2.6 illustrates this important point.

The operating system also provides the user with a number of utility programs which can be used for housekeeping tasks such as disk formatting, disk copying, etc.

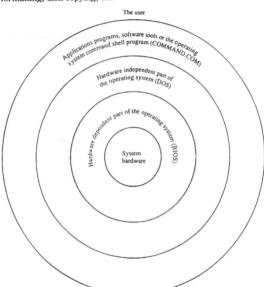

*Figure 2.6  Relationship between COMMAND.COM, DOS and BIOS*

In order to provide a means of interaction with the user (via keyboard entered commands and on-screen prompts and messages), the operating system incorporates a shell program (e.g. the COMMAND.COM program provided within MS-DOS).

In order to optimise the use of the available memory, most modern operating systems employ memory management techniques which allocate memory to transient programs and then release the memory when the program is terminated. A special type of 'terminate and stay resident' (TSR) program can remain resident in memory for execution whilst an application program is running.

**TIP**

TSRs can consume valuable memory which can, in some instances prevent applications programs from functioning correctly. Use the MEM /C or MEM /D command to determine which TSRs are present and how much of your valuable memory is being consumed!

# 3
# System Architecture and Construction

This chapter sets out to introduce the PC and provide an insight into the architecture, operation and construction of a 'generic PC'. This chapter also deals with the safety and static hazards associated with PC equipment.

## PC architecture

The term 'PC' now applies to such a wide range of equipment that it is difficult to pin down the essential ingredients of such a machine. However, at the risk of over-simplifying matters, a 'PC' need only satisfy two essential criteria:

(a) be based upon an Intel 16 or 32-bit processor (such as an 80x86, Pentium, or an equivalent device)

(b) be able to support the MS-DOS, PC-DOS, DR-DOS or a compatible operating system.

Other factors, such as available memory size, display technology, and disk storage, remain secondary.

The generic PC, whether a 'desktop' or 'tower' system, comprises three units; System Unit, Keyboard, and Display. The System Unit itself comprises three items; System Board, Power Supply, and Floppy/Hard Disk Drives.

The original IBM PC System Board employed approximately 100 IC devices including an 8088 CPU, an 8259A Interrupt Controller, an optional 8087 Maths Coprocessor, an 8288 Bus Controller, an 8284A Clock Generator, an 8253 Timer/Counter, an 8237A DMA Controller, and an 8255A Parallel Interface together with a host of discrete logic (including bus buffers, latches and transceivers). Figure 3.1 shows the simplified bus architecture of the system.

Much of this architecture was carried forward to the PC-XT and the PC-AT. This latter machine employed an 80286 CPU, 80287 Maths Coprocessor, two 8237A DMA Controllers, 8254-2 Programmable Timer, 8284A Clock Generator, two 8259A Interrupt Controllers, and a 74LS612N Memory Mapper.

In order to significantly reduce manufacturing costs as well as to save on space and increase reliability, more recent XT and AT-compatible microcomputers are based on a significantly smaller number of devices (many of which may be surface mounted types).

This trend has been continued with today's powerful '386 and '486-based systems. However, the functions provided by the highly integrated chipsets are merely a superset of those provided by the much large number of devices found in their predecessors.

## PC specifications

PC's tend to conform to one of the basic specifications shown in Table 3.1.

*Table 3.1  Typical PC specifications*

| Standard | Processor | RAM | Floppy disk | Hard disk | Graphics | Parallel port(s) | Serial port(s) | Clock speed |
|---|---|---|---|---|---|---|---|---|
| PC | 8088 | 256K | 1 or 2 360K | none | Text or CGA | 1 or 2 | 1 or 2 | 8 MHz |
| XT | 8088 or 80286 | 640K | 1 or 2 5.25" 360K | 10M | Text and CGA | 1 or 2 | 1 or 2 | 8 or 10MHz |
| AT | 80286 | 1M | 1 or 2 5.25" 1.2M | 20M | Text, CGA or EGA | 1 or 2 | 1 or 2 | 12 or 16MHz |
| 386SX-based | 80386SX | 1M to 8M | 1 or 2 3.5" 1.44M or 5.25" 1.2M | 40M | Text, VGA or SVGA | 1 or 2 | 1 or 2 | 16 or 20MHz |
| 386DX-based | 80386DX | 1M to 16M | 1 or 2 3.5" 1.44M or 5.25" 1.2M | 60M | Text, VGA or SVGA | 1 or 2 | 1 or 2 | 25, 33 or 40MHz |
| 486DX-based | 80486DX | 4M to 64M | 1 or 2 3.5" 1.44M | 100M | Text, VGA or SVGA | 1 or 2 | 1 or 2 | 25, 33 or 50MHz |
| PS/2 | 80286 or 80386 | 1M to 16M | 1 3.5" 720K or 1.44M | 44M, 70M or 117M | Text, EGA or VGA | 1 or 2 | 1 or 2 | 8, 10, 16 or 20MHz |

## TIP

With PC specifications things may not always be what they seem. For example, the XT specification is usually associated with an 8088 CPU operating at a very pedestrian 4.77MHz. A much improved version of the XT was, however, released two years *after* the launch of the AT. This machine has an 80286 processor and operates at 6MHz (it is about 2.5 times faster than its predecessor). This version of the XT is more correctly known as an 'XT-286' and its system board can be easily distinguished from a standard XT as both the CPU and the 80287 maths coprocessor are relocated to the *opposite* corner of the PCB when compared with an original XT.

## Architecture of a generic PC

Figure 3.1 shows the architecture of a generic 8088-based PC. There is more to this diagram than mere historical interest as all modern PCs can trace their origins to this particular arrangement. It is, therefore, worth spending a few moments developing an understanding of the configuration.

The 'CPU bus' (comprising lines A8 to A19 and AD0 to AD7 on the left side of Figure 3.1) is separated from the 'system bus' which links the support devices and expansion cards.

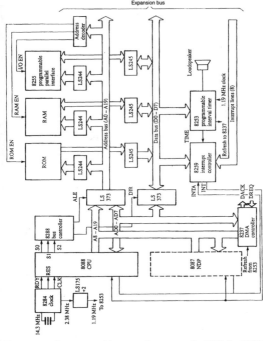

*Figure 3.1   System architecture for a generic 8088 (or 8086-based) PC*

The eight least significant address and all eight of the data bus lines share a common set of eight CPU pins. These lines are labelled AD0 to AD7. The term used to describe this form of bus (where data and address information take turns to be present on a shared set of bus lines) is known as 'multiplexing'. This saves pins on the CPU package and it allowed Intel to make use of standard 40-pin packages for the 8088 and 8086 processors.

The system address bus (available on each of the expansion connectors) comprises twenty address lines, A0 to A19. The system data bus comprises eight lines, D0 to D7. Address and data information is alternately latched onto the appropriate set of bus lines by means of the four 74LS373 8-bit data latches. The control signals, ALE (address latch enable) and DIR (direction) derived from the 8288 bus controlled are used to activate the two pairs of data latches.

The CPU bus is extended to the 8087 numeric data processor (maths coprocessor). This device is physically located in close proximity to the CPU in order to simplify the PCB layout.

The original PC required a CPU clock signal of 4.773MHz from a dedicated Intel clock generator chip. The basic timing element for this device is a quartz crystal which oscillates at a fundamental frequency of 14.318MHz. This frequency is internally divided by three in order to produce the CPU clock.

The CPU clock frequency is also further divided by two internally and again by two externally in order to produce a clock signal for the 8253 programmable interrupt timer. This device provides three important timing signals used by the system. One (known appropriately as TIME) controls the 8259 programmable interrupt controller, another (known as REFRESH) provides a timing input for the 8237 DMA controller, whilst the third is used (in conjunction with some extra logic) to produce an audible signal at the loudspeaker.

74LS244 8-bit bus drivers and 74LS245 8-bit bus transceivers link each of the major support devices with the 'system address bus' and 'system data bus' respectively. Address decoding logic (with input signals derived from the system address bus) generates the chip enable lines which activate the respective ROM, RAM and I/O chip select lines.

The basic system board incorporates a CPU, provides a connector for the addition of a maths coprocessor, incorporates bus and DMA control, and provides the system clock and timing signals. The system board also houses the BIOS ROM, main system RAM, and offers some limited parallel I/O. It does not, however, provide a number of other essential facilities including a video interface, disk and serial I/O. These important functions must normally be provided by means of adapter cards (note that some systems which offer only limited expansion may have some or all of these facilities integrated into the system board).

Adapter cards are connected to the expansion bus by means of a number of expansion slots (see Chapter 9 for further details). The expansion cards are physically placed so that any external connections required are available at the rear (or side) of the unit. Connections to internal sub-systems (such as hard and floppy disk drives) are usually made using lengths of ribbon cables and PCB connectors (see later).

## Typical system board layout

Figure 3.2 shows the system board layout of a generic 8088-based PC-XT. This general layout started with the original PC and has been carried forward with improvements and enhancements into a wide ange of PCs (including XT, XT-286, AT and compatible equipment).

The original PC's system board RAM was arranged in four banks, ach of which provides 64K of memory. This memory is supplied sing up to 36 conventional dual-in-line RAM chips. Bank 0 is the owest 64K of RAM (addresses 00000 to 0FFFF), Bank 1 the next 4K (addresses 10000 to 1FFFF), and so on. The XT uses a similar AM layout to the original PC but with larger capacity RAM chips (a otal of 512K on the system board). Additional memory can only be rovided by means of an appropriate adapter card.

The original AT motherboard ('AT Type 1') had its RAM organ-sed in two banks (Bank 0 and Bank 1). These accommodate up to 36 28K x 1 bit dual-in-line RAM chips. The later AT motherboard ('AT ype 2') and XT-286 machines use 'memory modules' (rather han individual RAM chips). See Chapter 6 for more information.

The major support devices (8288 bus controller, 8237A direct nemory access controller, etc) on all three basic specification ma-hines (PC, XT and AT) are clustered together on the right of the 'CB (as viewed from above). More modern machines use integrated upport chips and thus there are less (but more complex) devices resent on the motherboard. Furthermore, modern system boards nvariably use surface mounted components and pin-grid array (PGA) hips (rather than the conventionally soldered dual-in-line chips used n the original specification machines).

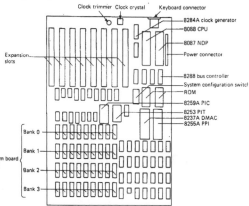

**Figure 3.2 Typical generic system motherboard layout**

**Figure 3.3 System board power connector**

# Wiring and cabling

Internal wiring within a PC tends to take one of three forms:

(a) power connections based on colour coded stranded wires (red black, yellow, etc)

(b) ribbon cables (flat, multi-core wiring which is often grey o beige in colour)

(c) signal wiring (miniature colour coded wires with strande conductors) used to connect front panel indicators, switches etc.

### TIP

Ribbon cables invariably have a coloured stripe at one end which denotes the position of pin-1 on the connector. Since some connectors are 'non-polarised' (i.e., it is possible to make the connection the 'wrong-way-round') you should always carefully check that the stripe is aligned towards the '1' marked on the PCB. Making the connection the 'wrong-way-round' can sometimes have disastrous consequences...

### Colour coding

The power supply wiring is invariably colour coded. The colour coding often obeys the following convention:

| | | |
|---|---|---|
| Red | +5V | Main system +5V supply rail. |
| Yellow | +12V | An ancillary supply rail used by disk drives, etc. |
| Black | ground/common/0V | This variously named rail links all ground and chassis points and also acts as the negativ 'return' for the +5V and +12V rails. |

Different colours may be used to denote other power supply voltag rails and signals. The colour scheme used by one popular 'clone manufacturer is shown in Table 3.2.

**Table 3.2 Typical colour coding convention for the system power connector in an AT-compatible machine** (you should no rely on this being the same in other machines)

| Power connector pin number (see Figure 3.3) | Voltage/signal | Colour |
|---|---|---|
| 1 | Power good | orange |
| 2 | +5V d.c. | red |
| 3 | +12V d.c. | yellow |
| 4 | -12V d.c. | blue |
| 5 | 0V/common | black |
| 6 | 0V/common | black |
| 7 | 0V/common | black |
| 8 | 0V/common | black |
| 9 | -5V d.c. | white |
| 10 | +5V d.c. | red |
| 11 | +5V d.c. | red |
| 12 | +5V d.c. | red |

# Making a connection

Several forms of connector are used within PC equipment; including PCB edge connectors (both direct and indirect types), IDC connectors, D-connectors, and DIN connectors.

## PCB edge connectors

PCB edge connectors (usually 34-way) are commonly used with 5.25" and some 3.5" disk drives. This type of connector is also found on many hard disk drives. The connector mates with the edge of the printed circuit board where the PCB tracks are brought out to gold plated contacts.

PCB edge connectors are also used for the conventional ISA (Industry Standard Architecture) expansion bus (see Chapter 9 for further details).

## IDC connectors

IDC (insulation displacement) connectors are commonly used on ribbon cables. These connectors (often 26-way or 34-way) use PCB mounted headers. The connector is 'forced' onto the ribbon cable and connection made (without soldering) by means of a special tool.

## D-type connectors

D-type connectors are invariably used for external connections. Most systems use one or more female 25-way D-connectors for the parallel printer interface together with one or more male 25-way or 9-way D-connectors for serial (RS-232) communications. D-connectors are also commonly used for connecting the display (see Chapter 13 for further information).

## DIN connectors

The PC's keyboard connection is invariably made using a 5-way DIN connector (see Figure 3.4). Several manufacturers (notably Amstrad) have used DIN connectors for other purposes (including display connection and system board power).

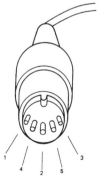
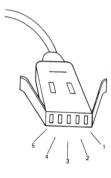

*Figure 3.4   Pin-numbering for the keyboard connector*

### TIP

Connectors can be a regular cause of problems on PC equipment. The older style direct contact edge connectors are particularly susceptible to problems which often first manifest themselves as intermittent faults causing random 'crashes' and 'lock-ups'.

### TIP

PCB edge connectors benefit from cleaning whenever a system is being overhauled. A PCB cleaning block (e.g., Maplin Electronic Component Supplies order code HX04E) and/or a can of aerosol PCB solvent cleaner (Maplin YJ45Y) is ideal for this purpose. In an emergency, or when no suitable cleaning materials are available, you should disconnect and reconnect the edge connector several times. The action of making and breaking the connection several times will often clear the offending oxide coating.

## Cooling

All PC systems produce heat and some systems produce more heat than others. Adequate ventilation is thus an essential consideration and fans are included within the system unit to ensure that there is adequate air flow. Furthermore, internal air flow must be arranged so that it is unrestricted as modern processors and support chips run at high temperatures. These devices are much more prone to failure when they run excessively hot than when they run cool or merely warm.

If the system unit fan fails to operate (and it is not thermostatically controlled) check the supply to it. If necessary replace the fan. If the unit runs slow or intermittently it should similarly be replaced.

### TIP

The '486 CPU produces a considerable amount of heat and often runs at an excessive temperature. You can significantly improve the reliability of the processor (and greatly extend its working life) by fitting a miniature CPU cooling fan. This inexpensive device (Watford Electronics) could save you a great deal of money!

### TIP

When fitting expansion cards and positioning internal ribbon cables, give some thought to the air flow within the system unit. In particular, it is worth trying to maximise the space between adapter cards (rather than have them sandwiched close together). You should also ensure that the ribbon cables do not impede the flow of air immediately behind the system unit fan.

## Dismantling a system

The procedure for dismantling a system depends upon the type of enclosure. The three examples that follow should at least give you some idea of the main points:

## Standard IBM PC, XT and AT system units

1. Exit from any program that may be running.
2. Type PARK to park the hard disk heads (if appropriate).
3. Remove the floppy disk(s) from the drive(s).
4. Switch the system unit power off (using the power switch at the rear of the system unit case).
5. Switch off at the mains outlet and disconnect the mains power lead.
6. Switch off and disconnect any peripherals that may be attached (including keyboard, mouse, printer, etc).
7. Disconnect the display power lead and video signal cable from the rear of the system unit. Remove the display and place safely on one side.
8. Remove the cover retaining screws from the rear of the system unit.
9. Carefully slide the system unit cover away from the rear and towards the front. When the cover will slide no further, tilt the cover upwards, remove the cover from the base and set aside.
10. You will now have access to the system board, power supply, disk drives, and adapter cards.

## Tower units

As steps 1 to 6 for a standard system plus:

7. Disconnect the display power lead and video signal cable from the rear of the system unit.
8. Remove the cover retaining screws from the rear of the system unit.
9. Carefully slide the system unit cover towards the rear until it is clear of the front fascia. Then lift the cover clear of the system unit. It is not usually necessary to remove the fascia.
10. You will now have access to the system board, power supply, disk drives, and adapter cards.

## Amstrad PC1512, PC1640

As steps 1 to 6 for a standard system plus:

7. Disconnect the display power lead and video signal cable from the rear of the system unit. Lift off the display from the recess in the upper case half and move to one side.
8. Depress the two tabs and then lift off the cover fitted to the expansion area at the rear of the system unit.
9. Remove the four long cross-point screws (two at the rear and two at the front fitted under the two snap-off plastic covers).
10. Remove the three smaller cross-point screws that retain the metal plate which secures the expansion cards.
11. Simultaneously slide the front plastic escutcheon forwards and the upper case half upwards, separating the two plastic mouldings in the process.
12. Remove the two-way PCB connector which links the battery holder with the system unit.
13. Remove the two-way PCB connector which links the front-panel power indicator to the system unit.
14. You will now have access to the system board, power supply, disk drives, and adapter cards.

### TIP

An egg-box (or similar container) makes an excellent receptacle for screws and small parts removed when you are dismantling a system.

### TIP

When a system uses a number of screws of similar size but of differing length, it is important to note the location of each screw so that it can be replaced correctly during re-assembly. A water-based felt-tip pen can be used to mark the screw sizes on the case.

### TIP

If you are building or assembling your own system, *always* start with the largest size enclosure. This will provide you with plenty of scope for expansion and allow you to upgrade more easily.

### Reassembly

System unit reassembly is usually the reverse of disassembly. It is, of course, essential to check the orientation of any non-polarised cables and connectors and also to ensure that screws have been correctly located and tightened. Under no circumstances should there be any loose connectors, components, or screws left inside a system unit!

## Safety first!

The voltages found in mains-operated PC equipment can be lethal. However, high voltages are normally restricted to the power supply and display. The lower voltages present on the system board, disk drives and adapter cards are perfectly safe.

When working *inside* the power supply or the display it is essential to avoid contact with any metal parts or components which may be at a high voltage. This includes all mains wiring, fuses and switches, as well as many of the components associated with the high-voltage a.c and d.c. circuits in the power supply.

It is always essential to switch-off and allow the capacitors to discharge *before* attempting to remove or replace components. Occasionally, you may need to test and/or make adjustments on 'live' circuits. In this event you can avoid electric shock hazards by only using tools which are properly insulated, and by using test leads fitted with insulated test prods.

### TIP

Another sensible precaution when making high-voltage measurements and adjustments is that of only working with one hand (you should keep the other one safely behind your back or in a pocket). This simple practice will ensure that you never place yourself in a position where electric current will pass from one hand and arm to the other via your heart. In such circumstances an electric shock *could be fatal*.

## Static hazards

Many of the devices used in modern PC equipment are susceptible
to damage from stray electrostatic charges. Static is, however, not a
problem provided you observe the following simple rules:

1. Ensure that your test equipment is properly earthed.
2. Preserve the anti-static wrapping supplied with boards and components and ensure that it is used for storage and also whenever boards or components have to be returned to suppliers.
3. Invest in an anti-static mat, grounding wire and wrist strap and
   use them whenever you remove or replace components fitted
   to a PCB.
4. Check your workshop or work area for potential static hazards (e.g., carpets manufactured from man-made fibres, cloth-
   ing made from synthetic materials, etc).

### TIP

When working within the system unit make sure that *you ground
yourself* by touching any grounded metal part (e.g., the case of
the power supply) *before* removing or replacing any parts or
adapter cards.

### TIP

When components are mounted on a PCB there are plenty of
paths which will allow static charges to drain safely away. Hence
you are unlikely to damage components by touching them when
they are in their correct locations on a PCB.

# 4
# Processor types and families

This chapter describes the main feature of each type of CPU used in a PC. It also explains how the CPU operates and how you can identify, remove and replace the device when it fails.

The CPU is crucial in determining the performance of a PC and the 80x86 family (see Table 4.1) has been consistently upgraded. The latest members of the family offer vastly improved performance when compared with their predecessors. Despite this, a core of common features has been retained in order to preserve compatabilty hence all current CPU devices provide a superset of the basic 8086 registers.

*Table 4.1  Intel 80x86 family*

| | 8086 | 8088 | 80186 | 80286 | 80386 (386) | 80486 (486) | Pentium |
|---|---|---|---|---|---|---|---|
| Data bus width (bits) | 16 | 8 | 16 | 16 | 32 | 32 | 32 |
| Internal data bus width (bits) | 16 | 16 | 16 | 16 | 32 | 32 | 32 |
| Clock rate typ. (MHz) | 5,8 | 5,8 | 6,8 | 12,16, 20 | 16,20, 25,33 | 25,33, 40,50 | 25,33, 50,66 |
| Linear memory addressing range (bytes) | 1M | 1M | 1M | 1M | 16M | 4G | 4G |
| I/O addressing range (bytes) | 64K | 64K | 64K | 64K | 64K | 64K | 64K |
| Internal FPU | No | No | No | No | No | Yes | Yes |
| Internal data cache | No | No | No | No | No | Yes | Yes |
| Protected mode | No | No | No | Yes | Yes | Yes | Yes |

# The 8086 and 8088

The original member of the 80x86 family, the 8086, was designed with modular internal architecture. This approach to microprocessor design has allowed Intel to produce a similar microprocessor with identical internal architecture but employing an 8-bit external bus. This device, the 8088, shares the same 16-bit internal architecture as its 16-bit bus counterpart. Both devices are packaged in 40-pin DIL encapsulations, the pin connections for which are shown in Figure 4.1. The CPU signal lines are described in Table 4.2.

*Table 4.2   8086 and 8088 signals*

| Signal | Function | Notes |
|--------|----------|-------|
| AD0-AD7 (8088) | Address/data lines | Multiplexed 8-bit address/data bus |
| AD0-AD15 (8088) | Addres/data lines | Multiplexed 16-bit address/data bus |
| A8-A19 (8088) | Address lines | Address bus |
| A16-A19 (8086) | Address lines | Address bus |
| S0-S7 | Status lines | S0-S2 are only available in Maximum Mode and are connected to the 8288 Bus Controller (U6). S3-S7 all share pins with other signals |
| INTR | Interrupt line | Level-triggered, active high interrupt request input |
| NMI | Non-maskable interrupt line | Positive edge-triggered non-maskable interrupt input |
| RESET | Reset line | Active high reset input |
| READY | Ready line | Active high ready input |
| TEST | Test | Input used to provide synchronisation with external processors. When a WAIT instruction is encountered, the 8088 examines the state of the TEST line. If this line is found to be high, the processor waits in an 'idle' state until the signal goes low. |
| QS0, QS1 | Queue status lines | Outputs from the processor which may be used to keep track of the internal instruction queue. |
| LOCK | Bus lock | Output from the processor which is taken low to indicate that the bus is not currently available to other potential bus masters. |
| RQ/GT0-RQ/GT1 | Request/Grant | Used for signalling bus requests and grants placed in the CL register. |

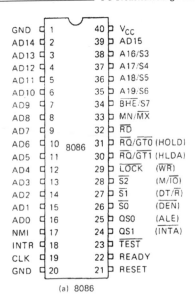

(a) 8086

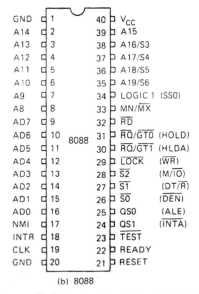

(b) 8088

*Figure 4.1  Pin connections for the 8086 and 8088 CPU*

## Architecture

The 8086/8088 can be divided internally into two functional blocks comprising an Execution Unit (EU) and a Bus Interface Unit (BIU), as shown in Figure 4.2. The Execution Unit is responsible for decoding and executing instructions whilst the Bus Interface Unit (BIU) prefetches instructions from memory and places them in an instruction queue where they await decoding and execution by the EU.

The Execution Unit comprises a general and special purpose register block, temporary registers, arithmetic logic unit (ALU), a flag (status) register, and control logic. It is important to note that the principal elements of the 8086 Execution Unit remains essentially common to each of the members of Intel's 80x86 microprocessor family but with additional 32-bit registers in the case of the 80386, 80486 and Pentium.

The BIU architecture varies according to the size of the external data bus. The BIU comprises four segment registers and an instruction pointer, temporary storage for instructions held in the instruction queue, and bus control logic.

## Addressing

The 8086 has 20 address lines and thus provides for a physical 1M byte memory address range (memory address locations 00000 to FFFFF hex.). The I/O address range is 64K bytes (I/O address locations 0000 to FFFF hex.).

The actual 20-bit physical memory address is formed by shifting the segment address four zero bits to the left (adding four least significant bits), which effectively multiplies the Segment Register contents by 16. The contents of the Instruction Pointer (IP), Stack Pointer (SP) or other 16-bit memory reference is then added to the result. This process is illustrated in Figure 4.3.

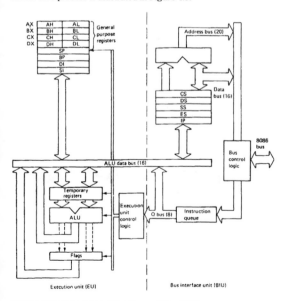

*Figure 4.2   Internal architecture of the 8086*

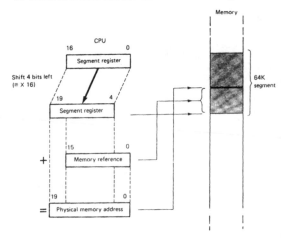

*Figure 4.3  Process of forming a 20-bit physical address*

As an example of the process of forming a physical address reference, Table 4.3 shows the state of the 8086 registers after the RESET signal is applied. The instruction referenced (i.e., the first instruction to be executed after the RESET signal is applied) will be found by combining the Instruction Pointer (offset address) with the Code Segment register (paragraph address). The location of the instruction referenced is FFFF0 (i.e. F0000 + FFF0). Note that the PC's ROM physically occupies addresses F0000 to FFFFF and that, following a power-on or hardware reset, execution commences from address FFFF0 with a jump to the initial program loader.

*Table 4.3  Contents of the 8086 registers after a reset*

| Register | Contents (hex.) |
|---|---|
| Flag | 0002 |
| Instruction Pointer | FFF0 |
| Code Segment | F000 |
| Data Segment | 0000 |
| Extra Segment | 0000 |
| Stack Segment | 0000 |

### TIP

The NEC V20 and V30 processors are pin-compatible replacements for the Intel 8088 and 8086 respectively. These chips are enhanced versions of their Intel counterparts and they offer an increase in processing speed for certain operations.

## The 80286

Intel's 80286 CPU was first employed in the PC-AT and PS/2 Models 50 and 60. The 80286 offers a 16M byte physical addressing range but incorporates memory management capabilities that can map up

*Component pad view* As viewed from underside of component when mounted on the board

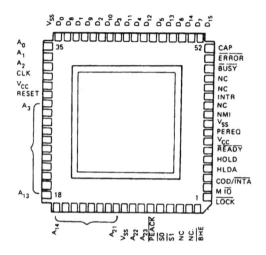

*PC Board view* As viewed from the component side of the PC board

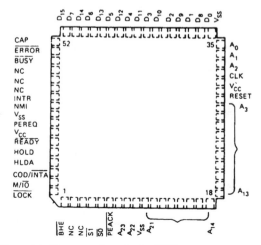

**Figure 4.4  Pin connections for the 80286**

to a Gigabyte of virtual memory. Depending upon the application, the 80286 is up to six times faster than the standard 5MHz 8086 while providing upward software compatability with the 8086 and 8088 processors.

The 80286 has fifteen 16-bit registers of which fourteen are identical to those of the 8086. The additional Machine Status Word (MSW) register controls the operating mode of the processor and also records when a task switch takes place.

The bit functions within the MSW are summarised in Table 4.4. The MSW is initialised with a value of FFF0H upon reset, the remainder of the 80286 registers being initialised as shown in Table 4.3. The 80286 is packaged in a 68-pin JEDEC type-A plastic leadless chip carrier (PLCC) as shown in Figure 4.4.

*Table 4.4  Bit functions in the 80286 machine status word*

| Bit | Name | Function |
| --- | --- | --- |
| 0 | Protected mode (PE) | Enables protected mode and can only be cleared by asserting the RESET signal. |
| 1 | Monitor processor (MP) | Allows WAIT instructions to cause a 'processor extension not present' exception (Exception 7). |
| 2 | Emulate processor (EP) | Causes a 'processor extension not present' exception (Exception 7) on ESC instructions to allow *emulation* of a processor extension. |
| 3 | Task switched (TS) | Indicates that the next instruction using a processor extension will cause Exception 7 (allowing software to test whether the current processor extension context belongs to the current task). |

# The 80386

The 80386 was designed as a *full* 32-bit device capable of manipulating data 32 bits at a time and communicating with the outside world through a 32-bit address bus. The 80386 offers a 'virtual 8086' mode of operation in which memory can be divided into 1 Mbyte chunks with a different program allocated to each partition.

The 80386 is available in two basic versions. The 80386SX operates internally as a 32-bit device but presents itself to the outside world through only 16 data lines. This has made the CPU extremely popular for use in low-cost systems which could still boast the processing power of a '386 (despite the obvious limitation imposed by the reduced number of data lines, the 'SX version of the 80386 runs at approximately 80% of the speed of its fully fledged counterpart).

## Architecture

The 80386 comprises a Bus Interface Unit (BIU), Code Prefetch Unit, Instruction Decode Unit, Execution Unit (EU), Segmentation Unit and Paging Unit. The Code Prefetch Unit performs the program 'lookahead' function.

When the BIU is not performing bus cycles in the execution of an instruction, the Code Prefetch Unit uses the BIU to fetch sequentially the instruction stream. The prefetched instructions are stored in a 16-byte 'code queue' where they await processing by the Instruction Decode Unit.

The prefetch queue is fed to the Instruction Decode Unit which translates the instructions into microcode. These microcoded instructions are then stored in a three-deep instruction queue on a first-in first-out (FIFO) basis. This queue of instructions awaits acceptance by the Execution Unit. Immediate data and opcode offsets are also taken from the prefetch queue.

## The 80486

The 80486 CPU is not merely an upgraded 80386 processor; its redesigned architecture offers significantly faster processing speeds when running at the *same* clock speed as its predecessor. Enhancements include a built-in maths coprocessor, internal cache memory and cache memory control.

### Additional signals and cache operation

The '486 CPU uses a large number of additional signals associated with parity checking (PCHK) and cache operation (AHOLD, FLUSH, etc). The cache comprises a set of four 2K blocks (128 x 16 bytes) of high-speed internal memory. Each 16-byte line of memory has a matching 21-bit 'tag'. This tag comprises a 17-bit linear address together with four protection bits. The cache control block contains 128 sets of seven bits. Three of the bits are used to implement the 'least recently used' (LRU) system for replacement and the remaining four bits are used to indicate valid data.

> ### TIP
>
> The '486's internal cache is responsible for a significant increase in processing speed. For example, a '486 operating at 25MHz can achieve a faster processing speed than a '386 operating at 33MHz!

## Interrupt handling

Interrupt service routines are sub-programs stored away from the main body of code that are available for execution whenever the relevant interrupt occurs. However, since interrupts may occur at virtually any point in the execution of a main program, the response must be automatic; the processor must suspend its current task and save the return address so that the program can be resumed at the point at which it was left. Note that the programmer must assume responsibility for preserving the state of any registers which may have their contents altered during execution of the interrupt service routine.

The Intel processor family uses a table of 256 four-byte pointers stored in the bottom 1K bytes of memory (addresses 0000H to 03FFH). Each of the locations in the Interrupt Pointer Table can be loaded with a pointer to a different interrupt service routine. Each pointer contains two bytes for loading into the Code Segment (CS) register and two bytes for loading into the Instruction Pointer (IP). This allows the programmer to place his or her interrupt service

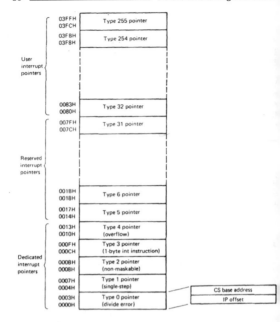

*Figure 4.5   Interrupt pointer table*

routines in any appropriate place within the 1M byte physical address space.

Each of the 256 interrupt pointers is allocated a different type number. A Type 0 interrupt has its associated interrupt pointer in the lowest four bytes of memory (0000H to 0003H). A Type 1 interrupt will have its pointer located in the next four bytes of memory (0004H to 0007H), and so on.

The structure of the Interrupt Pointer Table is shown in Figure 4.5. InterruptTypes 0 to 4 have dedicated functions whilst Types 5 to 31 are reserved. Hence there are 224 remaining locations in which interrupt pointers may be stored. The interrupting device places a byte on the data bus in response to an interrupt acknowledgement generated by the CPU. This byte gives the interrupt type and the CPU loads its Code Segment and Instruction Pointer registers with the words stored at the appropriate locations in the Interrupt Pointer Table and then commences execution of the interrupt service routine.

## Replacing the CPU

The processor chip (regardless of type) is invariably fitted in a socket and this makes removal and replacement quite straightforward provided that you have the correct tool for the job. Table 4.5 shows the packages and power supply requirements for various members of the 80x86 family.

Specialised tools will allow you to remove 40-pin DIL packages (8088 and 8086) and PLCC and PGA (80286 and later) chips. An 'extractor' vill allow you to grip the chip firmly in its stainless steel jaws whilst n 'inserter' will allow you to replace the chip by simply positioning he device and depressing a plunger or turning a knob. These tools are not cheap but are a worthwhile investment as it is virtually impossible to safely undertake this task by any other means.

The following describes the stages in removing and replacing a CPU chip:

1. Gain access to the system board (as described in Chapter 3).
2. Ensure that you observe the safety and static precautions at all times. Have some anti-static packing available to receive the CPU when it has been removed.
3. Locate the CPU and ensure that there is sufficient room to work all around it (you may have to move ribbon cables or adapter cards to gain sufficient clearance to use the extraction and insertion tools).
4. Check that you have selected the correct extraction tool. Open the jaws of the tool and carefully position it over the chip. Close the jaws and check that the device is gripped firmly (you may need to ease the jaws of the tool gently into place).
5. Lock the jaws into place and ease the chip out of the connector (you should pull straight but firmly but at right angles to the PCB).
6. Immediately deposit the chip in an anti-static container (do not touch any of the pins).
7. Pick up the replacement chip (using the insertion tool) from its anti-static packing. Position the insertion chip over the socket and ensure that it is correctly orientated.
8. Firmly press the plunger (or rotate the knob) on the insertion tool in order to insert the chip into its socket.
9. Re-assemble the system (replacing any adapter cards and cables that may have been removed in order to gain access or clearance around the CPU). Reconnect the system and test.

## TIP

In emergency, it is possible to remove and replace a DIL chip *without* using any specialised tools. The secret is to remove device by applying firm but *even* force to each end of the chip.

## TIP

Do not attempt to desolder a soldered-in DIL CPU chip unless you are *very* experienced. The system board can be very easily damaged by improper use of soldering tools. If you *do* attempt this task, make sure that you have a proper desoldering pump to remove the surplus solder from around the CPU pins *before* you attempt to lever up the chip.

**Table 4.5   Power supply requirements and packages for CPU chips**

| | 8086 | 8088 | 80186 |
|---|---|---|---|
| | | CPU type | |
| Supply current | 340mA–360mA | 340mA–360mA | 415mA–550mA |
| Supply power (typical) | 1.75W | 1.75W | 2.5W |
| Packages | DIP | DIP | PLCC, PGA |
| Pins | 40 | 40 | 68 |

| | 80286 | 80386 (386) | 80486 (486) |
|---|---|---|---|
| Supply current | 415mA–5500mA | 370mA–550mA | 750mA–900mA |
| Supply power (typical) | 2.5W | 2.5W | 5W |
| Packages | PLCC, PGA | PGA | PGA |
| Pins | 68 | 132 | 168 |

# 5
# Support Devices

Each of the major support devices present within a PC has a key role to play in off-loading a number of routine tasks that would otherwise have to be performed by the CPU. This chapter provides a brief introduction to each generic device together with internal architecture and pin connecting details.

*Table 5.1  Support chips used with 80x86 processors*

|  | CPU type | | | | |
| --- | --- | --- | --- | --- | --- |
|  | 8086 | 8088 | 80186 | 80286 | 80386 (386) |
| Clock generator | 8284A | 8284A | On-chip | 82284 | 82384 |
| Bus controller | 8288 | 8288 | On-chip | 82288 | 82288 |
| Inegrated support chip |  |  |  | 82230/ 82231, 82335 | 82230/ 82231, 82335 |
| Interrupt controller | 8259A | 8259A | On-chip | 8259A | 8259A |
| DMA controller | 8089/ 82258 | 8089/ 8237/ 82258 | On-chip/ 82258 | 8089/ 82258 | 8237/ 82258 |
| Timer/ counter | 8253/ 8254 | 8253/ 8254 | On-chip | 8253/ 8254 | 8253/ 8254 |
| Maths coprocessor | 8087 | 8087 | 8087 | 80287 | 80287/ 80387 |
| Chip select/ wait state logic | TTL | TTL | On-chip | TTL | TTL |

## Locating and identifying the support devices

The support devices are usually easy to identify as they occupy much larger packages than the RAM devices and other logic circuits. In many cases they may be socketed though they may also be soldered directly to the PCB (without a socket). The support devices are usually marked with the manufacturer's name (or logo), the device coding, and the date of manufacture.

The procedure for removing and replacing conventional DIL packaged support devices is the same as that described in Chapter 4. Where the functions of several support devices have been integrated into a single device, the chip will generally be surface mounted and soldered directly to the PCB. In this case, specialised SMT handling techniques will be required if the chip is to be removed and replaced.

**TIP**

Integrated circuits are usually clearly marked with their device code, however you can sometimes be confused by the four digit date code which is also marked on the chip. For example, a chip marked '8288 8806' is an 8288 chip manufactured in the sixth week of 1988.

**TIP**

You must carefully check the orientation of a chip whenever you remove and replace it. Pin-1 is often marked with a small circular indentation on the package. In addition, the end of the package adjacent to the lowest and highest numbered pins (e.g., 1 and 40) is invariably marked with a rectangular or semi-circular notch. To make things even easier, DIL i.c. also carry a notch which should align with the notch on the chip's package.

**TIP**

If you have to remove and replace a DIL support device that is soldered directly to the PCB, it is wise to fit the PCB with a DIL socket before replacing the suspect device. This will allow you to easily replace the device if it should ever fail in the future.

## 8087 Maths Coprocessor

The 8087, where fitted, is only active when mathematics related instructions are encountered in the instruction stream. The 8087, which is effectively wired in parallel with the 8086 or 8088 CPU, adds eight 80-bit floating point registers to the CPU register set. The 8087 maintains its own instruction queue and executes only those instructions which are specifically intended for it. The internal architecture of the 8087 is shown in Figure 5.1. The 8087 is supplied in a 40-pin DIL package, the pin connections for which are shown in Figure 5.2.

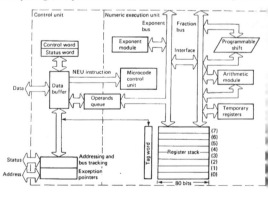

*Figure 5.1 Internal architecture of the 8087*

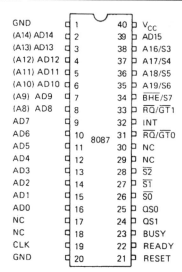

*Figure 5.2  Pin connections for the 8087*

The active-low TEST input of the 8086/8088 CPU is driven from the BUSY output of the 8087 NDP. This allows the CPU to respond to the WAIT instruction (inserted by the assembler/compiler) which occurs before each coprocessor instruction. An FWAIT instruction follows each coprocessor instruction which deposits data in memory for immediate use by the CPU. The instruction is then translated to the requisite 8087 operation (with the preceding WAIT) and the FWAIT instruction is translated as a CPU WAIT instruction.

During coprocessor execution, the BUSY line is taken high and the CPU (responding to the WAIT instruction) halts its activity until the line goes low. The two Queue Status (QS0 and QS1) signals are used to synchronise the instruction queues of the two processing devices.

80287 and 80387 chips provide maths coprocessing facilities within AT and '386-based PC's respectively. In '486-based systems there is no need for a maths coprocessor as these facilities have been incorporated within the CPU.

### TIP

A maths coprocessor can perform certain operations between 10 and 100 times faster than the main processor. Your system will greatly benefit from the addition of such a device if you regularly use maths-intensive applications (e.g., CAD, spreadsheets and statistical packages).

## 8237A Direct Memory Access Controller

The 8237A DMA Controller (DMAC) can provide service for up to four independent DMA channels, each with separate registers for Mode Control, Current Address, Base Address, Current Word Count

### TIP

You can find out whether a coprocessor is fitted to a system without dismantling it. If bit 1 of the byte stored at address 0410 hex. is set, a maths coprocessor is present. If bit 1 is reset, no coprocessor is fitted. You can check the bit in question using Debug (see Chapter 14) or by using the following QuickBASIC code:

```
DEF SEG = 0
byte=PEEK(&H410)
IF byte AND 2 THEN
   PRINT "Coprocessor fitted"
ELSE
   PRINT "No coprocessor present"
END IF
```

and Base Word Count (see Figure 5.3). The DMAC is designed to improve system performance by allowing external devices to directly transfer information to and from the system memory. The 8237A offers a variety of programmable control features to enhance data thoughput and allow dynamic reconfiguration under software control.

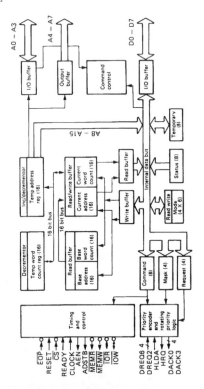

*Figure 5.3  Internal architecture of the 8237A*

```
        ┌──────┬─∪─┬──────┐
  IOR  ⊏│ 1         40 │⊐ A7
  IOW  ⊏│ 2         39 │⊐ A6
 MEMR  ⊏│ 3         38 │⊐ A5
 MEMW  ⊏│ 4         37 │⊐ A4
LOGIC 1 ⊏│ 5        36 │⊐ EOP
READY  ⊏│ 6         35 │⊐ A3
 HLDA  ⊏│ 7         34 │⊐ A2
ADSTB  ⊏│ 8         33 │⊐ A1
  AEN  ⊏│ 9         32 │⊐ A0
  HRQ  ⊏│ 10  8237A 31 │⊐ V_CC  (+5 V)
   CS  ⊏│ 11        30 │⊐ DB0
  CLK  ⊏│ 12        29 │⊐ DB1
RESET  ⊏│ 13        28 │⊐ DB2
DACK2  ⊏│ 14        27 │⊐ DB3
DACK3  ⊏│ 15        26 │⊐ DB4
DREQ3  ⊏│ 16        25 │⊐ DACK0
DREQ2  ⊏│ 17        24 │⊐ DACK1
DREQ1  ⊏│ 18        23 │⊐ DB5
DREQ0  ⊏│ 19        22 │⊐ DB6
(GND) V_SS ⊏│ 20    21 │⊐ DB7
        └──────────────┘
```

*Figure 5.4  Pin connections for the 8237A*

The 8237A provides four basic modes of transfer: Block, Demand, Single Word, and Cascade. These modes may be programmed as required, however channels may be autoinitialised to their original condition following an End Of Process (EOP) signal.

The 8237A is designed for use with an external octal address latch such as the 74LS373. A system's DMA capability may be extended by cascading further 8237A DMAC chips and this feature is exploited in the PC-AT which has two such devices.

The least significant four address lines of the 8237A are bi-directional: when functioning as inputs, they are used to select one of the DMA controllers sixteen internal registers. When functioning as outputs, on the other hand, a sixteen bit address is formed by taking the eight address lines (A0 to A7) to form the least significant address byte whilst the most significant address byte (A8 to A15) is multiplexed onto the data bus lines (D0 to D7). The requisite address latch enable signal (ADSTB) is available from pin-8. The upper four address bits (A16 to A19) are typically supplied by a 74LS670 4 x 4 register file. The requisite bits are placed in this device (effectively a static RAM) by the processor before the DMA transfer is completed.

DMA channel 0 (highest priority) is used in conjunction with the 8253 Programmable Interval Timer (PIT) in order to provide a memory refresh facility for the PC's dynamic RAM. DMA channels 1 to 3 are connected to the expansion slots for use by option cards.

The refresh process involves channel 1 of the PIT producing a negative going pulse with a period of approximately 15µs. This pulse sets a bistable which, in turn, generates a DMA request at the channel-0 input of the DMAC (pin-19). The processor is then forced into a wait state and the address and data bus buffers assume a tri-state (high impedance) condition. The DMAC then outputs a row refresh address and the row address strobe (RAS) is asserted. The 8237 increments its refresh count register and control is then returned to the processor. The process then continues such that all 256 rows are refreshed within a time interval of 4ms. The pin connections for the 8237A are shown in Figure 5.4.

# 8253 Programmable Interval Timer

The 8253 is a Programmable Interval Timer (PIT) which has three independent pre-settable 16-bit counters each offering a count rate of up to 2.6MHz. The internal architecture and pin connections for the 8253 are shown in Figures 5.5 and 5.6 respectively. Each counter consists of a single 16-bit presettable down counter. The counter can function in binary or BCD and its input, gate and output are configured by the data held in the Control Word Register. The down counters are negative edge triggered such that, on a falling clock edge, the contents of the respective counter is decremented.

The three counters are fully independent and each can have separate mode configuration and counting operation, binary or BCD. The contents of each 16-bit count register can be loaded or read using simple software referencing the relevant port addresses shown in Table 5.3. The truth table for the chip's active-low chip select (CS), read (RD), write (WR) and address lines (A1 and A0) is shown in Table 5.2.

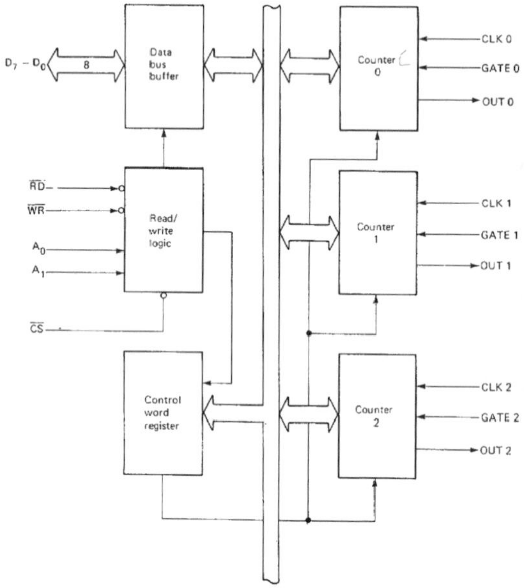

*Figure 5.5 Internal architecture of the 8253*

*Figure 5.6  Pin connections for the 8253*

*Table 5.2  Truth table for the 8253*

| CS | RD | WR | A1 | A0 | Function |
|----|----|----|----|----|----------|
| 0 | 1 | 0 | 0 | 0 | Load counter 0 |
| 0 | 1 | 0 | 0 | 1 | Load counter 1 |
| 0 | 1 | 0 | 1 | 0 | Load counter 2 |
| 0 | 1 | 0 | 1 | 1 | Write mode word |
| 0 | 0 | 1 | 0 | 0 | Read counter 0 |
| 0 | 0 | 1 | 0 | 1 | Read counter 1 |
| 0 | 0 | 1 | 1 | 0 | Read counter 2 |
| 0 | 0 | 1 | 1 | 1 | No-operation (tri-state) |
| 1 | x | x | x | x | Disable tri-state |
| 0 | 1 | 1 | x | x | No-operation (tri-state) |

## 8255A Programmable Peripheral Interface

The 8255A Programmable Peripheral Interface (PPI) is a general purpose I/O device which provides no less than 24 I/O lines arranged as three 8-bit I/O ports. The internal architecture and pin connections of the 8255A are shown in Figures 5.7 and 5.8 respectively. The Read/Write and Control Logic block manages all internal and external data transfers. The port addresses used by the 8255A are given in Table 5.3.

The functional configuration of each of the 8255's three I/O ports is fully programmable. Each of the control groups accepts commands from the Read/Write Control Logic, receives Control Words via the internal data bus and issues the requisite commands to each of the ports. At this point, it is important to note that the 24 I/O lines are, for control purposes, divided into two logical groups (A and B). Group A comprises the entire eight lines of Port A together with the four upper (most significant) lines of Port B. Group B, on the other hand, takes in all eight lines from Port B together with the four lower (least significant) lines of Port C. The upshot of all this is simply that Port C can be split into two in order to allow its lines to be used for status and control (handshaking) when data is transferred to or from Ports A or B.

**Table 5.3 Port addresses used in the PC family**

| Device | PC-XT | PC-AT etc |
|---|---|---|
| 8237A DMA controller | 000-00F | 000-01F |
| 8259A interrupt controller | 020-021 | 020-03F |
| 8253/8254 timer | 040-043 | 040-05F |
| 8255 parallel interface | 060-063 | n/a |
| 8042 keyboard controller | n/a | 060-06F |
| DMA page register | 080-083 | 080-09F |
| NMI mask register | 0A0-0A7 | 070-07F |
| Second 8259A interrupt controller | n/a | 0A0-0BF |
| Second 8237A DMA controller | n/a | 0C0-0DF |
| Maths coprocessor (8087, 80287) | n/a | 0F0-0FF |
| Games controller | 200-20F | 200-207 |
| Expansion unit | 210-217 | n/a |
| Second parallel port | n/a | 278-27F |
| Second serial port | 2F8-2FF | 2F8-2FF |
| Prototype card | 300-31F | 300-31F |
| Fixed (hard) disk | 320-32F | 1F0-1F8 |
| First parallel printer | 378-37F | 378-37F |
| SDLC adapter | 380-38F | 380-38F |
| BSC adapter | n/a | 3A0-3AF |
| Monochrome adapter | 3B0-3BF | 3B0-3BF |
| Enhanced graphics adapter | n/a | 3C0-3CF |
| Colours graphics adapter | 3D0-3DF | 3D0-3DF |
| Floppy disk controller | 3F0-3F7 | 3F0-3F7 |
| First serial port | 3F8-3FF | 3F8-3FF |

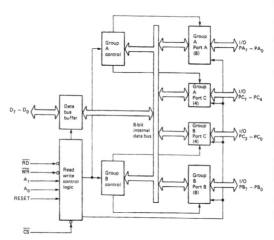

*Figure 5.7 Internal architecture of the 8255A*

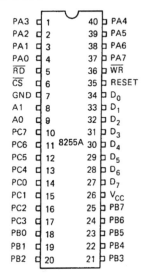

*Figure 5.8 Pin connections for the 8255A*

## 8259A Programmable Interrupt Controller

The 8259A Programmable Interrupt Controller (PIC) was designed specifically for use in real-time interrupt driven microcomputer systems. The device manages eight levels of request and can be expanded using further 8259A devices.

The sequence of events which occurs when an 8259A device is used in conjunction with an 8086 or 8088 processor is as follows:

(a) One or more of the interrupt request lines (IR0-IR7) are asserted (note that these lines are active-high) by the interrupting device(s).

(b) The corresponding bits in the IRR register become set.

(c) The 8259A evaluates the requests on the following basis:
    (i)     If more than one request is currently present, determine which of the requests has the highest priority.
    (ii)    Ascertain whether the successful request has a higher priority than the level currently being serviced.
    (iii)   If the condition in (ii) is satisfied, issue an interrupt to the processor by asserting the active-high INT line.

(d) The processor acknowledges the interrupt signal and responds by asserting the interrupt acknowledge by pulsing the interrupt acknowledge (INTA) line.

(e) Upon receiving the INTA pulse from the processor, the highest priority ISR bit is set and the corresponding IRR bit is reset.

(f) The processor then initiates a second interrupt acknowledge (INTA) pulse. During this second period for which the INTA line is taken low, the 8259 outputs a pointer on the data bus to be read by the processor.

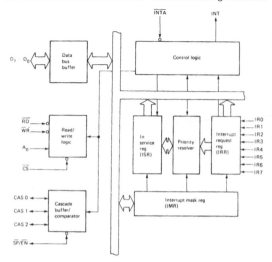

*Figure 5.9    Internal architecture of the 8259A*

```
        CS   ┌─┐ 1      28 ┌─ V_CC
        WR  ┌┤ │ 2      27 │┐ A_0
        RD  ┌┤ │ 3      26 │┐ INTA
        D_7 ┌┤ │ 4      25 │┐ IR7
        D_6 ┌┤ │ 5      24 │┐ IR6
        D_5 ┌┤ │ 6      23 │┐ IR5
        D_4 ┌┤ │ 7      22 │┐ IR4
        D_3 ┌┤ │ 8 8259A 21 │┐ IR3
        D_2 ┌┤ │ 9      20 │┐ IR2
        D_1 ┌┤ │ 10     19 │┐ IR1
        D_0 ┌┤ │ 11     18 │┐ IR0
      CAS 0 ┌┤ │ 12     17 │┐ INT
      CAS 1 ┌┤ │ 13     16 │┐ SP/EN
        GND ┌┤ │ 14     15 │┐ CAS 2
```

*Figure 5.10    Pin connections for the 8259A*

The internal architecture and pin connections for the 8259A are shown in Figures 5.9 and 5.10 respectively.

## 8284A Clock Generator

The 8284A is a single chip clock generator/driver designed specifically for use by the 8086 family of devices. The chip contains a crystal oscillator, divide-by-3 counter, ready and reset logic as shown in Figure 5.11. On the original PC, the quartz crystal is a series mode fundamental device which operates at a frequency of 14.312818MHz. The output of the divide-by-3 counter takes the form of a 33% duty cycle square wave at precisely one third of the fundamental frequency

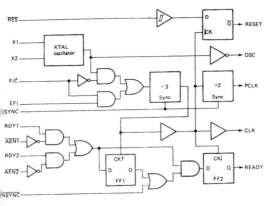

**Figure 5.11   Internal architecture of the 8284A**

```
       CSYNC  ⊏ 1        18 ⊐ V_CC
        PCLK  ⊏ 2        17 ⊐ X1
        AEN1  ⊏ 3        16 ⊐ X2
        RDY1  ⊏ 4        15 ⊐ ASYNC
       READY  ⊏ 5  8284A 14 ⊐ EFI
        RDY2  ⊏ 6        13 ⊐ F/C
        AEN2  ⊏ 7        12 ⊐ OSC
         CLK  ⊏ 8        11 ⊐ RES
         GND  ⊏ 9        10 ⊐ RESET
```

**Figure 5.12   Pin connections for the 8284A**

(i.e. 4.77MHz). This signal is then applied to the processor's clock (CLK) input. The clock generator also produces a signal at 2.38MHz which is externally divided to provide a 5.193MHz 50% duty cycle clock signal for the 8253 Programmable Interval Timer (PIT), as shown in Figure 5.13.

# 8288 Bus Controller

The 8288 bus controller decodes the status outputs from the CPU (S0 S1) in order to generate the requisite bus command and control signals. These signals are used as shown in Table 5.4.

The 8288 issues signals to the system to strobe addresses into the address latches, to enable data onto the buses, and to determine the direction of data flow through the data buffers. The internal architecture and pin connections for the 8288 are shown in Figures 5.14 and 5.15 respectively.

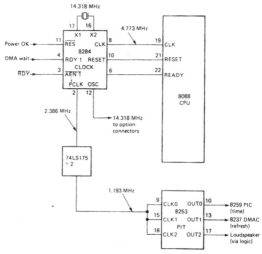

Figure 5.13  Clock signals in the PC

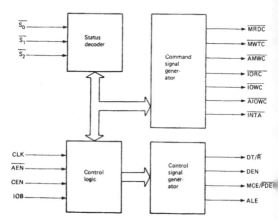

Figure 5.14  Internal architecture of the 8288

Table 5.4  8288 bus controller status inputs

| CPU status line | | | Condition |
|---|---|---|---|
| S2 | S1 | S0 | |
| 0 | 0 | 0 | Interrupt acknowledge |
| 0 | 0 | 1 | I/O read |
| 0 | 1 | 0 | I/O write |
| 0 | 1 | 1 | Halt |
| 1 | 0 | 0 | Memory read |
| 1 | 0 | 1 | Memory read |
| 1 | 1 | 0 | Memory write |
| 1 | 1 | 1 | Inactive |

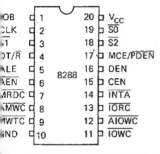

*Figure 5.15  Pin connections for the 8288*

## Integrated support devices

In modern PCs, the overall device count has been significantly reduced by integrating several of the functions associated with the original PC chip set within a single VLSI device or within the CPU itself. As an example, the Chips and Technology 82C100 XT Controller provides the functionality associated with no less than six of the original XT chip set and effectively replaces the following devices: 8237 DMA Controller, 8253 Counter/Timer, 8255 Parallel Interface, 8259 Interrupt Controller, 8284 Clock Generator, and 8288 Bus Controller.

In order to ensure software compatability with the original PC, the 82C100 contains a superset of the registers associated with each of the devices which it is designed to replace. The use of the chip is thus completely transparent as far as applications software is concerned.

# 6
# Semiconductor Memory

This chapter will help you understand the use of RAM and ROM within your PC. It also explains how you can locate and replace a faulty memory chip. In addition, several short utility programs have been included to help you locate useful system information stored in your computer's memory and protect the important data stored in your CMOS RAM.

## Memory basics

Semiconductor memory devices tend to fall into two main categories; 'read/write' and 'read-only'. Read/write memory is simply memory which can be read from and written to. In other words, the contents of the memory can be modified at will. Read-only memory, on the other hand, can only be read from; an attempt to write data to such a memory will have no effect on its contents.

Obvious examples of read-only and read/write memories with which the man in the street will be familiar are, respectively, compact disks and audio cassette tapes. Once recorded, compact disks cannot be modified whereas a pre-recorded audio tape cassette can be erased and re-recorded many times.

### Memory organisation

Each location in semiconductor ROM and RAM has its own unique address. At each address a byte (comprising eight bits) is stored. Each ROM, RAM (or bank of RAM devices) accounts for a particular block of memory, its size depending upon the capacity of the ROM or RAM in question.

As an example, a particular system may have a 'base memory' arranged in two blocks, each of nine 256K x 1-bit DRAM devices (the ninth chip provides a parity checking bit for each memory location, see page 35 for further information). The total capacity of this memory is 512K bytes (there are 256K bytes in each block, not counting the parity bits). The organisation of this memory (which occupies the address range from 00000 to 9FFFF) is shown in Table 6.1 where 'U1', 'U2' etc are the component designations for the individual RAM chips.

Now consider a 1M byte 'extended memory' board (see page 53) based on a total of 36 256K x 1-bit devices. The RAM chips will be organised on the basis of four blocks (each of eight chips with the remaining four devices providing the parity bits). The organisation of this memory is shown in Table 6.2.

### Table 6.1  512K byte memory example

| Block | Address range | Data bits | | | | | | | | Parity |
|---|---|---|---|---|---|---|---|---|---|---|
| | | D7 | D6 | D5 | D4 | D3 | D2 | D1 | D0 | |
| 0 | 00000 –3FFFF | U8 | U7 | U6 | U5 | U4 | U3 | U2 | U1 | U9 |
| 1 | 40000 –7FFFF | U17 | U16 | U15 | U14 | U13 | U12 | U11 | U10 | U18 |

**able 6.2  1M byte memory example**

| lock Address range | Data bits | | | | | | | | Parity |
|---|---|---|---|---|---|---|---|---|---|
| | D7 | D6 | D5 | D4 | D3 | D2 | D1 | D0 | |
| 100000 –13FFFF | U8 | U7 | U6 | U5 | U4 | U3 | U2 | U1 | U9 |
| 140000 –17FFFF | U17 | U16 | U15 | U14 | U13 | U12 | U11 | U10 | U18 |
| 180000 —1BFFFF | U26 | U25 | U24 | U23 | U22 | U21 | U20 | U19 | U27 |
| 1C0000 –1FFFFF | U35 | U34 | U33 | U32 | U31 | U30 | U29 | U28 | U36 |

## IOS ROM

he BIOS ROM is programmed during manufacture. The program-
ning data is supplied to the semiconductor manufacturer by the BIOS
riginator. This process is cost-effective for large-scale production
owever programming of the ROM is irreversible; once programmed,
evices cannot be erased in preparation for fresh programming.
Hence, the only way of upgrading the BIOS is to remove and discard
he existing chips and replace them with new ones. This procedure
s fraught with problems, not least of which is compatability of the
IOS upgrade with existing DOS software.

The BIOS ROM invariably occupies the last 64K or 128K bytes of
nemory (from F0000 to FFFFF or E0000 to FFFFF, respectively). It
s normally based on two chips; one for the odd addresses and one
or the even addresses.

## IOS variations

everal manufacturers (e.g., Compaq) have produced ROM BIOS
ode for use in their own equipment. This code must, of course, be
ompatible with IBM's BIOS code. Several other companies (e.g.,
American Megatrends (AMI), Award Software, and Phoenix Software)
ave developed generic versions of the BIOS code which has been
ncorporated into numerous clones and compatibles.

There are, of course, minor differences between these BIOS versions. Notably these exist within the power-on self-test (POST), the
et-up routines, and the range of hard disk types supported.

### TIP

Some users of the AMI BIOS dated 04/09/90 (or earlier) have
reported problems with the keyboard controller when running
Windows or OS/2. If you have difficulties check the BIOS date
and, if necessary, upgrade the BIOS ROMs to a later version.

## Upgrading your BIOS ROM

At some point, you may find it desirable to upgrade the BIOS ROM
on a machine. There are various reasons for doing this but most centre on the need to make your software recognise significant hardware upgrades (e.g., to make use of an IDE hard drive or when replacing the 360K or 720K floppy drives on an older machine with
newer 1.44M or 2.88M drives).

The following stages are required:
1. As far as possible, make sure that the new BIOS is compatible
   with your system (it might be wise to ask the supplier if he/
   she will offer a refund if you have any problems).

2. Note down your existing CMOS configuration (using your 'set up' program).
3. Power-down your system as described in Chapter 3 (page 25).
4. Locate the BIOS ROM chips (note their position and orientation).
5. Remove and replace the BIOS ROM chips (follow the procedure described in Chapter 4 (page 37).
6. Re-assemble the system and run the 'set-up' program, making any changes necessary.

### TIP

The BIOS ROM chips are usually marked 'Low' and 'High' (or 'Odd' and 'Even') in order to distinguish them from one another. Always make sure that you replace them in the correct sockets (i.e., locate the new 'Low' chip in the socket vacated by the old 'L' chip).

## Random Access Memory (RAM)

The PC system board's read/write memory provides storage for the DOS and BIOS as well as transient user programs and data. In addition, read/write memory is also used to store data which is displayed on the screen. Depending upon the nature of the applications software, this memory may be either character-mapped (text) or bit mapped (graphics). The former technique involves dividing the screen into a number of character-sized cells.

Each displayed character cell requires one byte of memory for storage of the character plus a further byte for 'attributes' (see Chapter 13). Hence a screen having 80 columns x 25 lines (corresponding to the IBM's basic text mode) will require 2000 bytes; 1000 for storage of the characters and a further plus 1000 for the attributes.

Bit-mapped graphic displays require a very much larger amount of storage. Each display pixel is mapped to a particular bit in memory and the bit may be a 1 or a 0 depending upon whether it is to be light or dark. Where a colour display is to be produced, several colour planes must be implemented and consequently an even larger amount of memory is required. A VGA graphics adapter, for example, may be fitted with up to 1M byte of video RAM. Chapter 13 provides more information on the size and organisation of video memory.

### Static versus dynamic memories

Semiconductor random access memories are divided into 'static' and 'dynamic' types. Static types are generally CMOS types (for low power consumption) and are based on bistable memory cells. Each cell will retain a stored bit (logic 1 or logic 0) for as long as the power is left connected.

Dynamic memories (DRAM) are generally NMOS types which utilise charge storage within a semiconductor junction (effectively a tiny capacitor). To prevent the stored charge leaking away (in which case the memory would lose its contents) the charge is periodically 'refreshed' by a continuous process of reading and writing. This process takes place automatically.

### DIL packaged DRAM

The data in Table 6.3 refers to a range of the most popular DIL packaged DRAM chips whilst Table 6.4 shows equivalent 64K x 1 bit and 256K x 1 bit devices. The pin connections for the most common DIL packaged DRAMs are shown in Figure 6.1. Note that access times are often included within a chip's coding. A chip marked TMS4164-15, for example, has an access time of 150ns whilst one marked MSM41256-10 has an access time of 100ns.

### Table 6.3 DRAM data

| Type | Size (bits) | Organisation | Package |
|------|-------------|--------------|---------|
| 4116 | 16384 | 16K words x 1 bit | 16-pin DIL |
| 4164 | 65536 | 64K words x 1 bit | 16-pin DIL |
| 4256 | 262144 | 25K words x 1 bit | 16-pin DIL |
| 4716 | 16384 | 16K words x 1 bit | 16-pin DIL |
| 4816 | 16384 | 16K words x 1 bit | 16-pin DIL |
| 4864 | 65536 | 64K words x 1 bit | 16-pin DIL |
| 4865 | 65536 | 64K words x 1 bit | 16-pin DIL |
| 41256 | 262144 | 256K words x 1 bit | 16-pin DIL |
| 41257 | 262144 | 256K words x 1 bit | 16-pin DIL |
| 41416 | 65536 | 16K words x 4 bit | 18-pin DIL |
| 48416 | 65536 | 16K words x 4 bit | 18-pin DIL |
| 50256 | 262144 | 256K words x 1 bit | 16-pin DIL |
| 50257 | 262144 | 256K words x 1 bit | 16-pin DIL |

### Table 6.4 DRAM equivalents

| Organisation | Manufacturer | Part number |
|--------------|--------------|-------------|
| 64K x 1 bit | AMD | AM9064 |
| | Fairchild | F64K |
| | Fujitsu | MB8264A/MB8265A |
| | Hitachi | HM4864/HM4864A |
| | Inmos | IMS2600 |
| | Intel | 2164A |
| | Matsushita | MN4164 |
| | Micron Tech. | MT4264 |
| | Mitsubishi | MSK4164 |
| | Mostek | MK4564 |
| | Motorola | MCM66665A |
| | National Semi. | NMC4164 |
| | NEC | uPD4164 |
| | Oki | MSM3764 |
| | Siemens | HYB4164 |
| | Texas Instr. | TMS4164 |
| | Toshiba | TMM4164 |
| | Tristar | KM4164A |
| 256K x 1 bit | Fujitsu | MB81256/MB81257 |
| | Hitachi | HM50256/HM50257 |
| | Micron Tech. | MT1256 |
| | Mitsubishi | MSM4256 |
| | Motorola | MCM6256 |
| | NEC | uPD41256/uPD41257 |
| | Oki | MSM37256 |
| | Texas Instr. | TMS4256/TMS4257 |
| | Toshiba | TMM41256 |
| | Western Elec. | WCM41256 |

*Figure 6.1   DRAM pin connections*

## SIMMs

In modern machines, DIL packaged DRAM devices have been re‐
placed by single in-line memory modules (SIMM). These units are
small cards which usually contain surface mounted DRAM chips and
which simply plug into the system board.

SIMMs are available in various sizes including 256K, 1M, 4M, 8M
and 16M byte. The most common type of SIMM (which first saw
light in the XT-286, see page 19) has nine DRAM devices and it lo‐
cates with a 30-pin header. Four of these 256K modules are required
to populate a full 1M memory map.

SIMMs are usually inserted into their headers at an angle of about
45 degrees and then simply snapped into place by standing them
upright. To remove a SIMM, you should open the locking tabs and
gently release the module from its header.

### TIP

Memory access times can be important if you have to replace
DRAM chips or modules. Access times vary from 150ns (or even
200ns) in some of the older devices to as little as 60ns with the
latest generation of SIMM modules. Check the supplier or manu‐
facturer's data when replacing your DRAM or SIMM.

### TIP

'Zero-wait state' memory offers the fastest access time. Slower
memory devices may require between 1 and 5 'wait states' (i.e.,
do-nothing cycles) to slow the CPU down to match the access
time of the RAM. You can often adjust the number of wait states
by means of system board jumper if you suspect that your RAM
is too slow for your CPU.

## Memory Terminology

### Conventional RAM

The PC's RAM extending from 00000 to 9FFFF is referred to as 'con‐
ventional memory' or 'base memory'. This 640K of read/write
memory provides storage for user programs and data as well as re‐
gions reserved for DOS and BIOS use.

### Upper memory area

The remaining memory within the 1M byte direct addressing space
(i.e., that which extends form A0000 to FFFFF is referred to as the
'upper memory area' (UMA). The UMA itself is divided into various
regions (depending upon the machine's configuration) including that
which provides storage used by video adapters.

## Video RAM

As its name implies, video RAM is associated with the video/graphics adapter. The video RAM occupies the lower part of the upper memory area and its precise configuration will depend upon the type of adapter fitted.

## Extended memory

Memory beyond the basic 1M byte direct addressing space is referred to as 'extended memory'. This memory can be accessed by a '286 or later CPU operating in 'protected mode'. In this mode, the CPU is able to generate 24-bit addresses (instead of the real mode's 20-bit addresses) by multiplying the segment register contents by 256 (instead of 16). This scheme allows the CPU to access addresses ranging from 000000 to FFFFFF (a total of 16M byte). When the CPU runs in protected mode, a program can only access the designated region of memory. A processor exception will occur if an attempt is made to write to a region of memory that is outside of the currently allocated block.

## Expanded memory

Expanded memory was originally developed for machines based on 8088 and 8086 CPU which could not take advantage of the protected mode provide by the '286 and later processors. Expanded memory is accessed through a 64K 'page frame' located within the upper memory area. This page frame acts as a window into a much larger area of memory.

Expanded memory systems are based on a standard developed by three manufacturers (Lotus, Intel and Microsoft). This 'LIM standard' is also known as the Expandend Memory Standard (EMS). In order to make use of EMS, a special expanded memory driver is required. EMS has largely been superseded by the advanced memory management facilities provided by the '386 and '486 CPU chips.

## CMOS RAM

The PC-AT and later machine's CMOS memory is 64 bytes of battery-backed memory contained within the real-time clock chip (a Motorola MC146818). Sixteen bytes of this memory are used to retain the real-time clock settings (date and time information) whilst the remainder contains important information on the configuration of your system. When the CMOS battery fails or when power is inadvertently removed from the real-time clock chip, all data will become invalid and you will have to use your set-up program to restore the settings for your system. As mentioned in Chapter 2, this can be a real problem *unless* you know what the settings should be.

The organisation of the CMOS memory is shown in Table 6.5 (note that locations marked 'reserved' may have different functions in some non-IBM systems).

*Table 6.5  CMOS memory organisation*

| Offset (hex) | Contents |
| --- | --- |
| 00 | seconds |
| 01 | seconds alarm |
| 02 | minutes |
| 03 | minutes alarm |
| 04 | hours |
| 05 | hours alarm |
| 06 | day of the week |
| 07 | day of the month |
| 08 | month |
| 09 | year |
| 0A | status register A |
| 0B | status register B |
| 0C | status register C |
| 0E | diagnostic status byte |
| 0F | shutdown status byte |
| 10 | floppy disk type (drives A and B) |
| 11 | reserved |
| 12 | fixed disk type (drives 0 and 1) |
| 13 | reserved |
| 14 | equipment byte |
| 15 | base memory (low byte) |
| 16 | base memory (high byte) |
| 17 | extended memory (low byte) |
| 18 | extended memory (high byte) |
| 19 | hard disk 0 extended type |
| 1A | hard disk 1 extended type |
| 1B-2D | reserved |
| 2E-2F | checksum for bytes 10 to 1F |
| 30 | actual extended memory (low byte) |
| 31 | actual extended memory (high byte) |
| 32 | date century byte (in BCD format) |
| 33-3F | reserved |

```
DIM cmos%(32)
CLS
PRINT "Offset", "Value"
PRINT "(hex)", "(hex)"
PRINT
FOR i% = 16 TO 31
  OUT &H70, i%
  cmos%(i%) = INP(&H71)
  PRINT HEX$(i%), HEX$(cmos%(i%))
NEXT i%
```

*Figure 6.2  QuickBASIC program to reveal the contents of the second 16 bytes of CMOS RAM*

```
Offset      Value       Comment
(hex)       (hex)

10          44          Both drives are 1.44M (type 4)
11          EB
12          F0          Hard drive 0 is type 15, no hard drive 1
13          9C
14          4F          2 floppy drives, use display adapter's BIOS
15          80
16          2           640K of base memory
17          0
18          D           3328K of extended memory (4M total)
19          2F          Hard drive 0 extended type 47
1A          0           No hard drive 1
1B          68
1C          3
1D          8
1E          0
1F          0
```

**Figure 6.3   Output produced by the program shown in Figure 6.2**

The QuickBASIC program shown in Figure 6.2 will reveal the contents of the second 16 bytes of CMOS RAM (offset addresses 10 to 1F inclusive). These 16 bytes will tell you how the system has been configured (i.e., how much base and extended memory is present and the types of floppy and hard drive). A typical set of CMOS data for these locations is shown in Figure 6.3.

### TIP

The QuickBASIC program shown in Figure 6.4 will allow you to backup and restore your CMOS RAM data. The source code together with a fully compiled (.EXE) version of the program has been included on the Diagnostic Software disk (see Chapter 17 for details).

## Down Memory Lane (or finding your way around)

The allocation of memory space within a PC can be usefully illustrated by means of a 'memory map'. An 8086 microprocessor can address any one of 1048576 different memory locations with its 20 address lines. It thus has a memory which ranges from 00000 (the lowest address) to FFFFF (the highest address). We can illustrate the use of memory using a diagram known as a 'memory map'.

Figure 6.5 shows a representative memory map for a PC in which the memory is allocated as shown in Table 6.6.

### TIP

Microsoft's Windows provides you with an excellent utility called MSD (Microsoft System Diagnostic). You will find this program in your WINDOWS directory (see Chapter 14 if you need to know how to change the directory and run a DOS program). MSD will provide you with a great deal of useful information on your system, including a complete 'on-screen' memory map. A sample memory map produced by MSD is shown in Figure 6.6.

```
REM ** PC Troubleshooting CMOS memory backup **
ON ERROR GOTO warning
DIM cmos%(64)
main:
DO
  CLS
  PRINT "CMOS memory utility"
  PRINT "[B] = backup"
  PRINT "[R] = restore"
  PRINT "[Q] = exit to DOS"
  DO
    r$ = UCASE$(INKEY$)
  LOOP UNTIL r$ <> "" AND INSTR("BRQ", r$)
  IF r$ = "Q" THEN CLS : END
  IF r$ = "B" THEN
    ' user has selected backup
    PRINT "Backing up CMOS data, please wait..."
    OPEN "A:\CMOS.DAT" FOR OUTPUT AS #1
    FOR i% = 16 TO 63
      OUT &H70, i%
      cmos%(i%) = INP(&H71)
      PRINT #1, cmos%(i%)
    NEXT i%
    CLOSE #1
    PRINT "Done!"
    GOSUB waitkey
  END IF
  IF r$ = "R" THEN
    ' user has selected restore
    PRINT "Restoring CMOS data, please wait..."
    OPEN "A:\CMOS.DAT" FOR INPUT AS #1
    FOR i% = 16 TO 63
      INPUT #1, cmos%(i%)
      OUT &H70, i%
      OUT (&H71), cmos%(i%)
    NEXT i%
    CLOSE #1
  PRINT "Done!"
  GOSUB waitkey
  END IF
LOOP
'
waitkey:
PRINT "Press any key to continue..."
DO
  r$ = INKEY$
LOOP UNTIL r$ <> ""
RETURN
warning:
PRINT "An error has occurred!"
GOSUB waitkey
DO
  r$ = INKEY$
LOOP UNTIL r$ <> ""
RESUME main
```

*Figure 6.4 QuickBASIC program to backup and restore the CMOS RAM*

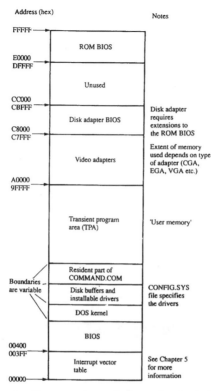

Address (hex)                                    Notes

FFFFF

        ROM BIOS

E0000
DFFFF

        Unused

CC000
CBFFF

        Disk adapter BIOS          Disk adapter
                                   requires
C8000                                            extensions to
C7FFF                                            the ROM BIOS

                                   Extent of memory
        Video adapters             used depends on type
                                   of adapter (CGA,
A0000                                            EGA, VGA etc.)
9FFFF

        Transient program          'User memory'
        area (TPA)

        Resident part of
        COMMAND.COM
Boundaries                                       CONFIG.SYS
are variable   Disk buffers and                  file specifies
        installable drivers         the drivers

        DOS kernel

        BIOS

00400
003FF

        Interrupt vector           See Chapter 5
        table                      for more
00000                                            information

*Figure 6.5  Representative memory map for a basic PC*

*Table 6.6  Memory allocation in a basic specification PC*

| Address range (hex) | Size (bytes) | Use |
|---|---|---|
| 00000-9FFFF | 640K | Conventional (base) memory |
| A0000-AFFFF | 64K | Video memory (graphics mode) |
| B0000-B7FFF | 32K | Video memory (monochrome text mode) |
| B8000-BFFFF | 32K | Video memory (colour text mode) |
| C0000-C7FFF | 32K | Display adapter ROM (EGA, VGA, etc) |
| C8000-DFFFF | 96K | Unused (page frame for extended memory etc) |
| E0000-FFFFF | 128K | BIOS ROM |

## TIP

The DOS MEM command will let you know which programs and drivers are present in memory at any time. The command will also tell you how much extended memory you have available. Use the /CLASSIFY or /DEBUG switches with the MEM command.

```
Microsoft Diagnostics version 2.00    6/27/93   11:10pm   Page
===============================================================

--------------------------- Memory ---------------------------

Legend:   Available " "   RAM "##"   ROM "RR"   Possibly Available "
EMS Page Frame "PP"   Free XMS   UMBs "XX"
1024K FC00 RRRRRRRRRRRRRRRR FFFF   Conventional Memory
      F800 RRRRRRRRRRRRRRRR FBFF                    Total: 640K
      F400 RRRRRRRRRRRRRRRR F7FF                Available: 560K
 960K F000 RRRRRRRRRRRRRRRR F3FF                          574208 by
      EC00 XXXXXXXXXXXXXXXX EFFF
      E800 #XXXXXXXXXXXXXXX EBFF   Extended Memory
      E400 ################ E7FF                    Total: 3328K
 896K E000 ################ E3FF
      DC00 ################ DFFF   Expanded Memory (EMS)
      D800 ################ DBFF   LIM Version: 4.00
      D400 PPPPPPPPPPPPPPPP D7FF   Page Frame Address: C800H
 832K D000 PPPPPPPPPPPPPPPP D3FF                    Total: 3104K
      CC00 PPPPPPPPPPPPPPPP CFFF                Available: 2928K
      C800 PPPPPPPPPPPPPPPP CBFF
      C400 RRRRRRRRRRRRRRRR C7FF   XMS Information
 768K C000 RRRRRRRRRRRRRRRR C3FF                  XMS Version: 3.00
      BC00 ################ BFFF               Driver Version: 3.00
      B800 ################ BBFF            A20 Address Line: Enabled
      B400              B7FF            High Memory Area: In use
 704K B000              B3FF                Available: 2928K
      AC00              AFFF        Largest Free Block: 2928K
      A800              ABFF        Total Free XMS UMB: 30K
      A400              A7FF   Largest Free XMS UMB: 30K
 640K A000              A3FF
                               VCPI Information
                                    VCPI Detected: Yes
                                          Version: 1.00
                                 Available Memory: 2928K
```

*Figure 6.6   A sample memory map produced by MSD*

### TIP

If you have a '386 or later system, you can use the EMM386 driver to tell you what is happening in your expanded memory. Just enter the command EMM386 (you must have EMM386.EXE for this to work) to view the LIM/EMS version, the size of your expanded memory and the segment address of its page frame.

## Using RAM and ROM to find out about your system

A number of memory locations can be useful in determining the current state of a PC or PC-compatible microcomputer. You can display the contents of these memory locations (summarised in Table 6.7) using the MS-DOS DEBUG utility (see Chapter 14) or using a short routine written in QuickBASIC.

As an example, the following DEBUG command can be used to display the contents of ten bytes of RAM starting at memory location 0410:

D0:0410L0A

(NB: the equivalent command using the DR-DOS SID utility is: D0:410,419)

A rather more user-friendly method of displaying the contents of RAM is shown in Figure 6.7. This QuickBASIC program prompts the user for a start address (expressed in hexadecimal) and the number of bytes to display.

Figure 6.8 shows a typical example of running the program in Figure 6.7 on a '486-based computer. The program has been used to display the contents of 10 bytes of RAM from address 0410 onwards.

*Table 6.7  Useful RAM locations*

| Address (hex) | Number of bytes | Function |
|---|---|---|
| 0410 | 2 | Installed equipment list |
| 0413 | 2 | Usable base memory |
| 0417 | 2 | Keyboard status |
| 043E | 1 | Disk calibration (see Chapter 10) |
| 043F | 1 | Disk drive motor status (see Chapter 10) |
| 0440 | 1 | Drive motor count (see Chapter 10) |
| 0441 | 2 | Disk status (see Chapter 10) |
| 0442 | 2 | Disk controller status (see Chapter 10) |
| 0449 | 1 | Current video mode (see Chapter 13) |
| 044A | 2 | Current screen column width (see Chapter 13) |
| 046C | 4 | Master clock count (incremented by 1 on each clock 'tick') |
| 0472 | 2 | Set to 1234 hex. during a keyboard reboot (this requires <CRTL-ALT-DEL> keys) |
| 0500 | 1 | Screen print byte (00 indicates normal ready status, 01 indicates that a screen print is in operation, FF indicates that an error has occurred during the screen print operation) |

```
DEF SEG = 0
CLS
INPUT "Start address (in hex)"; address$
address$ = "&H" + address$
address = VAL(address$)
INPUT "Number of bytes to display"; number
PRINT
PRINT "Address", "Byte"
PRINT "(hex)", "(hex)"
PRINT
FOR i% = 0 TO number - 1
  v = PEEK(address + i%)
  PRINT HEX$(address + i%), HEX$(v)
NEXT i%
PRINT
END
```

*Figure 6.7  QuickBASIC program to display RAM contents*

```
Start address (in hex)? 410
Number of bytes to display? 10
```

| Address<br>(hex) | Byte<br>(hex) |
|---|---|
| 410 | 63 |
| 411 | 44 |
| 412 | BF |
| 413 | 80 |
| 414 | 2 |
| 415 | 0 |
| 416 | 18 |
| 417 | 20 |
| 418 | 0 |
| 419 | 0 |

*Figure 6.8   Output produced by the program in Figure 6.7*

### What equipment's installed?

The machine's Installed Equipment List (see Table 6.8) can tell you what hardware devices are currently installed in your system. The equipment list is held in the word (two bytes) starting address 0410. Figure 6.9 and Table 6.9 show you how to decipher the Equipment List word.

*Table 6.8   Equipment list word at address 0410*

| Bit Number | Meaning |
|---|---|
| 0 | Set if disk drives are present |
| 1 | Unused |
| 2 and 3 | System Board RAM size: |

| | Bit 3 | Bit 2 | RAM size |
|---|---|---|---|
| | 0 | 0 | 16K |
| | 0 | 1 | 32K |
| | 1 | 1 | 64K/256K |

(NB: on modern systems this coding does not apply)

| 4 and 5 | Initial video mode: |
|---|---|

| | Bit 5 | Bit 4 | Mode |
|---|---|---|---|
| | 0 | 1 | 40 column colour |
| | 1 | 0 | 80 column colour |
| | 1 | 1 | 80 column monochrome |

| 6 and 7 | Number of disk drives plus 1: |
|---|---|

| | Bit 7 | Bit 6 | Number of drives |
|---|---|---|---|
| | 0 | 0 | 1 |
| | 0 | 1 | 2 |
| | 1 | 0 | 3 |
| | 1 | 1 | 4 |

| Bit Number | Meaning |
|---|---|
| 8 | Reset if DMA chip installed (standard) |
| 9 to 11 | Number of serial ports installed |
| 12 | Set if an IBM Games Adapter is installed |
| 13 | Set if a serial printer is installed |
| 14 and 15 | Number of printers installed |

| Address: (hex) | | 0411 | | | 0410 | |
|---|---|---|---|---|---|---|
| Contents: (hex) | | 4 | 2 | | 2 | D |
| (binary) | | 0100 | 0010 | | 0010 | 1101 |
| Bit position: | | 15 | 8 | | 7 | 0 |

*Figure 6.9   Deciphering the equipment list*

*Table 6.9   Example equipment list*

| Bit position | Status | Comment |
|---|---|---|
| 0 | 1 = set | disk drives are present |
| 1 | 1 = set | this bit is not used |
| 2 | 0 = reset | these bits have no meaning with |
| 3 | 0 = reset | systems having greater than 256K RAM |
| 4 | 0 = reset | initial video mode is 80 column |
| 5 | 1 = set | colour |
| 6 | 1 = set | two disk drives installed |
| 7 | 0 = reset | |
| 8 | 0 = reset | DMA controller fitted (standard) |
| 9 | 0 = reset | two serial ports installed |
| 10 | 1 = set | |
| 11 | 0 = reset | |
| 12 | 0 = reset | no IBM Games Adapter installed |
| 13 | 0 = reset | no serial printer installed |
| 14 | 1 = set | one printer attached |
| 15 | 0 = reset | |

## How much base memory is available?

The amount of usable base memory can be determined from the two bytes starting at address 0413. The extent of memory is found by simply adding the binary weighted values of each set bit position. Figure 6.10 and Table 6.10 shows how this works.

*Table 6.10   Determining the base memory*

| Bit position | Status | Value |
|---|---|---|
| 9 | Set | 512K |
| 8 | Reset | 256K |
| 7 | Set | 128K |
| 6 | Reset | 64K |
| 5 | Reset | 32K |
| 4 | Reset | 16K |
| 3 | Reset | 8K |
| 2 | Reset | 4K |
| 1 | Reset | 2K |
| 0 | Reset | 1K |

Adding together the values associated with each of the set bits gives (512+128) = 640K.

| Address: (hex) | | 0414 | | | 0413 | |
|---|---|---|---|---|---|---|
| Contents: (hex) | | 0 | 2 | | 8 | 0 |
| (binary) | | 0000 | 0010 | | 1000 | 0000 |
| Bit position: | | 15 | 8 | | 7 | 0 |

*Figure 6.10   Determining the usable base memory*

## What ROM's fitted?

The BIOS ROM release date and machine ID can be found by examining the area of read-only memory extending between absolute locations FFFF5 and FFFFC. The ROM release information (not found in all compatibles) is presented in American date format using ASCII characters. Various ROM release dates for various IBM models are shown in Table 6.11.

### Table 6.11   IBM major ROM release dates

| ROM date | PC version |
|----------|------------|
| 04/24/81 | Original PC |
| 10/19/81 | Revised PC |
| 08/16/82 | Original XT |
| 10/27/82 | PC upgrade to XT BIOS level |
| 11/08/82 | PC-XT |
| 06/01/83 | Original PC Junior |
| 01/10/84 | Original AT |
| 06/10/85 | Revised PC-AT |
| 09/13/85 | PC Convertible |
| 11/15/85 | Revised PC-AT |
| 01/10/86 | Revised PC-XT |
| 04/10/86 | XT 286 |
| 06/26/87 | PS/2 Model 25 |
| 09/02/96 | PS/2 Model 30 |
| 12/12/86 | Revised PS/2 Model 30 |
| 02/13/87 | PS/2 Models 50 and 60 |
| 12/05/87 | Revised PS/2 Model 30 |
| 03/30/87 | PS/2 Model 80 (16MHz) |
| 10/07/87 | PS/2 Model 80 (20 MHz) |
| 01/29/88 | PS/2 Model 70 |
| 12/01/89 | PS/1 |
| 11/21/89 | PS/2 Model 80 (25MHz) |

## What kind of machine?

The type of machine (whether PC-XT, AT, etc) is encoded in the form of an identification (ID) byte which is stored at address FFFFE. Table 6.12 gives the ID bytes for each member of the PC family (non-IBM machines may have ID bytes which differ from those listed).

### Table 6.12   ID bytes for various IBM machines

| ID Byte (hex) | Machine |
|---------------|---------|
| F8 | PS/2 Models 35, 40, 65, 70, 80 and 90 ('386 and '486 CPU) |
| F9 | PC Convertibles |
| FA | PS/2 Models 25, 30 ('8086 CPU) |
| FB | PC-XT (revised versions, post 1986) |
| FC | AT, PS/2 Models 50 and 60 ('286 CPU) |
| FD | PC Junior |
| FE | XT and Portable PC |
| FF | Original PC |

### Getting into the BIOS ROM

You can display the ROM release date and machine ID byte by using the MS-DOS DEBUG utility or by using the simple QuickBASIC program shown in Figure 6.11. An example of the output produced by this program is shown in Figure 6.12 (the machine in question has an ID byte of FC and a ROM release date of 06/06/92).

## Memory diagnostics

### ROM diagnostics

The PC'c BIOS ROM incorporates some basic diagnostic software which checks the BIOS ROM and DRAM during the initialisation process. The ROM diagnostic is based upon a known 'checksum' for

```
DEF SEG = &HFFF0
CLS
PRINT "ROM address", "Byte", "ASCII"
PRINT "(hex)", "(hex)"
PRINT
FOR i% = &HF0 TO &HFF
  v = PEEK(i%)
  PRINT HEX$(i%), HEX$(v), ;
  IF v > 31 AND v < 128 THEN
    PRINT CHR$(v)
  ELSE
    PRINT ""
  END IF
NEXT i%
PRINT
END
```

*Figure 6.11   QuickBASIC program to display the last 16 bytes of the BIOS ROM*

| ROM address (hex) | Byte (hex) | ASCII | Comment |
|---|---|---|---|
| F0 | EA | | |
| F1 | 5B | [ | |
| F2 | E0 | | |
| F3 | 0 | | |
| F4 | F0 | | |
| F5 | 30 | 0 | *ROM release date* |
| F6 | 36 | 6 | *06/06/92* |
| F7 | 2F | / | |
| F8 | 30 | 0 | |
| F9 | 36 | 6 | |
| FA | 2F | / | |
| FB | 39 | 9 | |
| FC | 32 | 2 | |
| FD | 0 | | |
| FE | FC | | *Machine ID byte* |
| FF | 0 | | |

*Figure 6.12   Output produced by the program shown in Figure 6.11*

the device. Each byte of ROM is successively read and a checksum is generated. This checksum is then compared with a stored checksum or is adjusted by padding the ROM with bytes which make the checksum amount to zero (neglecting overflow). If any difference is detected an error message is produced and the bootstrap routine is aborted.

## RAM diagnostics

In the case of RAM diagnostics the technique is quite different and usually involves writing and reading each byte of RAM in turn. Various algorithms have been developed which make this process more reliable (e.g., 'walking ones'). Where a particular bit is 'stuck' (i.e., refuses to be changed), the bootstrap routine is aborted and an error code is displayed. This error code will normally allow you to identify the particular device that has failed.

The power-on self-test (POST) code within the BIOS ROM checks the system (including system board ROM and RAM) during initialisation . The POST reports any errors detected using a numeric code (see Chapter 16 for a full list).

More complex RAM diagnostics involve continuously writing and reading complex bit patterns. These tests are more comprehensive than simple read/write checks. RAM diagnostics can also be carried out on a non-destructive basis. In such cases, the byte read from RAM is replaced immediately after each byte has been tested. It is thus possible to perform a diagnostic check some time after the system has been initialised and without destroying any programs and data which may be resident in memory at the time.

---

**TIP**

You can usually bypass the BIOS POST memory check by pressing the <ESC> key. This will abandon the memory self-test and continue initialising the system in the normal way.

---

## Parity checking

The integrity of stored data integrity can be checked by adding an extra 'parity bit'. This bit is either set or reset according to whether the number of 1's present within the byte are even or odd (i.e., 'even parity' and 'odd parity').

Parity bits are automatically written to memory during a memory write cycle and read from memory during a memory read cycle. A non-maskable interrupt (NMI) is generated if a parity error is detected and thus users are notified if RAM faults develop during normal system operation.

## The last resort...

Fault finding on semiconductor memories is relatively simple when software diagnostic routines are available. In some cases (e.g., failure of the boot ROM or a bus failure within a DRAM device), a faulty chip may prevent normal system initialisation. In such cases, a failed device may consume excessive power and run very warm. The following procedure will normally allow you to identify the defective chip:

(i) Leave the system running for 10 minutes, or more, then touch the centre of each chip in turn in order to ascertain its working temperature. If a device is running distinctly hot (i.e., so warm that it is too hot to touch or noticeably warmer than other similar devices) it should be considered a prime suspect. (If possible compare with the heat produced by an identical chip fitted in the same machine.).

(ii) Wherethe boot ROM or DRAM chips have been fitted in sockets, carefully remove and replace each suspected device in turn (disconnecting the power and observing the static precautions mentioned in Chapter 3). Replace each device with a known functional device.

(iii) Where the boot ROM or DRAM chips are soldered directly to the PCB, a current tracer (see Chapter 15) can be usefully employeed to pinpoint a failed device. The current tracer should be applied to the copper PCB at strategic points along the +5V supply rail to each device in turn.

Finally, if you do have to desolder a suspect boot ROM or DRAM chip, it is well worth fitting the PCB with a socket before replacing the chip. A low-profile DIL socket with the appropriate number of pins will only cost a few pence but it could save much aggravation in the event of another failure!

# 7
# The Parallel Printer Interface

The PC's parallel ports (LPT1 and LPT2) provide a very simple and effective interface which can be used to link your PC to a wide range of printers. This chapter explains the principles of parallel I/O and describes the Centronics interface standard before discussing basic fault finding and troubleshooting procedures which can be applied to the parallel printer interface.

## Parallel I/O

Parallel I/O is used to transfer bytes of data at a time between a microcomputer and a peripheral device (such as a printer). This method of I/O requires a minimum of hardware (e.g., a single 8255 parallel I/O device) and it is thus relatively easy and inexpensive to implement.

The 8255 (or equivalent) is used to interface the PC's system data bus to the external 8-bit data lines that link the computer to the printer. In addition, several other control signals are present in order to achieve 'handshaking', the aptly named process which controls the exchange of data between the computer system and the printer.

A basic handshake sequence is as follows:

(a) the PC indicates that it is ready to output data to the printer by asserting the STROBE line,

(b) the PC then waits for the printer to respond by asserting the ACK (acknowledge) line,

(c) when ACK is received by the PC, it places the outgoing data on the eight data lines,

(d) the cycle is then repeated until the printer's internal buffer is full of data.

The buffer may have to be filled several times during the printing of a large document. Each time, the port will output data at a fast rate but the printer will takes an appreciable amount of time to print each character and thus will operate at a very much slower rate. Clearly, your PC will be 'tied up' for less time if you have a larger printer buffer!

### TIP

You can read the status of the PC's parallel printer ports using a few QuickBASIC statements. As an example, the code Figure 7.1 will let you determine the status of LPT1 and also give you some idea of what is happening at the printer.

## The Centronics interface standard

The Centronics interface has become established as the most commonly used interface standard for the transfer of data between a PC

```
DEF SEG = &H40
DO
   status& = PEEK(9) * 256 + PEEK(8) + 1
   stat% = INP(status&)
   IF stat% = &H57 THEN PRINT "Printer not ready"
   IF stat% = &H77 THEN PRINT "Printer out of paper"
   IF stat% = &HF7 THEN PRINT "Printer off-line"
   GOSUB waitkey
LOOP UNTIL stat% = &HDF
PRINT "Printer ready"
DEF SEG
```

**Figure 7.1 QuickBASIC program which will allow you to determine the status of LPT1**

and a printer. The standard employs parallel data transmission (a byte is transferred at a time).

The standard is based on a 36-way Amphenol connector (see Figure 7.2 and Table 7.1). The interface is generally suitable for transfer of data at distances of up to 4m, or so. At greater distances, an RS-232 serial data link is usually more effective. Note that, whilst an Amphenol connector is usually fitted at the printer, the PC invariably has a standard female 25-way female D-type connector.

It is also worth noting that data transfer is essentially in one direction only (from the microcomputer to the printer). Indeed, some early PC's have printer ports which can only be configured in one direction (i.e., output only).

Handshaking between the microcomputer and printer is accomplished by means of the strobe, (STROBE), acknowledge (ACK), and busy (BUSY) lines. The BUSY line is asserted when a 'error' condition occurs (e.g., 'printer off-line', or 'paper out').

**Table 7.1 The Centronics printer interface signals and pin connections**

| Pin no. 36-way Amphenol connector | Pin no. 25-way female PC connector | Signal | Function |
|---|---|---|---|
| 1 | 1 | STROBE | Strobe. Pulsed low to initiate data transfer. |
| 2 | 2 | DATA1 | Data line 1 (bit 0) |
| 3 | 3 | DATA2 | Data line 2 (bit 1) |
| 4 | 4 | DATA3 | Data line 3 (bit 2) |
| 5 | 5 | DATA4 | Data line 4 (bit 3) |
| 6 | 6 | DATA5 | Data line 5 (bit 4) |
| 7 | 7 | DATA6 | Data line 6 (bit 5) |
| 8 | 8 | DATA7 | Data line 7 (bit 6) |
| 9 | 9 | DATA8 | Data line 8 (bit 7) |
| 10 | 10 | ACK | Acknowledge. Pulsed low to indicate that data has been received. |
| 11 | 11 | BUSY | Busy. Usually taken higher under the following conditions: (a) during data entry (b) during a printing operation (c) when the printer is 'off-line' (d) when an error condition exists. |
| 12 | 12 | PE | Paper end. Taken high to indicate that the printer is out of paper. |

*Table 7.1 Cont.*

| Pin no. 36-way Amphenol connector | Pin no. 25-way female PC connector | Signal | Function |
|---|---|---|---|
| 13 | 13 | SLCT | Select. Taken high to indicate that the printer is in the selected state. |
| 14 | 14 | AUTO FEED XT | Automatic feed. When this input is taken low, the printer is instructed to produce an automatic line feed after printing. This function can normally also be selected by means of an internal DIP switch |
| 15 | | n.c. | Not connected (unused) |
| 16 | | 0V | Logic ground |
| 17 | | CHASSIS GND | Printer chassis (usually isolated from logic ground) |
| 18 | | n.c. | Not connected (unused) |
| 19 to 30 | 18 to 25 | GND | Signal ground. Originally defined as 'twisted pair earth returns' for each of the data lines, pins 1 to 12 respectively, these lines are just simply connected to the common ground. |
| 31 | 16 | INIT | Initialise. Pulsed low to reset the printer controller. |
| 32 | 15 | ERROR | Taken low by the printer to indicate: (a) Paper-end status (b) Off-line status (c) Error status |
| 33 | | GND | Signal ground |
| 34 | | n.c. | Not connected (unused) |
| 35 | | LOGIC1 | Logic 1 (usually pulled to +5V by a fixed resistor) |
| 36 | 17 | SLCTIN | Select input. Data entry to the printer is only possible when this line is taken low. The function can normally be disabled using a DIP switch. |

Notes:
1. Signals, pin numbers, and signal directions are as seen by the printer.
2. The PC end of the interface is fitted with a 25-way D-connector (rather than a 36-way Amphenol connector).
3. All signals employ standard TTL levels and are 'TTL compatible'.
4. The ERROR and ACK are not supported on a number of machines.

## Printer Types and Emulations

A vast selection of different types of printer is available to the PC user including laser, thermal, ink-jet, and impact dot matrix types. Whatever the actual printing technology, printers tend to fall into one of two main categories; 'line printers' and 'page printers'. In the former case each line of text is built up in turn whilst in the later the full image of a page is received and processed before printing.

Most printers nowadays support a number of different standards or 'emulations'. These include the following:

1. The Diablo standard used with early daisy-wheel printers which only offer text printing capability.
2. The Epson standard which is widely used with impact dot-matrix printers and which offers a number of variants including FX, RX, LQ, GQ, etc.
3. As its name implies, the Hewlett-Packard LaserJet standard was designed for laser printers. The standard uses a simple language based on escape sequences (known as 'printer control language'). Printer control language (PCL) has been progressively enhanced as shown in Table 7.2.

*Table 7.2   Printer control language*

| Language | Machines supported |
| --- | --- |
| PCL3 | Original LaserJet printers. |
| PCL4 | LaserJet Plus and LaserJet II printers. |
| PCL5 | LaserJet III printers (this version supports 'scalable fonts') |

In addition, many printers now support the increasingly popular PostScript emulation. This will allow you to incorporate a vast range of scalable typefaces into your documents.

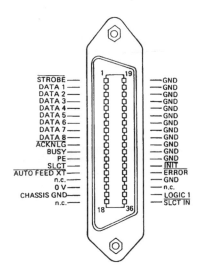

*Figure 7.2   36-way Centronics printer interface connector*

## Troubleshooting the parallel printer interface

Fault finding on a PC printer interface is usually quite straightforward and generally involves checking first that the printer is operating correctly (by using the printer 'self-test'), and that no error condition exists (e.g., 'paper out' or incorrect DIP switch setting). Printer cables and connectors often prove to be troublesome (particularly when they are regularly connected and disconnected) and it is always worth checking the cable first.

It will usually be a fairly easy matter to decide which part of the interface (printer, cable or the PC's parallel port) is at fault. Where text is printed but characters appear to be translated resulting in garbled output, one or more of the data line signals may be missing. In this case it is worth checking individual signal lines (D1 to D8) at each end of the cable.

Where the handshake signals are missing, you will usually be warned by an on-screen error message (such as 'printer not responding' or 'printer off-line'). Handshake lines (and, where appropriate, individual data lines) can be easily checked using a logic probe. An output line which is 'stuck' (i.e., permanently at logic 1 or logic 0) or is 'floating' (i.e., takes neither logical state) can be easily located.

It is always worth checking that you have selected the correct printer emulation and print options (e.g., paper size, lines per page, etc). Many software packages are supplied with printer configuration files or 'printer driver' files which ensure that the control codes generated by the software match those required by the printer.

### TIP

Standard printer output routines direct their output to the parallel printer port (LPT1). You can use the DOS MODE command (see Chapter 14) to redirect the output to an alternative output device (e.g., COM1).

### TIP

You can use the DOS PRINT command to redirect printing. Suppose, for example, that you need to send all your printed output to LPT2 whenever you use your system. All you need to do is include the following statement in your AUTOEXEC.BAT file:

PRINT /D:LPT2

### TIP

The DOS MODE command allows you to configure your printer. When used to configure the printer the MODE command syntax (DOS 3.3) is as follows:
MODE LPTn: c,l
The equivalent syntax for DOS 4 (and higher) is:
MODE LPTn: COLS=c LINES=l
where n = printer port number (1, 2 etc)
       c = columns (80 or 132)
       l = vertical spacing (6 or 8 lines per inch)

**TIP**

The DOS PRINT command lets you establish a print buffer in memory. The default size of the buffer is a mere 512 bytes (about eight lines of average text). You can increase the size of the buffer (and speed things up a bit when using the PRINT command to output files to your printer) by increasing the buffer size. If you have sufficient memory available, try incorporating the following line in your AUTOEXEC.BAT file:
PRINT /B:8192
The command establishes an 8K buffer (enough for two pages of normal text).

### Printer control codes

Special codes can be sent to a printer in order to determine the type style and page format. These codes can take the form of single byte characters (ASCII characters in the range 0 to 1F hex.) or a sequence of characters preceded by the ASCII Escape character (27 decimal or 1B hex.). In addition, dot matrix printers are normally capable of operating in text (character based) or graphics (bit image) modes. You can switch modes by means of escape sequences.

*Table 7.3   QuickBASIC commands that will allow you to control print styles on Epson-compatible printers*

| Command | Effect |
|---|---|
| LPRINT CHR$ (15); | condensed mode |
| LPRINT CHR$ (27); "G"; | double strike mode |
| LPRINT CHR$ (27); "E"; | emphasised mode |
| LPRINT CHR$ (27); "4"; | italic mode |
| LPRINT CHR$ (27); "S"; "0"; | subscript mode |
| LPRINT CHR$ (27); "S"; "1"; | superscript mode |
| LPRINT CHR$ (18); | cancel condensed mode |
| LPRINT CHR$ (27); "F"; | cancel emphasised mode |
| LPRINT CHR$ (27); "H"; | cancel double strike mode |
| LPRINT CHR$ (27); "5"; | cancel italic mode |
| LPRINT CHR$ (27); "T"; | cancel subscript/superscript mode |

**TIP**

You can configure an Epson-compatible printer using the simple QuickBASIC commands shown in Table 7.3. These commands can be entered in immediate mode or incorporated into a configuration program (don't forget to reset the printer when you have finished!)

**TIP**

When printing text on a LaserJet-compatible printer, it is often useful to be able to change the number of characters printed on each line. The simple QuickBASIC commands shown in Table 7.4 will let you select printing using either 80, 96, or 132 characters per line.

*Table 7.4 QuickBASIC commands that will allow you to se-
lect the number of characters per line on LaserJet compatible
printers*

| Command | Effect |
|---|---|
| LPRINT CHR\$ (27); "E"; | reset the printer (80 chars/line) |
| LPRINT CHR\$ (27); "(s0p12H)"; | select 96 chars/line |
| LPRINT CHR\$ (27); (s16.66H); | select 132 chars/line |

## Printing from Windows

When you wish to use a printer with Windows applications, you need
to do the following:

1. Install the printer driver file for the printer in question (this
   file will normally be present on one of your installation disks
   and Windows will copy it to the hard disk).
2. Select the port you wish to assign to the printer (e.g., LPT1,
   LPT2, COM1, or COM2).
3. Choose the printer and print options that you wish to use with
   the installed printer.
4. Select the 'active' printer for each port (you can have more
   than one printer installed but only one can be active on each
   port at any time).
5. Select the 'default printer' (i.e., the printer driver that is loaded
   automatically when Windows starts up).

Windows lets you select a 'default printer' and an 'active printer'
via the Control Panel window. You can also install further printer
drivers or set up various options to use with your existing printer
(select the 'Configure' option).

Finally, the Windows Print Manager allows you to establish a 'print
queue'. This lets your system carry out its printing as a 'background
operation' (you can carry on using the application whilst files in the
print queue are 'spooled' to your printer). Note that you can change
the order of this queue, pause the printing, and also delete files that
are currently waiting in the queue.

### TIP

Microsoft's Windows provides you with an excellent DOS utility
called MSD (Microsoft System Diagnostic). You will find this program in your WINDOWS directory (see Chapter 14 if you need
to know how to change the directory and run a DOS program)
MSD includes a printer test routine which will allow you to select a printer type and port before putting your printer through
its paces.

# 8
# The Serial Communications Ports

The PC's serial communication ports (COM1, COM2, etc) provide a means of linking your PC with the rest of the world. Data can be exchanged with remote host computers, 'bulletin boards', and a vast number of other PC users world-wide. This chapter explains the basic principles of serial I/O and describes the RS-232 interface standard before providing you with some useful fault finding and trouble-shooting information.

## Serial I/O devices

Serial I/O involves transmitting a stream of bits, one after another, from a PC to a peripheral device and vice versa. Since parallel (8, 16 or 32-bit) data is present on the system bus, serial I/O is somewhat more complex than parallel I/O.

Serial input data must be converted to parallel (byte wide) data which can be presented to the system data bus. Conversely, the parallel data on the bus must be converted into serial data before it can be output from the port. In the first case, conversion can be performed with a serial-input parallel-output (SIPO) shift register whilst in the second case a parallel-input serial-output (PISO) shift register is required.

Serial data may be transferred in either 'synchronous' or 'asynchronous' mode. In the former case, transfers are carried out in accordance with a common clock signal (the clock must be available at both ends of the transmission path). Asynchronous operation, on the other hand, involves transmission of data in small 'packets'; each packet containing the necessary information required to decode the data which it contains. Clearly this technique is more complex but it has the considerable advantage that a separate clock signal is not required.

As with programmable parallel I/O devices, a variety of different names are used to describe programmable serial I/O devices including 'asynchronous communications interface adaptor' (ACIA) and 'universal asynchronous receiver/transmitter' (UART). Both types of device have common internal features including registers for buffering the transmit and receive data and controlling the format of each data word. The most notable input and output signals used with serial I/O devices are shown in Table 8.1.

*Table 8.1  Signals produced by a serial I/O device*

| Signal | Function |
| --- | --- |
| D0 to D7 | Data input/output lines connected directly to the system data bus |
| RXD (or RD) | Received (incoming) serial data |
| TXD (or TD) | Transmitted (outgoing) serial data |
| CTS | Clear to send. This signal is taken low by the peripheral when it is ready to accept data from the microprocessor system |
| RTS | Request to send. This signal is taken low by the UART when it wishes to send data to the peripheral. |

Signals produced directly by serial I/O devices are invariably TTL compatible. Furthermore, such signals are unsuitable for anything other than the shortest of data transmission paths (e.g., between a keyboard and a system enclosure). Serial data transmission over any appreciable distance requires additional 'line drivers' to provide buffering and level shifting between the serial I/O device and the physical medium. Additionally, 'line receivers' are required to condition and modify the incoming signal to TTL levels.

# The RS-232 standard

The RS-232/CCITT V.24 interface is currently the most widely used standard for serial communication between microcomputers, peripheral devices, and remote host computers. Unfortunately, the standard is not generally well understood and end-users of microcomputers often experience considerable difficulty in connecting together equipment using the RS-232 interface.

The RS-232 standard was first defined by the Electronic Industries Association (EIA) in 1962 as a recommended standard (RS) for modem interfacing. The latest revision of the RS-232 standard (RS-232D, January 1987) brings it in-line with international standards CCITT V24, V28 and ISO IS2110. The RS-232D standard includes facilities for 'loop-back' testing which were not defined under the previous RS-232C standard.

## Terminology

The standard relates essentially to two types of equipment; Data Terminal Equipment (DTE) and Data Circuit Terminating Equipment (DCE). Data Terminal Equipment (i.e., a PC) is capable of sending and/or receiving data via the COM1 or COM2 serial interface. It is thus said to 'terminate' the serial link. Data Circuit Terminating Equipment (formerly known as Data Communications Equipment), on the other hand, facilitates data communications. A typical example is that of a 'modem' (modulator-demodulator) which forms an essential link in the serial path between a PC and a telephone line.

## TIP

You can normally distinguish a DTE device from a DCE device by examining the type of connector fitted. A DTE device is is normally fitted with a male connector whilst a DCE device is invariably fitted with a female connector.

## TIP

There is a subtle difference between the 'bit rate' as perceived by the computer and the 'baud rate' (i.e., the signalling rate in the transmission medium. The reason is simply that additional start, stop and parity bits must accompany the data so that it can be recovered from the *asynchronous* data stream. For example, a typical PC serial configuration might use a total of 11 bits to convey each 7-bit ASCII character. In this case, a line baud rate of 600 baud implies a useful data transfer rate of a mere 382 bits per second.

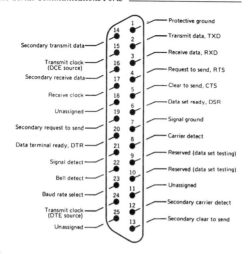

*Figure 8.1    Standard 25-way RS-232 D-connector*

## The RS-232 connector

A PC serial interface is usually implemented using a standard 25-way
D connector (see Figure 8.1). The PC (the DTE) is fitted with a male
connector and the peripheral device (the DCE) normally uses a female connector. When you need to link two PC's togther, they must
both adopt the role of DTE whilst thinking that the other is a DCE.
This little bit of trickery is enabled by means of a 'null-modem'. The
null-modem works by swapping over the TXD and RXD, CTS and
RTS, DTR and DSR signals.

## RS-232 signals

The signals present within the RS-232 interface fall into one of the
following three categories:

(a) **Data** (e.g., TXD, RXD)

RS-232 provides for two independent serial data channels (described as 'primary' and 'secondary'). Both of these channels
provide for full duplex operation (i.e., simultaneous transmission and reception).

(b) **Handshake control** (e.g., RTS, CTS)

Handshake signals provide the means by which the flow of
serial data is controlled allowing, for example, a DTE to open
a dialogue with the DCE prior to actually transmitting data
over the serial data path.

(c) **Timing** (e.g., TC, RC)

For synchronous (rather than the more usual asynchronous)
mode of operation, it is necessary to pass clock signals between the devices. These timing signals provide a means of
synchronising the received signal to allow correct decoding.

The *complete* set of RS-232D signals is summarised in Table 8.2, together with EIA and CCITT designations and commonly used signal

line abbreviations.

*Table 8.2 The complete set of RS-232 signals and pin connections*

| Pin | EIA inter-change circuit | CCITT equiv. | Common abbrev. | Direction | Signal/function |
|---|---|---|---|---|---|
| 1 | – | – | FG | – | Frame or protective ground |
| 2 | BA | 103 | TXD or TD | To DCE | Transmitted data |
| 3 | BB | 104 | RXD or RD | To DTE | Received data |
| 4 | CA | 105 | RTS | To DCE | Request to send |
| 5 | CB | 106 | CTS | To DTE | Clear to send |
| 6 | CC | 107 | DSR | To DTE | DCE ready |
| 7 | AB | 102 | SG | – | Signal ground/common |
| 8 | CF | 109 | DCD | To DTE | Received line signal detector (carrier detect) |
| 9 | – | – | – | – | Reserved for testing (positive test voltage) |
| 10 | – | – | – | – | Reserved for testing (negative test voltage) |
| 11 | – | – | (QM) | – | (Equaliser mode) |
| 12 | SCF/ CI | 122/ 112 | SDCD | To DTE | Secondary received line signal detector/ Data rate select (DCE source) |
| 13 | SCB | 121 | SCTS | To DTE | Secondary clear to send |
| 14 | SBA | 118 | STD | To DCE | Secondary transmitted data |
| 15 | DB | 114 | TC | To DCE | Transmitter signal element timing (DCE source) |
| 16 | SBB | 119 | SRD | To DTE | Secondary received data |
| 17 | DD | 115 | RC | To DTE | Receiver signal element timing (DCE souce) |
| 18 | LL | 141 | (DCR) | To DCE | Local loopback (Divided receive clock) |
| 19 | SCA | 120 | SRTS | To DCE | Secondary request to send |
| 20 | CD | 108.2 | DTR | To DCE | Data terminal ready |
| 21 | RL/ CG | 140/ 110 | SQ | To DCE/ | Remote loopback/ |
| | | | | To DTE | Signal quality detector |
| 22 | CE | 125 | RI | To DTE | Ring indicator |
| 23 | CH/ CI | 111/ 112 | – | To DCE/ | Data signal rate selector (DTE) |
| | | | | To DTE | Data signal rate selector (DCE) |

**Table 8.2 Cont.**

| Pin | EIA inter-change circuit | CCITT equiv. | Common abbrev. | Direction | Signal/function |
|-----|------|------|------|------|------|
| 24 | DA | 113 | TC | To DCE | Transmit signal element timing |
| 25 | TM | 142 | – | To DTE | Test mode |

Notes:

1. The functions given in brackets for lines 11 and 18 relate to the Bell 113B and 208A specifications.
2. Lines 9 and 10 are normally reserved for testing. A typical use for these lines is testing of the positive and negative voltage levels used to represent the MARK and SPACE levels.
3. For new designs using EIA interchange circuit SCF, CH and CI are assigned to pin-23. If SCF is not used, CI is assigned to pin-12.
4. Some manufacturers use spare RS-232 lines for testing and/ or special functions peculiar to particular hardware (some equipment even feeds power and analogue signals along unused RS-232C lines!).

In practice, few RS-232 implementations make use of the secondary channel and, since asynchronous (non-clocked) operation is almost invariably used with microcomputer systems, only eight or nine of the 25 RS-232 signals are used in the PC. These signals present on the PC's 9-way serial port connector are described in Table 8.3.

**Table 8.3 Subset of RS-232 signals used on the PC's 9-pin connector**

| Pin no: | EIA inter-change circuit | Signal | Function |
|-----|------|------|------|
| 1 | CF | DCD | Active when a data carrier is detected. |
| 2 | BB | RXD | Serial data received by the PC from the DCE. |
| 3 | BA | TXD | Serial data transmitted from PC to DCE. |
| 4 | CD | DTR | When active, the DTE is signalling that it is operational and that the PC may be connected to the communications channel. |
| 5 | AB | SG | Common signal return path. |
| 6 | CC | DSR | When active, the DCE is signalling that a communications path has been properly established. |
| 7 | CA | RTS | When active, the PC is signalling that it wishes to send data to the DCE. |
| 8 | CB | CTS | When active, the DCE is signalling that it is ready to accept data from the PC. |

(a) 4-way cable for dumb terminals

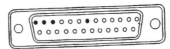

Pins used: 1–3 and 7 (pins 8 and 20 are jumpered)

(b) 9-way cable for asynchronous communications

Pins used: 1–8 and 20

(c) 15-way cable for synchronous communications

Pins used: 1–8, 13, 15, 17, 20, 22 and 24

(d) 25-way cable for universal applications

Pins used: 1–25

*Figure 8.2   Various possibilities for RS-232 data cables*

## TIP

There are various types of RS-232 data cable. Some may have as few as four connections, many have nine or fifteen, and some have all 25. When you purchase a cable it is worth checking how many connections are present within the cable. A cheaper 9-way cable will usually work provided your software does not make use of the 'ring indicator' facility. Figure 8.2 shows some of the possibilities for data cable wiring.

## Line signals and voltages

In most RS-232 systems, data is transmitted asynchronously as a series of small 'packets' each of which represents a single ASCII (or control) character.

ASCII characters are represented by seven bits. The upper case letter 'A', for example, is represented by the seven-bit binary word 1000001. In order to send the letter 'A' via an RS-232 system, extra bits must be added to signal the start and end of the data packet. These are known as the 'start bit' and 'stop bits' respectively. In addition, you can include a further bit to provide a simple 'parity' error detecting facility.

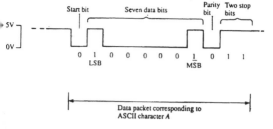

**Figure 8.3   Representation of ASCII character 'A' using TTL levels (1 start bit, 1 parity bit and 2 stop bits)**

One of the most commonly used schemes involves the use of one start bit, one parity bit, and two stop bits. The commencement of the data packet is signalled by the start bit which is always low irrespective of the contents of the packet. The start bit is followed by the seven data bits representing the ASCII character concerned. A parity bit is added to make the resulting number of 1's in the group either odd ('odd parity') or even ('even parity'). Finally, two stop bits are added. These are both high. The TTL representation of this character is shown in Figure 8.3.

## TIP

You can configure the serial ports using the DOS MODE command (see page 153). MODE allows you to set up the baud rate, the number of data bits, the number of stop bits, and the type of parity checking (even, odd or none).

The complete asynchronously transmitted data word thus comprises eleven bits (note that only seven of these actually contain data). The binary word can be represented as: 01000001011. In this case, even parity has been used and thus the ninth (parity bit) is reset (0).

The voltage levels employed in an RS-232 interface are markedly different from those used within a microcomputer system. A positive voltage (of between +3V and +25V) is used to represent a logic 0 (or 'SPACE') whilst a negative voltage (of between -3V and -25V) is used to represent a logic 1 (or 'MARK'). The line signal corresponding to the ASCII character 'A' is shown in Figure 8.4.

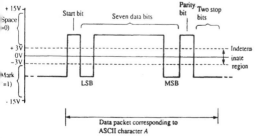

**Figure 8.4   Representation of ASCII character 'A' at standard RS-232 line voltage levels (comparethis diagram with Figure 8.3)**

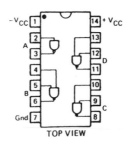

*Figure 8.5    1488 RS-232 line driver pin connections*

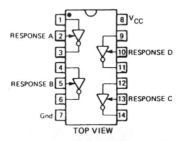

*Figure 8.6    1489 RS-232 line receiver pin connections*

The level shifting (from TTL to RS-232 signal levels and vice versa) is invariably accomplished using 'line driver' and 'line receiver' chips, the most common examples being the 1488 and 1489 devices (see Figure 8.5 and 8.6 respectively).

## RS-232 electrical characteristics

Table 8.4 summarises the principal electrical specification for the RS-232 standard whilst Figure 8.7 shows the normally acceptable range of RS-232 line voltage levels:

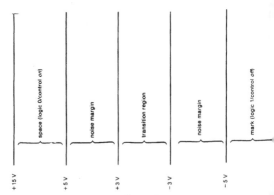

*Figure 8.7    Normally accepted range of voltages used in a RS-232 interface*

### Table 8.4 Electrical characteristics of the RS-232 interface

| | |
|---|---|
| Maximum line driver output voltage (open circuit): | ±25V |
| Maximum line driver output current (short circuit): | ±500mA |
| Minimum line impedance: | 3k (in parallel with 2.5nF) |
| Line driver SPACE output voltage ($3k \leq R_L \leq 7k$): | +5V to +15V |
| Line driver MARK output voltage ($3k \leq R_L \leq 7k$): | -5V to -15V |
| Line driver output (idle state): | MARK |
| Line receiver output with open circuit input: | logic 1 |
| Line receiver output with input ≥3V: | logic 0 |
| Line receiver output with input ≥ -3V: | logic 1 |

## Troubleshooting the communication ports

Troubleshooting the communication ports usually involves the following basic steps:

(a) Check the physical connection between the PC (the 'DTE') and the DCE (e.g., the modem). Where both devices are PC's (i.e., both configured as DTE) a patch box or null modem (see Figure 8.8) should be inserted for correct operation.

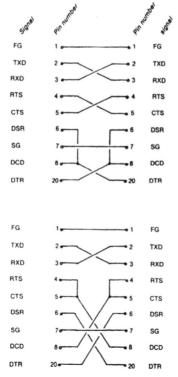

**Figure 8.8 Two forms of null-modem**

(b) Check that the correct cable has been used. Note that RS-232 cables are provided in a variety of forms; 4-way (for 'dumb' terminals), 9-way (for normal asynchronous data communications), 15-way (for synchronous comminications), and 25-way (for 'universal' applications) - see Figure 8.2.If in doubt, use full 25-way cable.

(c) Check that the same data word format and baud rate has been selected at each end of the serial link (note that this is most important and it often explains why an RS-232 link fails to operate even though the hardware and cables have been checked).

(d) Activate the link and investigate the logical state of the data (TXD and RXD) and handshaking (RTS, CTS etc) signal lines using a line monitor, breakout box, or interface tester. Lines may be looped back to test each end of the link.

(e) If in any doubt, refer to the equipment manufacturer's data in order to ascertain whether any special connections are required and to ensure that the interfaces are truly compatible. Note that some manufacturers have implemented quasi-RS-232 interfaces which make use of TTL signals. These are NOT electrically compatible with the normal RS-232 system even though they may obey the same communication protocols. They will also NOT interface directly with a standard PC COM port!

(f) The communications software should be initially configured for the 'least complex' protocol (e.g., basic 7-bit ASCII character transfer at 300 baud). When a successful link has been established, more complex protocols may be attempted in order to increase the data transfer rate or improve upon data checking.

## TIP

You can easily check your serial COM ports using a simple loopback test. You will need a female 25-pin or 9-pin D connector with three links soldered, as shown in Table 8.5. Connect the loopback plug to the port that you wish to test and then run the QuickBASIC program shown in Figure 8.9. The program reads consecutive keypresses and outputs them to the serial port. It then reads them from the serial port and displays them on the screen.

### Table 8.5  Loopback plug wiring

| Signals | Pins linked (9-way) | Pins linked (25-way) |
|---------|---------------------|----------------------|
| RXD and TXD | 2 to 3 | 3 to 2 |
| RTS and CTS | 7 to 8 | 4 to 5 |
| DTR and DSR | 4 to 6 | 20 to 6 |

```
' Loopback test routine using COM1 serial port
CLS
PRINT "Keyboard characters will be output to COM1"
PRINT "Screen shows from characters received from COM1"
PRINT "Press <ESC> to end the test..."
PRINT
OPEN "COM1:9600,E,7,1" FOR RANDOM AS #1

getkey:
K$ = INKEY$
IF K$ = "" THEN GOTO waitin
IF K$ = CHR$(3) OR K$ = CHR$(27) THEN GOTO finish
PRINT #1, K$;

waitin:
IF EOF(1) THEN GOTO getkey
C$ = INPUT$(LOC(1), #1)
PRINT C$;
GOTO getkey

finish:
CLOSE #1
CLS
END
```

*Figure 8.9  QuickBASIC loopback test program*

# 9
# The PC Expansion Bus

The availability of a standard expansion bus system within the PC must surely be one of the major factors in ensuring its continuing success. The bus is the key to expansion. It allows you to painlessly upgrade your system and configure it for almost any conceivable application. This chapter introduces you to the ISA and MCA bus standards and explains some of the pitfalls that can occur when you make use of the expansion bus.

## PC expansion schemes

Three basic standards are employed in conventional PC expansion bus schemes. The original, and still most widely used, standard is called 'Industry Standard Architecture' (ISA). This expansion scheme employs either one or two direct edge connectors and it can cater for an 8 or 16-bit system data bus.

The first ISA connector (62-way) provides access to the 8-bit data bus and the majority of control bus signals and power rails whilst the second connector (36-way) gives access to the remaining data bus lines together with some additional control bus signals. Applications which require only an 8-bit data path and a subset of the PC's standard control signals can make use of only the first connector. Applications which require access to a full 16-bit data path (not available in the early original PC and PC-XT machines) must make use of both connectors.

### MCA bus

With the advent of PS/2, a more advanced expansion scheme has become available. This expansion standard is known as 'Micro Channel Architecture' (MCA) and it provides access to the 16-bit DATA bus in the IBM PS/2 Models 50 and 60 whereas access to a full 32-bit data bus is available in the Model 80 which has an 80386 CPU.

An important advantage of MCA is that it permits data transfer at significantly faster rates than is possible with ISA. In fairness, the increase in data transfer rate may be unimportant in many applications and also tends to vary somewhat from machine to machine. As a rough guide, when a standard ISA bus AT machine is compared with an MCA PS/2 Model 50, data transfer rates can be expected to increase by around 25% for conventional memory transfers and by 100% (or more) for DMA transfers.

Since MCA interrupt signals are shared between expansion cards, MCA interrupt structure tends to differ from that employed within ISA where interrupt signals tend to remain exclusive to a particular expansion card. More importantly, MCA provides a scheme of bus arbitration in order to decide which of the 'feature cards' has rights to exercise control of the MCA bus at any particular time.

MCA's arbitration mechanism provides for up to 15 bus masters each one able to exercise control of the bus. As a further bonus, MCA provides an auxiliary video connector and programmable option configuration to relieve the tedium of setting DIP switches on system boards and expansion cards.

# EISA bus

Recently, a third bus standard has appeared. This standard is known as 'Extended Industry Standard Architecture' (EISA) and it is supported by a number of manufacturers seeking an alternative to the MCA standard.

EISA is a 32-bit expansion bus. To make the system compatible with ISA expansion cards, the standard is based on a two-level connector. The lowest level contacts (used by EISA cards) make connection with the extended 32-bit bus whilst the upper level contacts (used by ISA cards) provide the 8 and 16-bit connections.

# ISA bus

The PC's ISA bus is based upon a number of expansion 'slots' each of which is fitted with a 62-way direct edge connector together with an optional subsidiary 36-way direct edge connector. Expansion (or option) cards may be designed to connect only to the 62-way connector or may, alternatively, mate with both the 62-way and 36-way connectors.

Since only the 62-way connector was fitted on early machines (which then had an 8-bit data bus), cards designed for use with this connector are sometimes known as '8-bit expansion cards' or 'XT expansion cards'. The AT machine, however, provides access to a full 16-bit data bus together with additional control signals and hence requires the additional 36-way connector. Cards which are designed to make use of both connectors are generally known as '16-bit expansion cards' or 'AT expansion cards'.

The original PC was fitted with only five expansion slots (spaced approximately 25mm apart). The standard XT provided a further three slots to make a total of eight (spaced approximately 19mm apart). Some cards, particularly those providing hard disk storage, require the width occupied by two expansion slot positions on the XT. This is unfortunate, particularly where the number of free slots may be at a premium!

All of the XT expansion slots provide identical signals with one notable exception; the slot nearest to the power supply was employed in a particular IBM configuration (the IBM 3270 PC) to accept a Keyboard/Timer Adapter. This particular configuration employs a dedicated 'card select' signal (B8 on the connector) which is required by the system motherboard. Other cards that will operate in this position include the IBM 3270 Asynchronous Communications Adapter.

Like the XT, the standard AT also provides eight expansion slots. Six of these slots are fitted with two connectors (62-way and 36-way) whilst two positions (slots one and seven) only have 62-way connectors. Slot positions one and seven are designed to accept earlier 8-bit expansion cards which make use of the maximum allowable height throughout their length. If a 36-way connector had been fitted to the system motherboard, this would only foul the lower edge of the card and prevent effective insertion of the card in question.

Finally, it should be noted that boards designed for AT systems (i.e., those specifically designed to take advantage of the availability of the full 16-bit data bus) will offer a considerable speed advantage over those which are based upon the 8-bit PC-XT data bus provided by the original XT expansion connector. In some applications, this speed advantage can be critical.

# Expansion cards and connectors

Expansion cards for PC systems tend to vary slightly in their outline and dimensions (see Figure 9.1). However, the maximum allowable dimensions for the adapter and expansion cards fitted to PC (and PS/2) equipment are shown in Table 9.1.

**Table 9.1   Expansion card dimensions**

| Standard | Bus | Height | | Length | | Width | |
|---|---|---|---|---|---|---|---|
| | | inches | mm | inches | mm | inches | mm |
| EISA | AT | 5.0 | 127 | 13.2 | 334 | 0.5 | 12.7 |
| ISA | XT | 4.2 | 107 | 13.2 | 334 | 0.5 | 12.7 |
| ISA | AT | 4.8 | 122 | 13.2 | 334 | 0.5 | 12.7 |
| MCA | PS/2 | 3.8 | 96 | 13.2 | 334 | 0.5 | 12.7 |

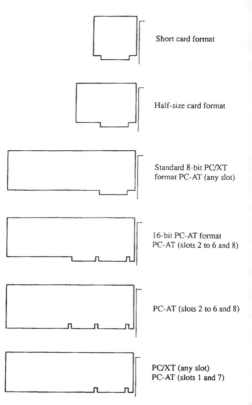

Short card format

Half-size card format

Standard 8-bit PC/XT format PC-AT (any slot)

16-bit PC-AT format PC-AT (slots 2 to 6 and 8)

PC-AT (slots 2 to 6 and 8)

PC/XT (any slot) PC-AT (slots 1 and 7)

*Figure 9.1   Outlines for various types of PC expansion card*

It is important to note that, although the XT-286 is based on an AT motherboard, it is fitted in an XT enclosure and thus expansion and adapter cards used in this machine must conform with the general height restriction imposed on XT cards (i.e. 4.2 inches maximum). Whilst many expansion card manufacturers are very conscious of this requirement, 4.8 inch height cards are still commonly available and XT users should thus exercise some caution when selecting expansion hardware.

Another difficulty is that some XT cards may fail to operate in AT equipment due to interrupt, DMA, addressing or other problems. In fairness, most manufacturers of adapters and expansion cards provide very clear indications of the systems with which their products are compatible. In any event, it is always wise to check with a manufacturer or distributor concerning compatability of a card with a particular microcomputer system.

With the exception of the eighth slot in the XT, the position in which an adapter or expansion card is placed should be unimportant. In most cases, this does hold true however, in certain circumstances it is worth considering in which slot one should place a card. The most important factor that should be taken into account is ventilation.

## TIP

Where cards are tightly packed together (particularly where ribbon cables may reduce airflow in the space between expansion cards) it is wise to optimise arrangements for cooling. Boards which are tightly packed with heat producing components should be located in the positions around which airflow can be expected to be the greatest. This generally applies to the sixth, seventh, or eighth slot in a system fitted with a fan. Furthermore, when introducing a new card to a system, it may be worth re-arranging those cards which are already fitted in order to promote the unimpeded flow of air.

## TIP

To minimise noise and glitches on the supply rails, it is usually beneficial to place boards which make large current demands or switch rapidly, in close proximity to the power supply (i.e. in slots six, seven, and eight). This precaution can be instrumental in reducing supply borne disturbances (glitches) and can also help to improve overall system integrity and reliability.

## TIP

Whilst timing is rarely a critical issue, some advantages can accrue from placing cards as close to the CPU (and coprocessor) as possible. Expansion memory cards should, therefore, be fitted in slot positions six, seven, and eight in preference to positions one, two, and three. In some cases this precaution may be instrumental in improving overall memory access times and avoiding parity errors.

## The 62-way ISA expansion bus connector

The 62-way PC expansion bus connector is a direct edge-type fitted to the system motherboard. One side of the connector is refererred to as A (lines are numbered A1 to A31) whilst the other is referred to as B (lines are numbered B1 to B31). The address and data bus lines are grouped together on the A-side of the connector whilst the control bus and power rails occupy the B-side (see Figure 9.2).

---

**TIP**

It is important to be aware that some early PC expansion bus pin numbering systems did not use letters A and B to distinguish the two sides of the expansion bus connector. In such cases odd numbered lines (1 to 61) formed one side of the connector whilst even numbered lines (2 to 62) formed the other.

---

Table 9.2 describes each of the signals present on the 62-way expansion bus connector.

*Table 9.2  Signals present on the 62-way ISA bus connector*

| Pin No. | Abbrev. | Direction | | Signal Function | |
|---------|---------|-----------|--|------------------|--|
| A1 | IOCHK | I | I/O Channel check | Taken low to indicate a parity error in a memory or I/O device. | |
| A2 | D7 | I/O | Data line 7 | Data bus line | |
| A3 | D6 | I/O | Data line 6 | Data bus line | |
| A4 | D5 | I/O | Data line 5 | Data bus line | |
| A5 | D4 | I/O | Data line 4 | Data bus line | |
| A6 | D3 | I/O | Data line 3 | Data bus line | |
| A7 | D2 | I/O | Data line 2 | Data bus line | |
| A8 | D1 | I/O | Data line 1 | Data bus line | |
| A9 | D0 | I/O | Data line 0 | Data bus line | |
| A10 | IOCHRDY | I | I/O channel ready | Pulsed low by a slow memory or I/O device to signal that it is not ready for data transfer. | |
| A11 | AEN | O | Address enable | Issued by the DMA controller to indicate that a DMA cycle is in progress. Disables port I/O during a DMA operation in which IOR AND IOW may be asserted. | |
| A12 | A19 | I/O | Address line 19 | Address bus line | |
| A13 | A18 | I/O | Address line 18 | Address bus line | |
| A14 | A17 | I/O | Address line 17 | Address bus line | |
| A15 | A16 | I/O | Address line 16 | Address bus line | |
| A16 | A15 | I/O | Address line 15 | Address bus line | |
| A17 | A14 | I/O | Address line 14 | Address bus line | |
| A18 | A13 | I/O | Address line 13 | Address bus line | |
| A19 | A12 | I/O | Address line 12 | Address bus line | |
| A20 | A11 | I/O | Address line 11 | Address bus line | |
| A21 | A10 | I/O | Address line 10 | Address bus line | |
| A22 | A9 | I/O | Address line 9 | Address bus line | |
| A23 | A8 | I/O | Address line 8 | Address bus line | |

### Table 9.2 Cont.

| Pin No. | Abbrev. | Direction | Signal | Function |
|---------|---------|-----------|--------|----------|
| A24 | A7 | I/O | Address line 7 | Address bus line |
| A25 | A | I/O | Address line 6 | Address bus line |
| A26 | A5 | I/O | Address line 5 | Address bus line |
| A27 | A4 | I/O | Address line 4 | Address bus line |
| A28 | A3 | I/O | Address line 3 | Address bus line |
| A29 | A2 | I/O | Address line 2 | Address bus line |
| A30 | A1 | I/O | Address line 1 | Address bus line |
| A31 | A0 | I/O | Address line 0 | Address bus line |
| B1 | GND | n.a. | Ground | Ground/common 0V |
| B2 | RESET | O | Reset | When taken high this signal resets all expansion cards. |
| B3 | +5V | n.a. | +5V d.c. | Supply voltage rail |
| B4 | IRQ2 | I | Interrupt request level 2 | Interrupt request (highest priority). |
| B5 | −5V | n.a. | −5V d.c. | Supply voltage rail |
| B6 | DRQ2 | I | Direct memory access request level 2 | Taken high when a DMA transfer is required. The signal remains high until the corresponding DACK line goes low. |
| B7 | −12V | n.a. | −12V d.c. | Supply voltage rail |
| B8 | 0WS | I | Zero wait state | Indicates to the microprocessor that the present bus cycle can be completed without inserting any additional wait cycles. |
| B9 | +12V | n.a. | +12V d.c. | Supply voltage rail |
| B10 | GND | n.a. | Ground | Ground/common 0V |
| B11 | MEMW | O | Memory write | Taken low to signal a memory write operation. |
| B12 | MEMR | 0 | Memory read | Taken low to signal a memory read operation. |
| B13 | IOW | O | I/O write | Taken low to signal an I/O write operation. |
| B14 | IOR | O | IO read | Taken low to signal an I/O read operation. |
| B15 | DACK3 | O | Direct memory access acknowledge level 3 | Taken low to acknowledge a DMA request on the corresponding level (see notes). |
| B16 | DRQ3 | I | Direct memory access request level 3 | Taken high when a DMA transfer is required. The signal remains high until the corresponding DACK line goes low. |

*Table 9.2 Cont.*

| Pin No. | Abbrev. | Direction | Signal | Function |
|---------|---------|-----------|--------|----------|
| B17 | DACK1 | O | Direct memory access acknowledge level 1 | Taken low to acknowledge a DMA request on the corresponding level (see notes). |
| B18 | DRQ1 | I | Direct memory access request level 1 | Taken high when a DMA transfer is required. The signal remains high until the corresponding DACK line goes low. |
| B19 | DACK0 | O | Direct memory access acknowledge level 0 | Taken low to acknowledge a DMA request on the corresponding level (see notes). |
| B20 | CLK4 | O | 4.77MHz clock | CPU clock divided by 3, 210ns period, 33 duty cycle. |
| B21 | IRQ7 | I | Interrupt request level 7 | Asserted by an I/O device when it requires service (see notes). |
| B22 | IRQ6 | I | Interrupt request level 6 | Asserted by an I/O device when it requires service (see notes). |
| B23 | IRQ5 | I | Interrupt request level 5 | Asserted by an I/O device when it requires service (see notes). |
| B24 | IRQ4 | I | Interrupt request level 4 | Asserted by an I/O device when it requires service (see notes). |
| B25 | IRQ3 | I | Interrupt request level 3 | Asserted by an I/O device when it requires service (see notes). |
| B26 | DACK2 | O | Direct memory access acknowledge level 2 | Taken low to acknowledge a DMA request on the corresponding level (see notes). |
| B27 | TC | O | Terminal count | Pulsed high to indicate that a DMA transfer terminal count has been reached. |
| B28 | ALE | O | Address latch enable | A falling edge indicates that the address latch is to be enabled. The signal is taken high during DMA transfers. |
| B29 | +5V | n.a. | +5V d.c. | Supply voltage rail |

| B30 | OSC | O | 14.31818MHz clock | Fast clock with 70 ns period, 50% duty cycle. |
| B31 | GND | n.a. | Ground | Ground/common 0V |

**Notes:**

(a) Signal directions are quoted relative to the system motherboard; I represents input, O represents output, and I/O represents a bidirectional signal used both for input and also for output (n.a. indicates not applicable).

(b) IRQ4, IRQ6 and IRQ7 are generated by the motherboard serial, disk, and parallel interfaces respectively.

(c) DACK0 (sometimes labelled REFRESH) is used to refresh dynamic memory whilst DACK1 to DACK3 are used to acknowledge other DMA requests.

## The 36-way ISA bus connector

The PC-AT and later machines are fitted with an additional expansion bus connector which provides access to the upper eight data lines, D8 to D15 as well as further control bus lines. The ISA AT-bus employs an additional 36-way direct edge-type connector. One side of the connector is referred to as C (lines are numbered C1 to C18) whilst the other is referred to as D (lines are numbered D1 to D18), as shown in Figure 9.2. The upper eight data bus lines and latched upper address lines are grouped together on the C-side of the connector (together with the memory read and write lines) whilst additional interrupt request, DMA request, and DMA acknowledge lines occupy the D-side.

Table 9.3 describes each of the signals present on the 32-way expansion bus.

*Table 9.3 Signals present on the 36-way ISA bus connector*

| Pin No. | Abbrev. | Direction | Signal | Function |
|---|---|---|---|---|
| C1 | SBHE | I/O | System bus high enable | When asserted this signal indicates that the high byte (D8 to D15) is present on the DATA bus. |
| C2 | LA23 | I/O | Latched address line 23 | Address bus line |
| C3 | LA22 | I/O | Latched address line 22 | Address bus line |
| C4 | LA21 | I/O | Latched address line 21 | Address bus line |
| C5 | LA20 | I/O | Latched address line 20 | Address bus line |
| C6 | LA23 | I/O | Latched address line 19 | Address bus line |
| C7 | LA22 | I/O | Latched address line 18 | Address bus line |
| C8 | LA23 | I/O | Latched address line 17 | Address bus line |
| C9 | MEMW | I/O | Memory write | Taken low to signal a memory write operation. |
| C10 | MEMR | I/O | Memory read | Taken low to signal a memory read operation. |
| C11 | D8 | I/O | Data line 1 | Data bus line |

*Table 9.3 Cont.*

| Pin No. | Abbrev. | Direction | Signal | Function |
|---|---|---|---|---|
| C12 | D9 | I/O | Data line 1 | Data bus line |
| C13 | D10 | I/O | Data line 1 | Data bus line |
| C14 | D11 | I/O | Data line 1 | Data bus line |
| C15 | D12 | I/O | Data line 1 | Data bus line |
| C16 | D13 | I/O | Data line 1 | Data bus line |
| C17 | D14 | I/O | Data line 1 | Data bus line |
| C18 | D15 | I/O | Data line 1 | Data bus line |
| D1 | MEMCS-16 | I | Memory chip-select 16 | Taken low to indicate that the current data transfer is a 16-bit (single wait state) memory operation. |
| D2 | IOCS16 | I | I/O chip-select 16 | Taken low to indicate that the current data transfer is a 16-bit (single wait state) I/O operation. |
| D3 | IRQ10 | I | Interrupt request level 10 | Asserted by an I/O device when it requires service. |
| D4 | IRQ11 | I | Interrupt request level 11 | Asserted by an I/O device when it requires service. |
| D5 | IRQ12 | I | Interrupt request level 12 | Asserted by an I/O device when it requires service. |
| D6 | IRQ13 | I | Interrupt request level 13 | Asserted by an I/O device when it requires service. |
| D7 | IRQ14 | I | Interrupt request level 14 | Asserted by an I/O device when it requires service. |
| D8 | DACK0 | O | Direct memory access acknowledge level 0 | Taken low to acknowledge a DMA request on the corresponding level. |
| D9 | DRQ0 | I | Direct memory access request level 0 | Taken high when a DMA transfer is required. The signal remains high until the corresponding DACK line goes low. |
| D10 | DACK5 | O | Direct memory access acknowledge level 5 | Taken low to acknowledge a DMA request on the corresponding level. |
| D11 | DRQ5 | I | Direct memory access request level 5 | Taken high when a DMA transfer is required. The signal remains high until the corresponding DACK line goes low. |

**Table 9.3 Cont.**

| Pin No. | Abbrev. | Direction | | Signal | Function |
|---|---|---|---|---|---|
| D12 | DACK6 | O | Direct memory access acknowledge level 6 | Taken low to acknowledge a DMA request on the corresponding level. | |
| D13 | DRQ6 | I | Direct memory access request level 6 | Taken high when a DMA transfer is required. The signal remains high until the corresponding DACK line goes low. | |
| D14 | DACK7 | O | Direct memory access acknowledge level 7 | Taken low to acknowledge a DMA request on the corresponding level. | |
| D15 | DRQ7 | I | Direct memory access request level 7 | Taken high when a DMA transfer is required. The signal remains high until the corresponding DACK line goes low. | |
| D16 | +5V | n.a. | +5V d.c. | Supply voltage rail | |
| D17 | MASTER | I | Master | Taken low by the I/O processor when controlling the system address, data and control bus lines. | |
| D18 | GND | n.a. | Ground | Ground/common 0V | |

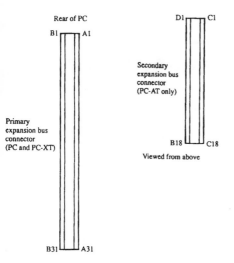

**Figure 9.2  ISA expansion bus connectors**

## Electrical characteristics

All of the signals lines present on the expansion connector(s) are TTL-compatible. In the case of output signals from the system motherboard, the maximum loading imposed by an expansion card adapter should be limited to no more than two low-power (LS) TTL devices. The following expansion bus lines are open-collector: MEMCS16, IOCS16, and 0WS.

The IOCHRDY line is available for interfacing slow memory or I/O devices. Normal processor generated read and write cycles use four clock (CLK) cycles per byte transferred. The standard PC clock frequency of 4.77MHz results in a single clock cycle of 210ns. Thus each processor read or write cycle requires 840ns at the standard clock rate. DMA transfers, I/O read and write cycles, on the other hand, require five clock cycles (1050us). When the IOCHRDY line is asserted, the processor machine cycle is extended for an integral number of clock cycles.

Finally, when an I/O processor wishes to take control of the bus, it must assert the MASTER line. This signal should not be asserted for more than 15μs as it may otherwise impair the refreshing of system memory.

## A word about power...

A fully populated AT-compatible system motherboard (including 80287 coprocessor) requires approximately 5A and 2A from the +5V and +12V rails respectively. An EGA graphics adapter and two standard floppy drives will demand an additional 2.4A and 1.5A from the +5V and +12V rails respectively. A cooling fan will require a further 0.3A, or so, from the +12V rail. The total load on the system power supply is thus 7.4A from the +5V rail and 4.1A from the +12V rail. With a standard XT power supply, reserves of only 7.6A from the +5V supply and a mere 400mA from the +12V supply will be available!

Problems which arise when systems have been upgraded or expanded are often caused by excessive loading on the power supply. Under marginal conditions the system will appear to operate satisfactorily but it may crash or lock-up at some later time when the system temperature builds up or when one or more of the power rail voltages momentarily falls outside its tolerance limits.

**TIP**

Never attempt to connect or remove an expansion card when the power is connected and the system is switched on. If this sounds rather obvious, I make no apologies for repeating it. In the heat of the moment it is all too easy to forget that a system is 'live'. Like me, you are only likely to make this mistake once - the cost and frustration will have a profound effect!

## Resolving conflict...

When you add an expansion card to a system potential conflicts must be avoided. This is because the existing hardware will be configured into I/O space with interrupt request (IRQ) and direct memory access (DMA) channels already established. It is vitally important that any new card does not disturb the existing configuration by attempting to use the same memory space, IRQ or DMA channels.

## TIP

When fitting expansion cards you should always carefully check the I/O address, IRQ, and DMA settings of your *existing* cards before you accept the manufacturer's default settings. In many cases the default settings will prove statisfactory but in others they won't!

# 10
# Floppy Disk Drives

Floppy disks provide you with a means of installing programs on your hard disk, exchanging data between computers, and backing-up the data stored on your hard disk. This chapter begins by introducing the most commonly used floppy disk formats and the structure of boot records and file allocation tables (FAT). It also describes the floppy disk interface and the functions of the PC's floppy disk controller (FDC). The chapter also explains how to remove and replace a floppy disk drive.

## Floppy disk formats

A variety of different floppy disk formats are supported by PCs (see Table 10.1 and Figure 10.1). To help you select the correct type of disks for your drive, they are generally marked 'DSDD', 'DSHD', 'HD', 'ED' etc. If there are no markings, the presence of additional notches and windows (on 5.25" and 3.5" disks respectively) will give you some clue as to the media type. As an example, a 'high density' 1.44M 3.5" disk has two small square windows on each side of the plastic housing. One window (fitted with a sliding shutter) is used to make the disk 'read-only' (i.e., it disables writing). The other window is used to indicate that the disk is a high density DSHD type. Optical sensors within the disk drive are used to detect the presence of the windows and configure the system accordingly.

When a disk is formatted, DOS writes a magnetic pattern on the surface of the disk. The pattern comprises 40 or 80 concentric 'tracks', each of which is divided into a number of 'sectors' depending upon the type of disk (see Table 10.1). The magnetic pattern is repeated on both sides of the disk (note that some obsolete disk formats are designed for 'single-sided' disks). In order to locate the data stored on the disk, DOS allocates numbers to the sides, tracks and sectors. In addition, DOS employs a basic unit of disk storage space known as a 'cluster'. Note that there are two sectors per cluster on a standard double-sided floppy disks formatted by DOS.

### TIP

Disks can be 'notched' and 'drilled' to make them appear to be of higher density rating than originally manufactured. However, don't be tempted to format a disk for a capacity that it hasn't been designed to support. This will put your data at risk; the disk may appear to format successfully but problems may well occur at some later date!

### Table 10.1  PC floppy disk formats

| Size | Formatted capacity (bytes) | Media type | Number of tracks | Number of sectors | DOS version (from) |
|------|----------------------------|------------|------------------|-------------------|--------------------|
| 5.25" | 360K | DSDD | 40 | 9 | 2.0 |
| 5.25" | 1.2M | HD | 80 | 15 | 3.0 |
| 3.5" | 720K | DSDD | 80 | 9 | 3.2 |
| 3.5" | 1.44M | HD | 80 | 18 | 3.2 |
| 3.5" | 2.88M | ED | 80 | 36 | 5.0 |

5.25 inch disk media format

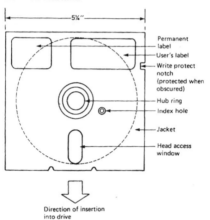

3.5 inch disk media format

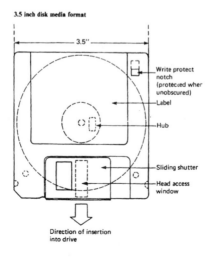

*Figure 10.1   5.25" and 3.5" disks*

### TIP

Don't be tempted to buy cheap unbranded floppy disks. Such disks are often of indeterminate quality and may have been rejected as part of a reputable manufacturer's production test procedures. If you do need a source of inexpensive disks you are actually better off using 'secondhand' branded disks. These are available from various sources and simply require reformatting before use.

### TIP

Floppy disks sometimes become contaminated with surface films (e.g., due to liquid spills). If you need to recover the data stored on such a disk, you should first remove the disk from its jacket or plastic housing, and then rinse it under a tap with warm running water. Do not use cleansers or detergents. When the surface of the disk has been thoroughly rinsed, you should dry the disk in warm (but not hot) air before replacing it in its jacket or plastic housing. During the cleaning process it is important to hold the disk by the edges or by the central hub ring. You should avoid touching the surface of the disk. Once the disk has been reassembled, you should copy the data to another disk (using **XCOPY** *.*, see page 155).

### TIP

Problems often occur when you attempt to read a high capacity disk on a drive which only supports lower density media (e.g. when reading data from a 1.2M disk in a 360K drive). DOS will usually report an error as the drive will not be able to differentiate the data from several tracks at once. If you do need to transfer data from a PC with a 1.2M drive to another with only a 360K drive it is essential to ensure that you format your disks to the media capacity format of the smaller drives. The DOS FORMAT command provides you with the necessary 'switches' to do this. For example: FORMAT A: /4 formats a 5.25" disk in a 1.2M drive A to the 360K 5.25" disk format. Similarly, FORMAT A: /N:9 /T:80 will format a 3.5" disk to 720K when placed in a 1.44M drive.

### TIP

During disk formatting, you may occasionally notice that the drive spends some considerable time towards the end of the process (the heads may appear to be stepping erratically). This is a sure sign that DOS has discovered some 'bad tracks' on the surface of your disk. If the problem is severe, the formatting will be aborted (this also happens if track 00 is found to be bad). However, if it is not severe, the format will eventually be completed but the disk may not deliver the capacity that you expect. In such a case, it is worth formatting the disk a second time. You should also use the DOS CHKDSK utility (see page 150) to reveal the number of bad sectors and the total amount of free space on the disk. Never be tempted to use a disk that is in any way dubious!

# The boot record

A floppy disk's 'boot record' occupies the very first sector of a disk. The boot record contains a number of useful parameters as well as code which will load and run (i.e., 'boot'). Boot disks must also contain two other programs, IBMIO.COM and IBMDOS.COM (or IO.SYS and MSDOS.SYS). These, in turn, are responsible for locating, loading and running the command interpreter (COMMAND.COM).

The parameters contained in the boot record (see Table 10.2) include details of the disk format (e.g., the number of bytes per sector and the number of sectors per cluster).

**Table 10.2   Contents of the boot record**

| Offset (dec.) | (hex.) | Length | Contents |
|---|---|---|---|
| 0 | 00 | 3 bytes | Jump instruction |
| 3 | 03 | 8 bytes | System identification |
| 11 | 0B | 1 word | Number of bytes per sector |
| 13 | 0D | 1 byte | Number of sectors per cluster |
| 14 | 0E | 1 word | Number of reserved sectors at beginning |
| 16 | 10 | 1 byte | Number of copies of the FAT |
| 17 | 11 | 1 word | Number of root directory entries |
| 19 | 13 | 1 word | Total number of sectors on disk |
| 21 | 15 | 1 byte | Media descriptor (see Table 10.4) |
| 22 | 16 | 1 word | Number of sectors per FAT |
| 24 | 18 | 1 word | Number of sectors per track |
| 26 | 1A | 1 word | Number of sides |
| 28 | 1C | 1 word | Number of reserved sectors |

## Booting the system

When a PC performs a 'warm boot' or 'cold boot' (using the <CTRL> <ALT> <DEL> keys or by pressing the 'reset' button respectively), the ROM BIOS code initialises the system and then attempts to read the boot sector of the floppy disk in drive A. If no disk is present in drive A, the ROM BIOS reads the first sector of the hard drive, C.

The 512 byte boot sector is read into memory starting at absolute address location 0000:7C00. The BIOS code then checks the last two bytes of data (loaded at address 0000:7DFE and 0000:7DFF respectively). If these two locations contain 55 and AA respectively, the boot program jumps to 0000:7C00 (i.e., the start of the *image* of the boot sector in RAM). The CPU then continues by executing the boot code which has been loaded from the floppy disk.

On a 'system disk' (i.e., disks formatted using the DOS command FORMAT A: /S, see page 153) the first three bytes of the boot sector are a jump instruction (EB 34 90 in Figure 10.2). This instruction is needed in order to branch forward, avoiding the disk parameters stored at the beginning of the sector (which do not, of course, constitute executable code).

## Using Debug to display the boot record

Fortunately DOS provides you with a handy means of examining (and, if necessary, editing) the boot sectors of your disks. The MS-DOS Debug utility (see page 174) can be used to read any part of the disk into memory and then Debug will let you display the contents of the block of memory in question. You are thus able to examine an *image* of the disk's tracks and sectors.

This isn't quite so complicated as it may sound. As an example, suppose that you have placed a floppy disk in drive A and you wish to examine the boot sector of the disk. The following Debug commands will load the boot sector and display the first 256 bytes of the boot record (see Chapter 14 for information on using Debug):

```
l 0 0 0 1      (loads the boot sector into memory)
d 0 1 100      (displays the first 256 bytes of the boot sector)
```

A typical result of using these commands (in this case revealing the boot record of a standard 1.44M floppy disk formatted using MS-DOS 5.0) is shown in Figure 10.2.

```
C:\DOS>debug
-l 0 0 0 1
-d 0 1 100
1DD1:0000  EB 3C 90 4D 53 44 4F 53-35 2E 30 00 02 01 01 00   .<.MSDOS5.0.....
1DD1:0010  02 E0 00 40 0B F0 09 00-12 00 02 00 00 00 00 00   ...@............
1DD1:0020  00 00 00 00 00 00 29 19-2F 2D 28 4E 4F 20 4E 41   ......)./-(NO NA
1DD1:0030  4D 45 20 20 20 20 46 41-54 31 32 20 20 20 FA 33   ME    FAT12   .3
1DD1:0040  C0 8E D0 BC 00 7C 16 07-BB 78 00 36 C5 37 1E 56   .....|...x.6.7.V
1DD1:0050  16 53 BF 3E 7C B9 0B 00-FC F3 A4 06 1F C6 45 FE   .S.>|.........E.
1DD1:0060  0F 8B 0E 18 7C 88 4D F9-89 47 02 C7 07 3E 7C FB   ....|.M..G...>|.
1DD1:0070  CD 13 72 79 33 C0 39 06-13 7C 74 08 8B 0E 13 7C   ..ry3.9..|t...|
1DD1:0080  89 0E 20 7C A0 10 7C F7-26 16 7C 03 06 1C 7C 13   .. |..|.&.|...|.
1DD1:0090  16 1E 7C 03 06 0E 7C 83-D2 00 A3 50 7C 89 16 52   ..|...|....P|..R
1DD1:00A0  7C A3 49 7C 89 16 4B 7C-B8 20 00 F7 26 11 7C 8B   |.I|..K|. ..&.|.
1DD1:00B0  1E 0B 7C 03 C3 48 F7 F3-01 06 49 7C 83 16 4B 7C   ..|..H....I|..K|
1DD1:00C0  00 BB 00 05 8B 16 52 7C-A1 50 7C E8 92 00 72 1D   ......R|.P|....r.
1DD1:00D0  B0 01 E8 AC 00 72 16 8B-FB B9 0B 00 BE E6 7D F3   .....r........}.
1DD1:00E0  A6 75 0A 8D 7F 20 B9 0B-00 F3 A6 74 18 BE 9E 7D   .u... .....t...}
1DD1:00F0  E8 5F 00 33 C0 CD 16 5E-1F 8F 04 8F 44 02 CD 19   ._.3..^.....D...
```

*Figure 10.2  Boot record displayed using Debug*

It is worth taking a close look at Figure 10.2. The 'offset' addresses are the rightmost four hex characters in the left hand column (i.e., 0000, 0010, 0020, etc). The bytes of data (shown in hex. format in the 16 columns of data) are EB, 3C, 90, etc. The ASCII representation of this data is shown in the rightmost column (note that non-printing ASCII characters are represented by a '.').

The contents of the first three bytes are thus:

| Offset: | 0000 | 0001 | 0002 |
|---------|------|------|------|
| Contents: | EB | 3C | 90 |

These three bytes constitute the 80x86 jump instruction to the start of the DOS boot code (mentioned earlier). The next eight bytes identify the operating system that was used to format the disk. As this information is 'ASCII-encoded' you will find the ASCII display in Figure 10.2 somewhat more useful than the hex data! This will tell you that the disk was formatted under MS-DOS 5.0.

The number of bytes per sector is contained in the word at offset 11 (0B hex). The word (two bytes) is thus:

| Offset: | 000B | 000C |
|---------|------|------|
| Contents: | 00 | 02 |

Don't be too surprised if this is not what you might at first expect; an 80x86 processor stores data in memory in 'low-byte-first' format. We need to reverse the data values to express them in 'conventional human' format. Hence the number of bytes per sector is 0200 hex (*not* 0002!). In other words, the disk uses the standard 512 bytes per sector...

If you continue deciphering the boot record you will find that the disk in question is formatted according to the parameters shown in Table 10.3.

***Table 10.3   Typical boot sector parameters for a 1.44M floppy disk***

| | |
|---|---|
| Operating system: | MS-DOS 5.0 |
| Bytes per sector: | 512 |
| Sectors per cluster: | 1 |
| Number of reserved sectors: | 1 |
| Number of FAT copies: | 2 |
| Number of root directory entries: | 224 |
| Total number of sectors: | 2880 |
| Media descriptor: | F0 (i.e., 1.44M, see Table 10.4) |
| Sectors per FAT: | 9 |
| Sectors per track: | 18 |
| Number of sides: | 2 |
| Reserved sectors: | 0 |

## TIP

The ability to load, examine (and modify) the boot sector of a floppy disk can be extremely useful. If you wish to modify the contents of a boot sector (or a FAT) it is *essential* to make a back-up copy of the disk *before* you make any changes. The penalty for ignoring this advice is that you might find that you can no longer access the information stored on the disk in question - DOS can be an extremely efficient policeman!

# The file allocation table

Each disk contains a 'file allocation table' (or FAT) which keeps a record of where the data is stored on the surface of the disk. As the FAT is crucial to being able to successfully locate the data stored on the disk, DOS keeps more than one copy of it. If one copy of the FAT is damaged or corrupted, the other may still be readable.

There are two different types of FAT which are distinguished by the length of the entries. The more common 12-bit format used on floppy disks and some older (and smaller) hard disks, uses three nibbles (three 4-bit hex characters) to identify the cluster numbers whilst the 16-bit format (used by larger hard disks) employs a single 16-bit word (four 4-bit hex characters) to represent the cluster numbers.

Special characters are used in the FAT to denote features such as unusable clusters (sectors which have been identified as 'bad tracks' during formatting), available clusters, and the last cluster in each file.

## Media descriptors

DOS recognises the type of disk and drive by means of a single byte code known as a 'media descriptor' (see Table 10.4). The media descriptor is placed in the first byte of the disk's FAT.

### Table 10.4   DOS media descriptors

| Disk capacity | DOS media descriptor |
| --- | --- |
| 160K | FE |
| 180K | FC |
| 320K | FF |
| 360K | FD |
| 72K or 1.2M | F9 |
| 1.44M or 2.88M | F0 |
| Hard disk | F8 |

## Using Debug to display the FAT

You can use the MS-DOS Debug utility to display the contents of a disk's FAT in just the same way as you can show the boot record. Assuming that the disk is placed in drive A, the following Debug commands will load and display the FAT (see Chapter 14 for information on using Debug):

l 100 0 1 1      (loads the FAT into memory)

d 100 l 100      (displays 256 bytes of the FAT)

A typical result of using these commands to display the FAT from a 1.44M floppy disk formatted using MS-DOS 5.0 is shown in Figure 10.3.

# Floppy disk controllers

The floppy disk interface is managed by a dedicated VLSI device, the floppy disk controller (FDC). This chip manages the storage and retrieval of data in the sectors and tracks which are written to the disk during the formatting process. The FDC is thus an extremely complex device, being capable of both formatting the disk (acting upon instructions from the DOS FORMAT utility, see page 153) and then writing/reading the data on it.

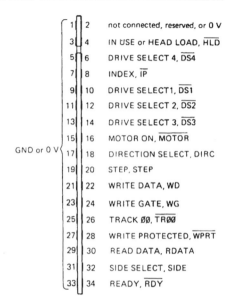

| | | |
|---|---|---|
| 1 | 2 | not connected, reserved, or 0 V |
| 3 | 4 | IN USE or HEAD LOAD, $\overline{\text{HLD}}$ |
| 5 | 6 | DRIVE SELECT 4, $\overline{\text{DS4}}$ |
| 7 | 8 | INDEX, $\overline{\text{IP}}$ |
| 9 | 10 | DRIVE SELECT 1, $\overline{\text{DS1}}$ |
| 11 | 12 | DRIVE SELECT 2, $\overline{\text{DS2}}$ |
| 13 | 14 | DRIVE SELECT 3, $\overline{\text{DS3}}$ |
| 15 | 16 | MOTOR ON, $\overline{\text{MOTOR}}$ |
| 17 | 18 | DIRECTION SELECT, DIRC |
| 19 | 20 | STEP, STEP |
| 21 | 22 | WRITE DATA, WD |
| 23 | 24 | WRITE GATE, WG |
| 25 | 26 | TRACK ØØ, $\overline{\text{TRØØ}}$ |
| 27 | 28 | WRITE PROTECTED, $\overline{\text{WPRT}}$ |
| 29 | 30 | READ DATA, RDATA |
| 31 | 32 | SIDE SELECT, SIDE |
| 33 | 34 | READY, $\overline{\text{RDY}}$ |

GND or 0 V (pins 1–33, odd)

Normally lower side ◀————    ————▶ Normally upper side

Note: Edge view of double sided PCB (0.1″ pad spacing)

**Figure 10.3  Disk drive pin connections**

The DOS and FDC act in concert to translate requests for logical files into physical tracks and sectors and also to maintain the FAT and disk directory. The FDC has various dedicated functions, which include:

1. Formatting the disk with the required number of tracks and sectors as determined by the DOS.
2. Accepting commands issued by DOS and translating these to appropriate actions within the disk drive, such as positioning the read/write head.
3. Maintaining various internal registers which:

    (a) reflect the current status of the controller,

    (b) indicate the current track over which the read/write head is positioned, and

    (c) hold the address of the desired sector position.

    Note that copies of the FDC status are held within the system RAM area (see page 114).

4. Providing an interface to the system bus so that:

    (a) during the write process, incoming parallel data from the bus is converted into a serial self-clocking data stream for writing to the floppy disk, and

      **(b)** during the read process, incoming serial data from the floppy disk is separated from the accompanying clock, and fed to a serial-to-parallel shift register before outputting to the data bus.

   **5.** Generating the necessary cyclic redundancy check (CRC) characters and appending these to the write data stream at the appropriate time.

```
DEF SEG = 0
CLS
PRINT "Disk controller status"
PRINT "Address", "Byte", " Status"
PRINT "(hex)", "(hex)", ;
FOR i = 7 TO 0 STEP -1
  PRINT i;
NEXT i
PRINT
PRINT
FOR address = &H43E TO &H443
  v = PEEK(address)
  GOSUB convert
  PRINT HEX$(address), HEX$(v), ;
  FOR i = 7 TO 0 STEP -1
    PRINT b(i);
  NEXT i
  PRINT
NEXT address
PRINT
END
'
convert:
x = v
FOR n = 0 TO 7
  b(n) = x - INT(x / 2) * 2
  x = INT(x / 2)
NEXT n
RETURN
```

*Figure 10.4   QuickBASIC program that displays the FDC status*

```
Disk controller status
Address      Byte        Status
(hex)        (hex)       7  6  5  4  3  2  1  0

43E          1           0  0  0  0  0  0  0  1
43F          81          1  0  0  0  0  0  0  1
440          25          0  0  1  0  0  1  0  1
441          0           0  0  0  0  0  0  0  0
442          4           0  0  0  0  0  1  0  0
443          0           0  0  0  0  0  0  0  0
```

*Figure 10.5   Typical output produced by the program of Figure 10.4*

Floppy Disk Drives

*Floppy Disk Drives* _____ 109

## The floppy disk bus

Each disk drive contains its own interface to the bus, which links all the drives in a system to the disk adapter and its FDC. The floppy disk bus uses a 34-way connector, the 17 odd-numbered lines of which are common ground. The typical designation and function of the signal lines are shown in Table 10.5. It should be noted that since the drive requires an appreciable current, the +12V and +5V power lines employ a separate 4-way connector.

*Table 10.5  Floppy disk bus pin connections*

| Pin number | Designation | Meaning | Function |
|---|---|---|---|
| 2 | n.c. | Not connected | |
| 4 | HEADLOAD | Head Load | Output from FDC, active low, when asserted it activates the head load solenoid |
| 6 | DS4 | Drive Select 4 | Output from FDC, active low, when asserted it activates the fourth drive |
| 8 | INDEX | Index | Input to FDC, active low, when asserted it indicates that the index hole has been detected by the appropriate sensor |
| 10 | DS1 | Drive Select 1 | Output from FDC, active low, when asserted it activates the first drive |
| 12 | DS2 | Drive Select 2 | Output from FDC, active low, when asserted it activates the second drive |
| 14 | DS3 | Drive Select 3 | Output from FDC, active low, when asserted it activates the third drive |
| 16 | MOTOR ON | Motor on | Output from FDC, active low, when asserted it turns the drive motor on |
| 18 | DIRC | Direction | Output from FDC, selects direction of head stepping, the head steps outwards when high and inwards when low |

*Table 10.5 Cont.*

| Pin number | Designation | Meaning | Function |
|---|---|---|---|
| 20 | STEP | Step | Output from FDC, steps the head on a rising edge pulse |
| 22 | WRITE DATA | Write data | Output from FDC, inactive high, pulsed low when data is written to the disk |
| 24 | WRITE GATE | Write gate | Output from FDC, write when low and read when high |
| 26 | TRACK 00 | Track zero | Input to FDC, low when the head is positioned over track zero (the outermost track) |
| 28 | WRITE PROT | Write protect | Input to FDC, active low |
| 30 | READ DATA | Read data | Input to FDC, inactive high, pulsed low when data is read from the disk |
| 32 | SIDE SELECT | Side select | Output from FDC, side select 0 or 1 |
| 34 | READY | Ready | Input to FDC, active low, when asserted indicates that the drive is ready for a read or write operation |

Note: There are some minor variations in the names given to the various lines and, in particular, drive selects are often numbered DS0 to DS3 rather than DS1 to DS4, HEAD LOAD and READY signals are not always provided.

## Disk drive troubleshooting

Troubleshooting disk drives can be just as complex a task as that associated with the system board. In addition, it must be recognised that the drive contains highly sophisticated electronic and mechanical components which require both careful and sympathetic handling. Hence it is recommended that, at least for the inexperienced reader, consideration be given to returning drives for overhaul and service by the manufacturer or importer as this may be more cost-effective in the long run. In any event, fault diagnosis within drives should only be carried out when one is certain that the disk interface and controller can be absolved from blame. Thus, whenever the drive in a single-drive system is suspect, it should first be replaced by a unit that is known to be good. In a two drive system it will, of course, be relatively easy to recognise a failure within one or other of the drives. Even so, it is worth interchanging the two drives before attempting to dismantle the suspect unit.

**TIP**

Floppy disk drives have links, jumpers or selectors which identify them as a particular drive in the system (i.e., A or B). The jumpers are usually located in a fairly obvious position at the rear of the drive close to the PCB edge connector. On 5.25" floppy drives, the jumpers are variously marked 'DS0, DS1, DS2, DS3', 'D1, D2, D3, D4', or 'DS1, DS2, DS3, DS4'. On 3.25" disk drives the jumpers will usually be marked 'DS0, DS1' or 'D0, D1'. The lowest numbered link position will correspond to drive A, and so on. Note that only one of these links should be in place on any particular drive. Furthermore, if you have a two-drive system, the drive select links must identify the two drives differently, i.e., one drive must be configured as drive A (with the lowest numbered link fitted) with the other should be drive B (with the next lowest number link fitted). If you ever have to swap drives around for test purposes don't forget to also change over the drive select links. There is, however, one important exception to all of this which relates to IBM AT-systems and compatibles which use the so-called 'twisted' floppy cable. This cable can easily be recognised as part of the ribbon will have been cut, then separated and twisted in order to swap several of the connections over. The result is simply that the cable makes the two drives appear different to the system even if they both use the same drive select links. The furthermost drive will normally be A whilst the drive on the other side of the twist will be B. Both may be fitted with their drive select links in the second lowest numbered position.

## The read/write heads

Great care should be exercised whenever operating on or near the read/write heads. These are the single most expensive component within the drive and are easily damaged. Fortunately, head adjustment is normally only required when either:

(a) the head itself, or

(b) the assembly on which the head is mounted, is replaced, or

(c) a particular drive is found to be incompatible with others when disks are exchanged.

Alignment requires the use of a special tool in conjunction with an analogue alignment disk and an oscilloscope. The alignment disk usually contains both continuous tones and bursts of tones which are used respectively to adjust radial alignment and azimuth. Fortunately, alignment disks are normally supplied with full instructions showing typical display patterns. These disks will normally allow you to perform the following operations:

(a) Accurately locate track 00.

(b) Adjust the index timing and hence check motor speed.

(c) Check the skew error of the head positioning mechanism.

(d) Align the head positioning mechanism with the track centre line

(e) Verify read output for correct head-to-disk compliance.

(f) Check the head azimuth.

### TIP

Many floppy and hard disk drives are discarded when they cause problems. There is often very little wrong with them that cannot easily be cured by cleaning or simple adjustment. Start with a thorough examination of the interior of the drive, remove any dust or oxide particles from the read/write heads and then use diagnostic software to exercise the drive and, if necessary, align the heads.

The read/write heads of disk units require regular cleaning to ensure trouble-free operation. In use, the disk surface is prone to environmental contaminants such as smoke, airborne dust, oils and fingerprints, and these can be transferred to the read/write heads along with oxide particles from the coating of the disk itself. Periodic cleaning is thus essential and, although this can easily be carried out by untrained personnel using one of several excellent head cleaning kits currently available, head cleaning is rarely given the priority it deserves. Thus, whenever a PC is being overhauled, routine cleaning of the heads may be instrumental in helping to avoid future problems.

### TIP

The read/write heads of a floppy disk drive are permanently in contact with the disk surface when the disk is in use. The heads can thus easily become contaminated with particles of dust and magnetic oxide. You can avoid this problem by cleaning your read/write heads regularly using a proprietary head cleaning disk and cleaning fluid. As a rough guide, you should clean the heads every month if you use your system for two, or more hours each day.

## Replacing a floppy disk drive

The procedure for removing and replacing a floppy disk drive is quite straightforward. You should adopt the following procedure:

1. Power-down and gain access to the interior of the system unit (as described in Chapter 3).
2. Locate the drive in question and remove the disk-drive power and floppy disk bus connectors from the rear of the drive.
3. Remove the retaining screws from the sides of the drive (four screws are usually fitted). In the case of the older AT-style system units in which the drives are mounted using plastic guides, you should remove the two retaining screws and metal tabs at the front of the system chassis.
4. Once the drive chassis is free, it can be gently withdrawn from the system unit. Any metal screening can now be removed in order to permit inspection. The majority of the drive electronics (read/write amplifiers, bus buffers and drivers) normally occupies a single PCB on one side of the drive.
5. The head load solenoid, head assembly and mechanical parts should now be clearly visible and can be inspected for signs of damage or wear. Before reassembly, the heads should be thoroughly inspected and cleaned using a cotton bud and proprietary alcohol-based cleaning solvent.

6. Re-assemble the system (replacing the drive, if necessary) and ensure that the disk bus and power cables are correctly connected before restoring power to the system.

---

## TIP

Take special care when replacing machined screws which locate directly with the diecast chassis of a disk drive. These screws can sometimes become cross-threaded in the relatively soft diecast material. If you are fitting a new drive, you must also ensure that you use screws of the correct length. A screw that is too long can sometimes foul the PCB mounted components.

---

## TIP

A 34-way male PCB header is usually fitted to 3.5" drives. Unfortunately, the matching female IDC connector can easily be attached the wrong way round. You should thus check that the connector has been aligned correctly when replacing or adding a disk drive to your system. Pin-1 (and/or pin-34) is usually clearly marked on the PCB. You should also notice a stripe along one edge of the ribbon cable. This stripe must be aligned with pin-1 on the connector.

---

## Diagnostic/alignment disks

For all but the most obvious mechanical faults in disk drives, software diagnostics quickly become essential. It is rarely possible to make meaningful assessments of the performance of drives without such an aid. Disk diagnostics vary widely in sophistication. As a minimum they should be capable of:

(a) Selecting a particular drive and verifying the operation of the disk controller by reading the status register.

(b) Performing step-in and step-out operations and testing for track 00.

(c) Reading and displaying the contents of a selected track.

(d) Writing a particular byte pattern in a selected track (or tracks), then reading and verifying the result.

(e) Measuring, and displaying, the rotational speed of the disk.

With some of the older types of drive it is wise to check the drive motor speed when a system is being overhauled since this can be instrumental in avoiding future problems. With older drives, motor speed adjustment is invariably provided by means of a small preset potentiometer mounted on the motor control PCB. Access to this control is often arranged so that speed adjustment can be carried out without having to dismantle, or even remove, the drive. The drive speed should be within +/-3rpm of 300rpm and should always be adjusted whenever it is outside this range. With care, it should be possible to adjust the speed to within +/-0.5rpm of the nominal 300rpm.

You can display the disk controller's status using a simple QuickBASIC program along the lines shown in Figure 10.4. This program displays the individual bits that indicate the status of the FDC (see Figure 10.5 and Table 10.6). A somewhat more comprehensive QuickBASIC disk drive test program has been included in Chapter 17.

*Table 10.6   Disk status byte at address 0441*

| Bit number | Meaning |
|---|---|
| 0 | Set if an invalid disk command has been requested |
| 1 | Set if address mark on disk is not found |
| 2 | Set if sector is not found (this error occurs if the disk is damaged or has not been formatted) |
| 3 | Set if a DMA error has occurred |
| 4 | Set if a CRC error has occurred |
| 5 | Set if the disk controller is not responding |
| 6 | Set if a track seek operation has failed |
| 7 | Set if the disk has 'timed out' (i.e., failed to respond in a preset time) |

# 11
# Hard Disk Drives

Your hard disk drive provides a means of storing a very large amount of data which can be accessed virtually instantaneously. Not only does a hard disk drive provide more storage than a large quanitity of high-density floppy disks, but it also transfers the data approximately ten times faster. Unfortunately, the failure of a hard drive can be catastrophic – in many cases you may find that your precious data is totally irretrievable.

This chapter begins by introducing each of the most commonly used types of hard disk. It continues by explaining the process of formatting a hard disk and describing the structure of master boot records and partition tables. The chapter also explains how to remove and replace a hard disk disk drive.

## Hard disk basics

Like floppy disks, the data stored on a hard disk takes the form of a magnetic pattern stored in the oxide coated surface of a disk. Unlike floppy disks, hard disk drives are sealed in order to prevent the ingress of dust, smoke and dirt particles. This is important since hard disks work to much finer tolerances (track spacing, etc) than do floppy drives. Furthermore, the read/write heads of a hard disk 'fly' above the surface of the disk when the platters are turning. Due to the high speed of rotation (typically 3600 rev/min) it is essential that none of the read/write heads comes into direct contact with the area of the disk surface used for data storage.

A typical 120Mbyte IDE drive has two platters which provide four data surfaces. The drive is thus fitted with four read/write heads (one for each data surface). The read/write heads are all operated from the same 'voice coil' actuator so that they step in and out together across the surface of the disk. In addition, the innermost cylinder is designated as a 'landing zone'. No data is stored in this region and thus it provides a safe place for the heads to 'land' and make contact with the disk surface.

When the drive is static or coming up to speed, the heads remain in the landing zone. When sufficient rotational speed has been achieved, the heads leave the surface of the disk and are then stepped across to the active part of the disk surface where reading and writing takes place. Finally, when the disk becomes inactive, the motor ceases to rotate and the heads return to the landing zone where they are 'parked'.

---

**TIP**

Some older hard disk drives do not park their read/write heads automatically. You can, however, park the heads using a simple program that steps the heads to the innermost track. Thereafter, it is safe to switch the power off. You can obtain a hard disk park utility (e.g. PARK.COM) from most shareware libraries.

### TIP

You can have your read/write heads parked automatically after a predetermined period of inactivity by means of an automatic parking utility (e.g., AUTOPARK.COM from Sydex). This memory-resident program will park the heads after a period which can be set from 1 to 60 minutes (5 minutes is the default).

### TIP

Never attempt to move a PC when the power is on and the system is active. A bump or knock can easily cause your drive's read/write heads to 'crash' against the oxide coated surface of the disk platters. If this happens, you may be unlucky enough to remove part of one or more of the tracks and your precious data will be forever lost!

## Hard disk types

A variety of different hard disk types are supported by PCs including ST506 (MFM), RLL, ESDI, and SCSI types. Since they all have different interfacing requirements, it is important to know which type you are dealing with! Typical data transfer rates and capacities for various types of hard disk drive are shown in Table 11.1.

*Table 11.1   Typical data transfer rates and capacities for various types of hard disk drive*

| Interface | Data transfer rate (bit/sec) | Capacity (Mbyte) |
|---|---|---|
| ST506 | 0.1 to 1M | 10 to 20 |
| ESDI | 1.2 to 1.8M | 40 to 320 |
| SCSI | 1 to 2M | 80 to 680 |
| IDE | 1 to 7M | 80 to 340 |

### ST506

The Shugart ST506 interface standard was popular in the late '70s and early '80s and it became the hard disk standard to be used in the first generations of PCs that were supplied with hard disks.

The ST506 uses 'modified frequency modulation' (MFM) to digitally encode its data. This method of recording digital information has now been superseded by 'run-length-limited' (RLL) encoding which uses the available disk space more efficiently. Note that MFM ST506 drives are normally formatted with 17 sectors per track whilst RLL drives generally use 26 sectors per track.

When RLL encoding is used, a limit is imposed on the number of consecutive 0 bits that can be recorded before a 1 bit is included. '2,7 RLL' uses strings of between 2 and 7 consecutive 0 bits whilst '3,9 RLL' is based on sequences of between 3 and 9 consecutive 0 bits before a 1 bit is inserted. 2,7 RLL and 3,9 RLL respectively offer a 50% and 100% increase in drive capacity.

ST506 drives, whether MFM or RLL types, require a complex hard disk controller card. Drives are connected to the card by means of two separate ribbon cables; a 34-way cable for control signals and a 20-way cable for data.

## ESDI

The 'enhanced small device interface' (ESDI) is an updated and improved standard based on the original ST506 interface. ESDI was first introduced by Maxtor in 1983 and its BIOS code is generally software-compatible with the earlier standard. You should note, however, that most ESDI drives are formatted to 32 sectors per track. Like ST506 drives, ESDI units require the services of a separate hard disk controller card. Both the ESDI and ST506 interface standards support up to four physical drives though usually no more than two drives are actually fitted.

## IDE

'Integrated drive electronics' (IDE) drives are designed to interface very easily with the ISA bus. The interface can either make use of a simple adapter card (without the complex controller associated with ST506 and ESDI drives) or can be connected directly to the system motherboard where the requisite 40-way IDC connector has been made available by the manufacturer.

In either case, the 40-way ISA bus extension is sometimes known as an 'AT attachment'. This system interface is simply a subset of the standard ISA bus signals and it can support up to two IDE drives in a 'daisy-chain' fashion (i.e., similar to that used for floppy disk drives). This makes IDE drives extremely cost-effective since they dispense with the complex hard disk controller/adapter card required by their predecessors.

IDE drives are 'low-level formatted' with a pattern of tracks and sectors already in-place when they reach you. This allows them to be formatted much more efficiently; the actual *physical* layout of the disk is hidden from BIOS which only sees the *logical* format presented to it by the integrated electronics. This means that the disk can have a much larger number of sectors on the outer tracks than on the inner tracks. Consequently, a much greater proportion of the disk space is available for data storage.

### TIP

If you are fitting two IDE drives in a system, one drive must be designated the 'master' and the other must be the 'slave'. You can do this simply by setting a jumper (in one of three positions) at the rear of the drive. The jumper is not usually fitted when there is only one IDE drive.

## SCSI

The only practical alternative to IDE drives are those based on the small computer systems interface' (SCSI). This interface standard is not particularly new but it does offer a powerful and highly flexible method of expansion which is particularly suited to mass storage applications.

SCSI is a local I/O bus which is commonly used to interface peripheral devices (such as hard disk and tape drives) to a host computer system. The SCSI bus supports a total of eight devices (including the host computer). Communication is allowed between two devices at any one time. Each device present must have its own unique SCSI ID (invariably selected by means of links or DIP switch settings).

When two devices communicate on the SCSI bus, the unit originating the operation is designated as the 'initiator'. The unit performing the operation, on the other hand, is known as the 'target'. Any desired combination of initiators and targets may be present in an SCSI bus system (provided, of course, that the total number of devices present does not exceed eight). Data transfers on the SCSI bus are asynchronous and follow a defined handshake protocol in which signals are exchanged on the Request (REQ) and Acknowledge (ACK) lines. The SCSI interface employs a total of nine control signals and nine data signals (including an optional parity bit).

### TIP

With most SCSI drives, you will find an 8-pin SCSI ID selector fitted at the rear of the drive. You should fit jumpers to this selector in order to establish the ID for the drive in question. If you have more than one SCSI drive fitted they must have different IDs!

### SCSI connector

The SCSI interface uses a 50-way connector arranged in two rows each of 25-ways. The connector pin assignment is shown in Table 11.2.

*Table 11.2  SCSI bus connections*

| Signal | Pin No. |
| --- | --- |
| DB(0) | 2 |
| DB(1) | 4 |
| DB(2) | 6 |
| DB(3) | 8 |
| DB(4) | 10 |
| DB(5) | 12 |
| DB(6) | 14 |
| DB(7) | 16 |
| DB(P) | 18 |
| GND | 20 |
| GND | 22 |
| GND | 24 |
| Terminator power | 26 |
| GND | 28 |
| GND | 30 |
| ATN | 32 |
| GND | 34 |
| BSY | 36 |
| ACK | 38 |
| RST | 40 |
| MSG | 42 |
| SEL | 44 |
| C/D | 46 |
| REQ | 48 |
| I/O | 50 |

Note: 1. All odd numbered pins, with the exception of pin-25, are connected to ground (GND). Pin-25 is not connected.
2. Pin-1 is marked by a triangle identation on the 50-way connector.

# Formatting a hard disk

Formatting a hard disk is essentially a three-stage process but you don't always have to perform all three stages. The first stage of the process, a 'low-level' or 'physical' format, allows the drive to be configured for a particular hard disk controller card. The low-level format writes tracks and sectors on the magnetic surface and allocates numbers to identify their physical position on the disk. At this stage, the sectors may be 'interleaved'.

## Interleaving

Although the 17 sectors of an ST-506 compatible hard disk are numbered 1 to 17, there is no reason why the sectors should be numbered consecutively. Indeed, there is a very good reason for not numbering them in a strict numerical sequence. It is worth attempting to explain this particular point.

A considerable improvement in data transfer rate can be achieved by not attempting to read the sectors of a hard disk in strict physical sequence. This is because the controller transfers a sector at a time and, when it is ready to read the next physical sector it is quite likely that the sector will have already passed under the read/write head. In this case it will be necessary to wait until the disk has completed a further revolution before it is possible to read the next wanted sector. A far better scheme would be to arrange the sectors so that the next wanted sector is one or two sectors further on.

In 1:1 interleaving (i.e., no interleaving) the sectors are numbered consecutively around the circumference of the disk. 2:1 interleaving numbers the sectors 1,10,2,11,3,12 etc, and 3:1 interleaving uses the sequence 1,7,13,2,8, etc.

## Performing a low-level format

There are three methods of performing a low-level format:

(a) Using formatting software supplied on disk and shipped with a drive and/or controller.

(b) Using the BIOS set-up program when it includes a 'hard disk' utility.

(c) Using a formatting program resident within the hard disk controller's ROM.

In the first case, you need only insert the disk in drive A, run the program and follow the on-screen instructions. In the last case, you may have to use Debug (using a command of the form G=C800:5, or equivalent) in order to execute the code stored in the disk controller's ROM.

In all three cases you will have to specify information on your drive including its type, number of heads, cylinders, landing zone, etc. You can usually also specify the interleaving that you wish to use.

## Partitioning

Once a low-level format has been completed, you can partition it so that it behaves as several *logical* drives. Partitioning was originally invented to work around one of DOS's early limitations. This was simply that, by virtue of the 16-bit sector numbering system, early versions of DOS could only support a hard disk of up to 32Mbyte.

To put this into context, assume that you have an 80Mbyte drive in a system operating under MS-DOS 3.3. You would probably have a 'primary partition' (C) of 32Mbyte, with two further 'extended partitions' (D and E) of 24Mbyte each. Note that, whilst they can be different sizes, neither of the extended partitions should excee 32Mbyte in size.

With the advent of MS-DOS 5.0 there is no longer any need partition a large drive into several smaller logical drives. You can, you wish, have a single 'primary DOS partition' and no 'extende DOS partitions' (note that MS-DOS 5.0 lets you have up to 23 logica drives within the extended DOS partition). The primary DOS part tion can occupy the entire drive.

### TIP

In order to start DOS from a hard disk, the disk must have a primary DOS partition that contains the three system files; IO.SYS, MSDOS.SYS and COMMAND.COM. This partition must be made the 'active partition'. You can have up to 23 logical drives (D to Z) in the remaining 'extended DOS partition'.

### TIP

SuperStor (and similar disk compression programs) creates a single very large compressed *file* which appears to DOS to be a logical drive C (the *real* drive C is renamed D). If you have a drive with a physical capacity of 40Mbyte, SuperStor will provide you with a logical drive C of about 80Mbyte capacity. This fake C drive is actually a compressed data file - not a disk partition.

## Using FDISK

The DOS FDISK utility creates and displays information about part tions and logical drives. It also sets the active partition and allow you to delete partitions and logical drives. FDISK provides simpl on-screen instructions. If the drive has been used before, it is wort displaying the existing partition information before you make an changes.

When you exit FDISK the system will restart and the new option will then take effect. If you have changed the size of your primar DOS partition, FDISK will prompt you to insert an MS-DOS syster disk in drive A (you can use the emergency boot disk described o page 125 for this).

After using FDISK you should use the DOS FORMAT comman to format any partition that you have created or changed. If you fai to do this DOS will display an 'invalid media' error message.

### TIP

FDISK destroys all existing files in the partitions that you modify. If you intend to use FDISK to change the partitions on your hard disk you must first backup your files to floppy disk.

**TIP**

If you are formatting the primary DOS partition of your hard disk, don't forget to transfer the DOS system files by using the /S switch within the FORMAT command. If, for example, you have created a primary DOS partition (C) with two logical drives (D and E) in the extended partition, you should use the following three DOS commands:

FORMAT C: /S
FORMAT D:
FORMAT E:

## The master boot record

Hard disk drives, like floppy disks, have a boot record which occupies the very first sector of the disk. On hard disks, this is known as the 'master boot record'. Apart from the basic parameter table, the structure of the boot sector is somewhat different from that used for a floppy disk.

You can examine the master boot record in the same way as for a floppy disk (see page 104). Note, however, that the Debug command to load the master boot sector for drive C into RAM is l 0 2 0 1 (not l 0 0 0 1 which applies to drive A).

### Booting the system

The master boot program (starting at byte 0) copies itself to a different location in memory and then inspects the partition table looking for a startable partition. If more than one startable partition exists or any Boot Indicator is not 80 or 0 then DOS will display an 'Invalid Partition Table' error message.

When the partition table has been successfully validated, the boot program obtains the Begin Head, Sector, and Cylinder for the startable partition and reads it from the hard disk to absolute memory location 0000:7C00. It checks the last two bytes of the master boot record (55 AA) and then jumps to location 0000:7C00. From this point on startup is identical to booting from a floppy (see page 103).

## The partition table

The 'partition table' starts at location 0000:01BE. This structure contains entries which have the format shown in Table 11.3. Like the master boot record, the partition table can be examined using simple Debug commands.

## Hard drive troubleshooting

Failure of one or more of the read/write heads, the drive electronics, the voice coil actuator, or a major problem with one or more of the disk surfaces can render a hard disk drive inoperable. Furthermore, whilst many of these faults are actually quite simple, specialist tools, test facilities and a 'clean area' are essential if a hard drive is to be successfully repaired.

For this reason, it is wise not to attempt to carry out an internal repair unless you are *completely* confident that you can dismantle, inspect, repair, align *and* reassemble the unit without a hitch. If you have any doubts about this it is better to return the unit for specialist attention.

Furthermore, modern drives offer significantly greater amounts of data storage and better overall performance than their predecessors and thus, in many cases, you will not wish to replace an older hard drive with an identical unit. On a 'cost-per-kbyte' basis, modern drives are considerably cheaper than their predecessors!

*Table 11.3 The partition table*

| Offset | Size | Field | Purpose |
|---|---|---|---|
| +0 | 1 | Boot Indicator | Indicates if partition is startable, as follows: |
| | | *Contents (hex)* | *Meaning* |
| | | 00 | Non-startable partition |
| | | 80 | Startable partition |
| +1 | 1 | Begin Head | Side on which partition starts |
| +2 | 1 | Begin Sector | Sector at which partition starts |
| +3 | 1 | Begin Cylinder | Cylinder at which partition starts |
| +4 | 1 | System ID | Identifies partition type, as follows: |
| | | *Contents (hex)* | *Meaning* |
| | | 00 | Empty partition entry |
| | | 01 | DOS FAT-12 |
| | | 02 | XENIX |
| | | 04 | DOS FAT-16 |
| | | 05 | Extended partition |
| | | 06 | DOS > 32M |
| | | 07 | HPFS |
| | | 64 | Novell |
| | | 75 | PCIX |
| | | DB | CP/M |
| | | FF | BBT |
| +5 | 1 | End Head | Side on which partition ends |
| +6 | 1 | End Sector | Sector at which partition ends |
| +7 | 1 | End Cylinder | Cylinder at which partition ends |
| +8 | 4 | Relative Sectors | Number of sectors before start of partition |
| +12 | 4 | Number Sectors | Number of sectors in partition |

## TIP

Modern applications packages make considerable demands on your precious hard disk space. As an example, most Windows applications require upwards of 6 to 10Mbytes of storage. Hence, as a general rule, you should consider *doubling* the hard disk space on any system that you have to repair. A failed 40Mbyte hard drive should be upgraded to 80Mbyte, a 60Mbyte drive by a 120Mbyte unit, and so on. If the user needs to further increase the storage capacity then he or she can install a disk compression program (such as SuperStor). This will roughly double the storage space again.

# Replacing a hard disk drive

The procedure for removing and replacing a hard disk is very similar to that which applies to a floppy disk drive (see page 112). The following procedure is recommended:

1. Power-down and gain access to the interior of the system unit (as described in Chapter 3).
2. Remove the hard disk's power and data connectors from the rear of the drive.
3. Remove the retaining screws from the sides of the drive (four screws are usually fitted).
4. Once the drive chassis is free, it can be gently withdrawn from the system unit.
5. Re-assemble the system (replacing the drive and, if necessary also the controller card). Ensure that the data and power cables are correctly connected before restoring power to the system.
6. If the drive is new and has not been formatted by the manufacturer or supplier, you will have to perform a 'low-level' format (see page 119). You must then use the DOS FDISK utility to set-up the partitions and prepare the disk for DOS. Finally you must the DOS FORMAT command to prepare the disk for data.

## TIP

One of the most common problems with hard disks is related to temperature. If you use your PC in an unheated room on a cold morning you may find that the hard disk does not operate correctly. You may also encounter a similar problems when it is very hot. Problems can often be reduced by ensuring that the hard disk is formatted at the normal working temperature of the machine. In other words, before you attempt to carry out a low-level (or high-level) format, you should wait for between 15 and 20 minutes for the machine's internal temperature to stabilise. Never attempt a low-level format first thing on a cold and frosty morning or last thing in the afternoon where the temperature has been building up all day. The difference in these two extremes can be greater than 20 deg.C. and, like you, your hard disk may well not perform consistently over the whole of this range!

## TIP

Never turn off your computer when it is performing a hard disk access (you should always check the hard disk indicator before switching off). Failure to observe this simple rule can cause many hours of frustration and may even require drastic action on your part to recover lost or corrupt data. If you are unlucky enough to be presented with a system which boots up with an error message relating to the hard disk or that tells you that there is no space available on the disk or that directories are missing or corrupt, it is worth trying to recall what happened when you *last used* the system. If you do suspect that something was not right when the PC was switched off (e.g., the user switched off while Windows was manipulating a giant swap file) it is worth running the DOS CHKDSK utility. If you discover a number of 'lost clusters' use CHKDSK again with the /F switch (see page 150) in order to convert the lost clusters to files and to update the disk accordingly. Having done this, you can examine the files (FELE0000.CHK, FILE0001.CHK, etc) using an ASCII text editor or word processor. If they contain nothing that is recognisable then you can delete them otherwise they can be renamed, saved and used to reconstruct the lost data file.

## TIP

If your hard disk fails don't immediately rush to reformat the disk. There are several things that you can do before you resort to this course of action. If DOS does not recognise the existence of your drive you should use the BIOS set-up routine and check the CMOS RAM settings (see pages 57 and 58). If DOS recognises your drive but you are not able to either write to or read from it, you should use the DOS CHKDSK utility (see page 150) to gain some insight into the structure of the disk (or at least how DOS currently perceives it). It is also worth examining the master boot record and partition table for further clues (see page 121).

### TIP

It is well worth having an 'emergency boot' disk available in the event that your PC may one day fail to boot from the hard disk. Assuming that you have placed a blank disk in drive A, you should enter the command FORMAT A:/S. This command will format the disk and copy the system files to it. If your DOS version does not copy COMMAND.COM to the disk when the /S switch is used, you should use the COPY command (see page 144) to copy COMMAND.COM to the disk. In addition, you may find it useful to also copy the following files (or their equivalents) to your emergency boot disk:

| | |
|---|---|
| FORMAT.COM | (the first seven files will be found in |
| XCOPY.EXE | your DOS directory) |
| EDITOR.EXE | |
| FDISK.COM | |
| DEBUG.EXE | |
| DISKCOPY.COM | |
| CHKDSK.COM | |
| CONFIG.SYS | (your existing system configuration file) |
| AUTOEXEC.BAT | (your existing auto-execute batch file) |

Armed with the above, you should be able to reformat and partition the hard disk (using FDISK and FORMAT), transfer files to the hard disk (using XCOPY), check the disk (using CHKDSK) and create/edit CONFIG.SYS and AUTOEXEC.BAT files. For good measure, DEBUG will allow you to examine the master boot record and partition table.

### TIP

You can improve file access times by using a 'disk optimiser' or 'defragmenter' utility. DR-DOS 6.0 provides a useful tool (DISKOPT) that will perform this task. DISKOPT makes all files contiguous, moves all free space to the end of the disk, and sorts all directories (if required).

### TIP

Take special care when replacing the screws used for mounting a hard disk drive. It is *very* important to use the correct *length* of screw. Internal damage can easily be caused by screws that are too long!

# 12
# Viruses

A virus is simply a program that has been designed to replicate itself in every system that it comes into contact with. It is more or less successful in this goal depending on several factors including the sophistication of the virus, the level of anti-virus protection present, and the 'habits' of the user.

Sooner or later all computer users have to come to terms with this particular nuisance. Don't think that it can't happen to you; just like hard disk failure *it can and will* happen to you sometime!

This chapter explain what a virus is and briefly describes the most common types of virus. It explains how your system can become infected by a virus as well as the simple steps that you can take to avoid infection. The chapter also describes the procedure for detecting and removing a virus from your system.

> **TIP**
>
> When your hard disk fails to boot or your system locks up for no apparent reason, don't always jump to the conclusion that you have a virus. In most cases you won't have!

## Types of virus

There are over 1300 known viruses in existence. Some of these originated more than a decade ago but may appear with monotonous regularity in a variety of new disguises. In addition, completely new (and often highly sophisticated) viruses appear from time to time. Table 12.1 describes the characteristics of some of the most common types.

Viruses tend to fall into one of several main categories depending upon their mode of operation (i.e., whether they attach themselves to files, overwrite boot sectors, or pretend to be something they are not). The following main types exist:

### Boot sector viruses

A boot sector virus copies itself to the boot sector of a hard disk or floppy disk. Boot sector viruses overwrite the original boot code and replace it with their own code. The virus thus becomes active every time the system is booted from an infected disk. The virus will then usually attempt to make copies of itself in the boot sectors of other disks.

### Software bombs

Software bombs are not really viruses. They are, however, a rather unpleasant form of malicious coding designed to cripple a program (or a system!) under a given set of circumstances (e.g., elapsed time, failure to enter a password). Unlike a virus, a software bomb does not attempt to replicate itself. It is simply embedded in the code to disable the software and/or the system on which it runs.

Software bombs can produce a variety of undesirable effects, some more unpleasant than others. The least problematic type simply erases itself from memory (together with any data that you were working on at the time). Others are liable to lock up your system (often until a cryptic password is entered) and some will delete programs and data files from your hard disk. The most extreme form of software bomb will effectively 'trash' your hard disk - yet another reason for making a regular backup!

## Trojan horses

Trojan horses are destructive programs disguised as legitimate software. Sometimes these programs may purport to add some extra features to your system (e.g., additional graphics capability) or they may appear to be copies of commercial software packages.

The unwitting user simply loads the program (the user is often asked to boot the system from the floppy disk on which the trojan horse is distributed) and then some time later finds that things are not what they should be!

## Polymorphic viruses

A polymorphic virus is one which mutates each time it successfully invades a system. The changing nature of this type of virus makes them much harder to detect.

---

### TIP

Beware the unsolicited disk that arrives in your mail. There has been at least one major case of a trojan horse distributed by an unscrupulous software company. Once installed this extremely unfriendly 'evaluation program' disabled your system and then invited you to pay for the privilege of purchasing an antidote. Until you did this, your system was unusable. The (very) small print that accompanied the disk did, in fact, warn users that they would be committing themselves to a very large cash out-lay when they installed the software. This is one reason why I immediately trash any unsolicited disks that arrive in my mail and I strongly advise that you do the same!

---

# Sources of viruses

Viruses can find their way into your system in a number of ways and from a variety of sources, including:

## Bulletin boards

Unless managed correctly, an open-access bulletin board can be an environment in which a virus can thrive. Most good system operators arrange for regular or automatic virus checks. These can be instrumental in reducing the incidence of infection.

## Networks

Like bulletin boards, networks must also be considered a 'public place' in which viruses can potentially thrive. Most network managers take steps to implement reliable anti-virus measures.

## Magazine cover disks

Even the magazine cover disk that proclaims that it has been 'tested for all known viruses' is not always what it seems. There have been several cases of viruses spread by cover disks even though the disk was 'checked' before duplication. So how did this happen? The important phrase is 'all known' - no scanning software can protect you from a virus strain that it doesn't know about!

### Pirated software

It should go without saying that pirate copies of commercial software passed from person to person carry a significant risk of being infected with viruses. Many viruses are spread this way.

---

**TIP**

It is illegal to make copies of commercial software and distribute these to others. People who indulge in this practice put themselves at risk not only of infecting their systems with viruses but also of prosecution for what amounts to theft. It just isn't worth it!

---

## Virus prevention

Fortunately, there are plenty of things that you can do to safeguard yourself from virus infection and avoid the frustration of having to 'clean up' when disaster strikes. A few basic precautions will help you to avoid the vast majority of virus infections but if you do find that your system has been invaded by one of these 'nasties' you can usually destroy them quickly and easily using one of several proprietary 'virus killers'.

You can prevent viruses infecting your system by adopting 'clean habits', notably:

(a) Only download software from reputable bulletin board systems
If you are unsure about downloaded software you should scan it (using a proprietary anti-virus package) before you run any of the downloaded programs.

(b) Never use pirated copies of games and commercial software (these carry a very high risk of virus infection).

(c) Don't install or copy files onto your system from any unsolicited disk.

(d) Never install programs on your system from anything other than original distribution disks (or your own personally made backup copies of them)

(e) Make sure that other users of your system do not import their own software or install any software onto your system that you don't know about. Make *them* adhere to *your* 'clean habits'!

(f) Purchase a reputable anti-virus package (e.g., Central Point's Anti-Virus, or McAfee Associates' SCAN, VSHIELD, etc). Use this to periodically scan your system and also to check any new disks that you are uncertain of.

**TIP**

You should ensure that your anti-virus software is regularly up-dated to take account of any new virus strains that have appeared. Most anti-virus producers provide such a service at nominal cost.

**TIP**

In severe cases of virus infection you may find it necessary to reformat your hard disk and replace the programs and data stored on it in just the same way as you would if the hard disk itself had failed. This 'last resort' will eradicate an existing virus completely and should serve to further emphasise the need to make regular backups of the data stored on your hard disk. You can use the DOS BACKUP command (see page 149) or one of several excellent proprietary backup packages to help you perform this task.

## Detecting and eliminating viruses

### Detecting a virus

Some viruses will forcibly announce their presence by displaying messages, corrupting screen data, or simply by 'dissolving' your screen. Others are a little more subtle in operation. In such cases you should look for the following 'tell-tale' signs:

1. Has your hard disk increased in size for no apparent reason?
2. Have you noticed an increase (albeit small) in the size of individual programs?
3. Is hard disk activity occurring when you don't expect it?
4. Has your system become noticeably slower recently?

Next you should ask yourself what you have done recently that could have been responsible for importing a virus:

5. Have you installed any new software recently?
6. Have you recently downloaded software from a bulletin board?
7. Have you transferred any programs from someone else's disks to your machine?
8. Has anyone else had access to your machine?

If you are sure that you are suffering a virus infection and not a hardware fault (you can confirm this using proprietary anti-virus software) the next stage is to eradicate the virus before it spreads.

### Eliminating a virus

To prevent the virus present on your hard disk becoming active when you boot your system, you will need a 'clean boot' disk. This is simply an emergency boot disk (see page 125) which must, of course, have been produced before your system was infected.

You should boot from this disk (in which case the your system will be 'clean' when the DOS prompt appears). You can then run a proprietary virus detection program to scan the complete system.

Scanning software will first check memory for any viruses that may have installed themselves into RAM. It will then check boot sectors, COM, EXE, overlay and data files for any viruses that may have attached themselves to your existing software.

This process may take some time as the scanning software works through the entire contents of your hard disk. When the scan has been completed, the anti-virus package will display a report on the types of virus (if any) that it has detected. If a virus is found, the scanning software may suggest the remedy. Alternatively, you may have to refer to a printed table in order to decide upon the best method for removing the virus. The technique will vary with the type of virus and, in particular, whether it invades boot sectors or attaches itself to files. In some cases (e.g., where the virus has overwritten some of your program code) you may have to re-install applications software in order to restore the code to its original state.

*Table 12.1  Some common virus types*

| Virus name | Virus type | Type of damage | Notes |
|---|---|---|---|
| AIDS | Trojan | Corrupts COM and EXE files and affects system operation | Several strains exist |
| Bad Boy | File | Self-installs in memory, infects COPMMAND.COM, affects program and data files | Several strains exist |
| Darth Vader | Trojan | Self-installs in memory, infects COMMAND.COM, affects program and data files | |
| Dir2 | Stealth | Self-installs in memory, infects COMMAND.COM and COM files | Programs increase in size by 1024 bytes |
| Friday 13th | File | Infects COM files | Several strains exist |
| Gotcha | File | Self-installs in memory, infects COM, EXE and overlay files | Several strains exist |
| Jerusalem | File | Self-installs in memory, affects COM, EXE and overlay files | Programs increase in by approx. 1700 bytes |
| Michelangelo | Boot | Self-installs in memory, corrupts boot sectors | |
| Stoned | Boot | Self-installs in memory, corrupts boot sectors | |
| Tequila | Stealth | Self-installs in memory, infects EXE files | Programs increase in size by 2468 bytes |
| USSR | File | Affects COMMAND.COM, COM and EXE files | Various strains exist |

# 13
# Displays

The PC supports a wide variety of different types of display. This chapter explains the most commonly used display standards and video modes. It also tells you how to get and set the current video mode and provides some basic information on how the PC produces a colour display.

## PC display standards

The video capability of a PC will depends not only upon the display used but also upon the type of 'graphics adapter' fitted. Most PCs will operate in a number of video modes which can be selected from DOS or from within an application.

The earliest PC display standards were those associated with the Monochrome Display Adapter (MDA) and Colour Graphics Adapter (CGA). Both of these standards are now obsolete although they are both emulated in a number of laptop PCs that use LCD displays.

MDA and CGA were followed by a number of other much enhanced graphics standards. These include Enhanced Graphics Adapter (EGA), Multi-Colour Graphics Array (MCGA), Video Graphics Array (VGA), and the 8514 standard used on IBM PS/2 machines.

The EGA standard is fast becoming obsolete and all new PC systems are supplied with either VGA, 'super VGA', or displays which conform to IBM's 8514 standard. The characteristics of the most commonly used graphics standards are summarised in Table 13.1.

### Table 13.1 Display adapter summary

| Display standard | Approx. year of introduction | Text capability (columns x lines) | Graphics capability (horz. x vert. pixels) |
|---|---|---|---|
| MDA | 1981 | 80 x 2e monochrome | None |
| HGA | 1982 | 80 x 25 monochrome | 720 x 320 monochrome |
| CGA | 1983 | 80 x 25 in 16 colours | 320 x 200 in two sets of 4 colours |
| EGA | 1984 | 80 x 40 in 16 colours | 640 x 350 in 16 colours |
| MCGA | 1987 | 80 x 30 in 16 colours | 640 x 480 in 2 colours, 320 x 200 in 256 colours |
| 8514/A (PS/2) | 1987 | 80 x 60 in 16 colours | 1024 x 768 in 256 colours |
| VGA | 1987 | 80 x 50 in 16 colours | 640 x 480 in 16 colours, 320 x 200 in 256 colours |
| SVGA (XGA) | 1991 | 132 x 60 in 16 colours | 1024 x 768 in 256 colours, 640 x 480 in 65536 colours |

### TIP

When purchasing or upgrading a display and/or a graphics adapter there are a number of important questions that you should put to the supplier. These include:
(a) What is the maximum resolution supported?
(b) How much memory is supplied with the adapter (or how much *additional* memory is needed)?
(c) How many colours can be displayed on screen at any one time? (This will give you a clue as to which display modes are supported.)
(d) What type of card (8-bit XT or 16-bit AT) is supplied?
(e) Do I need an interlaced display? (This will cost more.)
(f) Are drivers supplied for particular applications? (Reputable suppliers will provide software drivers for popular applications including Windows, AutoCAD, Ventura, OS/2 Presentation Manager, WordPerfect, etc.)

### TIP

When purchasing a display, it is important to check that it will cope with a range of different vertical and horizontal scanning frequencies. Most 'multi-sync' compatible monitors will operate with vertical scanning frequencies between 50Hz and 90Hz and horizontal scanning frequencies between 30kHz and 38kHz. If your chosen display cannot accept this range of scanning frequencies you will be unable to make use of the higher resolution text and graphics modes.

### TIP

When operating in a high resolution mode, a 'multi-sync' display may occasionally suffer a loss of synchronisation which will usually result in a series of jagged lines across the screen. Sometimes, a display will regain 'lock' after a few seconds. However in a severe case, the display may completely fail to synchronise. If this is the case, you can usually cure the problem by making adjustments to the 'h-sync' or 'hold' control. This control may be adjusted externally in some cases but in others you may have to disassemble the monitor in order to locate the requisite pre-set adjustment on the display's printed circuit board. The same applies to vertical synchronisation (in which case the display will 'roll'). If you do have to dismantle the display, it is vitally important that you follow the high-voltage safety precautions described on page 26.

## Video modes

It is important to realise at the outset that graphics adapters normally operate in one of several different modes. A VGA card will, for example, operate in 'text mode' using either 80 or 40 columns, and in 'graphics mode' using 4, 16 or 256 colours.

The graphics adapter contains one or more VLSI devices that organise the data which produces the screen display. You should recall that a conventional cathode ray tube (CRT) display is essentially a serial device (screen data is built up using a beam of electrons which continuously scans the screen). Hence the graphics adapter must store the screen image whilst the scanning process takes place.

## Getting and setting the video mode

To determine the current video mode, you can simply read the machine's video mode byte stored in RAM at address 0449 (see Chapter 5). This byte indicates the current video mode (using the hex. values shown in Table 13.2). You can examine the byte at this address using the Debug command D0:0449L1 (the equivalent SID command is D0:449,44A). Alternatively, you can make use of the QuickBASIC program shown in Figure 6.7 (see page 63).

If you need to change the video mode, you can make use of the DOS MODE command (see page 153).

---

### TIP

You can easily give your PC a 40 (rather than 80) column screen by using the command, MODE CO40. This command can be handy when the user suffers from impaired vision or when a screen has to be viewed from a distance. If you have a monochrome monitor you may find the command MODE BW80 useful when running certain DOS applications. Of course, either of these two MODE commands can be included in your AUTOEXEC.BAT file so that the required video mode will then become active whenever the system is switched on (see page 156 for how to create an AUTOEXEC.BAT file).

---

## Graphics adapter memory

The amount of memory required to display a screen in text mode is determined by the number of character columns and lines and also on the number of colours displayed. In modes 0 to 6 and 8, a total of 16K bytes is reserved for display memory whilst in mode 7 (monochrome 80 x 25 characters) the requirement is for only 4K bytes (colours are not displayed).

In modes 0 to 3, less than 16K bytes is used by the screen at any one time. For these modes, the available memory is divided into pages. Note that only one page can be displayed at any particular time. Displayed pages are numbered 0 to 7 in modes 0 and 1 and 0 to 3 in modes 2 and 3.

The extent of display memory required in a graphics mode depends upon the number of pixels displayed (horizontal x vertical) and also on the number of colours displayed. Provided that a display adapter has sufficient RAM fitted, the concept of screen pages also applies to graphics modes. Again, it is only possible to display one page at a time.

## Colour

The basic 16-colour palette for a PC used in the vast majority of DOS applications is based on a 4-bit 'intensity plus RGB' code (see Table 13.3). This simple method generates colours by switching on and off the individual red, green and blue electron beams. The intensity signal simply serves to brighten up or darken the display at the particular screen location. The result is the 16 basic PC colours that we have all grown to know and love!

The 16 colour palette is adequate for most text applications however, to produce more intermediate shades of colour, we need a larger

*Table 13.2  Video display modes and graphics adapter standards*

| Mode | Display type | Colours | Screen resolution (note 1) | MDA | CGA | EGA | MCGA | VGA | HGA (note 3) |
|---|---|---|---|---|---|---|---|---|---|
| 00 | Text | 16 | 40 x 25 | | • | • | • | • | • |
| 01 | Text | 16 | 40 x 25 | | • | • | • | • | • |
| 02 | Text | 16 | 80 x 25 | | • | • | • | • | • |
| 03 | Text | 16 | 80 x 25 | | • | • | • | • | • |
| 04 | Graphics | 4 | 320 x 200 | | • | • | • | • | • |
| 05 | Graphics | 4 | 320 x 200 | | • | • | • | • | • |
| 06 | Graphics | 2 | 640 x 200 | | • | • | • | • | • |
| 07 | Text | Mono | 80 x 25 | • | | • | • | • | • |
| 08 | Graphics | 16 | 160 x 200 | (note 2) | | | | | |
| 09 | Graphics | 16 | 320 x 200 | (note 2) | | | | | |
| 0A | Graphics | 4 | 640 x 200 | (note 2) | | | | | |
| 0B | (note 4) | | | | | | | | |
| 0C | (note 4) | | | | | | | | |
| 0D | Graphics | 16 | 320 x 200 | | • | • | • | | |
| 0E | Graphics | 16 | 640 x 200 | | | • | | | |
| 0F | Graphics | Mono | 640 x 350 | | | • | | • | |
| 10 | Graphics | 16 | 640 x 350 | | | | | • | |
| 11 | Graphics | 2 | 640 x 480 | | | | • | • | |
| 12 | Graphics | 16 | 640 x 480 | | | | • | • | |
| 13 | Graphics | 256 | 320 x 200 | | | | • | • | |

Notes:
1. Resolutions are quoted in (columns x lines) for text displays and (horizontal x vertical) pixels for graphics displays.
2. Applies only the PC Junior.
3. The Hercules Graphics Adapter card combines the graphics (but NOT colour) capabilities of the CGA adapter with the high quality text display of the MDA adapter.
4. Reserved mode.

**Table 13.3  The PC's 16 colour palette**

| Hex. code | Binary code | | | | Colour produced |
|---|---|---|---|---|---|
| | I | R | G | B | |
| 00 | 0 | 0 | 0 | 0 | Black |
| 01 | 0 | 0 | 0 | 1 | Blue |
| 02 | 0 | 0 | 1 | 0 | Green |
| 03 | 0 | 0 | 1 | 1 | Cyan |
| 04 | 0 | 1 | 0 | 0 | Red |
| 05 | 0 | 1 | 0 | 1 | Magenta |
| 06 | 0 | 1 | 1 | 0 | Yellow |
| 07 | 0 | 1 | 1 | 1 | White |
| 08 | 1 | 0 | 0 | 0 | Grey |
| 09 | 1 | 0 | 0 | 1 | Bright blue |
| 0A | 1 | 0 | 1 | 0 | Bright green |
| 0B | 1 | 0 | 1 | 1 | Bright cyan |
| 0C | 1 | 1 | 0 | 0 | Bright red |
| 0D | 1 | 1 | 0 | 1 | Bright magenta |
| 0E | 1 | 1 | 1 | 0 | Bright yellow |
| 0F | 1 | 1 | 1 | 1 | Bright white |

Note:
I = intensity, R = red, B = blue, G - green

palette. One way of doing this is to make use of a 6-bit code where each of the three basic colours (red, green and blue) is represented by two bits (one corresponding to bright and the other to normal). This allows each colour to have four levels and produces 64 possible colour combinations.

A better method (which generates a virtually unlimited colour palette) is to use 'analogue RGB' rather than 'digital RGB' signals. In this system (used in VGA, SVGA and XGA), the three basic colour signals (red, green and blue) are each represented by analogue voltages in the range 0V to 0.7V (at the video connector). The number of colours displayed using such an arrangement depends upon the number of bits used to represent the intensity of each colour before its conversion to an analogue signal.

## TIP

> The Display Check program will allow you to carry out a variety of checks and display adjustments. This program allows you to change the video mode between CGA, EGA, and VGA and examine the effect on both text and colour screen displays.

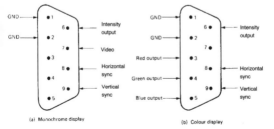

**Figure 13.1  Pin numbering for standard CGA and EGA displays**

# 14
# System Configuration

DOS provides you with various methods for configuring your system; individual DOS commands entered from the DOS command processor, batch files, hardware device drivers, and two vitally important files; CONFIG.SYS and AUTOEXEC.BAT. All of these can be instrumental in helping you to get the best out of your system.

This chapter is designed to give you a good understanding of the resources provided by your DOS. It begins by explaining some of the basic facilities provided including how to make backup copies of disks and how DOS uses I/O channels and file specifications. The chapter continues with a detailed description of each of the standard internal and external DOS commands and numerous examples have been included for you to follow.

The chapter includes a section on creating and using batch files as well as the CONFIG.SYS and AUTOEXEC.BAT files which are used to initialise your system. The chapter also shows you how to use some of the most popular device drivers, including how to set up a disk cache, a RAM drive, make use of extended and/or expanded memory, and how to configure the display and printer for international characters and fonts. The chapter concludes with an introduction to the powerful Debug utility provided as part of your DOS package.

## DOS basics

### Booting the system

DOS is automatically loaded from the hard disk (drive C) or the floppy disk placed in drive A whenever the system is 'booted' (i.e., whenever the power is applied and the CPU executes the BIOS code stored in the ROM). After successful loading, the title and version of the operating system is displayed on the screen. The message is then followed by a prompt that gives the currently selected drive (usually C> or C:\> in a system fitted with a hard disk drive). This prompt shows that the system is ready to receive a command from the user.

If an AUTOEXEC batch file is present, the commands that it contains are executed before control is passed to the user. Furthermore, if such a file contains the name of an executable program (i.e. a file with a COM or EXE extension) then this program will be loaded from disk and executed. The program may take one of several forms including a program that simply performs its function and is then cleared from memory, a 'terminate and stay resident' (TSR) program, or a fully-blown application.

In any event, it is important to remember that the currently selected drive remains the default drive unless explicitly changed by the user. As an example, consider a system that is booted with a system disk (floppy) placed in drive A. The default drive will then be A (unless an AUTOEXEC file is present that contains commands to change the current drive). The system prompt will indicate that A is the current drive. Thereafter, it is implicit that all commands which do not specify a drive refer, by default, to that drive. The SET PATH command (see page 146) can, however, be used to specify a directory path which will be searched if a command or filename does not appear in the current directory.

## TIP

To return to the root directory from within any level of sub-directory you need only type **CD\** (followed, of course, by the <ENTER> key). To return to just one level of sub-directory towards the root you can simply type **CD..** . To help you navigate the system use the **PROMPT $p$g** command (see page 146).

### Making back-up copies of disks

It is often necessary to make back-up copies of software supplied on distribution disks. Indeed, it should be considered essential to make at least one back-up copy of every disk in current use. This simple precaution can help to save much agonising when a disk becomes corrupt or is inadvertently subjected to a FORMAT command!

Having made a back-up copy, the distribution or master disk should be safely stored away and the working copy clearly labelled with the program name, version number and creation date, where appropriate. Assuming that a hard disk-based system is in use and that the DOS command utilities are placed in a sub-directory named DOS on drive C, the procedure for backing-up a floppy disk is as follows:

1. Boot the system from the hard disk in the normal way.
2. When the system prompt (C> or C:\>) appears, enter the command:
   **SET PATH=C:\DOS**
   (the command may be entered in either upper or lower case and should be immediately followed by the <ENTER> key.
   An alternative to using the SET PATH command is to make the DOS directory the current directory by entering the command:
   **CD DOS**
   Note, however, that this step can be omitted if the DOS command utilities are present in the root directory of drive C or if the SET PATH command has been included in the AUTOEXEC.BAT file.
3. Now enter the command:
   **DISKCOPY A: A:** (or **DISKCOPY A: B:** if you have two disk drives of similar size and capacity)
   The system will respond with a message of the form:
   **Insert SOURCE diskette in drive A:**
   **Press any key when ready . . .**
4. Insert the distribution or master disk in drive A and press a key. The system will read information from the master disk and transfer the contents of the disk to memory. At the start of this process a message of the form:
   **Copying 80 tracks, 18 sectors/track, 2 side(s)**
   will de displayed.
5. When all data has been transferred from the disk to memory, the system will prompt for insertion of the destination or target disk. The following message (or its equivalent) will appear:
   **Insert DESTINATION diskette in drive A:**
   **Press any key when ready . . .**
   The destination disk should then be inserted. This disk may be a blank (unformatted) disk or may be a disk which has

been previously written to. In the latter case, the disk write protection should be removed.

If the disk is blank (unformatted) it will be formatted during the process. In this case the following message will appear:

**Formatting while copying**

6. When the copying process has been completed (several disk swaps may be necessary on systems with limited RAM available) you will be prompted with the following message:

**Copy another diskette (Y/N)?**

Further disks may then be copied or the user may choose to exit from the DISKCOPY utility and return to the command prompt. In the latter case, the contents of the target disk may be checked by issuing the following command from the system prompt:

**DIR A:**

7. If it is necessary to abort the copying process at any stage, the user should use the <CTRL-C> key combination (see page 140). It should also be noted that early versions of DOS require the user to format disks before using DISKCOPY.

## I/O channels

In order to simplify the way in which DOS handles input and output, the system recognises the names of its various I/O devices (see Table 14.1). This may, at first, appear to be unnecessarily cumbersome but it is instrumental in allowing DOS to redirect data. This feature can be extremely useful when, for example, output normally destined for the printer is to be redirected to an auxiliary serial port.

*Table 14.1 DOS I/O channels*

| Channel | Meaning | Function | Notes |
|---|---|---|---|
| COM1: and COM2: | Communications | Serial I/O | Via RS-232 ports |
| CON: | Console | Keyboard (input) and screen (output) | This channel combines the functions associated with the keyboard and the display (i.e. a 'terminal'). |
| LPT1: LPT2: and LPT3: | Line printer | Parallel printer (output) | This interface conforms to the Centronics standard. |
| PRN: | Printer | Serial or parallel printer (output) | |
| NUL: | Null device | Simulated I/O | Provides a means of simulating a physical I/O channel without data transfer taking place. |

## TIP

The COPY command (see page 144) can be used to transfer data from one device to another. As an example, the command **COPY CON: PRN:** copies data from the keyboard (console input device) to the printer, **COPY CON: COM1 copies data from the keyboard to the serial port. In either case**, the end-of-file character, <CTRL-Z> or <F6>, must be entered to terminate input.

# DOS commands

DOS responds to command lines typed at the console and terminated with a <RETURN> or <ENTER> keystroke. A command line is thus composed of a command keyword, an optional command tail, and <RETURN>. The command keyword identifies the command (or program) to be executed. The command tail can contain extra information relevant to the command, such as a filename or other parameters. Each command line must be terminated using <RETURN> or <ENTER> (not shown in the examples which follow).

As an example, the following command can be used to display a directory of all bit-mapped picture files (i.e. those with a BMP extension) within a directory named GALLERY in drive C, indicating the size of each:

**DIR C:\GALLERY\\*.BMP**

Note that, in this example and the examples which follow, we have omitted the prompt generated by the system (indicating the current drive).

It should be noted that the command line can be entered in any combination of upper-case or lower-case characters. DOS converts all letters in the command line to upper-case before interpreting them. Furthermore, whilst a command line generally immediately follows the system prompt, DOS permits spaces between the prompt (e.g., \>) and the command word.

As characters are typed at the keyboard, the cursor moves to the right in order to indicate the position of the next character to be typed. Depending upon the keyboard used, a <BACKSPACE>, or <DELETE> key can be used to delete the last entered character and move the cursor backwards one character position. Alternatively, a combination of the CONTROL and H keys (i.e. <CTRL-H>) may be used instead. Various other control characters are significant in DOS and these are shown in Table 14.2.

## TIP

<CTRL-ALT-DEL> can be used to perform a 'warm' system reset. This particular combination should only be used in the last resort as it will clear system memory. Any program or data present in RAM will be lost!

## Repeating or editing DOS commands

If it is necessary to repeat or edit the previous command, the <F1> or right-arrow key may be used to reproduce the command line, character by character, on the screen. The left-arrow key permits backwards movement through the command line for editing purposes. The <F3> key simply repeats the last command in its entirety.

*Table 14.2  DOS control characters*

| Control character | Hex. | Function |
|---|---|---|
| <CTRL-C> | 03 | Terminates the current program (if possible) and returns control to the user. |
| <CTRL-G> | 07 | Sounds the audible warning device (bell) but can only be used as part of a program of batch file. |
| <CTRL-H> | 08 | Moves the cursor back by one space (i.e., the same as the <BACKSPACE> key) and deletes the character present in that position. |
| <CTRL-I> | 09 | Tabs the cursor right by a fixed number of columns (usually eight). Performs the same function as the <TAB> key. |
| <CTRL-J> | 10 | Issues a line feed and carriage return, effectively moving the cursor to the start of the next line. |
| <CTRL-L> | 12 | Issues a form feed instruction to the printer. |
| <CTRL-M> | 13 | Produces a carriage return (i.e., has the same effect as <RETURN>). |
| <CTRL-P> | 16 | Toggles screen output to the printer (i.e., after the first <CTRL-P> is issued, all screen output will be simultaneously echoed to the printer. A subsequent <CTRL-P> will disable the simultaneous printing of the screen output). Note that <CTRL-PRT.SC.> has the same effect as <CTRL-P>. |
| <CTRL-S> | 19 | Pauses screen output during execution of the TYPE command (<CTRL-NUM.LOCK> has the same effect). |
| <CTRL-Z> | 26 | Indicates the end of a file (can also be entered using <F6>). |

## File specifications

Many of the DOS commands make explicit reference to files. A file is simply a collection of related information stored on a disk. Program files comprise a series of instructions to be executed by the processor whereas data files simply contain a collection of records. A complete file specification has four distinct parts; a drive and directory specifier (known as a 'pathname'), a filename, and a filetype.

The drive specifier is a single letter followed by a colon (e.g., C:). This is then followed by the directory and sub-directory names (if applicable) and the filename and filetype.

The filename comprises 1 to 8 characters whilst the filetype takes the form of a 1 to 3 character extension separated from the filename by means of a full stop ('.'). A complete file specification (or 'filespec') thus takes the form:

**[pathname]:[filename].[filetype]**

s an example, the following file specification refers to a file named
OUSE and having a COM filetype found in the root directory of
e disk in drive A:

**A:\MOUSE.COM**

OS allows files to be grouped together within directories and sub-
rectories. Directory and sub-directory names are separated by
eans of the backslash (\) character. Directories and sub-directories
e organised in an heirarchical (tree) structure and thus complete
e specifications must include directory information.

The 'root' or base directory (i.e., that which exists at the lowest
vel in the heirarchical structure) is accessed by default when we
mply specify a drive name without further reference to a directory.
us:

**C:\MOUSE.COM**

fers to a file in the root directory whilst:

**C:\DOS\MOUSE.COM**

fers to a identically named file resident in a sub-directory called
OS'.

ub-directories can be extended to any practicable level. As an ex-
nple:

**C:\DOS\UTILS\MOUSE\MOUSE.COM**

fers to a file named MOUSE.COM present in the MOUSE sub-
rectory which itself is contained within the UTILS sub-directory
und within a directory named DOS.

When it is necessary to make explicit reference to the root direc-
ry, we can simply use a single backslash character as follows:

**C:\**

## ile extensions

he filetype extension provides a convenient mechanism for distin-
uishing different types of file and DOS provides various methods
r manipulating groups of files having the same filetype extension.
e could, for example, delete all of the back-up (BAK) present in the
ot directory of the hard disk (drive C) using a single command of
e form:

**ERA C:\*.BAK**

Alternatively, we could copy all of the executable (EXE) files from
e root directory of the disk in drive A to the root directory on drive
using the command:

**COPY A:\*.EXE C:\**

ommonly used filetype extensions are shown in Table 14.3.

## ildcard characters

OS allows the user to employ wildcard characters when specifying
es. The characters, '*' and '?', can be used to replace complete fields
d individual characters respectively within a file specification. DOS
ll search then carry out the required operation on all files for which
match is obtained.

The following examples illustrate the use of wildcard characters:

**A:\*.COM**

fers to all files having a COM extension present in the root direc-
ry of drive A.

**C:\TOOLS\*.***

fers to all files (regardless of name or extension) present in the
rectory named TOOLS on drive C.

**B:\TURBO\PROG?.C**

fers to all files having a C extension present in the TURBO direc-
ry on the disk in drive B which have PROG as their first four letters

and any alphanumeric character in the fifth character place. A match will occur for each of the following files:

**PROG1.C PROG2.C PROG3.C PROGA.C PROGB.C** etc

### Table 14.3 Common file extensions

| Extension | Type of file |
|---|---|
| ASC | An ASCII text file |
| ASM | An assembly language source file |
| BAK | A back-up file (often created automatically by a text editor which renames the source file with this extension and the revised file assumes the original file specification) |
| BAS | A BASIC program source file |
| BAT | A batch file which contains a sequence of operating system commands |
| BIN | A binary file (comprising instructions and data in binary format) |
| BMP | A bit-mapped picture file |
| C | A source code file written in the C language |
| CLP | A windows 'clipboard' file |
| COM | An executable program file in small memory format (i.e., confined to a single 64K byte memory segment) |
| CPI | A 'code page information' file |
| CRD | A Windows 'card index' file |
| DAT | A data file (usually presented in either binary or ASCII format) |
| DBG | A Debug text file |
| DOC | A document file (not necessarily presented in standard ASCII format) |
| EXE | An executable program file in large memory format (i.e., not confined to a 64K byte memory model) |
| HEX | A file presented in hexadecimal (an intermediate format sometimes used for object code) |
| INI | An initialisation file which may contain a set of inference rules and/or environment variables |
| LIB | A library file (containing multiple object code files) |
| LST | A listing file (usually showing the assembly code corresponding to each source code instruction together with a complete list of symbols) |
| OBJ | An object code file |
| OLD | A back-up file (replaced by a more recent version of the file) |
| PCX | A picture file |
| PIF | A Windows 'program interchange file' |
| SCR | A Debug script file |
| SYS | A system file |
| TMP | A temporary file |
| TXT | A text file (usually in ASCII format) |
| WRI | A document file produced by Windows 'Write' |
| \$\$\$ | A temporary file |

### Internal and external commands

It is worth making a distinction between DOS commands which form part the resident portion of the operating system (internal command) and those which involve other utility programs (external command) Intrinsic commands are executed immediately whereas extrins

ommands require the loading of transient utility programs from disk
nd hence there is a short delay before the command is acted upon.

In the case of external commands, DOS checks only the command
eyword. Any parameters which follow are passed to the utility pro-
ram without checking.

At this point we should perhaps mention that DOS only recognises
ommand keywords which are correctly spelled! Even an obvious
'ping error will result in the non-acceptance of the command and
e system will respond with an appropriate error message.

As an example, suppose you attempt to format a disk but type
**ORMATT** instead of **FORMAT**. Your system will respond with this
essage:

**Bad command or file name**

dicating that the command is unknown and that no file of that name
vith a COM, BAT, or EXE extension) is present in the current
rectory.

---

## TIP

To get on-line help from within MS-DOS 5.0 and DR-DOS 6.0
(and later operating systems) you can simple type the command name followed by /? . Hence **DIR /?** will bring you help
before using the directory command. With MS-DOS 5.0 (and
later) you can also type **HELP** followed by the command name
(i.e., **HELP DIR**). In DR-DOS 6.0 you can type **DIR /H.**

---

## nternal DOS commands

'e shall now briefly examine the function of each of the most com-
only used internal DOS commands. Examples have been included
herever they can help to clarify the action of a particular command.
he examples relate to the most commonly used versions of MS-
OS, PC-DOS, and DR-DOS however complete details of the com-
and syntax for MS-DOS version 5.0 are included in Chapter 16.

| ommand | Function |
|---|---|
| REAK | The BREAK command disables the means by which it is possible to abort a running program. This facility is provided by means of the <CTRL-C> or <CTRL-BREAK> key combinations and it normally only occurs when output is being directed to the screen or the printer. BREAK accepts two parameters, ON and OFF. |

Examples:

**BREAK ON**

enables full <CTRL-C> or <CTRL-BREAK> key checking (it is important to note that this will normally produce a dramatic reduction in the speed of execution of
a program).

**BREAK OFF**

restores normal <CTRL-C> or <CTRL-BREAK> operation (i.e. the default condition).

---

## TIP

**BREAK ON** will often result in a significant reduction in the speed
of execution of a program. You should only use this command
when strictly necessary!

CD          See CHDIR.

CHDIR       The CHDIR command allows users to display or chang
            the current directory. CHDIR may be appreviated
            CD.

            Examples:

            **CHDIR A:**

            displays the current directory path for the disk in dri
            A.

            **CHDIR C:\APPS**

            changes the directory path to APPS on drive C.

            **CD D:\DEV\PROCESS**

            changes the directory path to the sub-directory PRO(
            ESS within the directory named DEV on drive D.

            **CD\**

            changes the directory path to the root directory of th
            current drive.

            **CD..**

            changes the directory path one level back towards th
            root directory.

CLS         CLS clears the screen and restores the cursor positic
            to the top left-hand corner of the screen.

COPY        The COPY command can be used to transfer a file fro
            one disk to another using the same or a differen
            filename. The COPY command is effective when th
            user has only a single drive. The COPY command mu
            be followed by one or two file specifications. When on
            a single file specification is given, the command mak
            a single drive copy of a file. The copied file takes th
            same filename as the original and the user is prompte
            to insert the source and destination disks at the appr
            priate point. Where both source and destination fi
            specifications are included, the file is copied to the spe
            fied drive and the copy takes the specified name. Whe
            only a destination drive is specified (i.e. the destin
            tion filename is omitted) the COPY command copie
            the file to the specified drive without altering th
            filename. COPY may be used with the * and ? wildcar
            characters in order to copy all files for which a mate
            is found.

            Examples:

            **COPY A:\ED.COM B:**

            copies the file ED.COM present in the root director
            of the disk in drive A to the disk present in drive I
            The copy will be given the name ED.COM.

---

**TIP**

On a single drive system the only available floppy drive can be
used as both the source and destination when the COPY command is used. The single physical drive will operate as both
drive A and drive B and you will be prompted to insert the source
and destination disks when required.

---

**TIP**

COPY is unable to make copies files located within sub-directories. If you need this facility use XCOPY with the /s switch
(see page 155).

DATE
The DATE command allows the date to be set or displayed.
Examples:
**DATE**
displays the date on the screen and also prompts the user to make any desired changes. The user may press <RETURN> to leave the settings unchanged.
**DATE 12-27-93**
sets the date to 27th December 1993.

DEL
See ERASE.

DIR
The DIR command displays the names of files present within a directory. Variations of the command allow the user to specify the drive to be searched and the types of files to be displayed. Further options govern the format of the directory display.
Examples:
**DIR**
displays all files in the current default directory.
**A:\ DIR**
changes the default drive to A (root directory) and then displays the contents of the root directory of the disk in drive A.
**DIR \*.BAS**
displays all files with a BAS extension present in the current default directory drive.
**DIR C:\DEV.\***
displays all files named DEV (regardless of their type or extension) present in the root directory of drive C (the hard disk).
**DIR C:\MC\\*.BIN**
displays all files having a BIN extension present in the sub-directory named MC on drive C (the hard disk).
**DIR/W**
displays a directory listing in 'wide' format (excluding size and creation date/time information) of the current default directory.

## TIP

To prevent directory listings scrolling off the screen use DIR /P or DIR: MORE. These commands will pause the listing at the end of each screen and wait for you to press a key before continuing.

## TIP

MS-DOS 5.0 (and later) includes many options for use with the DIR command including sorting the directory listing and displaying hidden system files.

ERASE        The ERASE command is used to erase a filename from the directory and release the storage space occupied by a file. The ERASE command is identical to the DEL command and the two may be used interchangeably. ERASE may be used with the * and ? wildcard characters in order to erase all files for which a match occurs. Examples:

**ERASE PROG1.ASM**

erases the file named PROG1.ASM from the disk placed in the current (default) directory.

**ERASE B:\TEMP.DAT**

erases the file named TEMP.DAT from the root directory of the disk in drive B.

**ERASE C:\*.COM**

erases all files having a COM extension present in the root directory of the hard disk (drive C).

**ERASE A:\PROG1.***

erases all files named PROG1 (regardless of their type extension) present in the root directory of the disk currently in drive A.

MKDIR        The MKDIR command is used to make a new directory or sub-directory. The command may be abbreviated to MD.
Examples:

**MKDIR APPS**

creates a sub-directory named APPS within the current directory (note that the MKDIR command is often used after CHDIR).

PATH         The PATH command may be used to display the current directory path. Alternatively, a new directory path may be established using the SET PATH command.
Examples:

**PATH**

displays the current directory path (a typical response would be **PATH=C:\WINDOWS**).

**SET PATH=C:\DOS**

makes the directory path C:\DOS.

PROMPT       The PROMPT command allows the user to change the system prompt. The PROMPT command is followed by a text string which replaces the system prompt. Special characters may be inserted within the string as follows:

$d   current date
$e   escape character
$g   >
$h   backspace and erase
$l   <
$n   current drive
$p   current directory path
$q   =
$t   current time
$v   DOS version number
$$   $
$_   newline

Examples:

**PROMPT $t$g**

changes the prompt to the current time followed by a >.

**PROMPT Howard Associates PLC $_?**

changes the prompt to Howard Associates PLC followed by a carriage return and newline on which a ? is displayed.

**PROMPT**

restores the default system prompt (e.g. C:\>).

---

**TIP**

The most usual version of the PROMPT command is **PROMPT $p$g** which displays the current directory/sub-directory and helps to avoid confusion when navigating within DOS directories.

---

RD      See RMDIR.

RENAME     The RENAME command allows the user to rename a disk file. RENAME may be used with the * and ? wildcard characters in order to rename all files for which a match occurs. RENAME may be abbreviated to REN. Examples:

**RENAME PROG2.ASM PROG1.ASM**

renames PROG1.ASM to PROG2.ASM on the disk placed in

the current (default) directory.

**REN A:\HELP.DOC HELP.TXT**

renames the file HELP.DOC to HELP.TXT in the root directory of the disk in drive A.

**REN B:\CONTROL.* PROG1.***

renames all files with name PROG1 (regardless of type extension) to CONTROL (with identical extensions) found in the root directory of the disk in drive B.

RMDIR     The RMDIR command is used to remove a directory. RMDIR may be abbreviated to RD. The command cannot be used to remove the current directory and any directory to be removed must be empty and must not contain further sub-directories.

Example:

**RMDIR ASSEM**

removes the directory ASSEM from the current directory.

SET     The SET command is use to set the environment variables (see PATH).

TIME     The TIME command allows the time to be set or displayed.

Examples:

**TIME**

displays the time on the screen and also prompts the user to make any desired changes. The user may press <RETURN> to leave the settings unchanged.

**TIME 14:30**

sets the time to 2.30 p.m.

TYPE     The TYPE command allows the user to display the contents of an ASCII (text) file on the console screen. The TYPE command can be used with options which enable or disable paged mode displays. The <PAUSE> key or <CTRL-S> combination may be used to halt the display. You can press any key or use the <CTRL-Q> combination respectively to restart. <CTRL-C> may be used to abort the execution of the TYPE command and exit to the system.

Example:
**TYPE B:\PROG1.ASM**
will display the contents of a file called PROG1.ASM
stored in the root directory of the disk in drive B. The
file will be sent to the screen.
**TYPE C:\*.DOC**
will display the contents of all the files with a DOC
extension present in the root directory of the hard disk
(drive C).

## TIP

You can use the TYPE command to send the contents of a file
to the printer at the same time as viewing it on the screen. If you
need to do this, press <CTRL-P> before you issue the TYPE
command (but do make sure that the printer is 'on-line' and
ready to go!). To disable the printer 'echo' you can use the
<CTRL-P> combination a second time.

## TIP

The ability to redirect data is an extremely useful facility. DOS
uses the < and > characters in conjunction with certain commands to redirect files. As an example, **TYPE A:\README.DOC
>PRN** will redirect normal screen output produced by the TYPE
command to the printer. This is usually more satisfactory than
using the <PRT.SCREEN> key.

VER         The VER command displays the current DOS version.
VERIFY      The VERIFY command can be used to enable or dis-
            able disk file verification. VERIFY ON enables verifica-
            tion whilst VERIFY OFF disables verification. If
            VERIFY is used without ON or OFF, the system will
            display the state of verification (on or off).
VOL         The VOL command may be used to display the volume
            label of a disk.

## External DOS commands

Unlike internal commands, these commands will not function unless
the appropriate DOS utility program is resident in the current (default) directory. External commands are simply the names of utility
programs (normally resident in the DOS sub-directory). If you need
to gain access to these utilities from any directory or sub-directory,
then the following lines should be included in your AUTOEXEC.BAT
file (see page 166):
**SET PATH=C:\DOS**
The foregoing assumes that you have created a sub-directory called
DOS on the hard disk and that this sub-directory contains the DOS
utility programs. As with the internal DOS commands, the examples
given apply to the majority of DOS versions.

**Command    Function**
APPEND      The APPEND command allows the user to specify
            drives, directories and sub-directories which will be
            searched through when a reference is made to a par-
            ticular data file. The APPEND command follows the
            same syntax as the PATH command (see page 146).

ASSIGN    The ASSIGN command allows users to re-direct files
          between drives. ASSIGN is particularly useful when a
          RAM disk is used to replace a conventional disk drive.
          Examples:
          **ASSIGN A=D**
          results in drive D being searched for a file whenever a
          reference is made to drive A. The command may be
          countermanded by issuing a command of the form:
          **ASSIGN A=A**
          Alternatively, all current drive assignments may be
          over-ridden by simply using:
          **ASSIGN**

---

**TIP**

ASSIGN A=B followed by **ASSIGN B=A** can be used to swap
the drives over in a system which has two floppy drives. The
original drive assignment can be restored using **ASSIGN**.

---

ATTRIB    The ATTRIB command allows the user to examine and/
          or set the attributes of a single file or a group of files.
          The ATTRIB command alters the file attribute byte
          (which appears within a disk directory) and which
          determines the status of the file. (e.g. read-only).
          Examples:
          **ATTRIB A:\PROCESS.DOC**
          displays the attribute status of copies the file
          PROCESS.DOC contained in the root directory of the
          disk in drive A.
          **ATTRIB +R A:\PROCESS.DOC**
          changes the status of the file PROCESS.DOC contained
          in the root directory of the disk in drive A so that is a
          read-only file. This command may be countermanded
          by issuing a command of the form:
          **ATTRIB -R A:\PROCESS.DOC**

---

**TIP**

TIP: A crude but effective alternative to password protection is
is that of using ATTRIB to make all the files within a sub-directory hidden. As an example, **ATTRIB +H C:\PERSONAL** will
hide all of the files in the PERSONAL sub-directory. **ATTRIB -H
C:\PERSONAL** will make them visible once again.

---

BACKUP    The BACKUP command may be used to copy one or
          more files present on a hard disk to a number of floppy
          disks for security purposes. It is important to note that
          the BACKUP command stores files in a compressed
          format (i.e. not in the same format as that used by the
          COPY command). The BACKUP command may be
          used selectively with various options including those
          which allow files to be archived by date. The BACKUP
          command usually requires that the target disks have
          been previously formatted however, from DOS V3.3
          onwards, an option to format disks has been included.

Examples:
**BACKUP C:\*.\* A:**

backs up all of the files present on the hard disk. This command usually requires that a large number of (formatted) disks are available for use in drive A. Disks should be numbered so that the data can later be RESTOREd in the correct sequence.

**BACKUP C:\DEV\\*.C A:**

backs up all of the files with a C extension present within the DEV sub-directory on drive C.

**BACKUP C:\PROCESS\\*.BAS A:/D:01-01-93**

backs up all of the files with a BAS extension present within the PROCESS sub-directory of drive C that were created or altered on or after 1st January 1993.

**BACKUP C:\COMMS\\*.\* A:/F**

backs up all of the files present in the COMMS sub-directory of drive C and formats each disk as it is used.

CHKDSK    The CHKDSK command reports on disk utilisation and provides information on total disk space, hidden files, directories, and user files. CHKDSK also gives the total memory and free memory available. CHKDSK incorporates options which can be used to enable reporting and to repair damaged files.

CHKDSK provides two useful switches; /F fixes errors on the disk and /V displays the name of each file in every directory as the disk is checked. Note that if you use the /F switch, CHKDSK will ask you to confirm that you actually wish to make changes to the disk's file allocation table (FAT).

Examples:
**CHKDSK A:**

checks the disk placed in the A drive and displays a status report on the screen.

**CHKDSK C:\DEV\\*.ASM/F/V**

checks the specified disk and directory, examining all files with an ASM extension, reporting errors and attempting to correct them.

---

### TIP

If you make use of the /F switch, CHKDSK will ask you to confirm that you actually wish to correct the errors. If you do go ahead CHKDSK will usually change the disk's file allocation table (FAT). In some cases this may result in loss of data!

### TIP

The CHKDSK command has a nasty bug in certain versions of MS-DOS and PC-DOS. The affected versions are:

| DOS version | File name | File size | Date |
|---|---|---|---|
| PC-DOS 4.01 | CHKDSK.COM | 17771 bytes | 17 Jun 88 |
| MS-DOS 4.01 | CHKDSK.COM | 17787 bytes | 30 Nov 88 |
| PC-DOS 5.0 | CHKDSK.EXE | 16200 bytes | 09 Apr 91 |
| MS-DOS 5.0 | CHKDSK.EXE | 16184 bytes | 09 May 91 |

The bug destroys the directory structure when CHKDSK is used with the /F switch and the total allocation units on disk is greater than 65,278. The bug was corrected in maintenance release 5.0A dated 11 Nov 91 however the problem does not arise if the hard disk partition is less than 128Mbytes. If you have an affected DOS version it is well worth ugrading to avoid the disasterous consequences of this bug!

COMP      The COMP command may be used to compare two files on a line by line or character by character basis. The following options are available:

/A   use ... to indicate differences
/B   perform comparison on a character basis
/C   do not report character differences
/L   perform line comparison for program files
/N   add line numbers
/T   leave tab characters
/W   ignore white space at beginning and end of lines

Example:

**COMP /B PROC1.ASM PROC2.ASM**

carries out a comparison of the files PROC1.ASM and PROC2.ASM on a character by character basis.

DISKCOMP    The DISKCOMP command provides a means of comparing two (floppy) disks. DISKCOMP accepts drive names as parameters and the necessary prompts are generated when a single-drive disk comparison is made.

Examples:

**DISKCOMP A: B:**

compares the disk in drive A with that placed in drive B.

EXE2BIN    The EXE2BIN utility converts, where possible, an EXE program file to a COM program file (which loads faster and makes less demands on memory space).

Example:

**EXE2BIN PROCESS**

will search for the program PROCESS.EXE and generate a program PROCESS.COM.

### TIP

EXE2BIN will not operate on EXE files that require more than 64K bytes of memory (including space for the stack and data storage) and/or those that make reference to other memory segments (CS, DS, ES and SS must all remain the same during program execution).

FASTOPEN The FASTOPEN command provides a means of rapidly accessing files. The command is only effective when a hard disk is fitted and should ideally be used when the system is initialised (e.g. from within the AUTOEXEC.BAT file).

Example:

**FASTOPEN C:32**

enables fast opening of files and provides for the details of up to 32 files to be retained in RAM.

### TIP

FASTOPEN retains details of files within RAM and must not be used concurrently with ASSIGN, JOIN and SUBST.

FDISK The FDISK utility allows users to format a hard (fixed) disk. Since the command will render any existing data stored on the disk inaccessible, FDISK should be used with extreme caution. Furthermore, improved hard disk partitioning and formatting utilities are normally be supplied when a hard disk is purchased. These should be used in preference to FDISK whenever possible.

### TIP

To ensure that FDISK is not used in error, copy FDISK to a subdirectory that is not included in the PATH statement then erase the original version using the following commands:
**CD\**
**MD XDOS**
**COPY C:\DOS\FDISK.COM C:\XDOS**
**ERASE C:\DOS\FDISK.COM**
Finally, create a batch file, FDISK.BAT, along the following lines and place it in the DOS directory:
**ECHO OFF**
**CLS**
**ECHO ***** You are about to format the hard disk! *******
**ECHO All data will be lost - if you do wish to continue**
**ECHO change to the XDOS directory and type FDISK again.**

FIND The FIND command can be used to search for a characterstring within a file. Options include:
/C display the line number(s) where the search string has been located
/N number the lines to show the position within the file
/V display all lines which do not contain the search string

Example:

**FIND/C "output" C:/DEV/PROCESS.C**

searches the file PROCESS.C present in the DEV subdirectory for occurrences of output. When the serach string is located, the command displays the appropriate line number.

FORMAT    The FORMAT command is used to initialise a floppy or hard disk. The command should be used with caution since it will generally not be possible to recover any data which was previously present. Various options are available including:

/1     single-sided format
/8     format with 8 sectors per track
/B    leave space for system tracks to be added (using the SYS command)
/N:8  format with 8 sectors per track
/S     write system tracks during formatting (note that this must be the last option specified when more than one option is required)
/T:80  format with 80 tracks
/V    format and then prompt for a volume label

Examples:

**FORMAT A:**

formats the disk placed in drive A.

**FORMAT B:/S**

formats the disk placed in drive B as a system disk

---

### TIP

When you format a disk using the /S option there will be less space on the disk for user programs and data. As an example, the system files for DR-DOS 6.0 consume over 100K bytes of disk space!

---

JOIN      The JOIN command provides a means of associating a drive with a particular directory path. The command must be used with care and must not be used with ASSIGN, BACKUP, DISKCOPY, FORMAT etc.

KEYB    The KEYB command invokes the DOS keyboard driver. KEYB replaces earlier utilities (such as KEYBUK) which were provided with DOS versions prior to V3.3. The command is usually incorporated in an AUTOEXEC.BAT file and must specify the country letters required.

Example:

**KEYB UK**

selects the UK keyboard layout.

LABEL    The LABEL command allows a volume label (maximum 11 characters) to be placed in the disk directory.

Example:

**LABEL A: TOOLS**

will label the disk present in drive A as TOOLS. This label will subsequently appear when the directory is displayed.

MODE    The MODE command can be used to select a range of screen and printer options. MODE is an extremely versatile command and offers a wide variety of options.

Examples:

**MODE LPT1: 120,6**

initialises the parallel printer LPT1 for printing 120 columns at 6 lines per inch.

**MODE LPT2: 60,8**

initialises the parallel printer LPT2 for printing 60 columns at 8 lines per inch.

**MODE COM1: 1200,N,8,1**

initialises the COM1 serial port for 1200 baud operation with no parity, eight data bits and one stop bit.

**MODE COM2: 9600,N,7,2**

initialises the COM2 serial port for 9600 baud operation with no parity, seven data bits and two stop bits.

**MODE 40**

sets the screen to 40 column text mode

**MODE 80**

sets the screen to 80 column mode.

**MODE BW80**

sets the screen to monochrome 40 column text mode

**MODE CO80**

sets the screen to colour 80 column mode.

**MODE CON CODEPAGE PREPARE=**
**((850)C:\DOS\EGA.CPI)**

loads codepage 850 into memory from the file EGA.CPI located within the DOS directory (see 'Using DISPLAY.SYS' on page164).

### TIP

The MODE command can be used to redirect printer output from the parallel port to the serial port using **MODE LPT1:=COM1:**. Normal operation can be restored using **MODE LPT1:**.

PRINT  The PRINT command sends the contents of an ASCII text file to the printer. Printing is carried out as a background operation and data is buffered in memory. The default buffer size is 512 bytes however the size of the buffer can be specified using /B: (followed by required buffer size in bytes). When the utility is first entered, the user is presented with the opportunity to redirect printing to the serial port (COM1:). A list of files (held in a queue) can also be specified.
Examples:

**PRINT README.DOC**

prints the file README.DOC from the current directory.

**PRINT /B:4096 HELP1.TXT HELP2.TXT HELP3.TXT**

establishes a print queue with the files HELP1.TXT, HELP2.TXT, and HELP3.TXT and also sets the print buffer to 4K bytes. The files are sent to the printer in the specified sequence.

RESTORE  The RESTORE command is used to replace files on the hard disk which were previously saved on floppy disk(s) using the BACKUP command. Various options are provided (including restoration of files created before or after a specified date).
Examples:

**RESTORE C:\DEV\PROCESS.COM**

restores the files PROCESS.COM in the sub-directory named DEV on the hard disk partition, C. The user is prompted to insert the appropriate floppy disk (in drive A).

**RESTORE C:\BASIC /M**

restores all modified (altered or deleted) files present

in the sub-directory named BASIC on the hard disk partition, C.

SYS The SYS command creates a new boot disk by copying the hidden DOS system files. SYS is normally used to transfer system files to a disk which has been formatted with the /S or /B option. SYS cannot be used on a disk which has had data written to it after initial formatting.

TREE The TREE command may be used to display a complete directory listing for a given drive. The listing starts with the root directory.

XCOPY The XCOPY utility provides a means of selectively copying files. The utility creates a copy which has the same directory structure as the original. Various options are provided:

 /A only copy files which have their archive bit set (but do not reset the archive bits)

 /D only files which have been created (or that have been changed) after the specified date

 /M copy files which have their archive bit set but reset the archive bits (to avoid copying files unnecessarily at a later date)

 /P prompt for confirmation of each copy

 /S copy files from sub-directories

 /V verify each copy

 /W prompt for disk swaps when using a single drive machine

Example:

**XCOPY C:\DOCS\\*.\* A:/M**

copy all files present in the DOCS sub-directory of drive C:. Files will be copied to the disk in drive A:. Only those files which have been modified (i.e. had their archive bits set) will be copied.

---

**TIP**

Always use XCOPY in preference to COPY when sub-directories exist. As an example, **XCOPY C:\DOS\\*.\* A:\ /S** will copy all present in the DOS directory on drive C: *together with* all files present in any sub-directories, to the root directory of the disk in A:.

---

## Using batch files

Batch files provide a means of avoiding the tedium of repeating a sequence of operating system commands many times over. Batch files are nothing more than straightforward ASCII text files which contain the commands which are to be executed when the name of the batch is entered. Execution of a batch file is automatic; the commands are executed just as if they had been types in at the keyboard. Batch files may also contain the names of executable program files (i.e. those with a COM or EXE extension), in which case the specified program is executed and, provided the program makes a conventional exit to DOS upon termination, execution of the batch file will resume upon termination.

### Batch file commands

DOS provides a number of commands which are specifically intended for inclusion within batch files.

**Command** **Function**

ECHO     The ECHO command may be used to control screen
         output during execution of a batch file. ECHO may be
         followed by ON or OFF or by a text string which will
         be displayed when the command line is executed.
         Examples:
         **ECHO OFF**
         disables the echoing (to the screen) of commands
         contained within the batch file.
         **ECHO ON**
         re-enables the echoing (to the screen) of commands
         contained within the batch file. (Note that there is no
         need to use this command at the end of a batch file as
         the reinstatement of screen echo of keyboard gener-
         ated commands is automatic).
         **ECHO Sorting data - please wait!**
         displays the message:
         **Sorting data - please wait!**
         on the screen.

**TIP**

You can use **@ECHO OFF** to disable printing of the ECHO command itself. You will normally want to use this command instead of **ECHO OFF**.

FOR      FOR is used with IN and DO to implement a series of
         repeated commands.
         Examples:
         **FOR %A IN (IN.DOC OUT.DOC MAIN.DOC)**
         **DO COPY %A LPT1:**
         copies the files IN.DOC, OUT.DOC, and MAIN.DOC
         in the current directory to the printer.
         **FOR %A IN (*.DOC) DO COPY %A LPT1:**
         copies all the files having a DOC extension in the cur-
         rent directory to the printer. The command has the
         same effect as **COPY *.DOC LPT1:**.

IF       IF is used with GOTO to provide a means of branching
         within a batch file. GOTO must be followed by a label
         (which must begin with :).
         Example:
         **IF NOT EXIST SYSTEM.INI GOTO :EXIT**
         transfers control to the label :EXIT if the file
         SYSTEM.INI cannot be found in the current directory.

PAUSE    the pause command suspends execution of a batch file
         until the user presses any key. The message:
         **Press any key when ready...**
         is displayed on the screen.

REM      The REM command is used to preceed lines of text
         which will constitute remarks.
         Example:
         **REM Check that the file exists before copying**

## Creating batch files

Batch files may be created using an ASCII text editor or a word processor (operating in ASCII mode). Alternatively, if the batch file comprises only a few lines, the file may be created using the DOS COPY
command. As an example, let us suppose that we wish to create a

batch file which will:

1. Erase all of the files present on the disk placed in drive B.
2. Copy all of the files in drive A having a TXT extension to produce an identically named set of files on the disk placed in drive B.
3. Rename all of the files having a TXT extension in drive A to so that they have a BAK extension.

The required operating system commands are thus:

**ERASE B:\*.\***
**COPY A:\*.TXT B:\**
**RENAME A:\*.TXT A:\*.BAK**

The following keystrokes may be used to create a batch file named ARCHIVE.BAT containing the above commands (note that <ENTER> is used to terminate each line of input):

**COPY CON: ARCHIVE.BAT**
**ERASE B:\*.\***
**COPY A:\*.TXT B:\**
**RENAME A:\*.TXT A:\*.BAK**
**<CTRL-Z>**

If you wish to view the batch file which you have just created simply enter the command:

**TYPE ARCHIVE.BAT**

Whenever you wish to execute the batch file simply type:

**ARCHIVE**

Note that, if necessary, the sequence of commands contained within a batch file may be interrupted by typing:

**<CTRL-C>**

i.e., press and hold down the CTRL key and then press the C key)

The system will respond by asking you to confirm that you wish to terminate the batch job. Respond with **Y** to terminate the batch process or **N** if you wish to continue with it.

Additional commands can be easily appended to an existing batch file. Assume that we wish to view the directory of the disk in drive A after running the archive batch file. We can simply append the extra commands to the batch files by entering:

**COPY ARCHIVE.BAT + CON:**

The system displays the filename followed by the CON prompt. The extra line of text can now be entered using the following keystrokes (again with each line terminated by <ENTER>):

**DIR A:\**
**<CTRL-Z>**

## Passing parameters

Parameters may be passed to batch files by including the % character to act as a place holder for each parameter passed. The parameters are numbered strictly in the sequence in which they appear after the name of the batch file. As an example, suppose that we have created a batch file called REBUILD, and this file requires two file specifications to be passed as parameters. Within the text of the batch file, these parameters will be represented by %1 and %2. The first file specification following the name of the batch file will be %1 and the second will be %2. Hence, if we enter the command:

**REBUILD PROC1.DAT PROC2.DAT**

During execution of the batch file, %1 will be replaced by PROC1.DAT whilst %2 will be replaced by PROC2.DAT.

It is also possible to implement simple testing and branching within a batch file. Labels used for branching should preferably be stated in lower case (to avoid confusion with operating systems commands) and should be preceded by a colon when they are the first (or only) statement in a line. The following example which produces a sorted list of directories illustrates these points:

```
@ECHO OFF
IF EXIST %1 GOTO valid
ECHO Missing or invalid parameter
GOTO end
:valid
ECHO Index of Directories in %1
DIR %1 I FIND "<DIR>" I SORT
:end
```

The first line disables the echoing of subsequent commands contained within the batch file. The second line determines whether, or not, a valid parameter has been entered. If the parameter is invalid (or missing) the ECHO command is used to print an error message on the screen.

---

**TIP**

Simple menus can be created with batch files. As an example, the following batch files make a simple 'front-end' for three well-known applications:

| MENU.BAT | 1.BAT | 2.BAT | 3.BAT |
|---|---|---|---|
| ECHO OFF | CD ASEASY | CD DBASE | CD QBASIC |
| CLS | ASEASY | DBASE | QBASIC |
| CD\ | | | |
| ECHO **** MENU **** | | | |
| ECHO [1] = ASEASY | | | |
| ECHO [2] = DBASE | | | |
| ECHO [3] = QBASIC | | | |
| ECHO ************* | | | |

All four batch files must be placed in the root directory.

---

## Using CONFIG.SYS

When DOS starts, but before the commands within the AUTOEXEC.BAT file are executed, DOS searches the root directory of the boot disk for a file called CONFIG.SYS. If this file exists, DOS will attempt to carry out the commands in the file. As with any batch file, the configuration sequence can be abandoned by means of <CTRL-C> or <CTRL-BREAK>.

CONFIG.SYS is a plain ASCII text file with commands on separate lines. The file can be created using any text editor or word processor operating in ASCII mode (CONFIG.SYS can also be created using COPY CON: as described earlier for the creation of batch files).

Only the following subset of DOS commands are valid within CONFIG.SYS:

### CONFIG.SYS commands

| Command | Function |
|---|---|
| BREAK | Determines the response to a <CTRL-BREAK> sequence. If you set BREAK ON in CONFIG.SYS, DOS checks to see whether you have requested a break whenever a DOS call is made. If you set BREAK OFF, DOS checks for a break only when it is working with the video display, keyboard, printer, or a serial port. |
| BUFFERS | Sets the number of file buffers which DOS uses. This command can be used to significantly improve disk |

perfomance with early versions of DOS and when a disk cache (accessed via IBMCACHE.SYS or SMARTDRV.SYS) is not available. The use of buffers can greatly reduce the number of disk accesses that DOS performs (DOS only reads and writes full sectors). Data is held within a buffer until it is full. Furthermore, by reusing the least-recently used buffers, DOS retains information more likely to be needed next.

It is worth noting that each buffer occupies 512 bytes of RAM (plus 16 additional bytes overhead). Hence, the number of buffers may have to be traded-off against the amount of convenional RAM available (particularly in the case of machines with less than the standard 640K RAM).

In general, **BUFFERS=20** will provide adequate storage for most applications. **BUFFERS=40** (or greater) may be necessary for database or other applications which make intensive use of disk files.

DOS uses a default value for BUFFERS of between 2 and 15 (depending upon the disk and RAM configuration).

Later versions of DOS (e.g. DOS V4) provide a much improved BUFFERS command which includes support for expanded memory and look-ahead buffers which can store sectors ahead of those requested by a DOS read operation. The number of look-ahead buffers must be specified (in the range 0 to 8) and each buffer requires 512 bytes of memory and corresponds exactly to one disk sector. The use of exapnded memory can be enabled by means of a /X switch.
Example:
**BUFFERS=100,8 /X**
sets the number of buffers to 100 (requiring approximately 52K bytes of expanded memory) and also enables 8 look-ahead buffers (requiring a further 4K bytes of expanded memory).

**COUNTRY** Sets the country-dependent information

**DEVICE** Set the hardware device drivers to be used with DOS.
Example:
**DEVICE=C:\MOUSE\MOUSE.SYS**
enables the mouse driver (MOUSE.SYS) which contained in a sub-directory called MOUSE.
**DEVICE=C:\DOS\ANSI.SYS**
selects the ANSI.SYS screen driver (the ANSI.SYS file must be present in the DOS directory).
**DEVICE=C:\WINDOWS\HIMEM.SYS**
selects the Windows extended memory manager HIMEM.SYS (the HIMEM.SYS file must be present in the WINDOWS directory)
**DEVICE=C:\DOS\DISPLAY.SYS CON**
       **=(EGA,850,2)**
selects the DOS display driver and switches it to multilingual EGA mode (code page 850) with up to two code pages.

**TIP**

Drivers often provide a number of 'switches' which allow you to optimise them for a particular hardware configuration. Always consult the hardware supplier's documentation to ensure that you have the correct configuration for your system.

**TIP**

You may find it handy to locate all of your drivers in a common directory called DRIVERS, DEVICE or SYS. This will keep them separate from applications and help you to find them at some later date.

Finally, note that you can load as many device drivers as you need, but you must use a separate DEVICE line for each driver.

Example:

**DEVICE = C:\DRIVERS\ANSI.SYS**
**DEVICE = C:\DRIVERS\CDROM.SYS**

| | |
|---|---|
| FCBS | Set the number of file control blocks that DOS can have open at any time (note that this command is now obsolete). |
| FILES | Sets the maximum number of files that DOS can access at any time. |
| INSTALL | Installs memory-resident programs. |

Example:

**INSTALL = C:\DOS\FASTOPEN.EXE C:=100**

installs the DOS FASTOPEN utility and configures it to track the opening of up to 100 files and directories on drive C:.

**TIP**

Slightly less memory is used when memory-resident programs are loaded with this command than with AUTOEXEC.BAT. Don't, however, use INSTALL to load programs that use environment variables or shortcut keys or that require COMMAND.COM to be present to handle critical errors.

| | |
|---|---|
| LASTDRIVE | Specifies the highest disk drive on the computer. |
| REM | Treats a line as a comment/remark. |
| SHELL | Determines the DOS command processor (e.g. COMMAND.COM) |
| STACKS | Sets the number of stacks that DOS uses. |
| SWITCHES | Disables extended keyboard functions. |

## Using device drivers

DOS provides a number of device drivers and utility programs which can be installed from CONFIG.SYS. The following drivers will allow you to make the most of your own particular hardware configuration and to modify it to cater for hardware upgrades:

| Function | Device driver (generic name) |
|---|---|
| Disk caches | IBMCACHE.SYS, SMARTDRV.SYS |
| RAM drives | RAMDRIVE.SYS, VDISK.SYS |
| Additional disk drives | DRIVER.SYS |
| Memory management | XMAEM.SYS, EMM386.SYS, EMM386.EXE |
| Display adapter configuration | DISPLAY.SYS |
| Printer configuration | PRINTER.SYS |

Note: The names of device drivers tend to vary with different versions of DOS.

### Disk caching

A disk cache provides improved file access times and helps to reduce the number of physical disk accesses made by a program which makes regular use of disk files. Data is initially read from the disk into the cache. Subsequent file accesses make use of the cache rather than the disk itself. At some later time, data is written back to the disk. Generally a cache will hold more information than is likely to be requested at any one time by the program. Redundant disk accesses are eliminated as data in the cache can be manipulated directly without having to access data on the disk.

A disk cache remembers what sections of the disk have been used most frequently. When the cache must be recycled, the program keeps the more frequently used areas and discards those less frequently used. Some experimentation will normally be required in order to obtain the optimum size of a disk cache. This also varies according to the requirements of a particular application program.

### TIP

Because of its 'intelligent' features, a disk cache will normally outperform a disk buffer (created using the BUFFERS directive). Furthermore, a disk cache offers some advantages over a RAM drive since its operation is 'transparent' and you are less likely to lose all your data due to power failure. If your applications program makes frequent use of disk files, it is well worth setting up a cache.

### Using IBMCACHE.SYS

IBMCACHE.SYS is a file that accompanies any IBM PS/2 machine that uses extended memory (this excludes Models 25 and 30). The program is installed by inserting from the Reference Disk. The cache can be changed after installation either by re-running IBMCACHE or by editing the reference to IBMCACHE in CONFIG.SYS.

Example:

**DEVICE = C:\IBMDOS\IBMCACHE.SYS 32 /E /P4**

configures the cache size to 32K using extended memory and allows four sectors to be read at a time. IBMCACHE.SYS is resident in the IBMDOS directory.

### Using SMARTDRV.SYS

MS-DOS and DR-DOS offer an alternative disk-caching utility called SMARTDRV.SYS which is installed by means of an appropriate directive within CONFIG.SYS.

Example:
**DEVICE = C:\WINDOWS\SMARTDRV.SYS 512 /A**
configures the cache size to 512K using expanded memory with
SMARTDRV.SYS resident in the WINDOWS directory.
(Note that 256K is the default cache size for SMARTDRV).

## Using RAMDRIVE.SYS (or VDISK.SYS)

RAMDRIVE.SYS (or VDISK.SYS) is used to simulate a disk drive in
RAM. The simulated drive behaves exactly like a conventional drive
but with vastly improved access time. RAMDRIVE.SYS is installed
using the DEVICE command from within CONFIG.SYS. A RAM drive
can be established in conventional memory, extended memory, or
expanded memory as appropriate.

Examples:
**DEVICE = C:\DOS\VDISK.SYS**
establishes a RAM drive of 64K (the default size) with 128 bytes
per sector (the default sector size) and 64 directory entries (the
default number of directory entries) within *conventional* base
memory.
**DEVICE = C:\DOS\RAMDRIVE.SYS 128 512 96 /X**
establishes a RAM drive of 128K with 512 bytes per sector and 96
directory entries within *expanded* memory.
**DEVICE = C:\DOS\VDISK.SYS 256 256 128 /E**
establishes a RAM drive of 256K with 256 bytes per sector and 128
directory entries within *extended* memory.
**DEVICE = C:\DRIVERS\RAMDRIVE.SYS 512 256 96 /A**
creates a 512K RAM disk with 256-byte sectors and 96 directory
entries in *expanded* memory.
**DEVICE = C:\DRIVERS\RAMDRIVE.SYS 1024 512 128 /E**
creates a 1M RAM disk with 512-byte sectors and 128 directory
entries in *extended* memory.

### TIP

Where RAM space is at a premium, use a small sector size
(e.g. 128 bytes). This works because DOS does not allow files
to share the same sector - a 513 byte file would occupy *two*
sectors with 511 bytes wasted! If, however, memory is not limited, it is better to use a relatively large sector size in order to
reduce access time.

### TIP

Remember that the data stored in a RAM drive will be lost when
the power is removed from the system. It is *vital* to back-up
your data before switching off!

## TIP

A RAM drive can provide a quick method of copying disks on a system which has only one disk drive. You simply use VDISK or RAMDRIVE to establish a RAM drive with identical features to your existing (single) drive and then perform a DISKCOPY. The parameters for standard drives are:

| Drive type | RAMDRIVE or VDISK parameters |
|---|---|
| 5.25" 360K | 360 512 112 /E or /A, as required |
| 5.25" 1.2M | 1200 512 224 /E or /A, as required |
| 3.5" 720K | 720 512 112 /E or /A, as required |
| 3.5" 1.44M | 1440 512 224 /E or /A, as required |
| 3.5" 2.88M | 2880 512 240 /E or /A, as required |

## Using DRIVER.SYS

DRIVER.SYS can be used to configure a system for use with a non-standard or an external disk drive.

Examples:

**DEVICE = C:\DOS\DRIVER.SYS /D:2 /F:0 /S:9 /T:40**

designates a third floppy disk drive in a system which already has two disk drives (the parameter following the /D switch is the 'physical drive number') having a capacity of 360K, 9 sectors per track, and 40 tracks.

**DEVICE = C:\DOS\DRIVER.SYS /D:2 /F:0 /S:9 /T:40**
**DEVICE = C:\DOS\DRIVER.SYS /D:2 /F:0 /S:9 /T:40**

specifies two further disk drives (D: and E:), each 360K, 9 sectors per track, with 40 tracks. Each time the driver is loaded, the physical disk drive is assigned an additional valid drive letter automatically (D: the first time, E: the second time, and so on).

**DEVICE = C:\DOS\DRIVER.SYS /F:1 /T:80 /S:15 /H:2 /C**

specifies a conventional 1.2M 5.25" floppy disk drive (incorporating a disk change line).

**DEVICE = C:\DOS\DRIVER.SYS /F:2 /T:80 /S:9 /H:2 /C**

specifies a conventional 720K 3.5" floppy disk drive (incorporating a disk change line).

**DEVICE = C:\DOS\DRIVER.SYS /F:7 /T:80 /S:18 /H:2 /C**

specifies a conventional 1.44M 3.5" floppy disk drive (incorporating a disk change line).

## Using EMM386

The EMM386 memory manager requires an 80386 (or later) CPU and provides a means of accessing the unused parts of the upper memory area. The memory manager also allows you to use your system's extended memory to simulate expanded memory. Note that EMM386 is provided as EMM386.SYS with MS-DOS 4.0 and DR-DOS 6.0 but as EMM386.EXE with MS-DOS 5.0 (and later).

Examples:

**DEVICE = C:\DOS\EMM386.SYS**

installs the memory manager and takes 256K bytes (the default) of extended memory to provide expanded memory (MS-DOS 4.0).

**DEVICE = C:\DOS\EMM386.SYS 1024**

installs the memory manager and takes 1M byte of extended memory to provide expanded memory (MS-DOS 4.0).

**DEVICE = C:\DOS\EMM386.EXE 1024 RAM**

provides access to the upper memory area and also uses 1024K of your computer's extended memory as expanded memory (MS-DOS 5.0 and later).

**DEVICE = C:\DOS\EMM386.EXE NOEMS**

provides access to all available portions of the upper memory area but without functioning as an expanded memory emulator (MS-DOS 5.0 and later).

**DEVICE = C:\DRDOS\EMM386.SYS /F=NONE /B=AUTO /E=E800-FFFF**

autoscans upper memory from C000 to FFFF (the default) but specifically excludes the area from E800 to FFFF. No LIM page frame is set up and the DOS kernel is loaded into upper memory or, if there is not enough upper memory, it is loaded into high memory (DR-DOS 6.0).

**DEVICE = C:\DRDOS\EMM386.SYS /FRAME=C400 / KB=2048 /BDOS=FFFF**

autoscans upper memory from C000 to FFFF (the default) and sets up a LIM window with 2M byte available. BDOS is located to segment address FFFF in high memory (DR-DOS 6.0).

## TIP

The optimum sequence in which device drivers should appear within your CONFIG.SYS file is as follows:
1. HIMEM.SYS
2. An expanded memory manager (if your system is fitted with expanded memory).
3. Any device drivers that use extended memory.
4. EMM386.EXE (do not use EMM386 if you are using an expanded memory manager).
5. Any device drivers that use expanded memory.
6. Any device drivers that use the upper memory area.

## Using DISPLAY.SYS

DISPLAY.SYS enables you to switch code pages without restarting DOS and PRINTER.SYS enables you to download a font table to supported printers so that they can print non-English language and graphic characters.

The DISPLAY.SYS utility caters for different display types and for specified code pages. You do not have to include DISPLAY.SYS if you do not use code-page switching. Valid display types are:

| Display type | Meaning |
| --- | --- |
| MONO | Monochrome adapter |
| CGA | Color-graphics adapter |
| EGA | Enhanced color-graphics adapter or PS/2 or VGA |
| LCD | Convertible LCD |

Valid code pages are:

| Code page | Country |
| --- | --- |
| 437 | United States |
| 850 | Multilingual |
| 860 | Portugal |
| 863 | Canadian-French |
| 865 | Norway |

The number of pages specified within the DISPLAY.SYS command is the maximum number of *additional* code pages that the adapter can use (see also the MODE command on page 153).

Example:

**DEVICE = C:\DOS\DISPLAY.SYS CON: = (EGA,850,2)**

specifies an EGA (or VGA) display using the multilingual code page 850 with two code pages.

**DEVICE = C:\SYS\DISPLAY.SYS CON = (EGA,437,1)**
specifies an EGA (or VGA) display using 437 as the starting page
together with one additional code page.
**DEVICE = C:\SYS\DISPLAY.SYS CON = (EGA,850,863,2)**
selects an EGA (or VGA) display and a code page of 863 (French-
Canadian) together with the multilingual code page, 850.

### TIP

If your existing code page is not 437 (United States or United
Kingdom) always use 850 as the new code page and two as
the number of additional code pages.

### TIP

If you use ANSI.SYS and DISPLAY.SYS together in your
CONFIG.SYS file, the ANSI.SYS command must be used *before* the DISPLAY.SYS directive. ANSI.SYS will not take affect
when the order is reversed.

## Using PRINTER.SYS

You can use PRINTER.SYS to print the required code page characters on supported printers (or on printers that provide emulation for
the supported types). Note that MS-DOS 3.3 supports code pages on
only two printers:

IBM ProPrinter Model 4201
IBM Quietwriter III Model 5202

MS-DOS 4.0 and MS-DOS 5.0 provide additional support for the following printers:

IBM ProPrinter Model 4202
IBM ProPrinter Model 4207
IBM ProPrinter Model 4208

Valid code pages are:

| Code page | Country |
|-----------|-----------------|
| 437 | United States |
| 850 | Multilingual |
| 860 | Portugal |
| 863 | Canadian-French |
| 865 | Norway |

Example:
**DEVICE = C:\DOS\PRINTER.SYS LPT1 = (4201,850,2)**
specifies the IBM ProPrinter Model 4201 connected to the parallel printer port and using the multilingual code page as the built-in
character set. You can specify two code pages for the printer and
then switch between them.

## Using AUTOEXEC.BAT

The AUTOEXEC.BAT file allows you to automatically execute a series of programs and DOS utilites to add further functionality to your
system when the system is initialised. AUTOEXEC.BAT normally
contains a sequence of DOS commands but in addition it can also
contain the name of an application or shell that will be launched automatically when the system is booted. This is a useful facility if you
always use the same shell or application whenever you power-up your
system or if you wish to protect the end-user from the need to remember rudimentary DOS commands (such as CD, etc).

AUTOEXEC.BAT is typically used to:
1. Set up the system prompt (see page146).
2. Define the path for directory searches (using SET PATH, see page 146).
3. Execute certain DOS utilities (e.g., SHARE).
4. Load a mouse driver (e.g., MOUSE.COM).
5. Change directories (e.g., from the root directory to a 'working' directory).
6. Launch an application or shell program (e.g., PCSHELL, Windows, etc).

The example CONFIG.SYS and AUTOEXEC.BAT files which follow should give you plenty of food for thought!

## TIP

Microsoft's Windows and some DOS programs (e.g., AutoCAD) have their own built-in mouse drivers and can thus communicate directly with the mouse. However, if you regularly use a mouse with DOS applications, you will probably wish to include reference to your mouse driver within the AUTOEXEC.BAT file.

## TIP

Don't be afraid to experiment with your CONFIG.SYS and AUTOEXEC.BAT files but do make sure that you keep back-up copies of your original files (CONFIG.BAK, CONFIG.OLD, etc). Each time, use the MEM command with the /PROGRAM, /DEBUG, or /CLASSIFY switches to see the effect of your drivers and memory managers

## Example CONFIG.SYS and AUTOEXEC.Files

2Mb notebook for Windows applications, MS-DOS 5.0

| File | Content | Notes |
|------|---------|-------|
| ==== | ======= | ===== |
| CONFIG.SYS | DEVICE=C:\WINDOWS\HIMEM.SYS | load the Windows high memory device driver |
| | DOS=HIGH | load DOS into high memory |
| | FILES=40 | allow for up to 40 files |
| | BUFFERS=10 | provide 10 file buffers |
| | STACKS=9,256 | create 9 stacks each of 256 bytes |
| AUTOEXEC.BAT | PROMPT $P$G | prompt with current directory path |
| | PATH=C:\DOS;C:\WINDOWS | search DOS and Windows directories for executable files |
| | TEMP=C:\TEMP | directory for Windows swap files |
| | C:\DOS\SHARE.EXE | permits file sharing and locking |
| | C:\WINDOWS\SMARTRDV.EXE | establish a disk cache |
| | CD WINDOWS | change to the Windows directory... |
| | WIN | and run Windows! |

COMMENT: Windows performance will be disappointing with limited memory however the disk cache will improve disk access time.

4Mb business machine for Windows applications, MS-DOS 5.0

| File | Content | Notes |
|------|---------|-------|
| CONFIG.SYS | DEVICE=C:\WINDOWS\HIMEM.SYS | load the Windows high memory device driver |
| | DOS=HIGH | load DOS in high memory |
| | FILES=64 | allow for up to 64 files |
| | BUFFERS=16 | provide 16 file buffers |
| | STACKS=9,256 | set up 9 stacks each of 256 bytes |
| | SHELL=C:\DOS\COMMAND.COM C:\DOS E:/:1024 /P | specify the command interpreter and a 1K environment |
| AUTOEXEC.BAT | PROMPT $P$G | prompt with current directory path |
| | SET PATH=C:\DOS;C:\WINDOWS | search DOS and Windows directories for executable files |
| | SET TEMP=C:\TEMP | directory for Windows swap files |
| | LOADHIGH=C:\DOS\SHARE.EXE | permits file sharing and locking |
| | C:\WINDOWS\SMARTRDV.EXE | establishes a disk cache |
| | SET COMSPEC=C:\DOS\COMMAND.COM | specify the location of the command interpreter |
| | CD WINDOWS | change to the Windows directory... |
| | WIN | and run Windows! |

COMMENT: With more memory space available it is possible to allocate more buffers and provide for more files.

4Mb business machine for Windows and DOS applications, MS-DOS 5.0

| File | Content | Notes |
|------|---------|-------|
| ===== | ======= | ===== |
| CONFIG.SYS | DEVICE=C:\WINDOWS\HIMEM.SYS | load the Windows high memory device driver |
| | DEVICE=C:\WINDOWS\EMM386.EXE RAM NOEMS | load the memory manager |
| | DOS=HIGH,UMB | load DOS into a UMB |
| | DEVICEHIGH=C:\WINDOWS\MOUSE.SYS /Y | load the moouse driver into high memory |
| | SHELL=C:\DOS\COMMAND.COM C:\DOS /E:1024 /P | specify the command interpreter and a 1K environment |
| | FILES=64 | allow for up to 64 files |
| | BUFFERS=16 | provide 16 file buffers |
| | STACKS=9,256 | set up 9 stacks each of 256 bytes |
| AUTOEXEC.BAT | PROMPT $P$G | prompt with current directory path |
| | SET PATH=C:\DOS;C:\WINDOWS | search DOS and Windows directories for executable files |
| | SET TEMP=C:\TEMP | directory for Windows swap files |
| | LOADHIGH=C:\DOS\SHARE.EXE | permits file sharing and locking |
| | C:\WINDOWS\SMARTDRV.EXE | establishes a disk cache |
| | LOADHIGH C:\DOS\KEYB UK,,C:\DOS\KEYBOARD.SYS | specify a UK keyboard layout |
| | LOADHIGH C:\DOS\DOSKEY | remember last used commands |
| | SET COMSPEC=C:\DOS\COMMAND.COM | specify the location of the command interpreter |

COMMENT: A more elaborate configuration is required for this system which is used for both DOS and Windows applications.

4Mb machine for network use, MS-DOS 5.0

| File | Content | Notes |
|------|---------|-------|
| CONFIG.SYS | DEVICE=C:\WINDOWS\HIMEM.SYS | load the Windows high memory device driver |
| | DEVICE=C:\WINDOWS\EMM386.EXE RAM NOEMS | load the memory manager |
| | DOS=HIGH,UMB | loads DOS in high memory |
| | DEVICEHIGH=C:\WINDOWS\MOUSE.SYS /Y | load the mouse driver into high memory |
| | SHELL=C:\DOS\COMMAND.COM C:\DOS /E:1024 /P | specify the command interpreter and a 1K environemnt |
| | FILES=80 | allow for up to 80 files |
| | BUFFERS=16 | provide 16 file buffers |
| | STACKS=9,256 | set up 9 stacks each of 256 bytes |
| AUTOEXEC.BAT | PROMPT $P$G | prompt with directory path |
| | SET PATH=C:\DOS;C:\WINDOWS | search DOS and Windows directories for executable files |
| | SET TEMP=C:\TEMP | directory for Windows swap files |
| | LOADHIGH=C:\DOS\SHARE.EXE | permits file sharing and locking |
| | C:\WINDOWS\SMARTRDV.EXE | establishes a disk cache |
| | LOADHIGH C:\DOS\KEYB UK,,C:\DOS\KEYBOARD.SYS | specify a UK keyboard layout |
| | LOADHIGH C:\DOS\DOSKEY | remember last used commands |
| | LOADHIGH C:\NETWARE\IPX.COM | load Netware drivers into high memory (if available) |
| | LOADHIGH C:\NETWARE\NETX.COM | |
| | SET COMSPEC=C:\DOS\COMMAND.COM | specify the location of the command interpreter |

COMMENT: Notice the Netware drivers, IPX.COM and NETX.COM. Both are loaded into high memory.

2Mb home computer for games, MS-DOS 5.0

| File | Content | Notes |
|===|=======|=====|
| CONFIG.SYS | DEVICE=C:\DOS\HIMEM.SYS | load the Windows high memory device driver |
| | DEVICE=C:\WINDOWS\EMM386.EXE 1024 RAM | load the memory manager |
| | DOS=HIGH,UMB | loads DOS in high memory |
| | DEVICEHIGH=C:\WINDOWS\MOUSE.SYS /Y | load the mouse driver into high memory |
| | FILES=20 | allow for only 20 files |
| | BUFFERS=10 | provide 10 file buffers |
| | STACKS=2,256 | set up 2 stacks each of 256 bytes |
| AUTOEXEC.BAT | PROMPT $P$G | prompt with directory path |
| | SET PATH=C:\DOS;C:\GAMES | search DOS and Games directories for executable files |

COMMENT: Many modern games require an appreciable amount of base memory (as much as 600K bytes in some cases). This configuration maximises the amount of base RAM available for use by a games program.

2Mb laptop for DOS, DR-DOS 6.0

| File | Content | Notes |
|===|===|===|
| CONFIG.SYS | DEVICE=C:\DRDOS\EMM386.SYS | load the memory manager |
| | HIDEVICE=C:\DRDOS\ANSI.SYS | load the ANSI screen driver |
| | FILES=48 | allow for 48 files |
| | BUFFERS=25 | provide 25 file buffers |
| | FASTOPEN=512 | reduces file access time |
| | HISTORY=ON,256,OFF | remember last used commands |
| | COUNTRY=001,C:\DRDOS\COUNTRY.SYS | specify a US keyboard |
| AUTOEXEC.BAT | PROMPT $P$G | prompt with directory path |
| | SET PATH=C:\DOS;C:\UTILITY;C:\APPS | search DOS, Utility and Apps directories for executable files |

COMMENT: Some of the DOS programs and utilities used on this system make use of the ANSI.SYS screen driver.

1Mb '286 based notebook for DOS, DR-DOS 6.0

| File | Content | Notes |
|===|===|===|
| CONFIG.SYS | DEVICE=C:\DRDOS\HIDOS.SYS | use high memory for DOS facilities |
| | BREAK=ON | enable break key checking |
| | HIBUFFERS=20 | provide 20 buffers |
| | FILES=60 | allow for 60 files |
| | FASTOPEN=512 | reduce file access time |
| | LASTDRIVE=F | allow for drives A to F |
| | HISTORY=ON,256,OFF | remember last used commands |
| | COUNTRY=044,C:\DRDOS\COUNTRY.SYS | specify a UK keyboard |
| | SHELL=C:\COMMAND.COM C:\ /P /E:512 | specify the command interpreter |
| | HIDOS=ON | locate DOS structures in high memory |
| | HIDEVICE=C:\DRDOS\ANSI.SYS | load ANSI.SYS in high memory |
| | HINSTALL=C:\DRDOS\KEYB.COM UK+ | load UK keyboard driver into high memory |
| | HINSTALL=C:\DRDOS\CURSOR.EXE | load large cursor driver |
| | | |
| AUTOEXEC.BAT | @ECHO OFF | |
| | ECHO ================= | display message |
| | ECHO     Property of: | |
| | ECHO     John Smith | |
| | ECHO     Tel: 0224-768123 | |
| | ECHO ================= | |
| | PATH C:\DRDOS; C:\MOUSE; C:\UTILITY | search DOS, MOUSE and UTILITY directory |
| | PROMPT $P$G | prompt with directory path |
| | MOUSE | load mouse driver |

COMMENT: This system is used with a variety of utilities and batch files (break key checking has been enabled so that the user can escape if things go wrong). The system uses a hard disk with partitions A to F. The large cursor driver is useful on a machine with an LCD display.

**TIP**

Within CONFIG.SYS, the command that loads DOS into high memory (DOS=HIGH,UMB) *must* follow the command that loads the the high memory device driver, HIMEM.SYS.

**TIP**

You can easily include a message within the AUTOEXEC.BAT file to name the owner of the system:
ECHO OFF
ECHO *********************************
ECHO *    This system belongs to: *
ECHO *        A. N. Other        *
ECHO *      Tel: 081-123-45678    *
ECHO *********************************

## Using DEBUG

One of the most powerful (but often neglected) tools available within the MS-DOS environment is the debugger, DEBUG.COM. This program provides a variety of facilities including single-stepping a program to permit examination of the CPU registers and the contents of memory after execution of each instruction.

The debug command line can accept several arguments. Its syntax is as follows:

**DEBUG [filespec] [parm1] [parm2]**

where [filespec] is the specification of the file to be loaded into memory, [parm1] and [parm2] are optional parameters for the specified file.

As an example, the following MS-DOS command will load debug along with the file MYPROG.COM (taken from the disk in drive B) ready for debugging:

**DEBUG B:\MYPROG.COM**

When debug has been loaded, the familiar MS-DOS prompt is replaced by a hyphen (-). This indicates that DEBUG is awaiting a command from the user. Commands comprise single letters (in either upper or lower case). Delimiters are optional between commands and parameters. They must, however, be used to separate adjacent hexadecimal values.

<CTRL-BREAK> can be use to abort a DEBUG command whilst <CTRL-NUM.LOCK> can be used to pause the display (any other keystroke restarts the output). Commands may be edited using the keys available for normal MS-DOS command editing.

**TIP**

All Debug commands accept parameters (except the Q command). You can separate parameters with commas or spaces, but these separators are required only between two hexadecimal values Therefore the following commands are equivalent:
  D CS:100 110
  DCS:100 110
  D,CS:100,110

## TIP

Hard copy of Debug sessions can sometimes be very useful. If you need this facility, just type <CTRL-P> before the DEBUG command and then all your screen output will be echoed to your printer. Press <CTRL-P> a second time in order to cancel the printer echo.

### Debug commands

| Command | Meaning | Function |
|---|---|---|
| A [addr] | Assemble | Assemble mnemonics into memory from the specified address. If no address is specified, the code will be assembled into memory from address CS:0100. The <ENTER> key is used to terminate assembly and return to the debug prompt.<br>Examples:<br>**A 200**<br>starts assembly from address CS:0200.<br>**A 4E0:100**<br>starts assembly from address 04E0:0100 (equivalent to a physical address of 04F00). |
| C range addr | Compare | Compare memory in the specified range with memory starting at the specified address. |
| D [addr] | Dump | Dump (display) memory from the given starting address. If no start address is specified, the dump will commence at DS:0100.<br>Examples:<br>**D 400**<br>dumps memory from address DS:0400<br>**D CS:0**<br>dumps memory from address CS:0000 |
| D [range] | | Dump (display) memory within the specified range.<br>Example:<br>**D DS:200 20F**<br>displays 16 bytes of memory from DS:0200 to DS:0210 inclusive. |
| E addr [list] | Enter | Enter (edit) bytes into memory starting at the given address. If no list of data bytes is specified, byte values are displayed and may be sequentially overwritten. <SPACE> may be used to advance, and <> may be used to reverse the memory pointer.<br>Example:<br>**E 200,3C,FF,1A,FE**<br>places byte values of 3C, FF, 1A and FE into four consecutive memory locations commencing at DS:0200. |
| F range list | Fill | Fills memory in the given range with data in the list. The list is repeated until all memory locations have been filled.<br>Examples:<br>**F 100,10F,FF** |

|  |  | fills 16 bytes of memory with FF commencing at address DS:0100 |
|  |  | **F 0,FFFF,AA,FF** |
|  |  | fills 65536 bytes of memory with alternate bytes of AA and FF |
| G [=addr] | Go | Executes the code starting at the given address. If no address is specified, execution commences at address CS:IP. |
|  |  | Example: |
|  |  | **G =100** |
|  |  | executes the code starting at address CS:0100. |
| G [=addr] [addr] [addr] |  | Executes the code starting at the given address with the specified breakpoints. |
|  |  | Example: |
|  |  | **G =100 104 10B** |
|  |  | executes the code starting at address CS:0100 and with breakpoints at addresses CS:0104 and CS:010B. |
| H value value | Hexadecimal | Calculates the sum and difference of two hexadecimal values. |
| I port | Port input | Inputs a byte value from the specified I/O port address and display the value. |
|  |  | Example: |
|  |  | **I 302** |
|  |  | inputs the byte value from I/O port address 302 and displays the value returned. |
| L [addr] | Load | Loads the file previously specified by the Name (N) command. The file specification is held at address CS:0080. If no load address is specified, the file is loaded from address CS:0100. |
| M range addr | Move | Moves (replicates) memory in the given range so that it is replicated starting at the specified address. |
| N filespec | Name | Names a file to be used for a subsequent Load (L) or Write (W) command. |
|  |  | Example: |
|  |  | **N B:\MYPROG.COM** |
|  |  | names the file MYPROG.COM stored in the root directory of drive B for a subsequent load or write command. |
| O port byte | Port output | Output a given byte value to the specified I/O port address. |
|  |  | Example: |
|  |  | **O 303 FE** |
|  |  | outputs a byte value of FE from I/O port address 303. |
| P [=addr] [instr] | Proceed | Executes a subroutine, interrupt, loop or string operation and resumes control at the next instruction. Execution starts at the specified address and continues for the specified number of instructions. If no address is specified, execution commences at the address given by CS:IP. |
| Q | Quit | Exits debug and return control to the current MS-DOS shell. |
| R [regname] | Register | Displays the contents of the specified register and allows the contents to be modi- |

| | | |
|---|---|---|
| | | fied. If a name is not specified, the contents of all of the CPU registers (including flags) is displayed together with the next instruction to be executed (in hexadecimal and in mnemonic format). |
| S range list | | Search memory within the specified range for the listed data bytes.<br>Example:<br>**S 0100 0800 20,1B**<br>searches memory between address DS:0100 and DS:0800 for consecutive data values of 20 and 1B. |
| T [=addr]<br>[instr] | Trace | Traces the execution of a program from the specified address and executing the given number of instructions. If no address is specified, the execution starts at address CS:IP. If a number of instructions is not specified then only a single instruction is executed. A register dump (together with a disassembly of the next instruction to be executed) is displayed at each step.<br>Examples:<br>**T**<br>traces the execution of the single instruction referenced by CS:IP.<br>**T =200,4**<br>traces the execution of four instructions commencing at address CS:0200. |
| U [addr] | Unassemble | Unassemble (disassemble) code into mnemonic instructions starting at the specified address. If no address is specified, disassembly starts from the address given by CS:IP.<br>Examples:<br>**U**<br>disassembles code starting at address CS:IP.<br>**U 200**<br>disassembles code starting at address CS:0200. |
| U [range] | | Unassemble (disassemble) code into mnemonic instructions within the specified range of addresses.<br>Example:<br>**U 200 400**<br>disassembles the code starting at address CS:0200 and ending at address CS:0400. |
| W [addr] | Write | Writes data to disk from the specified address. The file specification is taken from a previous Name (N) command. If the address is not specified, the address defaults to that specified by CS:IP. The file specification is located at CS:0080. |

Notes:
**(a)** Parameters enclosed in square brackets ([ and ]) are optional.
**(b)** The equal sign (=) must preceed the start address used by the following commands; Go (G), Proceed (P), and Trace (T).
**(c)** Parameters have the following meanings:

**Parameter   Meaning**

addr       Address (which may be quoted as an offset or as the
           contents of a segment register or segment address
           followed by an offset). The following are examples
           of acceptable addresses:
           **CS:0100**
           **04C0:0100**
           **0200**

byte       A byte of data (i.e. a value in the range 0 to FF). The
           following are examples of acceptable data bytes:
           **0**
           **1F**
           **FE**

filespec   A file specification (which may include a drive letter
           and sub-directory, etc.) The following are examples
           of acceptable file specifications:
           **MYPROG.COM**
           **B:MYPROG.COM**
           **B:\PROGS\MYPROG.COM**

instr      The number of instructions to be executed within a
           Trace (T) or Proceed (P) command.

list       A list of data bytes, ASCII characters (which must be
           enclosed in single quotes), or strings (which must
           be enclosed in double quotes). The following exam-
           ples are all acceptable data lists:
           **3C,2F,C2,00,10**
           **'A',':','/'**
           **"Insert disk and press ENTER"**

port       A port address. The following are acceptable exam-
           ples of port addresses:
           E      (the DMA controller)
           30C    (within the prototype range)
           378    (the parallel printer)
           (see page 46 for more information)

range      A range of addresses which may be expressed as an
           address and offset (e.g. CS:100,100) or as an address
           followed by a size (e.g. DS:100 L 20).

regname    A register name (see (d)). The following are accept-
           able examples of register names:
           **AX**
           **DS**
           **IP**

value      A hexadecimal value in the range 0 to FFFF.

(d)        The following register and flag names are used within
           debug:

           AX, BX, CX, DX    16-bit general purpose registers
           CS, DS, ES, SS    Code, data, extra and stack
                             segment registers
           SP, BP, IP        Stack, base and instruction
                             pointers
           SI, DI            Source and destination index
                             registers
           F                 Flag register

(e)        The following abbreviations are used to denote the
           state of the flags in conjunction with the Register (R)
           and Trace (T) commands:

| Flag | Abbreviation | Meaning/status |
|------|-------------|----------------|
| Overflow | OV | Overflow |
|  | NV | No overflow |
| Carry | CY | Carry |
|  | NC | No carry |
| Zero | ZR | Zero |
|  | NZ | Non-zero |
| Direction | DN | Down |
|  | UP | Up |
| Interrupt | EI | Interrupts enabled |
|  | DI | Interrupts disabled |
| Parity | PE | Parity even |
|  | PO | Parity odd |
| Sign | NG | Negative |
|  | PL | Positive |
| Auxiliary carry | AC | |
|  | NC | |

(f)  All numerical values within Debug are in hexadecimal.

## A Debug walkthrough

The following 'walkthrough' has been provided in order to give you an insight into the range of facilities offered by Debug. We shall assume that a short program TEST.EXE has been written to test a printer connected to the parallel port. The program is designed to generate a single line of upper and lower case characters but, since an error is present, the compiled program prints only a single character. The source code for the program (TEST.ASM) is shown in Figure 14.1:

The first stage in the debugging process is to invoke Debug from MS-DOS using the command:

**DEBUG TEST.EXE**

The command assumes that TEST.EXE is present in the current directory and that DEBUG.EXE is accessible either directly or via previous use of the SET PATH command.

```
COMMENT |
******************************************************************************
File:         TEST
History:      Started 8/8/92
Purpose:      Displays ASCII characters as a line on the printer, LPT1
Format:       No calling conventions
******************************************************************************|
                TITLE    test         ;
                DOSSEG                ; Conventional segment allocation
                .MODEL   SMALL        ;
                .STACK   100h         ; 256 byte stack

; *** Data ***

                .DATA
message         DB       "Printer Test Program",13,10
lmessage        EQU      $ - message

; *** Code ***

                .CODE
start:          mov      ax,@DATA     ;
                mov      ds,ax        ; segment location of data
                mov      bx,1         ; handle for standard output
                mov      cx,lmessage  ; length of message
                mov      dx,OFFSET message   ; address of messaage
                mov      ah,40h       ; DOS write function
                int      21h          ; call DOS
                mov      dl,41h       ; First character to print is A
                mov      cl,3Eh       ; Number of characters to print
                mov      ah,05h       ; Set up the function code
                int      21h          ; and print the character
prch:           inc      dl           ; Get the next character
                loop     prch         ; and go round again
                mov      al,0         ; Set up the return error-level
                mov      ah,4Ch       ; DOS exit function
                int      21h          ; call DOS
                END      start
```

**Figure 14.1   Source code for the program TEST.ASM**

```
do
1CF5:00  00 00 00 00 BA C2 20 54  00 00 FC 65 7E 6C 7C 18  . . . . . . T e
1CF5:00  00 04 E2 54 38 E7 E7 10  00 B4 B0 73 74 DB FE 7C  . . . A . > . !
1CF5:00  ...                                                L . ! P r i n t e r  T e s t
1CF5:00  ...                                                    P r o g r a m
```

*Figure 14.2  Using Debug's Dump (D) command to display TEST.COM in memory*

After the Debug hyphen prompt appears, we can check that our code has loaded, we use the Dump (D) command. Entering the command D0 produces the display shown in Figure 14.2:

The extreme left hand column gives the address (in segment register:offset format). The next sixteen columns comprise hexadecimal data showing the bytes stored at the sixteen address locations starting at the address shown in the left hand column. The sixteen bytes in the block (addresses 1CF5:0000 to 1CF5:000F) all have values of 00. The value of the byte at 1CF5:0010 is B8, whilst that at 1CF5:0011 is F8, and so on. The last byte in the block (address 1CF5:007F) has the value 18.

An ASCII representation of the data is shown in the right hand column of the screen dump. Byte values that do not correspond to printable ASCII characters are shown simply as a full-stop. Hence B8 and F8 (which are both non-printable characters) are shown by full-stops whilst 21H appears as !, and 41H as A.

```
1CF5:0010  B8F81C      MOV    AX,1CF8
1CF5:0013  8ED8        MOV    DS,AX
1CF5:0015  BB0100      MOV    BX,0001
1CF5:0018  B91600      MOV    CX,0016
1CF5:001B  BA0400      MOV    DX,0004
1CF5:001E  B440        MOV    AH,40
1CF5:0020  CD21        INT    21
1CF5:0022  B241        MOV    DL,41
1CF5:0024  B13E        MOV    CL,3E
1CF5:0026  B405        MOV    AH,05
1CF5:0028  CD21        INT    21
1CF5:002A  FEC2        INC    DL
1CF5:002C  E2FC        LOOP   002A
1CF5:002E  B000        MOV    AL,00
1CF5:0030  B44C        MOV    AH,4C
1CF5:0032  CD21        INT    21
-
```

*Figure 14.3 Using Debug's Unassemble (U) command to disassemble TEST.COM*

The hexadecimal/ASCII dump shown earlier is not particularly useful and a more meaningful representation can be achieved by using the Unassemble (U) command. Since the program commences 16 bytes from the start of the block (i.e. at 1CF5:0010) we shall unassemble the code from the address by specifying an offset of 10. We shall end the code disassembly at address offset 32 (this corresponds to the return to DOS). Hence the command we require is U10,32 and this results in the display of Figure 14.3 which shows the sixteen instructions starting from address 1CF5:0010:

The first instruction occupies three bytes of memory (addresses 1CF5:0010, 1CF5:0011 and 1CF5:0012). The instruction comprises a move of 16-bits of immediate data (1CF8) into the AX register. The last program instruction is at address 1CF5:0032 and is a software interrupt relating to address 21 in the interrupt vector table.

At this point it is worth mentioning that the Unassemble command can sometimes produce some rather odd displays. This is simply because the command is unable to distinguish valid program code from data; Unassemble will quite happily attempt to disassemble something which is not actually a program!

Having disassembled the program code resident in memory we can check it against the original source code file. Normally, however, this will not be necessary unless the object code file has become changed or corrupted in some way.

The next stage is that of tracing program execution. The Debug Trace (T) command could be employed for this function however it is better to make use of the Proceed (P) command to avoid tracing execution of the DOS interrupt routines in order to keep the amount of traced code manageable.

The Proceed command expects its first parameter to be the address of the first instruction to be executed. This must then be followed by a second parameter which gives the number of instructions to be traced. In this case, and since our program terminates normally, we can supply any sufficiently large number of instructions as the second parameter to the Proceed command. Hence the required command is P=100,100 and the resulting trace dump is shown in Figure 14.4:

The state of the CPU registers is displayed as each instruction is executed together with the next instruction in disassembled format. Taking the results of executing the first instruction (MOV AX,1CF8) as an example, we see that 1C has appeared in the upper byte of AX

```
AX=1CF8  BX=0000  CX=004A  DX=0000  SP=0100  BP=0000  SI=0000  DI=0000
DS=1CF8  ES=1CF5  SS=1CFA  CS=1CF5  IP=0013  NV UP EI PL NZ NA PO NC
1CF5:0013 8ED8          MOV     DS,AX

AX=1CF8  BX=0000  CX=004A  DX=0000  SP=0100  BP=0000  SI=0000  DI=0000
DS=1CF8  ES=1CF5  SS=1CFA  CS=1CF5  IP=0015  NV UP EI PL NZ NA PO NC
1CF5:0015 BB0100        MOV     BX,0001

AX=1CF8  BX=0001  CX=004A  DX=0000  SP=0100  BP=0000  SI=0000  DI=0000
DS=1CF8  ES=1CF5  SS=1CFA  CS=1CF5  IP=0018  NV UP EI PL NZ NA PO NC
1CF5:0018 B91600        MOV     CX,0016

AX=1CF8  BX=0001  CX=0016  DX=0000  SP=0100  BP=0000  SI=0000  DI=0000
DS=1CF8  ES=1CF5  SS=1CFA  CS=1CF5  IP=001B  NV UP EI PL NZ NA PO NC
1CF5:001B BA0400        MOV     DX,0004

AX=1CF8  BX=0001  CX=0016  DX=0004  SP=0100  BP=0000  SI=0000  DI=0000
DS=1CF8  ES=1CF5  SS=1CFA  CS=1CF5  IP=001E  NV UP EI PL NZ NA PO NC
1CF5:001E B440          MOV     AH,40

AX=40F8  BX=0001  CX=0016  DX=0004  SP=0100  BP=0000  SI=0000  DI=0000
DS=1CF8  ES=1CF5  SS=1CFA  CS=1CF5  IP=0020  NV UP EI PL NZ NA PO NC
1CF5:0020 CD21          INT     21
Printer Test Program

AX=0016  BX=0001  CX=0016  DX=0004  SP=0100  BP=0000  SI=0000  DI=0000
DS=1CF8  ES=1CF5  SS=1CFA  CS=1CF5  IP=0022  NV UP EI PL NZ NA PO NC
1CF5:0022 B241          MOV     DL,41

AX=0016  BX=0001  CX=0016  DX=0041  SP=0100  BP=0000  SI=0000  DI=0000
DS=1CF8  ES=1CF5  SS=1CFA  CS=1CF5  IP=0024  NV UP EI PL NZ NA PO NC
1CF5:0024 B13E          MOV     CL,3E

AX=0016  BX=0001  CX=003E  DX=0041  SP=0100  BP=0000  SI=0000  DI=0000
DS=1CF8  ES=1CF5  SS=1CFA  CS=1CF5  IP=0026  NV UP EI PL NZ NA PO NC
1CF5:0026 B405          MOV     AH,05

AX=0516  BX=0001  CX=003E  DX=0041  SP=0100  BP=0000  SI=0000  DI=0000
DS=1CF8  ES=1CF5  SS=1CFA  CS=1CF5  IP=0028  NV UP EI PL NZ NA PO NC
1CF5:0028 CD21          INT     21
A
AX=0541  BX=0001  CX=003E  DX=0041  SP=0100  BP=0000  SI=0000  DI=0000
DS=1CF8  ES=1CF5  SS=1CFA  CS=1CF5  IP=002A  NV UP EI PL NZ NA PO NC
1CF5:002A FEC2          INC     DL

AX=0541  BX=0001  CX=003E  DX=0042  SP=0100  BP=0000  SI=0000  DI=0000
DS=1CF8  ES=1CF5  SS=1CFA  CS=1CF5  IP=002C  NV UP EI PL NZ NA PE NC
1CF5:002C E2FC          LOOP    002A

AX=0541  BX=0001  CX=0000  DX=007F  SP=0100  BP=0000  SI=0000  DI=0000
DS=1CF8  ES=1CF5  SS=1CFA  CS=1CF5  IP=002E  NV UP EI PL NZ NA PO NC
1CF5:002E B000          MOV     AL,00

AX=0500  BX=0001  CX=0000  DX=007F  SP=0100  BP=0000  SI=0000  DI=0000
DS=1CF8  ES=1CF5  SS=1CFA  CS=1CF5  IP=0030  NV UP EI PL NZ NA PO NC
1CF5:0030 B44C          MOV     AH,4C

AX=4C00  BX=0001  CX=0000  DX=007F  SP=0100  BP=0000  SI=0000  DI=0000
DS=1CF8  ES=1CF5  SS=1CFA  CS=1CF5  IP=0032  NV UP EI PL NZ NA PO NC
1CF5:0032 CD21          INT     21

Program terminated normally
-
```

*Figure 14.4  Debug program trace of TEST.COM*

(AH), F8 has appeared in the lower byte of AX (AL) and the instruction pointer (IP) has moved on to offset address 0013. The next instruction to be executed (located at the address which IP is pointing to) is MOV DS,AX. The state of the CPU flags is also shown within the register dump. In this particular case, none of the flags has been changed as a result of executing the instruction.

In order to obtain a hard copy of the program trace, a <CTRL-P> command can be issued immediately before issuing the Proceed (P) command. From that point onwards, screen output was echoed to the printer. Since the program directs is own output to the printer, this also appears amidst the traced output. The screen output, 'Printer Test Program' appears after execution of the seventh instruction (INT 21).

A single character, A, is printed after the eleventh instruction. Thereafter, the program executes the loop formed by the instructions at offset addresses 002A and 002C. However, no printing takes place within this loop even though the DL register is incremented through the required range of ASCII codes (41 to 7F). Clearly the loop is not returning to the INT 21 instruction which actually makes the required calls into DOS.

```
p=10,100

AX=1CF8  BX=0000  CX=004A  DX=0000  SP=0100  BP=0000  SI=0000  DI=0000
DS=1CE5  ES=1CE5  SS=1CFA  CS=1CF5  IP=0013  NV UP EI PL NZ NA PO NC
1CF5:0013 8ED8          MOV     DS,AX

AX=1CF8  BX=0000  CX=004A  DX=0000  SP=0100  BP=0000  SI=0000  DI=0000
DS=1CF8  ES=1CE5  SS=1CFA  CS=1CF5  IP=0015  NV UP EI PL NZ NA PO NC
1CF5:0015 BB0100        MOV     BX,0001

AX=1CF8  BX=0001  CX=004A  DX=0000  SP=0100  BP=0000  SI=0000  DI=0000
DS=1CF8  ES=1CE5  SS=1CFA  CS=1CF5  IP=0018  NV UP EI PL NZ NA PO NC
1CF5:0018 B91600        MOV     CX,0016

AX=1CF8  BX=0001  CX=0016  DX=0000  SP=0100  BP=0000  SI=0000  DI=0000
DS=1CF8  ES=1CE5  SS=1CFA  CS=1CF5  IP=001B  NV UP EI PL NZ NA PO NC
1CF5:001B BA0400        MOV     DX,0004

AX=1CF8  BX=0001  CX=0016  DX=0004  SP=0100  BP=0000  SI=0000  DI=0000
DS=1CF8  ES=1CE5  SS=1CFA  CS=1CF5  IP=001E  NV UP EI PL NZ NA PO NC
1CF5:001E B440          MOV     AH,40

AX=40F8  BX=0001  CX=0016  DX=0004  SP=0100  BP=0000  SI=0000  DI=0000
DS=1CF8  ES=1CE5  SS=1CFA  CS=1CF5  IP=0020  NV UP EI PL NZ NA PO NC
1CF5:0020 CD21          INT     21
Printer Test Program

AX=0016  BX=0001  CX=0016  DX=0004  SP=0100  BP=0000  SI=0000  DI=0000
DS=1CF8  ES=1CE5  SS=1CFA  CS=1CF5  IP=0022  NV UP EI PL NZ NA PO NC
1CF5:0022 B241          MOV     DL,41

AX=0016  BX=0001  CX=0016  DX=0041  SP=0100  BP=0000  SI=0000  DI=0000
DS=1CF8  ES=1CE5  SS=1CFA  CS=1CF5  IP=0024  NV UP EI PL NZ NA PO NC
1CF5:0024 B13E          MOV     CL,3E

AX=0016  BX=0001  CX=003E  DX=0041  SP=0100  BP=0000  SI=0000  DI=0000
DS=1CF8  ES=1CE5  SS=1CFA  CS=1CF5  IP=0026  NV UP EI PL NZ NA PO NC
1CF5:0026 B405          MOV     AH,05

AX=0516  BX=0001  CX=003E  DX=0041  SP=0100  BP=0000  SI=0000  DI=0000
DS=1CF8  ES=1CE5  SS=1CFA  CS=1CF5  IP=0028  NV UP EI PL NZ NA PO NC
1CF5:0028 CD21          INT     21
A
AX=0541  BX=0001  CX=003E  DX=0041  SP=0100  BP=0000  SI=0000  DI=0000
DS=1CF8  ES=1CE5  SS=1CFA  CS=1CF5  IP=002A  NV UP EI PL NZ NA PO NC
1CF5:002A FEC2          INC     DL

AX=0541  BX=0001  CX=003E  DX=0042  SP=0100  BP=0000  SI=0000  DI=0000
DS=1CF8  ES=1CE5  SS=1CFA  CS=1CF5  IP=002C  NV UP EI PL NZ NA PE NC
1CF5:002C E2FA          LOOP    0028
BCDEFGHIJKLMNOPQRSTUVWXYZ[\]^_`abcdefghijklmnopqrstuvwxyz{|}~
AX=057E  BX=0001  CX=0000  DX=007F  SP=0100  BP=0000  SI=0000  DI=0000
DS=1CF8  ES=1CE5  SS=1CFA  CS=1CF5  IP=002E  NV UP EI PL NZ NA PO NC
1CF5:002E B000          MOV     AL,00

AX=0500  BX=0001  CX=0000  DX=007F  SP=0100  BP=0000  SI=0000  DI=0000
DS=1CF8  ES=1CE5  SS=1CFA  CS=1CF5  IP=0030  NV UP EI PL NZ NA PO NC
1CF5:0030 B44C          MOV     AH,4C

AX=4C00  BX=0001  CX=0000  DX=007F  SP=0100  BP=0000  SI=0000  DI=0000
DS=1CF8  ES=1CE5  SS=1CFA  CS=1CF5  IP=0032  NV UP EI PL NZ NA PO NC
1CF5:0032 CD21          INT     21

Program terminated normally
-
```

***Figure 14.5   Program trace of the corrected TEST.COM code***

Fortunately, we can easily overcome this problem from within the
debugger without returning to the macro assembler. We simply need
to modify the LOOP instruction at offset address 002C. To do this we
can make use of the Assemble (A) command to over-write the existing instruction. The required command is:

**A 2C**

The CS:IP prompt is then displayed (in this case it shows 1CF5:002C)
after which we simply enter:

**LOOP 28**

The CS:IP prompt is incremented however, since we need to make
no further changes to the code, we can simply escape from the Debug line assembler by simply pressing <RETURN>.

Having modified our code, we can again trace the program using
the Proceed (P) command exactly as before. The traced output produced by the modified program is shown in Figure 14.5. Note that
we have now succeeded in producing a line of printed output showing the full range of characters.

```
COMMENT |
**********************************************************************
File:           TEST
History:        Started 8/8/92
Purpose:        Displays ASCII characters as a line on the printer, LPT1
Format:         No calling conventions
**********************************************************************|

                TITLE    test            ;
                DOSSEG                    ; Conventional segment allocation
                .MODEL   SMALL
                .STACK   100h             ; 256 byte stack

; *** Data ***

                .DATA
message         DB       "Printer Test Program",13,10
lmessage        EQU      $ - message

; *** Code ***

                .CODE
start:          mov      ax,@DATA         ;
                mov      ds,ax            ; segment location of data
                mov      bx,1             ; handle for standard output
                mov      cx,lmessage      ; length of message
                mov      dx,OFFSET message    ; address of messaage
                mov      ah,40h           ; DOS write function
                int      21h              ; call DOS
                mov      dl,41h           ; First character to print is A
                mov      cl,3Eh           ; Number of characters to print
                mov      ah,05h           ; Set up the function code
prch:           int      21h              ; and print the character
                inc      dl               ; Get the next character
                loop     prch             ; and go round again
                mov      al,0             ; Set up the return error-level
                mov      ah,4Ch           ; DOS exit function
                int      21h              ; call DOS
                END      start
```

*Figure 14.6   Corrected source code for TEST.ASM*

Since no further errors have been found, we can exit from Debug, load the macro assembler, make the necessary changes to our source code, assemble and link to produce a modified EXE program file. The corrected source code is shown in Figure 14.6.

## Using Debug's line assembler

Debug has an inbuilt line assembler which can be used to generate simple programs. The assembler is accessible from within Debug (as described in the previous section) but can also be accessed by means of a 'script file' which can be generated by any word processor or text editor capable of producing an ASCII text file (or even by means of the DOS COPY command).

During execution, Debug will take its input (redirected from the keyboard) from the script file. The script file will contain a sequence of Debug commands (which can include assembly language statements).

The two examples which follow show how Debug's assembler can be used to generate programs to respectively perform a 'warm' and 'cold' reboot:

### Warm reboot

The following script file can be used with Debug to generate a program (WARM.COM). This program directs the program counter to the start of ROM BIOS but avoids the power-on memory check routine.

Assuming that the script file is to be produced by means of the DOS COPY command, the following keyboard entries will be required:

```
COPY CON WARM.DBG
A
XOR AX,AX
MOV ES,AX
MOV DI,0472
MOV AX,1234
STOSW
JMP FFFF:0000
(leave one blank line here)
NWARM.COM
RCX
10
W
Q
^Z
```

It is important to note that a newline (enter) should be used to terminate each line and the input should be terminated (after the newline which follows 'Q') by means of <CTRL-Z> (shown as ^Z). The <CTRL-Z> should also be followed by a newline.

The keystrokes will generate a file (WARM.DBG) which can be used as input to Debug by means of the following command:

**DEBUG < WARM.DBG**

Debug will assemble the statements contained in the script file in order to generate an executable file, WARM.COM. This program can be executed directly from the DOS prompt by typing WARM followed by enter (NB: this will reboot your system!).

## Cold reboot

If a cold boot is required, the assembly code should be modified by changing the MOV AX,1234 to MOV AX,0. The following keyboard entries are required:

```
COPY CON COLD.DBG
A
XOR AX,AX
MOV ES,AX
MOV DI,0472
MOV AX,0
STOSW
JMP FFFF:0000
(leave one blank line here)
NCOLD.COM
RCX
10
W
Q
^Z
```

Again, note that the input should be terminated (after the newline which follows 'Q') by means of <CTRL-Z> (shown as ^Z) followed by enter.

The keystrokes will generate a file (COLD.DBG) which can be used as input to Debug by means of the following command:

**DEBUG < COLD.DBG**

Debug will assemble the statements contained in the script file in order to generate an executable file, COLD.COM. This program can be executed directly from the DOS prompt by typing COLD followed by enter. This should again reboot your system but this time the initial memory check routines will be performed.

# 15
# Tools and Test Equipment

This chapter describes the tools and test equipment necessary to locate basic hardware faults. Fault location to board or 'replaceable unit' level requires nothing more than a screwdriver, a multimeter and a diagnostic disk. Component level fault-finding, on the other hand, is much more demanding and requires an appreciable investment in specialised tools and test equipment. Despite this, you can achieve a great deal with only a modest initial outlay; more complex tools and test equipment can be acquired as you develop confidence.

## Tools

To help you prioritise your spending at the outset, I have included 'minimum' and 'extended' lists for both tools and test equipment. The 'minimum' list of tools represents the minimum complement of items necessary for basic service work (e.g., fault-finding to board level on conventional circuit boards). The 'extended' list, on the other hand, includes many items that may only be used infrequently as well as those that are required for repairs to boards using surface mounted components.

### Minimum list of tools

One small pair of side cutters
One small pair of pliers
One pair combination pliers and cutters
Set of flat-bladed screwdrivers
Set of cross-point screwdrivers
Set of trimming/adjusting tools
Set of hexagon keys
One miniature soldering iron (15 to 25W) with set of bits
One desoldering tool
Set of i.c. extracting tools
One anti-static mat (with grounding leads)

### Extended list of tools

As 'minimum' list plus the following additional items:
One pair of wire strippers
One medium mains tester screwdriver
Set of jeweller's screwdrivers
One trimming knife
One pair of good quality tweezers
One bench magnifying glass
One Anglepoise (or similar) adjustable bench lamp
One combination wire-wrapping/unwrapping tool
Set of open ended metric spanners (M2.5 to M6)
One portable soldering iron (12V or rechargeable type)
One temperature controlled soldering iron
One i.c. desoldering tools (with set of bits)
One PCB cleaner
One solder wick

> **TIP**
>
> Good quality tools can be expected to last a lifetime provided they are properly used and cared for. It is therefore wise to purchase the best quality that you can afford – there is little sense in buying inferior items that will need replacing every few years.

## Test equipment

As you might expect, test equipment tends to vary not only in specification but also in price. At one extreme are such everyday items as basic analogue multimeters costing less than £20. At the other extreme can be found sophisticated logic analysers costing around £5000.

Fortunately, only a few basic items of test equipment are required to successfully diagnose the vast majority of hardware faults. The three most commonly used items in my workshop are a digital multimeter, a logic probe, and a breakout box – an invaluable trio of instruments which cost me less than £80!

> **TIP**
>
> Choosing the right test instrument for the job can be all-important. Familiarity is the key to getting the best from your test gear and, at least in the initial stages, it is wise to learn how to use one instrument at a time.

Items on the 'minimum' list become essential if you are to adequately cope with every hardware fault that you are likely to encounter. There is, however, no reason why you should not make a start with only a good multi-range meter and a logic probe. Other items of test equipment (including those on the 'extended' list) can be acquired over a period of time. In any event, it is best not to be in too much of a hurry to extend the range of facilities available – you will soon get to know which instrument you derive most benefit from and this will help point the way to future purchases.

### Minimum list of test equipment

Multi-range meter (good quality analogue or digital type)
Logic probe
Breakout box (RS-232)
Null-modem (or null-modem cable)
Test prods
Selection of IC test clips
Selection of leads and connectors

### Extended list of test equipment

Oscilloscope (preferably dual beam 50MHz type)
Oscilloscope probes
Logic pulser
Current tracing probe
Logic test clip
Line monitor (RS-232)
Patch box (RS-232)
Gender changer (RS-232)
Null-modem (RS-232)

## Multi-range meters

A good quality multi-range meter is undoubtedly an excellent investment if you intend to regularly tackle hardware faults. The instrument can be used for checking voltage (a.c. and d.c.), current (a.c. or d.c.) and resistance ('ohms'). As many as eight or nine measuring functions may be provided with a maximum of six or eight ranges on each. Besides the normal voltage, current and resistance functions, some meters also include facilities for checking transistors and measuring capacitance. Meters may also be either analogue or digital types but will usually operate from internal batteries so that they are independent of the mains supply.

Analogue instruments employ conventional moving coil meters and the display takes the form of a pointer moving across a calibrated scale. This arrangement is not so convenient to use as that provided by digital instruments. It does, however, offer some advantages, not the least of which is that it is very difficult to make adjustments using a digital readout to monitor varying circuit conditions, and in this application the analogue meter is therefore superior. Its scale can be easily interpreted; a movement in one direction represents an increase and in the other a decrease. The principal disadvantage of many analogue meters is the rather cramped and sometimes confusing scale calibration. To determine the exact reading requires first an estimation of the pointer's position and then the application of some mental arithmetic based on the range switch setting.

Digital meters, on the other hand, are usually extremely easy to read and have displays that are clear, unambiguous, and capable of providing a very high resolution. It is thus possible to distinguish readings that are very close. This is just not possible with an analogue instrument. Another very significant difference between analogue and digital instruments is the input resistance that they present to the circuit under investigation when taking voltage measurements.

### TIP

The resistance of a reasonable quality non-electronic analogue meter can be as low as 50k ohm on the 2.5V range. With a digital instrument the input resistance is typically 10M ohm on the 2V (1.999V max) range. The digital instrument is thus to be preferred when accurate readings are to be taken. While this may be of little concern when checking the voltages of supply rails and in TTL circuits generally, it does become extremely important when measurements are to be made on circuits which use CMOS devices.

Low-cost digital multimeters have been made possible by the advent of mass-produced LSI devices and liquid crystal displays. A three-digit display is the norm, consisting of three full digits which can display 0 to 9 and a fourth (most significant) digit which can only display 1. Thus, the maximum display indication, ignoring the range switching and decimal point, is 1999; anything greater over-ranges the display. Nearly all digital meters contain automatic zero and polarity indicating facilities and some also have auto-ranging. This feature, which is usually only found in the more sophisticated instruments, automatically changes the range setting so that maximum resolution is obtained without over-ranging. There is thus no need for manual operation of the range switch once the indicating mode has been selected. This is an manual operation of the range switch once the indicating mode has been selected. This is an extremely useful facility since it frees the user from the need to make repeated adjustments to the range switch while measurements are being made.

For portable applications an LCD instrument is, by virtue of its small size, low weight, and minimal power consumption, much to be preferred. Most LCD meters will provide around 200 hours of continuous operation from one set of batteries but a comparable LED instrument may only operate for some 20 to 30 hours. As with analogue multimeters, it is wise to select an instrument that has a clear display and sensible range switching.

## TIP

Many digital multimeters use a multiplicity of push-buttons and this can be particularly confusing when a combination of several push-buttons have to be used to select a particular range. In general, instruments that employ a conventional rotary switch, augmented if necessary by one or two push-buttons or slide switches, are much easier to use.

## TIP

The most common use of a multimeter is checking supply rail voltages. The nominal 5V rail should normally be within the range 4.75V to 5.25V and the 12V rail between 11.4V and 12.6V. Voltages outside this range don't always indicate a fault – in some cases they can indicate that the power supply is inadequately rated!

## Oscilloscopes

An oscilloscope will allow you to display time-related voltage waveforms such as those which appear on a clock or bus line. Such an item represents a considerable capital investment however it can become invaluable in a number of applications such as disk drive head alignment, checking for 'glitches' and supply borne noise, faulty bus lines and certain timing problems.

The oscilloscope display is generally provided by a cathode ray tube (CRT) which has a typical screen area of around 80mm x 100mm. The CRT is fitted with a graticule, which may be either integral with the tube face or a separate translucent sheet. The graticule is usually ruled with a 1cm grid to which further bold lines may be added to mark the major axes on the central viewing area. Accurate voltage and time measurements may be made with reference to the graticule, applying a sale factor derived from the appropriate range switch. A word of caution is appropriate at this stage, however.

## TIP

Before taking accurate measurements from the CRT screen it is essential to ensure that the relevant front panel controls are set to the 'calibrate' (CAL) position. If you failt to do this, any readings which you take are liable to be inaccurate! (Many oscilloscopes have an in-built calibrate facility – consult your operations manual for details).

For personal computer servicing, it is essential to have an oscilloscope with a vertical bandwidth of at least 30MHz and a reliable trigger (preferably incorporating a 'delayed trigger' facility). The timebase ranges should similarly extend to at least 0.1μs/cm, or less. Ideally the oscilloscope should have a dual trace capability although this is not absolutely essential. A vertical amplifier sensitivity of 10mV/cm is quite adequate and an input impedance of 1M ohm shunted by about 30pF is the norm.

### TIP

The use of a correctly designed and matched 'scope probe is essential in order to avoid the effects of capacitive loading. Many probes provide switched 'x1' and 'x10' facilities and they should normally be used in the latter position.

## Logic probes

Surprisingly, the most regularly used item of test gear in my own workshop is also the least expensive. It is, as you may have guessed, nothing more than a simple hand-held logic probe. The supply to the probe (usually +5V and 'ground') is connected via a short length of cable terminated in a pair of crocodile clips. These may be attached to the positive supply and 0 V rails at suitably accessible points on the circuit under investigation. Most probes will accept supplies in the range 4.75 V to 18V and are usually protected against inadvertent polarity reversal.

### TIP

Some manufacturers supply their logic probes with a range of interchangeable probe tips. These can be an asset when the probe is to be attached to a wide variety of components.

*Table 15.1   Logic probe indications*

| LED indicator | | | State | Waveform |
|---|---|---|---|---|
| Low | Pulse | High | | |
| OFF | OFF | ON | Steady logic 1 | |
| ON | OFF | OFF | Steady logic 0 | |
| OFF | OFF | OFF | Open circuit or undefined level | |
| OFF | BLINK | OFF | Pulse train of near 50% duty cycle at >1 MHz | |
| ON | BLINK | ON | Pulse train of near 50% duty cycle at <1 MHz | |
| OFF | BLINK | ON | Pulse train of high mark:space ratio | |
| ON | BLINK | OFF | Pulse train of low mark:space ratio | |

As with other items of test equipment, there is some variation in the facilities offered by logic probes but invariably three LEDs are provided to indicate the logical state of the probe tip, which may be either 'HIGH' (logic 1), 'LOW' (logic 0), or PULSE (alternating between the two states). The relative brightness of the 'HIGH' and 'LOW' indicators gives an approximate indication of the duty cycle of the pulse train. The indications provided by a typical low-cost logic probe are shown in Table 15.1.

More sophisticated logic probes provide pulse-stretching facilities so that pulses of very short duration can be recognised. Other types incorporate a 'memory' mode that can catch a narrow pulse and display it continuously until the mode is cancelled or the probe is disconnected from its supply. Note that when using such a probe it is usually necessary to ensure that the probe tip is connected to the circuit at the point under investigation before switching to the 'memory' mode. If this precaution is not observed, the action of connecting the floating probe tip is likely to produce an erroneous trigger pulse.

Logic probes are usually available in two varieties (or may be switched into one of two modes): either TTL or CMOS. In the TTL mode 'HIGH' and 'LOW' signal levels are defined as greater than 2.25V and less than 0.8V respectively, whereas in the CMOS mode these levels are represented by 70 per cent and 30 per cent of the probe supply voltage. While it is possible to use a high input impedance TTL logic probe for fault tracing in CMOS circuits, the use of a CMOS probe in TTL circuits is not generally to be recommended.

Typical logic probe indications for an 8086 (or similar) CPU are shown in Table 15.2. Similar indications will apply to the named signal lines for 80286 and later processors but note that some older logic probes may fail to respond at the fast clock rates of some of the more recent processors. In such cases an oscilloscope will be required in order to test for activity on the various CPU lines.

---

**TIP**

A 'stuck' or 'floating' bus line is easy to detect using a logic probe. However, before checking the bus lines for activity it is worth checking the clock, interrupt and reset lines (see Table 15.2).

---

## Logic pulsers

Like logic probes, pulsers are simple hand-held instruments that derive their power supply from the circuit under investigation. A narrow pulse of short duration is generated whenever a push-button is depressed. Alternatively, a continuous train of pulses is generated if the button is held down. When the button is released, the probe assumes a high impedance state. The output of the probe can typically source or sink currents of up to several hundred milliamps (equivalent to 50 or more conventional TTL loads). The pulse width is made fairly narrow, being typically 1 μs and 10 μs in the TTL and CMOS modes respectively.

The primary function of the logic pulser is to achieve a momentary change of state at a node in a circuit. More sophisticated pulsers use comparator techniques to sense the state of the node before applying a pulse of the correct (opposite) polarity. If the test point is high the pulse goes low, and vice versa. After the pulse has been emitted another comparison is made and, if a change of node state has occurred, the next pulse generated will be of opposite polarity.

This useful facility permits continuous triggering of the circuit under investigation regardless of its actual logic state.

*Table 15.2   Typical logic probe indications for an 8086 (or similar) CPU*

| Pin Number | Signal | State |
|---|---|---|
| 1 | GND | 0V |
| 2 | A14 | Pulsing |
| 3 | A13 | Pulsing |
| 4 | A12 | Pulsing |
| 5 | A11 | Pulsing |
| 6 | A10 | Pulsing |
| 7 | A9 | Pulsing |
| 8 | A8 | Pulsing |
| 9 | A7/D7 | Pulsing |
| 10 | A6/D6 | Pulsing |
| 11 | A5/D5 | Pulsing |
| 12 | A4/D4 | Pulsing |
| 13 | A3/D3 | Pulsing |
| 14 | A2/D2 | Pulsing |
| 15 | A1/D1 | Pulsing |
| 16 | A0/D0 | Pulsing |
| 17 | NMI | Low |
| 18 | INTR | Low |
| 19 | Clock | Pulsing |
| 20 | GND | 0V |
| 21 | RESET | Low |
| 22 | READY | Pulsing |
| 23 | TEST | High |
| 24 | QS1 | Pulsing |
| 25 | QS0 | Pulsing |
| 26 | S0 | Pulsing |
| 27 | S1 | Pulsing |
| 28 | S2 | Pulsing |
| 29 | LOCK | Pulsing |
| 30 | RQ/GT1 | High |
| 31 | RQ/GT0 | High |
| 32 | RD | Pulsing |
| 33 | MN/MX | 0V |
| 34 | SSO | High |
| 35 | A19/S6 | Pulsing |
| 36 | A18/S5 | Pulsing |
| 37 | A17/S4 | Pulsing |
| 38 | A16/S3 | Pulsing |
| 39 | A15 | Pulsing |
| 40 | Vcc | +5V |

When using a logic pulser it should be remembered that, since an appreciable current may be sourced or sunk by the device, the return current flowing in the supply common lead will also be considerable. Thus, to prevent erroneous triggering, it is essential to derive the pulser's supply from a low impedance point on the supply rails and not merely clip the leads to the nearest available integrated circuit. While this latter technique may prove satisfactory for use with logic probes, it is definitely not recommended where logic pulsers are concerned. A suitable connecting point is directly across the terminals of an electrolytic supply decoupling capacitor of 100 μF minimum.

## IC test clips

The clearance between the pins of a conventional dual-in-line integrated circuit is of the order of 1.3mm, or less. In view of this, the use of conventional test prods is likely to be a hazardous process since there is a considerable risk of inadvertent short circuits when making a connection to a device. Spring-loaded dual-in-line test clips facilitate the attachment of a variety of test instruments using conventional hook-type test prods. Test clips come in a variety of sizes and it is wise to have several available including 16-pin, 28-pin and 40-pin types.

## Logic monitors

Various forms of logic state monitor are available, ranging from simple clip-on indicators to sophisticated multi-channel bench instruments. In all cases, however, LEDs are used to display the logical state of each of the pins of the IC under investigation. It is then possible to monitor, simultaneously, the logical state of all of the inputs and outputs of a digital IC.

Simple logic monitors generally contain 16 LEDs and can be used in conjunction with 8-pin, 14-pin and 16-pin devices. These are invariably circuit powered, automatically deriving their supplies from the highest and lowest voltages appearing at the 16 points of connection. Since only one LED is available for each pin, a single logic threshold is recognised. This is usually the same as that for a logic probe 'HIGH' (i.e. greater than 2.25V or 70 per cent of the supply voltage for TTL and CMOS monitors respectively). Pulse trains appear as LEDs with less than full intensity, the relative brightness giving an approximate indication of the duty cycle. More complex logic monitors may provide remote display facilities, a choice of logic thresholds (appropriate to either TTL or CMOS), and up to 40 display channels.

## Current tracers

When fault tracing it is sometimes advantageous to be able to measure the current at strategic points in a circuit. Such a measurement becomes necessary when, for example, we are concerned with the supply current drawn by an IC. Where devices are mounted in sockets, conventional multi-range meters may be used. The procedure involves first removing the IC from its socket, bending the relevant pin through 90 degrees, then re-inserting the IC and connecting the milliammeter between the bent-out pin and the appropriate point in the circuit. This method is, of course, inappropriate when an IC is soldered into the PCB. There is, however, no need to cut the PCB tracks if a current tracer is available. Such an instrument can measure, to a reasonable approximation, the current flowing in standard size PCB tracks without the need to break the circuit.

Two forms of current tracer are available; one operates by sensing the magnetic field in the vicinity of the track and the other measures the voltage drop across a short length of track. For accurate measurements, the PCB is assumed to be standard 35μm (306g/m²) track and calibration is usually supplied for 1 mm or 2 mm width track. Current tracers will typically respond to currents of 10mA or less, and it is thus possible to check the operating current of a single TTL gate with a reasonable degree of accuracy. More sophisticated current tracers of the magnetic sensing variety may be used to 'follow' the path of direct current in the PCB. Such devices can thus be extremely useful in detecting such PCB faults as dry joints, hair-line cracks, solder splashes, shorted tracks, and open-circuit plated through holes.

### TIP

A reasonably sensitive multimeter can be used to provide a rough indication of the relative magnitude of current present in a PCB track. Simply connect the probe tips to the ends of each track in turn and select a low voltage range (e.g. 200mV full-scale). A high voltage drop will indicate the presence of a larger than normal current.

## Logic comparators

It is often necessary to determine whether or not a logic gate is functioning correctly and, while a simple method of checking an IC using a logic probe has already been described, this may not cover every case and a more rigorous substitution test may be preferred. Such a test would verify all of the gates contained within a single IC at the same time without the need to transfer a logic probe from pin to pin.

Substitution testing is a relatively easy matter when devices are mounted in sockets but it may not even be considered when a device has to be desoldered (particularly when a double-sided PCB is involved!). We have therefore to leave the IC in circuit. However, since we have immediate access to all of its pins it is possible to duplicate its operation externally, using a known good device and then compare the results obtained. A device that performs this function is a logic comparator and such an instrument can permit rapid in-circuit dynamic testing of a wide variety of logic devices.

The output of the gate on test is compared with that derived from a reference gate using an exclusive-OR gate when both gates are fed with the same inputs. If the gate on test is producing the same logic function as that of the reference gate, the output of the exclusive-OR gate will be at logic 0. If, on the other hand, there is a difference between the outputs of the gate on test and the reference gate, the output provided by the exclusive-OR gate will be at logic 1.

The logic comparator is normally connected to the suspect device by means of an IC test clip and multi-way ribbon cable. To be useful, the logic comparator must be accompanied by a wide range of known reference devices. So if you are lucky enough to own such an instrument it is worth building up a reasonable stock of logic gates, over and above those one would normally keep in stock for replacement purposes.

## Diagnostic adapters

Finally, several manufacturers make use of specialised adapter cards to diagnose faults on systems which refuse to boot normally (i.e., when the system won't even run the diagnostic code within the BIOS ROM). As the display will not normally be operational in such an eventuality, these adapter cards provide their output on an external display or on a printer.

Diagnostic adapter cards provide a very effective means of fault-finding a system that fails the standard bootstrap diagnostics or that manifestly fails to execute any of the BIOS code. Unfortunately, such items are not widely available and furthermore their usefulness is generally restricted to a particular machine type or family.

# Data communications test equipment

Several specialised test instruments and accessories are required for testing asynchronous serial data communications systems. The following items are available from a number of manufacturers and suppliers:

## Patch boxes

These low-cost devices facilitate the cross connection of RS-232 (or equivalent) signal lines. The equipment is usually fitted with two D-type connectors (or ribbon cables fitted with a plug and socket) and all lines are brought out at patching area into which links may be plugged. In use, these devices are connected in series with the RS-232 serial data path and various patching combinations are tested until a functional interface is established. If desired a dedicated cable may then be manufactured in order to replace the patch box.

## Gender changers

Gender changers normally comprise an extended RS-232 connector which has a male connector at one end and a female connector at the other. Gender changers permit mixing of male and female connector types (note that the convention is male at the DTE and female at the DCE).

## Null modems

Like gender changers, these devices are connected in series with an RS-232C serial data path. Their function is simply that of changing the signal lines so that a DTE is effectively configured as a DCE. Null modems can easily be set up using a patch box or purchased as a dedicated null-modem cable.

## Line monitors

Line monitors display the logical state (in terms of MARK or SPACE) present on the most commonly used data and handshaking signal lines. Light emitting diodes (LED) provide the user with a rapid indication of which signals are present and active within the system.

## Breakout boxes

Breakout boxes provide access to the signal lines and invariably combine the features of patch boxes and line monitors. In addition, switches or jumpers are usually provided for linking lines on either side of the box. Connection is almost invariably via two 25-way ribbon cables terminated with connectors.

## Interface testers

Interface tests are somewhat more complex than simple breakout boxes and generally incorporate facilities for forcing lines into MARK or SPACE states, detecting glitches, measuring baud rates, and also displaying the format of data words. Such instruments are, not surprisingly, rather expensive but could be invaluable for anyone who is regularly carrying out fault finding on asynchronous serial equipment.

# 16
# Reference Section

## Glossary of terms

### Accelerator

A board which replaces the CPU with circuitry to increase the speed of processing.

### Access time

The time taken to retrieve data from a memory/storage device, i.e. the elapsed time between the receipt of a read signal at the device and the placement of valid data on the bus. Typical access times for semiconductor memory devices are in the region 100ns to 200ns whilst average access times for magnetic disks typically range from 10ms to 50ms.

### Accumulator

A register within the central processing unit (CPU) in which the result of an operation is placed.

### Acknowledge (ACK)

A signal used in serial data communications which indicates that data has been received without error.

### Active high

A term used to describe a signal which is asserted in the high (logic 1) state.

### Active low

A term used to describe a signal which is asserted in the low (logic 0) state.

### Address

A reference to the location of data in memory or within I/O space. The CPU places addresses (in binary coded form) on the address bus.

### Address bus

The set of lines used to convey address information. The IBM-PC bus has twenty address lines (A0 to A19) and these are capable of addressing more than a million address locations. One byte of data may be stored at each address.

### Address decoder

A hardware device (often a single integrated circuit) which provides chip select or chip enable signals from address patterns which appear on an address bus.

## Address selection

The process of selecting a specific address (or range of addresses). In order to prevent conflicts, expansion cards must usually be configured (by means of DIP switches or links) to unique addresses within the I/O address map.

## Amplifier

A circuit or device which increases the power of an electrical signal.

## Analogue

The representation of information in the form of a continuously variable quantity (e.g. voltage).

## AND

Logical function which is asserted (true) when all inputs are simultaneously asserted.

## ANSI character set

The American National Standard Institute's character set which is based on an eight-bit binary code and which provides 256 individual characters. See also ASCII.

## Archive

A device or medium used for storage of data which need not be instantly accessible (e.g. a tape cartridge).

## ASCII

A code which is almost universally employed for exchanging data between microcomputers. Standard ASCII is based on a seven-bit binary code and caters for alphanumeric characters (both upper and lower case), punctuation, and special control characters. Extended ASCII employs an eighth bit to provide an additional 128 characters (often used to represent graphic symbols).

## Assembly language

A low-level programming language which is based on mnemonic instructions. Assembly language is often unique to a particular microprocessor or microprocessor family.

## Asserted

A term used to describe a signal when it is in its logically true state (i.e. logic 1 in the case of an active high signal or logic 0 in the case of an active low signal).

## Asynchronous transmission

A data transmission method in which the time between transmitted characters is arbitrary. Transmission is controlled by start and stop bits (no additional synchronising or timing information is required).

## AUTOEXEC.BAT

A file which contains a set of DOS commands and/or program names which is executed automatically whenever the system is initialised and provides a means of configuring a system.

### Backup

A file or disk copy made in order to avoid the accidental loss, damage, or erasure of programs and/or data.

### Basic input output system (BIOS)

The BIOS is the part of the operating system which handles communications between the microcomputer and peripheral devices (such as keyboard, serial port, etc). The BIOS is supplied as firmware and is contained in a read-only memory (ROM).

### Batch file

A file containing a series of DOS commands which are executed when the file name is entered after the DOS prompt. Batch files are given a BAT file extension. A special type of batch file (AUTOEXEC.BAT) is executed (when present) whenever a system is initialised. See also AUTOEXEC.BAT.

### Baud rate

The speed at which serial data is transferred between devices.

### Binary file

A file which contains binary data (i.e. a direct memory image). This type of file is used for machine readable code, program overlays, and graphics screens.

### Bit

A contraction of 'binary digit'; a single digit in a binary number.

### Boot

The name given to the process of loading and initialising an operating system (part of the operating system is held on disk and must be loaded from disk into RAM on power-up).

### Boot record

A single-sector record present on a disk which conveys information about the disk and instructs the computer to load the requisite operating system files into RAM (thus booting the machine).

### Buffer

In a hardware context, a buffer is a device which provides a degree of electrical isolation at an interface. The input to a buffer usually exhibits a much higher impedance than its output (see also 'Driver'). In a software context, a buffer is a reserved area of memory which provides temporary data storage and thus may be used to compensate for a difference in the rate of data flow or time of occurrence of events.

### Bus

An electrical highway for signals which have some common function. Most microprocessor systems have three distinct buses; an address bus, data bus and control bus. A local bus can be used for high-speed data transfer between certain devices (e.g. CPU, graphics processors and video memory).

# Byte

A group of eight bits which are operated on as a unit.

# Cache

A high-speed random-access memory which is used to store copies of the data from the most recent main memory or hard disk accesses. Subsequent accesses fetch data from this area rather than from the slower main memory or hard disk.

# Central processing unit (CPU)

The part of a computer that decodes instructions and controls the other hardware elements of the system. The CPU comprises a control unit, arithmetic/logic unit and internal storage. In microcomputers, a microprocessor acts as the CPU. See also Microprocessor.

# Channel

A path along which signals or data can be sent.

# Character set

The complete range of characters (letters, numbers and punctuation) which are provided within a system. See also ANSI and ASCII.

# Checksum

Additional binary digits appended to a block of data. The value of the appended digits is derived from the sum of the data present within the block. This technique provides a means of error checking (validation).

# Chip

The term commonly used to describe an integrated circuit.

# Clock

A source of timing signals used for synchronising data transfers within a microprocessor or microcomputer system.

# Cluster

A unit of space allocated on the surface of a disk. The number of sectors which make up a cluster varies according to the DOS version and disk type. See also Sector.

# Command

An instruction (entered from the keyboard or contained within a batch file) which will be recognised and executed by a system. See also Batch file.

# Common

A return path for a signal (often ground).

# CONFIG.SYS

A file which contains DOS configuration commands which are used to configure the system at start-up. The CONFIG.SYS file specifies device drivers which are loaded during initialisation and which extend the functionality of a system by allowing it to communicate with additional items of hardware. See Device Driver.

### Controller

A sub-system within a microcomputer which controls the flow of data between the system and an I/O or storage device (e.g. a CRT controller, hard disk controller, etc). A controller will generally be based on one, or more, programmable VLSI devices.

### Coprocessor

A second processor which shares the same instruction stream as the main processor. The coprocessor handles specific tasks (e.g. mathematics) which would otherwise be performed less efficiently (or not at all) by the main processor.

### Cylinder

The group of tracks which can be read from a hard disk at any instant of time (i.e. without stepping the head in or out). In the case of a floppy disk (where there are only two surfaces), each cylinder comprises two tracks. In the case of a 20Mbyte hard disk, there are normally two platters (i.e. four surfaces) and thus four tracks will be present within each cylinder.

### Daisy chain

A method of connection in which signals move in a chained fashion from one device to another. This form of connection is commonly used with disk drives.

### Data

A general term used to describe numbers, letters and symbols present with a computer system. All such information is ultimately represented by patterns of binary digits.

### Data bus

A highway (in the form of multiple electrical conductors) which conveys data between the different elements within a microprocessor system.

### Data file

A file which contains data (rather than a program) and which are used by applications such as spreadsheet and database applications. Note that data may or may not be stored in directly readable ASCII form.

### Device

A hardware component such as a memory card, sound card, modem, or graphics adapter.

### Device driver

A term used to describe memory resident software (specified in the CONFIG.SYS system file) which provides a means of interfacing specialised hardware (e.g. expanded memory adapters). See CONFIG.SYS.

### Direct memory access

A method of fast data transfer in which data moves between a peripheral device (e.g. a hard disk) and main memory without direct control of the CPU.

## Directory

A catalogue of disk files (containing such information as filename, size, attributes, and date/time of creation). The directory is stored on the disk and updated whenever a file is amended, created, or deleted. A directory entry usually comprises 32 bytes for each file.

## Disk operating system (DOS)

A group of programs which provide a low-level interface with the system hardware (particularly disk I/O). Routines contained within system resident portions of the operating system may be used by the programmer. Other programs provided as part of the system include those used for formatting disks, copying files, etc.

## Double word

A data value which comprises a group of 32-bits (or two words). See also Word.

## Driver

In a software context, a driver is a software routine which provides a means of interfacing a specialised hardware device. See also Device driver. In a hardware context, a driver is an electrical circuit which provides an electrical interface between an output port and an output transducer. A driver invariably provides power gain (i.e. current gain and/or voltage gain). See also Amplifier.

## Expanded memory (EMS memory)

Memory which is additional to the conventional 'base' memory available within the system. This memory is 'paged' into the base memory space whenever it is accessed. The EMS specification uses four contiguous 16K pages of physical memory (64K total) to access up to 32M of expanded memory space.

## Extended memory (XMS memory)

Memory beyond the 1M byte range ordinarily recognised by MS-DOS. The XMS memory specification resulted from collaboration between Lotus, Intel and Microsoft (sometimes known as LIM specification).

## File

Information (which may comprise ASCII encoded text, binary coded data and executable programs) stored on a floppy or hard disk. Files may be redirected from one logical device to another using appropriate DOS commands.

## File attributes

Information which indicates the status of a file (e.g. hidden, read-only, system, etc).

## Filter

In a software context, a filter is a software routine which removes or modifies certain data items (or data items within a defined range). In a hardware context, a filter is an electrical circuit which modifies the frequency distribution of a signal. Filters are often categorised as low-pass, high-pass, band-pass, or band-stop depending upon the shape of their frequency response characteristic.

### Firmware

A program (software) stored in read-only memory (ROM). Firmware provides non-volatile storage of programs.

### Fixed disk

A disk which cannot be removed from its housing. Note that, whilst the terms 'hard' and 'fixed' are often used interchangeably, some forms of hard disk are exchangeable.

### Font

A set of characters (letters, numbers and punctuation) with a particular style and size.

### Format

The process in which a magnetic disk is initialised so that it can accept data. The process involves writing a magnetic pattern of tracks and sectors to a blank (uninitialised) disk. A disk containing data can be reformatted, in which case all data stored on the disk will be lost. An MS-DOS utility program (FORMAT.COM) is supplied in order to carry out the formatting of floppy disks (a similiar utility is usually provided for formatting the hard disk).

### Graphics adapter

An option card which provides a specific graphics capability (e.g. CGA, EGA, HGA, VGA). Graphics signal generation is not normally part of the functionality provided within a system mother board.

### Handshake

An interlocked sequence of signals between peripheral devices in which a device waits for an acknowledgement of the receipt of data before sending new data.

### Hard disk

A non-flexible disk used for the magnetic storage of data and programs. See also Fixed disk.

### Hardware

The physical components (e.g. system board, keyboard, etc) which make up a microcomputer system.

### High state

The more positive of the two voltage levels used to represent binary logic states. A high state (logic 1) is generally represented by a voltage in the range 2.0V to 5.0V.

### High memory

The first 64K of extended memory. This area is used by some DOS applications and also by Windows. See Extended memory.

### Input/output (I/O)

Devices and lines used to transfer information to and from external (peripheral) devices.

## Integrated circuit

An electronic circuit fabricated on a single wafer (chip) and packaged as a single component.

## Interface

A shared boundary between two or more systems, or between two or more elements within a system. In order to facilitate interconnection of systems, various interface standards are adopted (e.g. RS-232 in the case of asynchronous data communications).

## Interleave

A system of numbering the sectors on a disk in a non-consecutive fashion in order to optimise data access times.

## Interrupt

A signal generated by a peripheral device when it wishes to gain the attention of the CPU. The Intel 80x86 family of microprocessors support both software and hardware interrupts. The former provide a means of invoking BIOS and DOS services whilst the latter are generally managed by an interrupt controller chip (e.g. 8259).

## Joystick

A device used for positioning a cursor, pointer, or output device using switches or potentiometers which respond to displacement of the stick in the X and Y directions.

## Keyboard buffer

A small area in memory which provides temporary storage for keystrokes. See Buffer.

## Kilobyte (K)

1024 bytes (note that $2^{10} = 1024$).

## Logical device

A device which is normally associated with microcomputer I/O, such as the console (which comprises keyboard and display) and printer.

## Low state

The more negative of the two voltage levels used to represent the binary logic states. A low state (logic 0) is generally represented by a voltage in the range 0V to 0.8V.

## Megabyte (M)

1048576 bytes (note that $2^{20} = 1048576$). The basic addressing range of the 8086 (which has 20 address bus lines) is 1M byte.

## Memory

That part of a microcomputer system into which information can be placed and later retrieved. Storage and memory are interchangeble terms. Memory can take various forms including semiconductor (RAM and ROM), magnetic (floppy and hard disks), and optical disks. Note that memory may also be categorised as read-only (in which case data cannot subsequently be written to the memory) or read/write (in which case data can both be read from and written to the memory).

### Memory resident program

See TSR.

### Microprocessor

A central processing unit fabricated on a single chip.

### Modem

A contraction of modulator-demodulator; a communications interface device that enables a serial port to be interfaced to a conventional voice-frequency telephone line.

### Modified frequency modulation (MFM)

A method of data encoding employed with hard disk storage. This method of data storage is 'self-clocking'.

### Motherboard

The motherboard (or system board) is the mother printed circuit board which provides the basic functionality of the microcomputer system including CPU, RAM, and ROM. The system board is fitted with connectors which permit the installation of one, or more, option cards (e.g. graphics adapters, disk controllers, etc).

### Multimedia

A combination of various media technologies including sound, video, graphics and animation.

### Multitasking

A process in which several programs are running simultaneously.

### NAND

Inverse of the logical AND function.

### Negative acknowledge (NAK)

A signal used in serial data communications which indicates that erroneous data has been received.

### Network

A system which allows two or more computers to be linked via a physical communications medium (e.g. coaxial cable) in order to exchange information and share resources.

### Nibble

A group of four bits which make up one half of a byte. A hexadecimal character can be represented by such a group.

### Noise

Any unwanted signal component which may be appear superimposed on a wanted signal.

### NOR

Inverse of the logical OR function.

## Operating system

A control program which provides a low-level interface with the system hardware. The operating system thus frees the programmer from the need to produce hardware specific I/O routines (e.g. those associated with disk filing). See also Disk operating system.

## Option card

A printed circuit board (adapter card) which complies with the physical and electrical specification for a particular system and which provides the system with additional functionality (e.g. asynchronous communications facilities).

## OR

Logical function which is asserted (true) when any one or more of its inputs are asserted.

## Page

A contiguous area of memory of defined size (often 256 bytes but can be larger, see Expanded memory).

## Paragraph

Sixteen consecutive bytes of data. The segment address can be incremented to point to consecutive paragraphs of data.

## Parallel interface

A communications interface in which data is transferred a byte at a time between a computer and a peripheral device, such as a printer.

## Peripheral

An external hardware device whose activity is under the control of the microcomputer system.

## Port

A general term used to describe an interface circuit which facilitates transfer of data to and from external devices (peripherals).

## Program

A sequence of executable microcomputer instructions which have a defined function. Such instructions are stored in program files having EXE or COM extensions.

## Propagation delay

The time taken for a signal to travel from one point to another. In the case of logic elements, propagation delay is the time interval between the appearance of a logic state transition at the input of a gate and its subsequent appearance at the output.

## Protocol

A set of rules and formats necessary for the effective exchange of data between intelligent devices.

## Random access

An access method in which each word can be retrieved in the same amount of time (i.e. the storage locations can be accessed in any desired order). This method should be compared with sequential access in which access times are dependent upon the position of the data within the memory.

## Random access memory (RAM)

A term which usually refers to semiconductor read/write memory (in which access time is independent of actual storage address). Note that semiconductor read-only memory (ROM) devices also provide random access.

## Read

The process of transferring data to a processor from memory or I/O.

## Read-only memory (ROM)

A memory device which is permanently programmed. Erasable-programmable read only memory (EPROM) devices are popular for storage of programs and data in stand-alone applications and can be erased under ultraviolet light to permit reprogramming.

## Register

A storage area within a CPU, controller, or other programmable device, in which data (or addresses) are placed during processing. Registers will commonly hold 8, 16 or 32-bit values.

## Run length limited (RLL)

A method of data encoding employed with hard disk storage. This method is more efficient than conventional MFM encoding.

## Root directory

The principal directory of a disk (either hard or floppy) which is created when the disk is first formatted. The root directory may contain the details of further sub-directories which may themselves contain yet more sub-directories, and so on.

## Sector

The name given to a section of the circular track placed (during formatting) on a magentic disk. Tracks are commonly divided into ten sectors. See also Format.

## Segment

64K bytes of contiguous data within memory. The starting address of such a block of memory may be contained within one of the four segment registers (DS, CS, SS, or ES).

## Serial interface

A communications interface in which data is transferred a bit at a time between a computer and a peripheral device, such as a modem. In serial data transfer, a byte of data (i.e. eight bits) is transmitted by sending a stream of bits, one after another. Furthermore, when such data is transmitted asynchronously (i.e. without a clock), additional bits must be added for synchronistaion together with further bits for error (parity) checking (if enabled).

## Server

A computer which provides network accessible services (e.g. hard disk storage, printing, etc).

## Shell

The name given to an item of software which provides the principal user interface to a system. The DOS program COMMAND.COM provides a simple DOS shell however later versions of MS-DOS and DR-DOS provide much improved graphical shells (DOSSHELL and VIEWMAX respectively).

## Signal

The information conveyed by an electrical quantity.

## Signal level

The relative magnitude of a signal when considered in relation to an arbitrary reference (usually expressed in volts, V).

## Software

A series of computer instructions (i.e. a program).

## Sub-directory

A directory which contains details of a group of files and which is self contained within another directory (or within the root directory).

## System board

See motherboard.

## System file

A file that contains information required by DOS. Such a file is not normally shown in a directory listing.

## Terminal emulation

The ability of a microcomputer to emulate a hardware terminal.

## TSR

A terminate-and-stay-resident program (i.e. a program which, once loaded, remains resident in memory and which is available for execution from within another application).

## Upper memory

The 384K region of memory which extends beyond the 640K of conventional memory. This region of memory is not normally available to applications and is reserved for system functions such as the video display memory. Some applications (such as Windows running in enhanced mode) can access unused portions of the upper memory area).

## Validation

A process in which input data is checked in order to identify incorrect items. Validation can take several forms including range, character, and format checks.

### Verification

A process in which stored data is checked (by subsequent reading) to see whether it is correct.

### Virtual memory

A technique of memory management which uses disk swap files emulate random-access memory. The extent of RAM can be increased by this technique by an amount which is equivalent to the total size of the swap files on the hard disk.

### Visual display unit (VDU)

An output device (usually based on a cathode ray tube) on which text and/or graphics can be displayed. A VDU is normally fitted with an integral keyboard in which case it is sometimes referred to as a console.

### Volume label

A disk name (comprising up to 11 characters). Note that hard disks may be partitioned into several volumes, each associated with its own logical drive specifier (i.e. C:, D:, E:, etc).

### Word

A data value which comprises a group of 16-bits and which constitutes the fundamental size of data which an 8086 processor can accept and manipulate as a unit.

### Write

The process of transferring data from a CPU to memory or to an I/O device.

## Hex, binary, decimal and ASCII/IBM extended character set

| Hex. | Binary | Decimal | ASCII/IBM (see note on p.212) |
|------|----------|---------|-------------------------------|
| 00 | 00000000 | 0 | |
| 01 | 00000001 | 1 | ^A |
| 02 | 00000010 | 2 | ^B |
| 03 | 00000011 | 3 | ^C |
| 04 | 00000100 | 4 | ^D |
| 05 | 00000101 | 5 | ^E |
| 06 | 00000110 | 6 | ^F |
| 07 | 00000111 | 7 | ^G |
| 08 | 00001000 | 8 | ^H |
| 09 | 00001001 | 9 | ^I |
| 0A | 00001010 | 10 | ^J |
| 0B | 00001011 | 11 | ^K |
| 0C | 00001100 | 12 | ^L |
| 0D | 00001101 | 13 | ^M |
| 0E | 00001110 | 14 | ^N |
| 0F | 00001111 | 15 | ^O |
| 10 | 00010000 | 16 | ^P |
| 11 | 00010001 | 17 | ^Q |
| 12 | 00010010 | 18 | ^R |
| 13 | 00010011 | 19 | ^S |
| 14 | 00010100 | 20 | ^T |

| 15 | 00010101 | 21 | ^U |
| 16 | 00010110 | 22 | ^V |
| 17 | 00010111 | 23 | ^W |
| 18 | 00011000 | 24 | ^X |
| 19 | 00011001 | 25 | ^Y |
| 1A | 00011010 | 26 | ^Z |
| 1B | 00011011 | 27 | ^[ |
| 1C | 00011100 | 28 | ^\ |
| 1D | 00011101 | 29 | ^] |
| 1E | 00011110 | 30 | ^^ |
| 1F | 00011111 | 31 | ^ |
| 20 | 00100000 | 32 | |
| 21 | 00100001 | 33 | ! |
| 22 | 00100010 | 34 | " |
| 23 | 00100011 | 35 | # |
| 24 | 00100100 | 36 | $ |
| 25 | 00100101 | 37 | % |
| 26 | 00100110 | 38 | & |
| 27 | 00100111 | 39 | ' |
| 28 | 00101000 | 40 | ( |
| 29 | 00101001 | 41 | ) |
| 2A | 00101010 | 42 | * |
| 2B | 00101011 | 43 | + |
| 2C | 00101100 | 44 | , |
| 2D | 00101101 | 45 | - |
| 2E | 00101110 | 46 | . |
| 2F | 00101111 | 47 | / |
| 30 | 00110000 | 48 | 0 |
| 31 | 00110001 | 49 | 1 |
| 32 | 00110010 | 50 | 2 |
| 33 | 00110011 | 51 | 3 |
| 34 | 00110100 | 52 | 4 |
| 35 | 00110101 | 53 | 5 |
| 36 | 00110110 | 54 | 6 |
| 37 | 00110111 | 55 | 7 |
| 38 | 00111000 | 56 | 8 |
| 39 | 00111001 | 57 | 9 |
| 3A | 00111010 | 58 | : |
| 3B | 00111011 | 59 | ; |
| 3C | 00111100 | 60 | < |
| 3D | 00111101 | 61 | = |
| 3E | 00111110 | 62 | > |
| 3F | 00111111 | 63 | ? |
| 40 | 01000000 | 64 | @ |
| 41 | 01000001 | 65 | A |
| 42 | 01000010 | 66 | B |
| 43 | 01000011 | 67 | C |
| 44 | 01000100 | 68 | D |
| 45 | 01000101 | 69 | E |
| 46 | 01000110 | 70 | F |
| 47 | 01000111 | 71 | G |
| 48 | 01001000 | 72 | H |
| 49 | 01001001 | 73 | I |
| 4A | 01001010 | 74 | J |
| 4B | 01001011 | 75 | K |
| 4C | 01001100 | 76 | L |
| 4D | 01001101 | 77 | M |
| 4E | 01001110 | 78 | N |
| 4F | 01001111 | 79 | O |
| 50 | 01010000 | 80 | P |

| | | | |
|---|---|---|---|
| 51 | 01010001 | 81 | Q |
| 52 | 01010010 | 82 | R |
| 53 | 01010011 | 83 | S |
| 54 | 01010100 | 84 | T |
| 55 | 01010101 | 85 | U |
| 56 | 01010110 | 86 | V |
| 57 | 01010111 | 87 | W |
| 58 | 01011000 | 88 | X |
| 59 | 01011001 | 89 | Y |
| 5A | 01011010 | 90 | Z |
| 5B | 01011011 | 91 | [ |
| 5C | 01011100 | 92 | \ |
| 5D | 01011101 | 93 | ] |
| 5E | 01011110 | 94 | ^ |
| 5F | 01011111 | 95 | _ |
| 60 | 01100000 | 96 | ` |
| 61 | 01100001 | 97 | a |
| 62 | 01100010 | 98 | b |
| 63 | 01100011 | 99 | c |
| 64 | 01100100 | 100 | d |
| 65 | 01100101 | 101 | e |
| 66 | 01100110 | 102 | f |
| 67 | 01100111 | 103 | g |
| 68 | 01101000 | 104 | h |
| 69 | 01101001 | 105 | i |
| 6A | 01101010 | 106 | j |
| 6B | 01101011 | 107 | k |
| 6C | 01101100 | 108 | l |
| 6D | 01101101 | 109 | m |
| 6E | 01101110 | 110 | n |
| 6F | 01101111 | 111 | o |
| 70 | 01110000 | 112 | p |
| 71 | 01110001 | 113 | q |
| 72 | 01110010 | 114 | r |
| 73 | 01110011 | 115 | s |
| 74 | 01110100 | 116 | t |
| 75 | 01110101 | 117 | u |
| 76 | 01110110 | 118 | v |
| 77 | 01110111 | 119 | w |
| 78 | 01111000 | 120 | x |
| 79 | 01111001 | 121 | y |
| 7A | 01111010 | 122 | z |
| 7B | 01111011 | 123 | { |
| 7C | 01111100 | 124 | \| |
| 7D | 01111101 | 125 | } |
| 7E | 01111110 | 126 | ~ |
| 7F | 01111111 | 127 | |
| 80 | 10000000 | 128 | Ç |
| 81 | 10000001 | 129 | ü |
| 82 | 10000010 | 130 | é |
| 83 | 10000011 | 131 | â |
| 84 | 10000100 | 132 | ä |
| 85 | 10000101 | 133 | à |
| 86 | 10000110 | 134 | å |
| 87 | 10000111 | 135 | ç |
| 88 | 10001000 | 136 | ê |
| 89 | 10001001 | 137 | ë |
| 8A | 10001010 | 138 | è |
| 8B | 10001011 | 139 | ï |
| 8C | 10001100 | 140 | î |

| 8D | 10001101 | 141 | ì |
| 8E | 10001110 | 142 | Ä |
| 8F | 10001111 | 143 | Å |
| 90 | 10010000 | 144 | É |
| 91 | 10010001 | 145 | æ |
| 92 | 10010010 | 146 | Æ |
| 93 | 10010011 | 147 | ô |
| 94 | 10010100 | 148 | ö |
| 95 | 10010101 | 149 | ò |
| 96 | 10010110 | 150 | û |
| 97 | 10010111 | 151 | ù |
| 98 | 10011000 | 152 | ÿ |
| 99 | 10011001 | 153 | Ö |
| 9A | 10011010 | 154 | Ü |
| 9B | 10011011 | 155 | ¢ |
| 9C | 10011100 | 156 | £ |
| 9D | 10011101 | 157 | ¥ |
| 9E | 10011110 | 158 | ₧ |
| 9F | 10011111 | 159 | ƒ |
| A0 | 10100000 | 160 | á |
| A1 | 10100001 | 161 | í |
| A2 | 10100010 | 162 | ó |
| A3 | 10100011 | 163 | ú |
| A4 | 10100100 | 164 | ñ |
| A5 | 10100101 | 165 | Ñ |
| A6 | 10100110 | 166 | ª |
| A7 | 10100111 | 167 | º |
| A8 | 10101000 | 168 | ¿ |
| A9 | 10101001 | 169 | ⌐ |
| AA | 10101010 | 170 | ¬ |
| AB | 10101011 | 171 | ½ |
| AC | 10101100 | 172 | ¼ |
| AD | 10101101 | 173 | ¡ |
| AE | 10101110 | 174 | « |
| AF | 10101111 | 175 | » |
| B0 | 10110000 | 176 | ▓ |
| B1 | 10110001 | 177 | ▒ |
| B2 | 10110010 | 178 | ▓ |
| B3 | 10110011 | 179 | │ |
| B4 | 10110100 | 180 | ┤ |
| B5 | 10110101 | 181 | ╡ |
| B6 | 10110110 | 182 | ╢ |
| B7 | 10110111 | 183 | ╖ |
| B8 | 10111000 | 184 | ╕ |
| B9 | 10111001 | 185 | ╣ |
| BA | 10111010 | 186 | ║ |
| BB | 10111011 | 187 | ╗ |
| BC | 10111100 | 188 | ╝ |
| BD | 10111101 | 189 | ╜ |
| BE | 10111110 | 190 | ╛ |
| BF | 10111111 | 191 | ┐ |
| C0 | 11000000 | 192 | └ |
| C1 | 11000001 | 193 | ┴ |
| C2 | 11000010 | 194 | |
| C3 | 11000011 | 195 | ├ |
| C4 | 11000100 | 196 | ─ |
| C5 | 11000101 | 197 | ┼ |
| C6 | 11000110 | 198 | ╞ |
| C7 | 11000111 | 199 | ╟ |
| C8 | 11001000 | 200 | ╚ |

| | | | |
|------|-----------|-----|---|
| C9 | 11001001 | 201 | ╔ |
| CA | 11001010 | 202 | |
| CB | 11001011 | 203 | ╦ |
| CC | 11001100 | 204 | ╠ |
| CD | 11001101 | 205 | = |
| CE | 11001110 | 206 | ╬ |
| CF | 11001111 | 207 | ╧ |
| D0 | 11010000 | 208 | |
| D1 | 11010001 | 209 | ╤ |
| D2 | 11010010 | 210 | ╥ |
| D3 | 11010011 | 211 | |
| D4 | 11010100 | 212 | ╘ |
| D5 | 11010101 | 213 | ╒ |
| D6 | 11010110 | 214 | ╓ |
| D7 | 11010111 | 215 | ╫ |
| D8 | 11011000 | 216 | ╪ |
| D9 | 11011001 | 217 | |
| DA | 11011010 | 218 | ┌ |
| DB | 11011011 | 219 | █ |
| DC | 11011100 | 220 | ▄ |
| DD | 11011101 | 221 | ▌ |
| DE | 11011110 | 222 | |
| DF | 11011111 | 223 | ▀ |
| E0 | 11100000 | 224 | α |
| E1 | 11100001 | 225 | β |
| E2 | 11100010 | 226 | Γ |
| E3 | 11100011 | 227 | π |
| E4 | 11100100 | 228 | Σ |
| E5 | 11100101 | 229 | σ |
| E6 | 11100110 | 230 | μ |
| E7 | 11100111 | 231 | τ |
| E8 | 11101000 | 232 | Φ |
| E9 | 11101001 | 233 | θ |
| EA | 11101010 | 234 | Ω |
| EB | 11101011 | 235 | δ |
| EC | 11101100 | 236 | ∞ |
| ED | 11101101 | 237 | φ |
| EE | 11101110 | 238 | ∈ |
| EF | 11101111 | 239 | ∩ |
| F0 | 11110000 | 240 | ≡ |
| F1 | 11110001 | 241 | ± |
| F2 | 11110010 | 242 | ≥ |
| F3 | 11110011 | 243 | ≤ |
| F4 | 11110100 | 244 | ⌠ |
| F5 | 11110101 | 245 | ⌡ |
| F6 | 11110110 | 246 | ÷ |
| F7 | 11110111 | 247 | ≈ |
| F8 | 11111000 | 248 | ° |
| F9 | 11111001 | 249 | ∙ |
| FA | 11111010 | 250 | · |
| FB | 11111011 | 251 | √ |
| FC | 11111100 | 252 | ⁿ |
| FD | 11111101 | 253 | ² |
| FE | 11111110 | 254 | ■ |
| FF | 11111111 | 255 | |

Note: IBM and compatible equipment does not use standard ASCII characters below 32 decimal. These non-displayable ASCII characters are referred to as control characters. When output to the IBM display, these characters appear as additional graphics characters (not shown in the table).

# IBM POST and diagnostic error codes

### Indeterminate (01x)

01x            indeterminate problem

### Power supply (02x)

02x            power supply fault

### System board (1xx)

| | |
|---|---|
| 101 | interrupt failure |
| 102 | BIOS ROM checksum error (PC, XT); timer (AT, MCA) |
| 103 | BASIC ROM checksum error (PC, XT); timer interrupt (AT, MCA) |
| 104 | interrupt controller (PC, XT); protected mode (AT, MCA) |
| 105 | timer (PC, XT); keyboard controller (MCA) |
| 106 | system board |
| 107 | system board adapter card or maths coprocessor, NMI test (MCA) |
| 108 | system board; timer bus (MCA) |
| 109 | DMA test; memory |
| 110 | system board memory (ISA); system board parity check (MCA) |
| 111 | adapter memory (ISA); memory adapter parity check (MCA) |
| 112 | adapter; watchdog time-out (MCA) |
| 113 | adapter; DMA arbitration time-out (MCA) |
| 114 | external ROM checksum (MCA) |
| 115 | 80386 protect mode |
| 121 | unexpected hardware interrupt |
| 131 | cassette wrap test (PC) |
| 132 | DMA extended registers |
| 133 | DMA verify logic |
| 134 | DMA arbitration logic |
| 151 | real-time clock (or CMOS RAM) |
| 152 | system board (ISA); real time clock or CMOS (MCA) |
| 160 | system board ID not recognised (MCA) |
| 161 | system options (dead battery) (CMOS chip lost power) |
| 162 | system options (run Setup) (CMOS does not match system) |
| 163 | time and date (run Setup) (clock not updating) |
| 164 | memory size (run Setup) (CMOS does not match system) |
| 165 | adapter ID mismatch (MCA) |
| 166 | adapter time-out; card busy (MCA) |
| 167 | system clock not updating (MCA) |
| 199 | incorrect user device list |

### Memory (2xx)

| | |
|---|---|
| 201 | memory error (number preceding 201 indicates specific location) |
| 202 | memory address line 0-15 |
| 203 | memory address line 16-23; line 16-31 (MCA) |

| | |
|---|---|
| 204 | relocated memory (PS/2) |
| 205 | error in first 128K (PS/2 ISA); CMOS (PS/2 MCA) |
| 207 | ROM failure |
| 211 | system board memory; system board 64K (MCA) |
| 215 | memory address error; 64K on daughter/SIP 2 (70) |
| 216 | system board memory; 64K on daughter/SIP 1 (70) |
| 221 | ROM to RAM copy (MCA) |
| 225 | wrong speed memory on system board (MCA) |

## Keyboard (3xx)

| | |
|---|---|
| 301 | keyboard did not respond correctly, or stuck key detected (the hexadecimal number preceding 301 is the scan code for the faulty key) keyboard interface (MCA) |
| 302 | user-indicated error from keyboard test (PC, XT) |
| 302 | keyboard locked (AT, models 25, 30) |
| 303 | keyboard/system board interface |
| 304 | keyboard or system unit error; keyboard clock (MCA) |
| 305 | keyboard fuse on system board (50, 60, 80); +5V error (70) |
| 341 | keyboard |
| 342 | keyboard cable |
| 343 | enhancement card or cable |
| 365 | keyboard (replace keyboard) |
| 366 | interface cable (replace cable) |
| 367 | enhancement card or cable (replace) |

## Monochrome display (4xx)

| | |
|---|---|
| 401 | memory, horizontal sync frequency or vertical sync test |
| 408 | user-indicated display attributes |
| 416 | user-indicated character set |
| 424 | user-indicated 80 x 25 mode |
| 432 | monochrome card parallel port test |

## Color/graphics display (5xx)

| | |
|---|---|
| 501 | memory, horizontal sync frequency or vertical sync test |
| 508 | user-indicated display attributes |
| 516 | user-indicated character set |
| 524 | user-indicated 80 x 25 mode |
| 532 | user-indicated 40 x 25 mode |
| 540 | user-indicated 320 x 200 graphics mode |
| 548 | user-indicated 640 x 200 graphics mode |
| 556 | light pen test |
| 564 | user-indicated screen paging test |

## Diskette drives and/or adapter (6xx)

| | |
|---|---|
| 601 | diskette/adapter test failure; drive or controller (MCA) |
| 602 | diskette test (PC, XT); diskette boot record (MCA) |

| 603 | diskette size error |
|-----|---------------------|
| 606 | diskette verify function |
| 607 | write protected diskette |
| 608 | bad command; diskette status returned |
| 610 | diskette initialisation (PC, XT) |
| 611 | timeout; diskette status returned |
| 612 | bad NEC; diskette status returned |
| 613 | bad DMA; diskette status returned |
| 614 | DMA boundary error |
| 621 | bad seek; diskette status returned |
| 622 | bad CRC; diskette status returned |
| 623 | record not found; diskette status returned |
| 624 | bad address mark; diskette status returned |
| 625 | bad NEC seek; diskette status returned |
| 626 | diskette data compare error |
| 627 | diskette change line error |
| 628 | diskette removed |
| 630 | drive A: index stuck high |
| 631 | drive A: index stuck low |
| 632 | drive A: track 0 stuck off |
| 633 | drive A: track 0 stuck on |
| 640 | drive B: index stuck high |
| 641 | drive B: index stuck low |
| 642 | drive B: track 0 stuck off |
| 643 | drive B: track 0 stock on |
| 650 | drive speed |
| 651 | format failure |
| 652 | verify failure |
| 653 | read failure |
| 654 | write failure |
| 655 | controller |
| 656 | drive |
| 657 | write protect stuck protected |
| 658 | change line stuck changed |
| 659 | write protect stuck unprotected |
| 660 | change line stuck unchanged |

## Math coprocessor (7xx)

| 702 | exception errors test |
|-----|------------------------|
| 703 | rounding test |
| 704 | arithmetic test 1 |
| 705 | arithmetic test 2 |
| 706 | arithmetic test 3 |
| 707 | combination test |
| 708 | integer store test |
| 709 | equivalent expressions |
| 710 | exceptions |
| 711 | save state |
| 712 | protected mode test |
| 713 | voltage/temperature sensitivity test |

## Parallel printer adapter (9xx)

| 901 | data register latch |
|-----|---------------------|
| 902 | control register latch |
| 903 | register address decode |
| 904 | address decode |
| 910 | status line wrap connector |
| 911 | status line bit 8 wrap |
| 912 | status line bit 7 wrap |

| 913 | status line bit 6 wrap |
|---|---|
| 914 | status line bit 5 wrap |
| 915 | status line bit 4 wrap |
| 916 | interrupt wrap |
| 917 | unexpected interrupt |
| 92x | feature register |

## Alternate printer adapter (10xx)

| 10xx | adapter test failure |
|---|---|
| 1002 | jumpers (IBM models 25, 30) |

## Communications device asynchronous communications adapter System board, asynchronous port (MCA), 16550 internal modem (PS/2) (11xx)

| 1101 | adapter test failure |
|---|---|
| 1102 | card-selected feedback |
| 1103 | port 102 register test |
| 1106 | serial option |
| 1107 | communications cable or system board (MCA) |
| 1108 | IRQ 3 |
| 1109 | IRQ 4 |
| 1110 | modem status register not clear |
| | 16550 chip register |
| 1111 | ring-indicate |
| | 16550 control line internal wrap test |
| 1112 | trailing edge ring-indicate |
| | 16550 control line external wrap test |
| 1113 | receive and delta receive line signal detect |
| | 16550 transmit |
| 1114 | receive line signal detect |
| | 16550 receive |
| 1115 | delta receive line signal detect 16550 transmit and |
| | receive |
| | data unequal |
| 1116 | line control register: all bits cannot be set |
| | 16550 interrupt function |
| 1117 | line control register: all bits cannot be reset |
| | 16550 baud rate test |
| 1118 | transmit holding and/or shift register stuck on |
| | 16550 interrupt-driven receive external data wrap test |
| 1119 | data ready stuck on |
| | 16550 FIFO |
| 1120 | interrupt enable register: all bits cannot be set |
| 1121 | interrupt enable register: all bits cannot be reset |
| 1122 | interrupt pending stuck on |
| 1123 | interrupt ID register stuck on |
| 1124 | modem control register: all bits cannot be set |
| 1125 | modem control register: all bits cannot be reset |
| 1126 | modem status register: all bits cannot be set |
| 1127 | modem status register: all bits cannot be reset |
| 1128 | interrupt ID |
| 1129 | cannot force overrun error |
| 1130 | no modem status interrupt |
| 1131 | invalid interrupt pending |
| 1132 | no data ready |

| 1133 | no data available interrupt |
| 1134 | no transmit holding interrupt |
| 1135 | no interrupts |
| 1136 | no received line status interrupt |
| 1137 | no receive data available |
| 1138 | transmit holding register |
| 1139 | no modem status interrupt |
| 1140 | transmit holding register to empty |
| 1141 | no interrupts |
| 1142 | no IRQ4 interrupt |
| 1143 | no IRQ3 interrupt |
| 1144 | no data transferred |
| 1145 | maximum baud rate |
| 1146 | minimum baud rate |
| 1148 | timeout error |
| 1149 | invalid data returned |
| 1150 | modem status register error |
| 1151 | no DSR and delta DSR |
| 1152 | no DSR |
| 1153 | no delta DSR |
| 1154 | modem status register |
| 1155 | no CTS and delta CTS |
| 1156 | no CTS |
| 1157 | no delta CTS |

### Alternate communications device, asynchronous communications adapter (ISA), dual asynchronous communications (DAC) adapter (MCA), 16550 internal modem (12xx)

| 12xx | Same as 1100-1157ISA systems, except for PS/2 codes listed below |
| 1202 | jumpers (models 25,30) |
| 1202 or 06 | serial device (e.g. Dual asynchronous adapter) |
| 1208 or 09 | serial device (e.g. Dual asynchronous adapter) |
| 1212 | dual async adapter or system board |
| 1218 or 19 | dual async adapter or system board |
| 1227 | dual async adapter or system board |
| 1233 or 34 | dual async adapter or system board |

### Game control adapter (13xx)

| 1301 | adapter failure |
| 1302 | joystick test |

### Color/graphics printer (14xx)

| 1401 | printer test failure |
| 1402 | not ready; out of paper |
| 1403 | no paper; interrupt failure |
| 1404 | matrix printer test failure; system board time-out |
| 1405 | parallel adapter |
| 1406 | presence test |

### Synchronous data link control (SDLC) communications adapter (15xx)

| 1501 | adapter test failure |
| 1510 | 8255 port B |
| 1511 | 8255 port A |
| 1512 | 8255 port C |

| | |
|---|---|
| 1513 | 8253 timer #1 did not reach terminal count |
| 1514 | 8253 timer #1 output stuck on |
| 1515 | 8253 timer #0 did not reach terminal count |
| 1516 | 8253 timer #0 output stuck on |
| 1517 | 8253 timer #2 did not reach terminal count |
| 1518 | 8253 timer #2 output stuck on |
| 1519 | 8273 port B error |
| 1520 | 8273 port A error |
| 1521 | 8273 command/read time-out |
| 1522 | interrupt level 4 (timer and modem change) |
| 1523 | ring indicator stuck on |
| 1524 | received clock stuck on |
| 1525 | transmit clock stuck on |
| 1526 | test indicate stuck on |
| 1527 | ring indicate not on |
| 1528 | receive clock not on |
| 1529 | transmit clock not on |
| 1530 | test indicate not on |
| 1531 | data set ready not on |
| 1532 | carrier detect not on |
| 1533 | clear-to-send not on |
| 1534 | data set ready stuck on |
| 1535 | carrier detect stuck on |
| 1536 | clear-to-send stuck on |
| 1537 | level 3 (transmit/receive) interrupt |
| 1538 | receive interrupt results error |
| 1539 | wrap data miscompare error |
| 1540 | DMA channel 1 transmit error |
| 1541 | DMA channel 1 receive error |
| 1542 | 8273 error-checking or status-reporting error |
| 1547 | level 4 stray interrupt |
| 1548 | level 3 stray interrupt |
| 1549 | interrupt presentation sequence time-out |

### Display station emulation adapter (DSEA) (16xx)

(NB: try removing non-IBM adapters and then repeat the POST checks)

| | |
|---|---|
| 1604 or 08 | DSEA or system twin-axial network problem |
| 1624 or 34 | DSEA |
| 1644 or 52 | DSEA |
| 1654 or 58 | DSEA |
| 1662 | interrupt level switches set wrong or defective DSEA |
| 1664 | DSEA |
| 1668 | see 1662 |
| 1669 or 74 | if early version of IBM diagnostics diskette, replace with version 3.0 (or later) and repeat diagnostic checks |
| 1674 | station address which is set wrong or defective DSEA |
| 1684 or 88 | feature not installed, device address switches set wrong, or DSEA |

### Fixed (hard) disk/adapter (17xx)

| | |
|---|---|
| 1701 | drive not ready (PC, XT) |
| | fixed disk/adapter test (AT, PS/2) |
| 1702 | time-out (PC, XT); fixed disk/adapter (AT, PS/2) |
| 1703 | drive (PC, XT, PS/2) |

| | |
|------|------|
| 1704 | controller (PC, XT),<br>adapter, or drive error (AT, PS/2) |
| 1705 | no record found |
| 1706 | write fault |
| 1707 | track 0 error |
| 1708 | head select error |
| 1709 | bad ECC (AT) |
| 1710 | read buffer overrun |
| 1711 | bad address mark |
| 1712 | bad address mark (PC, AT);<br>error of undetermined cause (AT) |
| 1713 | data compare error |
| 1714 | drive not ready |
| 1730 | adapter |
| 1731 | adapter |
| 1732 | adapter |
| 1750 | drive verify |
| 1751 | drive read |
| 1752 | drive write |
| 1753 | random read test |
| 1754 | drive seek test |
| 1755 | controller |
| 1756 | controller ECC test |
| 1757 | controller head select |
| 1780 | hard disk drive C fatal; time-out |
| 1781 | hard disk drive D fatal; time-out |
| 1782 | hard disk controller (no IPL from hardfile) |
| 1790 | drive C non-fatal error (can attempt to run IPL<br>from drive) |
| 1791 | drive D non-fatal error (can attempt to run IPL<br>from drive) |

## Expansion unit (PC, XT only) (18xx)

| | |
|------|------|
| 1801 | Expansion Unit POST error |
| 1810 | enable/disable |
| 1811 | extender card wrap test failure while disabled |
| 1812 | high-order address lines failure while disabled |
| 1813 | wait state failure while disabled |
| 1814 | enable/disable could not be set on |
| 1815 | wait state failure while enabled |
| 1816 | extender card wrap test failure while enabled |
| 1817 | high-order address lines failure while enabled |
| 1818 | disable not functioning |
| 1819 | wait request switch not set correctly |
| 1820 | receiver card wrap test or an adapter card in<br>expansion unit |
| 1821 | receiver high-order address lines |

## BiSynchronous communications (BSC) adapter (20xx)

| | |
|------|------|
| 2001 | adapter test failure |
| 2010 | 8255 port A |
| 2011 | 8255 port B |
| 2012 | 8255 port C |
| 2013 | 8253 timer #1 did not reach terminal count |
| 2014 | 8253 timer #1 output stuck on |
| 2015 | 8253 timer #2 did not reach terminal count |
| 2016 | 8253 timer #2 output stuck on |
| 2017 | 8251 data-set-ready failure to come on |

| | |
|---|---|
| 2018 | 8251 clear-to-send not sensed |
| 2019 | 8251 data-set-ready stuck on |
| 2020 | 8251 clear-to-send stuck on |
| 2021 | 8251 hardware reset |
| 2022 | 8251 software reset command |
| 2023 | 8251 software error-reset command |
| 2024 | 8251 transmit-ready did not come on |
| 2025 | 8251 receive-ready did not come on |
| 2026 | 8251 could not force overrun error status |
| 2027 | interrupt-transmit; no timer interrupt |
| 2028 | interrupt-transmit; replace card or planar |
| 2029 | interrupt-transmit; replace card only |
| 2030 | interrupt-transmit; replace card or planar |
| 2031 | interrupt-transmit; replace card only |
| 2033 | ring-indicate stuck on |
| 2034 | receive-clock stuck on |
| 2035 | transmit clock stuck on |
| 2036 | test indicate stuck on |
| 2037 | ring indicate not on |
| 2038 | receive clock not on |
| 2039 | transmit clock not on |
| 2040 | test indicate not on |
| 2041 | data-set-ready stuck on |
| 2042 | carrier detect not on |
| 2043 | clear-to-send not on |
| 2044 | data-set-ready stuck on |
| 2045 | carrier detect stuck on |
| 2046 | clear-to-send stuck on |
| 2047 | unexpected transmit |
| 2048 | unexpected receive interrupt |
| 2049 | transmit data did not equal receive data |
| 2050 | 8251 detected overrun error |
| 2051 | lost data set ready during data wrap |
| 2052 | receive time-out during data wrap |

## Alternative bisynchronous communications adapter (21xx)

| | |
|---|---|
| 21xx | as for 2000 to 2052 |

## Cluster adapter (22xx)

| | |
|---|---|
| 22xx | adapter test failure |

## Plasma monitor adapter (23xx)

| | |
|---|---|
| 23xx | adapter test failure |

## Enhanced graphics adapter systems board video (MCA) (24xx)

| | |
|---|---|
| 2401 | adapter test failure |
| 2402 | monitor if colors change, otherwise system board |
| 2408 | user-indicated display attributes |
| 2409 | monitor |
| 2410 | system board |
| 2416 | user-indicated character set |
| 2424 | user-indicated 80 x 25 mode |
| 2432 | user-indicated 40 x 25 mode |
| 2440 | user-indicated 320 x 200 graphics mode |
| 2448 | user-indicated 640 x 200 graphics mode |

| 2456 | light pen test |
|---|---|
| 2464 | user-indicated screen paging test |

## Alternate enhanced graphics adapter (25xx)

| 25xx | adapter test failure |
|---|---|

## PC/370-M adapter (26xx)

| 2601 to 75 | memory card |
|---|---|
| 2677 to 80 | processor card |
| 2681 | memory card |
| 2682 | processor card |
| 2694 | processor card |
| 2695 | memory card |
| 2697 | processor card |

## PC/3277 (27xx)

| 27xx | emulator test failure |
|---|---|

## 3278/79 emulator, 3270 connection adapter (28xx)

| 28xx | adapter test failure |
|---|---|

## Color/graphics printer (29xx)

| 29xx | printer test failure |
|---|---|

## LAN (local area network) adapter (30xx)

| 3001 | adapter ROM failure |
|---|---|
| 3002 | RAM |
| 3003 | digital loopback |
| 3005 | 4V or 12V |
| 3006 | interrupt conflict |
| 3007 | analog |
| 3008 | reset command |
| 3015 | refer to PC Network Service Manual |
| 3020 | replace adapter with jumper W8 enabled |
| 3040 | LF translator cable |
| 3041 | refer to PC Network Service Manual |

## Primary PC network adapter (30xx)

| 3001 | adapter test failure |
|---|---|
| 3002 | ROM |
| 3003 | ID |
| 3004 | RAM |
| 3005 | HIC |
| 3006 | 12V dc |
| 3007 | digital loopback |
| 3008 | host-detected HIC failure |
| 3009 | sync fail and no-go bit |
| 3010 | HIC test OK and no-go bit |
| 3011 | go bit and no CMD 41 |
| 3012 | card not present |
| 3013 | digital fall-through |
| 3015 | analog |
| 3041 | hot carrier on other card |
| 3042 | hot carrier on this card |

## Alternate LAN adapter (31xx)

| 31xx | as for 3000 to 3041 |
| 3115 or 40 | LF translator cable |

## PC display adapter (32xx)

| 32xx | adapter test failure |

## Compact printer (PC, XT only) (33xx)

| 33xx | printer test failure |

## Enhanced display station emulator adapter (35xx)

| 3504 | adapter connected to twin-axial cable during off-line test |
| 3508 | work station address in use by another work station, or diagnostic diskette from another PC was used |
| 3509 | diagnostic program failure; retry on new diskette |
| 3540 | work station address invalid, not configured at controller; twin-axial cable failure or not connected; or diagnostic diskette from another PC was used |
| 3588 | feature not installed or device I/O address switches set wrong |
| 3599 | diagnostic program failure; retry on new diskette |

## IEEE 488 adapter (36xx)

| 3601 | adapter test failure (base address and read registers incorrect, following initialisation |
| 3602 | write to SPMR |
| 3603 | write to ADR or IEEE-488 adapter addressing problems |
| 3610 | adapter cannot be programmed to listen |
| 3611 | adapter cannot be programmed to talk |
| 3612 | adapter cannot take control with IFC |
| 3613 | adapter cannot go to standby |
| 3614 | adapter cannot take control asynchronously |
| 3615 | adapter cannot take control asynchronously |
| 3616 | adapter cannot pass control |
| 3617 | adapter cannot be addressed to listen |
| 3618 | adapter cannot be unaddressed to listen |
| 3619 | adapter cannot be addressed to talk |
| 3620 | adapter cannot be unaddressed to talk |
| 3621 | adapter cannot be addressed to listen with extended addressing |
| 3622 | adapter cannot be unaddressed to listen with extended addressing |
| 3623 | adapter cannot be addressed to talk with extended addressed |
| 3624 | adapter cannot be unaddressed to talk with extended addressing |
| 3625 | adapter cannot write to self |
| 3626 | adapter cannot generate handshake error |
| 3627 | adapter cannot detect DCL message |
| 3628 | adapter cannot detect SDC message |
| 3629 | adapter cannot detect END with EOI |

| | |
|---|---|
| 3630 | adapter cannot detect EOT with EOI |
| 3631 | adapter cannot detect END with 0-bit EOS |
| 3632 | adapter cannot detect END with 7-bit EOS |
| 3633 | adapter cannot detect GET |
| 3634 | mode 3 addressing not functioning |
| 3635 | adapter cannot recognise undefined command |
| 3636 | adapter cannot detect REM, REMC, LOK, or LOKC |
| 3637 | adapter cannot clear REM or LOK |
| 3638 | adapter cannot detect SRQ |
| 3639 | adapter cannot conduct serial poll |
| 3640 | adapter cannot conduct parallel poll |
| 3650 | adapter cannot DMA to 7210 |
| 3651 | data error on DMA to 7210 |
| 3652 | adapter cannot DMA from 7210 |
| 3653 | data error on DMA from 7210 |
| 3658 | uninvoked interrupt received |
| 3659 | adapter cannot interrupt on ADSC |
| 3660 | adapter cannot interrupt on ADSC |
| 3661 | adapter cannot interrupt on CO |
| 3662 | adapter cannot interrupt on DO |
| 3663 | adapter cannot interrupt on DI |
| 3664 | adapter cannot interrupt on ERR |
| 3665 | adapter cannot interrupt on DEC |
| 3666 | adapter cannot interrupt on END |
| 3667 | adapter cannot interrupt on DET |
| 3668 | adapter cannot interrupt on APT |
| 3669 | adapter cannot interrupt on CPT |
| 3670 | adapter cannot interrupt on REMC |
| 3671 | adapter cannot interrupt on LOKC |
| 3672 | adapter cannot interrupt on SRQI |
| 3673 | adapter cannot interrupt on terminal count on DMA to 7210 |
| 3674 | adapter cannot interrupt on terminal count on DMA from 7210 |
| 3675 | spurious DMA terminal count interrupt |
| 3697 | illegal DMA configuration setting detected |
| 3698 | illegal interrupt level configuration setting detected |

## Data acquisition adapter (38xx)

| | |
|---|---|
| 3801 | adapter test failure |
| 3810 | timer read test |
| 3811 | timer interrupt test |
| 3812 | delay, BI 13 test |
| 3813 | rate, BI 13 test |
| 3814 | BO 14, ISIRQ test |
| 3815 | BO 0, count-in test |
| 3816 | BI STB, count-out test |
| 3817 | BO 0, BO CTS test |
| 3818 | BO 1, BI 0 test |
| 3819 | BO 2, BI 1 test |
| 3820 | BO 3, BI 2 test |
| 3821 | BO 4, BI 3 test |
| 3822 | BO 5, BI 4 test |
| 3823 | BO 6, BI 5 test |
| 3824 | BO 7, BI 6 test |
| 3825 | BO 8, BI 7 test |
| 3826 | BO 9, BI 8 test |

| 3827 | BO 10, BI 9 test |
| 3828 | BO 11, BI 10 test |
| 3829 | BO 12, BI 11 test |
| 3830 | BO 13, BI 12 test |
| 3831 | BO 15, AI CE test |
| 3832 | BO STB, BO GATE test |
| 3833 | BI CTS, BI HOLD test |
| 3834 | AI CO, BI 15 test |
| 3835 | counter interrupt test |
| 3836 | counter read test |
| 3837 | AO 0 ranges test |
| 3838 | AO 1 ranges test |
| 3839 | AI 0 values test |
| 3840 | AI 1 values test |
| 3841 | AI 2 values test |
| 3842 | AI 3 values test |
| 3843 | analog input interrupt test |
| 3844 | AI 23 address or value test |

## Professional graphics controller adapter (39xx)

| 3901 | adapter test failure |
| 3902 | ROM1 self-test |
| 3903 | ROM2 self-test |
| 3904 | RAM self-test |
| 3905 | cold start cycle power |
| 3906 | data error in communications RAM |
| 3907 | address error in communications RAM |
| 3908 | bad data detected while read/write to 6845-like register |
| 3909 | bad data detected in lower hex-E0 bytes while reading or writing 6845 equivalent registers |
| 3910 | PGC display bank output latches |
| 3911 | basic clock |
| 3912 | command control error |
| 3913 | vertical sync scanner |
| 3914 | horizontal sync scanner |
| 3915 | intech |
| 3916 | LUT address error |
| 3917 | LUT red RAM chip error |
| 3918 | LUT green RAM chip error |
| 3919 | LUT blue RAM chip error |
| 3920 | LUT data latch |
| 3921 | horizontal display |
| 3922 | vertical display |
| 3923 | light pen |
| 3924 | unexpected error |
| 3925 | emulator addressing error |
| 3926 | emulator data latch |
| 3927 | base for error codes 3928-3930 (emulator RAM) |
| 3928 | emulator RAM |
| 3929 | emulator RAM |
| 3930 | emulator RAM |
| 3931 | emulator H/V display problem |
| 3932 | emulator cursor position |
| 3933 | emulator attribute display problem |
| 3934 | emulator cursor display |
| 3935 | fundamental emulation RAM problem |
| 3936 | emulation character set problem |

| | |
|------|------|
| 3937 | emulation graphics display |
| 3938 | emulation character display problem |
| 3939 | emulation bank select |
| 3940 | display RAM U2 |
| 3941 | display RAM U4 |
| 3942 | display RAM U6 |
| 3943 | display RAM U8 |
| 3944 | display RAM U10 |
| 3945 | display RAM U1 |
| 3946 | display RAM U3 |
| 3947 | display RAM U5 |
| 3948 | display RAM U7 |
| 3949 | display RAM U9 |
| 3950 | display RAM U12 |
| 3951 | display RAM U14 |
| 3952 | display RAM U16 |
| 3953 | display RAM U18 |
| 3954 | display RAM U20 |
| 3955 | display RAM U11 |
| 3956 | display RAM U13 |
| 3957 | display RAM U15 |
| 3958 | display RAM U17 |
| 3959 | display RAM U19 |
| 3960 | display RAM U22 |
| 3961 | display RAM U24 |
| 3962 | display RAM U26 |
| 3963 | display RAM U28 |
| 3964 | display RAM U30 |
| 3965 | display RAM U21 |
| 3966 | display RAM U23 |
| 3967 | display RAM U25 |
| 3968 | display RAM U27 |
| 3969 | display RAM U29 |
| 3970 | display RAM U32 |
| 3971 | display RAM U34 |
| 3972 | display RAM U36 |
| 3973 | display RAM U38 |
| 3974 | display RAM U40 |
| 3975 | display RAM U31 |
| 3976 | display RAM U33 |
| 3977 | display RAM U35 |
| 3978 | display RAM U37 |
| 3979 | display RAM U39 |
| 3980 | PGC RAM timing |
| 3981 | PGC read/write latch |
| 3982 | SR bus output latches |
| 3983 | addressing error (vertical column of memory; U2 at top) |
| 3984 | addressing error (vertical column of memory; U4 at top) |
| 3985 | addressing error (vertical column of memory; U6 at top) |
| 3986 | addressing error (vertical column of memory; U8 at top) |
| 3988 | addressing error (vertical column of memory; U10 at top) |
| 3989 | horizontal bank latch errors |
| 3990 | horizontal bank latch errors |
| 3991 | horizontal bank latch errors |
| 3992 | RAG/CAG PGC |

| 3993 | multiple write modes, nibble mask errors |
| 3994 | row nibble (display RAM) |
| 3995 | PGC addressing |

### 5278 display attachment unit and 5279 display (44xx)

| 44xx | display attachment test failure |

### IEEE-488 interface adapter (45xx)

| 45xx | adapter test failure |

### ARTIC multiport/2 interface adapter (46xx)

| 4611 | adapter |
| 4612 or 13 | memory module |
| 4630 | adapter |
| 4640 or 41 | memory module |
| 4650 | interface cable |

### Internal modem (48xx)

| 48xx | modem test failure |

### Alternate internal modem (49xx)

| 49xx | modem test failure |

### Financial communication system (56xx)

| 56xx | system test failure |

### Chip set (Phoenix BIOS only) (70xx)

| 7000 | CMOS failure |
| 7001 | shadow RAM failure (ROM not shadowed to RAM) |
| 7002 | CMOS configuration data error |

### Voice communications adapter (71xx)

| 7101 | adapter test failure |
| 7102 | instruction or external data memory |
| 7103 | PC to VCA interrupt |
| 7104 | internal data memory |
| 7105 | DMA |
| 7106 | internal registers |
| 7117 | interactive shared memory |
| 7108 | VCA to PC interrupt |
| 7109 | DC wrap |
| 7111 | external analog wrap and tone output |
| 7114 | telephone attachment test |

### 3.5-inch diskette drive (73xx)

| 7301 | diskette drive/adapter test failure |
| 7306 | diskette change line error |
| 7307 | write-protected diskette |
| 7308 | bad command; drive error |
| 7310 | disk initialization error; track zero bad |
| 7311 | time-out; drive error |
| 7312 | bad disk controller chip |
| 7313 | bad DMA controller; drive error |
| 7314 | DMA boundary error |

| 7315 | bad index timing; drive error |
| 7316 | speed error |
| 7321 | bad seek; drive error |
| 7322 | bad CRC; drive error |
| 7323 | record not found; drive error |
| 7324 | bad address mark; drive error |
| 7325 | bad drive controller chip; seek error |

## 8514/A display adapter/A (74xx)

| 74xx | adapter test failure |
| 7426 | monitor |
| 744x to 747x | 8514 memory module |

## Pageprinter (76xx)

| 7601 | adapter test failure |
| 7602 | adapter card |
| 7603 | printer |
| 7604 | printer cable |

## PS/2 speech adapter (84xx)

| 84xx | adapter test failure |

## 2Mb extended memory adapter (85xx)

| 85xx | adapter test failure |
| 850x or 851x | 80286 Expanded Memory Adapter/A (model 50) |
| 852x | 80286 Expanded Memory Adapter/A, memory module (model 50) |

## PS/2 pointing device (mouse) (86xx)

| 8601 | pointing device; mouse time-out (MCA) |
| 8602 | pointing device; mouse interface (MCA) |
| 8603 | system board; mouse interrupt (MCA) |
| 8604 | pointing device or system board |

## MIDI adapter (89xx)

| 89xx | adapter test failure |

## Multiprotocol communications adapter (100xx)

| 10002 or 06 | any serial device, but most likely multiprotocol adapter |
| 10007 | multiprotocol adapter or communications cable |
| 10008 or 09 | any serial device, but most likely multiprotocol adapter |
| 10012 | multiprotocol adapter or system board |
| 10018 or 19 | multiprotocol adapter or system board |
| 10042 or 56 | multiprotocol adapter or system board |

## Modem and communications adapter/A (101xx)

| 101xx | system board |
| 10102 | card-selected feedback |
| 10103 | port 102 register test |
| 10106 | serial option |
| 10108 | IRQ 3 |
| 10109 | IRQ 4 |
| 10110 | 16450 chip register |

| | |
|-------|------------------------------------------------|
| 10111 | 16450 control line internal wrap test |
| 10113 | transmit |
| 10114 | receive |
| 10115 | transmit and receive data not equal |
| 10116 | interrupt function |
| 10117 | baud rate test |
| 10118 | interrupt driven receive external data wrap test |
| 10125 | reset result code |
| 10126 | general result code |
| 10127 | S register write/read |
| 10128 | echo on/off |
| 10129 | enable/disable result codes |
| 10130 | enable number/word result codes |
| 10133 | connect results for 300 baud not received |
| 10134 | connect results for 1,200 baud not received |
| 10135 | local analog loopback 300-baud test |
| 10136 | local analog loopback 1,200-baud test |
| 10137 | no response to escape/reset sequence |
| 10138 | S register 13 incorrect parity or number of data bits |
| 10139 | S register 15 incorrect bit rate |

## ESDI fixed disk or adapter (104xx)

| | |
|-------|------------------------------------------------|
| 10450 | write/read test |
| 10451 | read verify test |
| 10452 | seek test |
| 10453 | wrong device type indicated |
| 10454 | controller failed sector buffer test |
| 10455 | controller |
| 10456 | controller diagnostic command |
| 10461 | format error |
| 10462 | controller head select |
| 10463 | write/read sector error |
| 10464 | drive primary map unreadable |
| 10465 | controller ECC 8-bit |
| 10466 | controller ECC 9-bit |
| 10467 | soft seek error |
| 10468 | hard seek error |
| 10469 | soft seek error count exceeded |
| 10470 | controller attachment diagnostic error |
| 10471 | controller wrap mode interface |
| 10472 | controller wrap mode drive select |
| 10473 | error during ESDI read verify test |
| 10480 | drive C, ESDI adapter or system board |
| 10481 | drive D seek failure, ESDI adapter or system board |
| 10482 | ESDI fixed disk adapter |
| 10483 | ESDI fixed disk adapter; controller reset; drive select 0 |
| 10484 | controller head select 3 selected bad |
| 10485 | controller head select 2 selected bad |
| 10486 | controller head select 1 selected bad |
| 10487 | controller head select 0 selected bad |
| 10488 | controlled rg-cmd complete 2 |
| 10489 | controlled wg-cmd complete 1 |
| 10490 | drive C format; read failure; controller |
| 10491 | drive D format; read failure |
| 10499 | controller |

## 5.25-inch external diskette drive or adapter (107xx)

107xx               drive or adapter test failure

## SCSI adapter (112xx)

112xx               adapter test failure

## Processor card for model 70, type 3 (129xx)

12901               processor portion of processor board
12902               cache portion of processor board

## Plasma display and adapter (149xx)

14901 or 02       system board or plasma display
14922               system board or display adapter
14932               display adapter

## 6157 Streaming tape drive or tape attachment adapter (165xx)

165xx               adapter test failure
16520               streaming tape drive
16540               tape attachment adapter

## Primary token-ring network PC adapter (166xx)

166xx               adapter test failure

## Alternative token-ring network PC adapter (167xx)

167xx               adapter test failure

## Adapter memory module (194xx)

194xx               adapter test failure

## SCSI fixed disk and controller (210xx)

210xx               disk or controller test failure

## SCSI CD-ROM system (215xx)

215xx               CD-ROM system test failure

# Addresses of suppliers

## Memory upgrades, chips and SIMMs

Advanced Business Computers (Europe) Ltd.
36A, Kilburn High Road,
London,
NW6 5UA
Tel: (071) 372 1917
Fax: (071) 625 7649

Dealex Ltd.
64, Chapel View,
South Croydon,
Surrey,
CR2 7LF
Tel: (081) 668 4199
Fax: (081) 668 7429

Memory Direct Ltd.
42-44 Birchett Road,
Aldershot,
Hants,
GU11 1LT
Tel: (0252) 316060

Portables and Upgrades Ltd.
Dram House,
Latham Close,
Bredbury Industrial Park,
Stockport,
SK6 2SD
Tel: (061) 406 6486
Fax: (061) 494 9125

Powermark PLC,
Premier House,
112 Station Road,
Edgware,
Middlesex,
HA8 7AQ
Tel: (081) 951 3355
Fax: (081) 905 6233

Richnight Ltd.
197, Brighton Road,
Purley,
Surrey,
CR8 4HF
Tel: (081) 668 4199
Fax: (081) 668 7249

## Motherboards, system upgrades

A+P Computers Ltd.
35 Walnut Tree Close,
Guildford,
Surrey,
GU1 4UN
Tel: (0483) 304118
Fax: (0483) 304124

A.C.C. Tronics Ltd.
Unit 6,
Chancel Way,
Moor Lane Industrial Estate,
Witton,
Birmingham,
B6 7AU
Tel: (021) 344 4911

Atom Computer Services Ltd.
1-7 Mount Street,
Stapleford,
Nottingham,
NG9 8AW
Tel: (0602) 491891
Fax: (0602) 491640

Computer Mates (UK) Ltd.
Pinewood Studios,
Iver Heath,
Bucks,
SL0 0NH
Tel: (0753) 553535
Fax: (0753) 553530

DS Computers,
Unit 206, Belgravia Workshops,
157 Marlborough Road,
London,
N19 4NF
Tel: (071) 281 5096
Fax: (071) 281 7364

Hobbykit Ltd.
Unit 19,
Capitol Industrial Park,
Capitol Way,
London, NW9 0EQ
Tel: (081) 205 7485
Fax: (081) 205 0603

Novatech,
Blueprint 1400,
Dundas Spur,
Portsmouth,
PO3 5RW
Tel: (0705) 664144
Fax: (0705) 664244

PGP Computers,
Unit 14A,
Sunrise Business Park,
Blandford Forum,
Dorset,
DT11 8ST
Tel: (0258) 451347
Fax: (0258) 456046

Stak Trading,
Stak House,
Butlers Leap,
Rugby,
CV21 3RQ
Tel: (0788) 577497
Fax: (0788) 544584

Watford Electronics Ltd.
Finway,
off Dallow Road,
Luton,
LU1 1TR
Tel: (0582) 487777
Fax: (0582) 488588

## Software

Elite Software Products Ltd.
102-104 High Street,
Coleshill,
Warks,
B46 3BL
Tel: (0675) 464488
Fax: (0675) 464685
(Agents for Addstor Inc. and distributors
of SuperStor hard disk data compression software)

WCD Ltd.
Rowlandson House,
289-293 Ballards Lane,
Finchley,
London,
N12 8NP
Tel: (081) 343 9899
Fax: (081) 343 8428
(Distributors of Landmark Research International's diagnostic software products including PC probe, AlignIt, Kickstart, ROM POST, Service Diagnostics, etc)

## Systems, cards and accessories

Chipboards PLC,
Almac House,
Chruch Lane,
Bisley,
Surrey
GU24 9DR
Tel: (0483) 797959
Fax: (0483) 797702

Dabs Press,
22 Warwick Street,
Prestwich,
Manchester,
M25 7HN
Tel: (061) 773 8632
Fax: (0772) 623000

Evesham Micros Ltd.
Unit 9,
St Richards Road,
Evesham,
Worcs,
WR11 6TD
Tel: (0386) 765180
Fax: (0386) 765354

Olympian Computer Systems,
Imperial House,
64 Willoughby Lane,
London,
N17 0SP
Tel: (081) 365 1526
Fax: (081) 365 1858

RSC Corporate,
75-77 Queens Road,
Watford,
Herts,
WD1 2QN
Tel: (0923) 243301
Fax: (0923) 237946

Scan International,
Genesis House,
Stopes Road,
Little Lever,
Bolton,
Lancs,
BL3 1NP
Tel: (061) 724 4910
Fax: (061) 725 9059

Silica Systems,
1-4, The Mews,
Hatherley Road,
Sidcup,, Kent,
DA14 4DX
Tel: (081) 309 1111
Fax: (081) 308 0608

SJP,
181 Melton Road,
Leicester,, LE4 6QT
Tel: (0533) 697270

SMC Computers,
26 Farnham Road,
Slough,
Berks,, SL1 3TA
Tel: (0753) 550333
Fax: (0753) 524443

Unimart Computers Ltd.
Unit 15,
Maple Industrial Estate,
Maple Way,
Feltham,
Middx,, TW13 7AW
Tel: (081) 893 2959
Fax: (081) 893 2961

# 17
# Diagnostic Software

This chapter provides you with the QuickBASIC source code for a number of complete diagnostic programs. These simple utilities will help you check and modify the configuration of your system as well as carry out routine tests and adjustments of such items as disk drives, printers and monitors.

Microsoft's QuickBASIC (or QBASIC) is currently 'bundled' with MS-DOS and it is eminently suitable for the complete beginner to programming.

---

### TIP

When keying in the diagnostic programs into your computer QuickBASIC will usually tell you if you make a mistake. The most common mistakes are:

**(a)** confusing letter O with figure 0 (they look alike and they are adjacent on the keyboard)

**(b)** confusing letter I with figure 1 (they look alike)

**(c)** confusing : with ;

**(d)** missing out one or more lines of text

**(e)** duplicating one or more lines of text

**(f)** missing off trailing $, #, :, ; and % signs (these are more important than you might think)

**(g)** missing spaces (although QuickBASIC is usually reasonably forgiving as far as this is concerned

**(h)** mis-spelling keywords like FILEATTR (two T's), ALIAS (one L), etc

---

### TIP

If you have the full version of QuickBASIC (rather than the cut-down version supplied as part of the MS-DOS package), you can compile the programs and make them into 'stand-alone' .EXE files. You will then be able to use them without first having to load QBASIC.

---

If you don't have access to Microsoft QuickBASIC, or if you would prefer not to type in the programs, a disk with the source code and fully compiled versions of the latest version of each of the program listings is available direct from the author for £4 (U.K. and E.C. countries) or £5 (U.S. and overseas). The nominal charge covers the cost of disk, duplication, postage and packing.

The disk also contains several other utility programs (including CMOS memory back-up) together with a collection of useful batch files.

When ordering, please state which one of the following formats is required:

(a) 3.5" 1.44M   (state 'FORMAT A')

(b) 3.5" 720K   (state 'FORMAT B')

(c) 5.25" 360K   (state 'FORMAT C')

Please allow up to 28 days for delivery and make sure that you have clearly printed your name and address. Cheques, money and postal orders should be made payable to 'MIKE TOOLEY'. Orders should be sent to:

Mike Tooley
Dean of Technology
Brooklands College
Heath Road
Weybridge
Surrey
KT13 8TT
England

All five programs may be freely adapted, copied and modified. You are encouraged to use them as the basis of your own personalised diagnostic programs. Finally, if you have any suggestions, modifications and/or improvements please let me know so that I can incorporate them in future releases.

## Disk check

This program will allow you to quickly check the performance of the floppy and hard drives fitted to your system. The program will also provide you with some useful information about the organisation of your disk drives including the number of sectors per cluster, the number of bytes per sector, the number of clusters per disk, and the total capacity of the disk.

The program will also allow you to carry out a disk write/read test. You should have a formatted disk with at least 32K free in each of the floppy drives that you wish to test. Similarly, you must have at least 32K free on each hard disk that is to be tested. Note that the test file created (TEST.DAT) is erased from the disk at the end of the test. The write/read test is repeated a total of ten times and any errors reported (DOS would normally report these errors anyway).

```
' *************************************************
' ** Name:      DISK.BAS        Version: 0.17   **
' ** Function:  Checks drives A: to D:          **
' ** Language:  Microsoft QuickBASIC            **
' ** Notes:     Program creates a file, TEST.DAT **
' **            on the specified drive which must **
' **            have at least 32K bytes free     **
' *************************************************
'
' Initialise
'
TYPE RegType
AX AS INTEGER
BX AS INTEGER
CX AS INTEGER
DX AS INTEGER
BP AS INTEGER
SI AS INTEGER
DI AS INTEGER
DS AS INTEGER
```

```
    FLAGS AS INTEGER
    END TYPE
    '
    ON ERROR GOTO warning
    ' Initialise in text mode
    SCREEN 0
    COLOR 15, 1
    ul$ = STRING$(40, CHR$(205))
    DIM InputRegs AS RegType, OutputRegs AS RegType
    ' Display main menu
    DO
    main:
    CLS
    PRINT ul$
    PRINT " DISK CHECK "
    PRINT ul$; ""
    PRINT " Select option..."
    PRINT " [T] = write/read test"
    PRINT " [V] = get DOS version"
    PRINT " [D] = disk information"
    PRINT " [Q] = quit"
    DO
      r$ = UCASE$(INKEY$)
    LOOP UNTIL r$ <> "" AND INSTR("TVDQ", r$)
    IF r$ = "Q" THEN CLS : SCREEN 0: END
    '
    PRINT ul$
    IF r$ = "T" THEN GOSUB test
    IF r$ = "V" THEN GOSUB version
    IF r$ = "D" THEN GOSUB info
    LOOP
    '
    test:
    GOSUB which
    ' Use root directory
    file$ = drive$ + ":\TEST.DAT"
    ' Reset error flag
    flag% = 0
    ' Repeat the write/read test ten times
    FOR no% = 1 TO 10
      GOSUB tidy
      LOCATE 10, 2
      PRINT "Writing data to "; file$
      LOCATE 11, 2
      PRINT "["; no%; "]"
      OPEN file$ FOR OUTPUT AS #1
      FOR ch% = 0 TO 4096
        PRINT #1, ch%
      NEXT ch%
      CLOSE #1
      GOSUB tidy
      LOCATE 10, 2
      PRINT "Reading data from "; file$
      LOCATE 11, 2
      PRINT "["; no%; "]"
      OPEN file$ FOR INPUT AS #1
      FOR dat% = 0 TO 4096
        INPUT #1, ch%
        IF ch% <> dat% THEN flag% = 1
      NEXT dat%
```

```
  CLOSE #1
NEXT no%
GOSUB tidy
IF flag% = 1 THEN
  LOCATE 10, 2
  PRINT "An error has occured - check the disk!"
  ELSE
  LOCATE 10, 2
  PRINT "Test completed without error."
  LOCATE 11, 2
  PRINT "Erasing "; file$
  KILL file$
END IF
GOSUB waitkey
RETURN
'
version:
' Get DOS version
InputRegs.AX = &H3000
CALL INTERRUPT(&H21, InputRegs, OutputRegs)
majorver% = OutputRegs.AX AND 255
minorver% = OutputRegs.AX / 256
LOCATE 10, 2
PRINT "DOS version..."; majorver%; "."; minorver%
GOSUB waitkey
RETURN
'
info:
GOSUB which
IF drive$ = "A" THEN InputRegs.DX = &H1
IF drive$ = "B" THEN InputRegs.DX = &H2
IF drive$ = "C" THEN InputRegs.DX = &H3
IF drive$ = "D" THEN InputRegs.DX = &H4
InputRegs.AX = &H1C00
CALL INTERRUPT(&H21, InputRegs, OutputRegs)
sectors = OutputRegs.AX AND 255
bytes = OutputRegs.CX
clusters = OutputRegs.DX
IF clusters <= 0 THEN clusters = clusters + 65536
' Determine disk capacity
capacity = INT(sectors * bytes * clusters / 1000)
' Erase any existing screen data
GOSUB tidy
' Display the disk information
LOCATE 10, 2: PRINT "Information for drive:  "; drive$
LOCATE 11, 2: PRINT "Sectors per cluster:   "; sectors
LOCATE 12, 2: PRINT "Bytes per sector:      "; bytes
LOCATE 13, 2: PRINT "Clusters per disk:     "; cluster:
LOCATE 14, 2: PRINT "Disk capacity:         "; capacit:
GOSUB waitkey
RETURN
'
which:
' Specify drive to be used
LOCATE 10, 2
PRINT "Which drive [A],[B],[C] or [D]?"
DO
  r$ = UCASE$(INKEY$)
LOOP UNTIL r$ <> "" AND INSTR("ABCD", r$)
drive$ = r$
```

```
LOCATE 10, 2
PRINT STRING$(39, " ")
RETURN
'
tidy:
' Erase any existing screen data
FOR cline% = 10 TO 14
  LOCATE cline%, 2
  PRINT STRING$(39, " ")
NEXT cline%
RETURN
'
waitkey:
PRINT ul$
PRINT " Press any key to continue..."
GOSUB keywait
RETURN
'
keywait:
DO
  r$ = INKEY$
LOOP UNTIL r$ <> ""
RETURN
'
warning:
PRINT ul$
PRINT " An error has occured!"
GOSUB waitkey
RESUME main
```

## Display check

This program will allow you to carry out various checks and adjustments on a variety of PC displays including basic text mode displays (80 x 25 monochrome), CGA, EGA, and VGA colour types.

The program has two menu screens and it initialises in 'Text' mode. You can then either display a chequerboard (80 x 25 grid) by pressing <T> or move to the 'setup display' sub-menu by pressing <S>. Here you have a choice of a 'Text Mode', 'CGA' (320 x 200, 4 colours), 'EGA' (640 x 200, 16 colours), and 'VGA' (640 x 350, 16 colours).

Once the required display mode has been selected, you should exit to the main menu and continue with one or more of the checks. Assuming that you have selected a graphics mode (CGA, EGA, or VGA) you can select from:

(i)   Alignment test   –   this test displays a series of concentric circles and it is used for adjusting height, width, vertical linearity, and horizontal linearity.

(ii)  Grid test        –   this test displays a grid (horizontal and vertical lines) and it is used to check monitor convergence.

(iii) Dot test         –   this test displays a matrix of single- pixel dots. It can be used to check dynamic focus (all dots should be the same size).

(iv)  Colour bars      –   this test displays 16 colours bars (4 in CGA mode) and can be used for performing colour adjustments.

(v) Text display     –   this test displays a chequerboard of text characters (ASCII 32 and 219 respectively). You should check that the 80 x 25 display fills the display with an adequate margin all round.

```
' *****************************************************
' **  Name:      DISPLAY.BAS                       **
' **  Function:  Checks Text/CGA/EGA/VGA displays  **
' **  Language:  Microsoft QuickBASIC              **
' **  Notes:     Requires appropriate display      **
' **             adapter card                       **
' *****************************************************
'
' Initialise
'
ON ERROR GOTO warning
' Initialise in text mode
SCREEN 0
COLOR 15, 1
xc = 0
mode$ = "Text"
ul$ = STRING$(40, CHR$(205))
' Display main menu
DO
main:
CLS
PRINT ul$
PRINT " DISPLAY CHECK      Current mode = "; mode$
PRINT ul$; ""
PRINT " Select option..."
IF xc <> 0 THEN
  PRINT " [A] = alignment test"
  PRINT " [G] = grid test"
  PRINT " [D] = dot test"
  PRINT " [C] = colour bars"
END IF
PRINT " [T] = text display"
PRINT " [S] = setup display mode"
PRINT " [Q] = quit"
DO
  r$ = UCASE$(INKEY$)
LOOP UNTIL r$ <> "" AND INSTR("AGDTCSQ", r$)
IF r$ = "Q" THEN CLS : SCREEN 0: END
'
PRINT ul$
IF xc <> 0 THEN
  IF r$ = "A" THEN GOSUB alignment
  IF r$ = "G" THEN GOSUB grid
  IF r$ = "D" THEN GOSUB dot
  IF r$ = "C" THEN GOSUB colours
END IF
IF r$ = "T" THEN GOSUB text
IF r$ = "S" THEN GOTO setup
LOOP
'
alignment:
CLS
FOR x = xc / 4 TO xc STEP xc / 4
  CIRCLE (xc, yc), x
NEXT x
```

```
LINE (0, yc)-(2 * xc, yc)
LINE (xc, 0)-(xc, 2 * yc)
GOSUB keywait
RETURN
'
grid:
CLS
FOR y = 0 TO 2 * yc STEP yc / 10
  LINE (0, y)-(2 * xc, y)
NEXT y
FOR x = 0 TO 2 * xc STEP xc / 15
  LINE (x, 0)-(x, 2 * yc)
NEXT x
GOSUB keywait
RETURN
'
dot:
CLS
FOR y = 0 TO 2 * yc STEP yc / 10
  FOR x = 0 TO 2 * xc STEP xc / 15
    PSET (x, y)
    NEXT x
  NEXT y
GOSUB keywait
RETURN
'
text:
CLS
IF mode$ <> "CGA" THEN xlim = 80 ELSE xlim = 40
FOR x = 1 TO xlim STEP 2
  FOR y = 1 TO 25 STEP 2
    LOCATE y, x
    PRINT CHR$(219);
  NEXT y
NEXT x
FOR x = 2 TO xlim STEP 2
  FOR y = 2 TO 25 STEP 2
    LOCATE y, x
    PRINT CHR$(219);
  NEXT y
NEXT x
GOSUB keywait
RETURN
'
colours:
IF mode$ <> "CGA" THEN
  COLOR 0, 0
  CLS
  x = 0
  xold = 0
  inc = xc / 8
  FOR colour = 0 TO 15
    x = x + inc
    LINE (xold, 0)-STEP(x, 2 * yc), colour, BF
    xold = x
  NEXT colour
ELSE
' CGA uses 4 colours...
  COLOR 0, 0, 1
  CLS
  x = 0
```

```
  xold = 0
  inc = xc / 2
  FOR colour = 0 TO 3
    x = x + inc
    LINE (xold, 0)-STEP(x, 2 * yc), colour, BF
    xold = x
  NEXT colour
END IF
GOSUB keywait
IF mode$ <> "CGA" THEN COLOR 15, 1 ELSE COLOR 1, 2, 1
RETURN
'
setup:
DO
' Display setup menu
CLS
PRINT ul$
PRINT " DISPLAY SETUP       Current mode = "; mode$
PRINT ul$; ""
PRINT " Select option..."
PRINT " [T] = Text Mode (80 col., 16 colours)"
PRINT " [C] = CGA (320 x 200, 4 colours)"
PRINT " [E] = EGA (640 x 200, 16 colours)"
PRINT " [V] = VGA (640 x 350, 16 colours)"
PRINT " [X] = exit to main menu"
DO
  r$ = UCASE$(INKEY$)
LOOP UNTIL r$ <> "" AND INSTR("TCEVX", r$)
IF r$ = "X" THEN GOTO main
PRINT ul$
IF r$ = "T" THEN
  SCREEN 2: SCREEN 0: COLOR 15, 1: xc = 0: yc = 0: mode$ = "Text"
END IF
IF r$ = "C" THEN SCREEN 1: COLOR 1, 2, 1: xc = 160: yc = 100: mode$ = "CGA"
IF r$ = "E" THEN SCREEN 8: COLOR 15, 1: xc = 320: yc = 100: mode$ = "EGA"
IF r$ = "V" THEN SCREEN 9: COLOR 15, 1: xc = 320: yc = 175: mode$ = "VGA"
LOOP
'
waitkey:
PRINT ul$
PRINT " Press any key to continue..."
GOSUB keywait
RETURN
'
keywait:
DO
  r$ = INKEY$
LOOP UNTIL r$ <> ""
RETURN
'
warning:
PRINT ul$
PRINT " An error has occured!"
GOSUB waitkey
RESUME main
```

## Printer check

This program will allow you to carry out a number of checks on an Epson-compatible printer connected to the PC's parallel port. You can print the standard (ASCII) and extended (non-ASCII) character sets (characters corresponding to codes from 32 to 127 and 128 to 255 respectively), print directly from the keyboard, send line feed and form feed characters, exercise the printer continuously, and print a 'style sheet' for the printer.

You can also use the 'setup' option (press <S>) from the main menu in order to select the required print style and repeat any of the main menu tests, as required. The 'setup' option allows you to select condensed, double strike, emphasised, italic, normal, subscript, and superscript print modes (and allowable combinations of these basic styles).

```
' ****************************************************
' ** Name:      PRINTER.BAS      Version: 0.15    **
' ** Function:  Checks Epson compatible printers  **
' ** Language:  Microsoft QuickBASIC              **
' ** Notes:     Use parallel printer port LPT1    **
' ****************************************************
'
' Initialise
'
ON ERROR GOTO warning
SCREEN 0
COLOR 15, 1
ul$ = STRING$(31, CHR$(205))
'
' Check printer is on-line and ready
'
DEF SEG = &H40
status& = PEEK(9) * 256 + PEEK(8) + 1
IF INP(status&) <> 223 THEN
  CLS
  PRINT " Printer not ready!"
  DO
  LOOP UNTIL INP(status&) = 223
END IF
DEF SEG
' Reset printer to start
GOSUB cancel
' Set up print style flags
nf$ = "*": cf$ = "": bf$ = "": ef$ = ""
if$ = "": sbf$ = "": spf$ = ""
'
' Display main menu
'
DO
main:
CLS
PRINT ul$
PRINT " PRINTER CHECK"
PRINT ul$; ""
PRINT " Select option..."
PRINT " [A] = print standard ASCII character set"
PRINT " [E] = print extended character set"
PRINT " [K] = print from keyboard"
```

```
PRINT " [L] = send line feed"
PRINT " [F] = send form feed"
PRINT " [C] = continuous printing"
PRINT " [P] = print style check sheet"
PRINT " [S] = setup printer"
PRINT " [Q] = quit"
DO
  r$ = UCASE$(INKEY$)
LOOP UNTIL r$ <> "" AND INSTR("AEKLFCPSQ", r$)
IF r$ = "Q" THEN GOSUB cancel: CLS : END
'
PRINT ul$
IF r$ = "A" THEN GOSUB standard
IF r$ = "E" THEN GOSUB extended
IF r$ = "K" THEN GOSUB keyboard
IF r$ = "L" THEN GOSUB linefeed
IF r$ = "F" THEN GOSUB formfeed
IF r$ = "C" THEN GOSUB continuous
IF r$ = "P" THEN GOSUB style
IF r$ = "S" THEN GOTO setup
LOOP
'
standard:
PRINT " Standard ASCII character set..."
LPRINT
LPRINT "Standard ASCII character set..."
LPRINT
FOR char = 32 TO 79
  LPRINT CHR$(char);
NEXT char
LPRINT
FOR char = 80 TO 127
  LPRINT CHR$(char);
NEXT char
LPRINT
RETURN
'
extended:
PRINT " Extended character set..."
LPRINT
LPRINT "Extended character set (non-ASCII)..."
LPRINT
FOR char = 128 TO 191
  LPRINT CHR$(char);
NEXT char
LPRINT
FOR char = 192 TO 255
  LPRINT CHR$(char);
NEXT char
LPRINT
RETURN
'
keyboard:
PRINT " Printing from keyboard."
PRINT " Press [#] to quit..."
PRINT ul$
LPRINT
DO
  LOCATE , , 1      'turn cursor on for text entry
  r$ = INPUT$(1)
```

```
   IF r$ = "#" THEN
     LOCATE , , 0
     LPRINT
     GOSUB waitkey
     RETURN
   END IF
   PRINT r$;
   LPRINT r$;
LOOP
'
linefeed:
PRINT " Sending line feed..."
LPRINT CHR$(13);
RETURN
'
formfeed:
PRINT " Sending form feed..."
LPRINT CHR$(12);
RETURN
'
continuous:
PRINT " Continuous printing."
PRINT " Press [#] to quit..."
PRINT ul$
LPRINT
DO
  r$ = INKEY$
  LPRINT "H";
LOOP WHILE r$ <> "#"
LPRINT
RETURN
'
style:
PRINT " Printing style check sheet..."
GOSUB cancel
LPRINT CHR$(12);
FOR lin% = 1 TO 4
  LPRINT
NEXT
LPRINT STRING$(64, "_")
LPRINT
LPRINT "Style check sheet: "; TIME$; " "; DATE$
LPRINT
LPRINT STRING$(64, "_")
LPRINT
test$ = ""
FOR char = 1 TO 40
  test$ = test$ + CHR$(char + 64)
NEXT char
' normal mode
GOSUB cancel
LPRINT "Normal:       "; test$
LPRINT
' condensed mode
LPRINT CHR$(15);
LPRINT "Condensed:    "; test$
LPRINT
GOSUB cancel
' double-strike mode
LPRINT CHR$(27); "G";
```

```
LPRINT "Double-strike: "; test$
LPRINT
GOSUB cancel
' italic mode
LPRINT CHR$(27); "4";
LPRINT "Italic:        "; test$
LPRINT
GOSUB cancel
' emphasized mode
LPRINT CHR$(27); "E";
LPRINT "Emphasized:    "; test$
LPRINT
GOSUB cancel
' superscript mode
LPRINT CHR$(27); "S"; "0";
LPRINT "Superscript:   "; test$
LPRINT
GOSUB cancel
' subscript mode
LPRINT CHR$(27); "S"; "1";
LPRINT "Subscript:     "; test$
LPRINT
GOSUB cancel
LPRINT
LPRINT STRING$(64, "_")
LPRINT CHR$(12);
RETURN
'
setup:
DO
  '
  ' Display setup menu
  '
  CLS
  PRINT ul$
  PRINT " PRINTER SETUP"
  PRINT ul$; ""
  PRINT " Select option..."
  PRINT " [C] = condensed print "; cf$
  PRINT " [B] = double strike   "; bf$
  PRINT " [E] = emphasized      "; ef$
  PRINT " [I] = italic print    "; if$
  PRINT " [N] = normal print    "; nf$
  PRINT " [S] = subscript       "; sbf$
  PRINT " [T] = superscript     "; spf$
  PRINT " [X] = exit to main menu"
  DO
    r$ = UCASE$(INKEY$)
  LOOP UNTIL r$ <> "" AND INSTR("CBENISTX", r$)
  IF r$ = "X" THEN GOTO main
  '
  PRINT ul$
  IF r$ = "C" THEN LPRINT CHR$(15); : cf$ = "*": nf$ = ""
  IF r$ = "B" THEN LPRINT CHR$(27); "G"; : bf$ = "*": nf$ = ""
  IF r$ = "E" THEN LPRINT CHR$(27); "E"; : ef$ = "*": nf$ = ""
  IF r$ = "I" THEN LPRINT CHR$(27); "4"; : if$ = "*": nf$ = ""
  IF r$ = "N" THEN
    GOSUB cancel
    nf$ = "*"
    cf$ = "": bf$ = "": ef$ = "": if$ = "": sbf$ = "": spf$ = ""
```

```
END IF
IF r$ = "S" THEN
    LPRINT CHR$(27); "s"; "0";
    sbf$ = "*": spf$ = "": nf$ = ""
  END IF
  IF r$ = "T" THEN
    LPRINT CHR$(27); "s"; "1";
    spf$ = "*": sbf$ = "": nf$ = ""
  END IF
LOOP
'
cancel:
LPRINT CHRS(18); : cf$ = ""          ' cancel condensed mode
LPRINT CHR$(27); "F"; : ef$ = "" ' cancel emphasized mode
LPRINT CHR$(27); "H"; : bf$ = "" ' cancel double strike mode
LPRINT CHR$(27); "5"; : if$ = ""  \ cancel italic mode
LPRINT CHR$(27); "T"; : sbf$ = "": spf$ = "": ' cancel sub/super
RETURN
'
waitkey:
PRINT ul$
PRINT " Press any key to continue..."
DO
  r$ = INKEY$
LOOP UNTIL r$ <> ""
RETURN
'
warning:
PRINT ul$
PRINT " An error has occured!"
GOSUB waitkey
RESUME main
```

## Soak test

This program will allow you to soak test your system. It will continuously cycle through a serious of routines which will exercise the items that you specify. You can interrupt program execution at the end of the current cycle by pressing <Q> at any point in the cycle (note that you will have to wait for the current cycle to complete before the program terminates and returns you to the DOS prompt).

The program will first request information on your system including the number of floppy and hard disk drives fitted, the type of display and whether you wish to test a printer connected to the parallel port (if you select this last option you must have a printer connected which is on-line and ready to go).

The program will also prompt you for your system clock speed. You should select from 4 to 12MHz (slow), 12MHz to 25MHz (medium), and 25MHz to 66MHz (fast). If you don't know the system clock speed, you should select the middle option (respond by pressing <B>).

You should have a formatted disk with at least 32K free in each of the floppy drives that you wish to test. Similarly, you must have at least 32K free on each hard disk that has been included in the system specification.

After responding to the various prompts and questions, your system configuration will be displayed and you will be asked to confirm your selection. If the selection is correct, the program will cycle through the various tests with each part exercised in turn until you decide to quit the program.

Finally, it is important to note that you don't have to put the whole system to test. You can exclude particular items from the soak test by simply omitting them from the initial system specification.

```
' ****************************************************
' **  Name:      SOAK.BAS        Version: 0.17    **
' **  Function:  Performs system soak test        **
' **  Language:  Microsoft QuickBASIC             **
' **  Notes:     Program creates files on each    **
' **             drive (32K bytes of free space   **
' **             required on each drive)          **
' ****************************************************
'
' Initialise
'
ON ERROR GOTO warning
' Initialise in text mode
SCREEN 0
COLOR 15, 1
ul$ = STRING$(40, CHR$(205))
' Display main menu
r$ = ""
main:
DO
  CLS
  PRINT ul$
  PRINT " SYSTEM SOAK TEST"
  PRINT ul$; ""
  PRINT " Please provide system information..."
  '
  PRINT " Number of floppy disk drives?"
  PRINT " (0, 1, or 2)"
  DO
    r$ = INKEY$
  LOOP UNTIL r$ <> "" AND INSTR("012", r$)
  fdrives = VAL(r$)
  '
  PRINT " Number of hard disk drives?"
  PRINT " (0, 1, or 2)"
  DO
    r$ = INKEY$
  LOOP UNTIL r$ <> "" AND INSTR("012", r$)
  hdrives = VAL(r$)
  '
  PRINT " Type of graphics adapter?"
  PRINT " (C=CGA, E=EGA, V=VGA)"
  DO
    r$ = UCASE$(INKEY$)
  LOOP UNTIL r$ <> "" AND INSTR("CEV", r$)
  display$ = r$
  '
  PRINT " Parallel printer check (Y/N)?"
  DO
    r$ = UCASE$(INKEY$)
  LOOP UNTIL r$ <> "" AND INSTR("YN", r$)
  testprint$ = r$
  '
  PRINT " System clock speed range?"
  PRINT " (A=4-12MHz, B=12-25MHz, C=25-66MHz)"
```

```
DO
  r$ = UCASE$(INKEY$)
LOOP UNTIL r$ <> "" AND INSTR("ABC", r$)
speed$ = r$
'
' Display users specification
'
CLS
PRINT ul$
PRINT " SELECTED SYSTEM SPECIFICATION"
PRINT ul$; ""
d$(1) = "": d$(2) = "": d$(3) = "": d$(4) = ""
'
PRINT " Number of floppy disk drives: "; fdrives
IF fdrives > 0 THEN
  IF fdrives = 1 THEN d$(1) = "A"
  IF fdrives = 2 THEN d$(1) = "A": d$(2) = "B"
  PRINT " Floppy drive(s): "; d$(1); d$(2)
END IF
'
PRINT " Number of hard disk drives: "; hdrives
IF hdrives > 0 THEN
  IF hdrives = 1 THEN d$(3) = "C"
  IF hdrives = 2 THEN d$(3) = "C": d$(4) = "D"
  PRINT " Hard drive(s): "; d$(3); d$(4)
END IF
'
PRINT " Display type: "; display$; "GA"
'
IF testprint$ = "Y" THEN
  PRINT " Parallel printer checking enabled"
ELSE
  PRINT " Parallel printer checking disabled"
END IF
'
IF speed$ = "A" THEN
  lim% = 10000
  PRINT " Clock speed range 4-12MHz (slow)"
END IF
IF speed$ = "B" THEN
  lim% = 20000
  PRINT " Clock speed range 12-25MHz (medium)"
END IF
IF speed$ = "C" THEN
  lim% = 30000
  PRINT " Clock speed range 25-66MHz (fast)"
END IF
'
  PRINT ul$
  PRINT " Is this configuration correct (Y/N)?"
  DO
    r$ = UCASE$(INKEY$)
  LOOP UNTIL r$ <> "" AND INSTR("YN", r$)
LOOP WHILE r$ = "N"
'
' Warn user to prepare for soak tests...
'
CLS
PRINT ul$
PRINT " ABOUT TO CARRY OUT SOAK TESTS"
PRINT ul$
```

```
IF print$ = "Y" THEN
  PRINT "WARNING: Check printer is on-line and ready!"
END IF
FOR n% = 1 TO 2
  IF d$(n%) <> "" THEN
    PRINT " WARNING: Insert a formatted disk with "
    PRINT "          at least 32K available in "; d$(n%
  END IF
NEXT n%
FOR n% = 3 TO 4
  IF d$(n%) <> "" THEN
    PRINT " WARNING: You must have at least 32K "
    PRINT "          free space on drive "; d$(n%)
  END IF
NEXT n%
GOSUB waitkey
'
cycle% = 1
  DO
  CLS
  PRINT ul$
  PRINT " SOAK TESTING SYSTEM"
  PRINT ul$
  PRINT " Soak test cycle: "; cycle%
  PRINT " Press <Q> during cycle to quit at"
  PRINT " end of current cycle."
  '
  ' First test; sound speaker
  '
  LOCATE 8, 2
  FOR n% = 1 TO 4
    BEEP
    GOSUB delay1
  NEXT n%
  '
  ' Second test; write to display using text mode
  '
  CLS
  FOR c% = 53 TO 48 STEP -1
    FOR location% = 0 TO (25 * 80)
      PRINT CHR$(c%);
    NEXT location%
  NEXT c%
  '
  ' Third test; write to display using graphics mode
  '
  ' Set-up graphics mode...
  IF display$ = "C" THEN
    SCREEN 1: COLOR 1, 2, 1: xc = 160: yc = 100
  END IF
  IF display$ = "E" THEN
    SCREEN 8: COLOR 15, 1: xc = 320: yc = 100
  END IF
  IF display$ = "V" THEN
    SCREEN 9: COLOR 15, 1: xc = 320: yc = 175
  END IF
  ' Display colour bars
  CLS
  IF display$ <> "C" THEN
    COLOR 0, 0
    CLS
```

```
  x = 0
  xold = 0
  inc = xc / 8
  FOR colour = 0 TO 15
    x = x + inc
    LINE (xold, 0)-STEP(x, 2 * yc), colour, BF
    xold = x
  NEXT colour
ELSE
  ' CGA uses only 4 colours...
  COLOR 0, 0, 1
  CLS
  x = 0
  xold = 0
  inc = xc / 2
  FOR colour = 0 TO 3
    x = x + inc
    LINE (xold, 0)-STEP(x, 2 * yc), colour, BF
    xold = x
  NEXT colour
END IF
' Hold display on screen for a while
GOSUB delay2
' Reset screen mode to text
SCREEN 2: SCREEN 0: COLOR 15, 1
'
' Fourth test; exercise each disk drive in turn
'
CLS
PRINT ul$
PRINT " Checking disk drives, please wait..."
PRINT ul$
FOR n% = 1 TO 4
  IF d$(n%) <> "" THEN
    ' Use root directory
    file$ = d$(n%) + ":\TEST.DAT"
    ' Reset error flag
    flag% = 0
    GOSUB tidy
    LOCATE 6, 2
    PRINT "Writing data to "; file$
    OPEN file$ FOR OUTPUT AS #1
    FOR ch% = 0 TO 4096
      PRINT #1, ch%
    NEXT ch%
    CLOSE #1
    GOSUB tidy
    LOCATE 6, 2
    PRINT "Reading data from "; file$
    OPEN file$ FOR INPUT AS #1
    FOR dat% = 0 TO 4096
      INPUT #1, ch%
      IF ch% <> dat% THEN flag% = 1
    NEXT dat%
    CLOSE #1
    GOSUB tidy
    IF flag% = 1 THEN
      LOCATE 6, 2
      PRINT "An error has occured!"
    ELSE
      LOCATE 6, 2
```

```
      PRINT "Drive "; d$(n%); " tested without error.
      LOCATE 7, 2
      PRINT "Erasing "; file$
      KILL file$
    END IF
  END IF
  GOSUB delay2
NEXT n%
'
' Fifth test: write to parallel printer
'
IF testprint$ = "Y" THEN
  LPRINT
  FOR c% = 32 TO 95
    LPRINT CHR$(c%);
  NEXT c%
  LPRINT
  FOR c% = 96 TO 159
    LPRINT CHR$(c%);
  NEXT c%
  LPRINT
  FOR c% = 160 TO 223
    LPRINT CHR$(c%);
  NEXT c%
  LPRINT
  FOR c% = 224 TO 255
    LPRINT CHR$(c%);
  NEXT c%
  LPRINT " Soak test cycle ="; cycle%
END IF
'
cycle% = cycle% + 1
'
' Does user want to  quit?
'
r$ = UCASE$(INKEY$)
IF r$ = "Q" THEN COLOR 15, 0: CLS : END
LOOP
'
' Utility subroutines
'
tidy:
' Erase any existing screen data
FOR cline% = 6 TO 10
  LOCATE cline%, 2
  PRINT STRING$(39, " ")
NEXT cline%
RETURN
'
waitkey:
PRINT ul$
PRINT " Press any key to continue...'
GOSUB keywait
RETURN
'
keywait:
DO
  r$ = INKEY$
LOOP UNTIL r$ <> ""
RETURN
'
```

```
delay1:
t% = 0
FOR t% = 0 TO lim%: NEXT t%
RETURN
'
delay2:
u% = 0
FOR u% = 0 TO 20
  GOSUB delay1
NEXT u%
RETURN
'
warning:
PRINT ul$
PRINT " An error has occured!"
GOSUB waitkey
RESUME main
```

## System check

This utility will tell you a lot about about your system. It will display
the system type (PC, XT, AT or PS/2), the system identification byte,
the current video mode and number of screen columns, the amount
of conventional (base) RAM present, the number of floppy drives,
serial ports and printers connected. The program will also let you
know whether a PC games adapter, DMA controller, maths
coprocessor and internal modem is present. The program also displays the ROM creation date.

The program will also provide you with an approximate indication
of the clock speed of your system compared with a basic specification AT machine. Note that the value indicated is *not* the clock speed
of your system. Instead, it is the clock rate that an AT specification
computer would have to operate at in order to achieve an equivalent
processing speed. Indications will range from about 22MHz for a fairly
basic 80386SX machine to well over 200MHz for an 80486DX operating at 33MHz.

```
' *****************************************************
' ** Name:      SYSTEM.BAS      Version: 0.1       **
' ** Function:  Checks and displays system info.   **
' ** Language:  Microsoft QuickBASIC               **
' ** Notes:     Assumes conventional ROM BIOS      **
' **            organisation                       **
' *****************************************************
'
' Initialise
'
ON ERROR GOTO warning
' Initialise in text mode
SCREEN 0
COLOR 15, 1
ul$ = STRING$(40, CHR$(205))
' Display main menu
DO
main:
CLS
PRINT ul$
PRINT " SYSTEM BOARD CHECK
PRINT ul$; ""
```

```
PRINT " Select option..."
PRINT " [I] = system information"
PRINT " [S] = speed check"
PRINT " [Q] = quit"
DO
  r$ = UCASE$(INKEY$)
LOOP UNTIL r$ <> "" AND INSTR("ISQ", r$)
IF r$ = "Q" THEN CLS : SCREEN 0: END
'
PRINT ul$
IF r$ = "S" THEN GOSUB speed
IF r$ = "I" THEN GOSUB information
LOOP
'
speed:
LOCATE 10, 2
PRINT "Checking clock speed..."
start! = TIMER
FOR i = 1 TO 10576
NEXT i
time! = TIMER
elapsed = time! - start!
LOCATE 10, 2
PRINT "Equiv. clock speed (AT): "; INT(60 / elapsed); "MHz'
GOSUB waitkey
RETURN
'
information:
' Get system ID byte from ROM
DEF SEG = &HF000
ident% = PEEK(&HFFFE)
' Determine type standard (PC, XT, AT etc)
IF ident% = 255 THEN type$ = "PC"
IF ident% = 254 OR ident% = 251 THEN type$ = "XT"
IF ident% = 253 THEN type$ = "PC Junior"
IF ident% = 252 THEN type$ = "AT or PS/2"
IF ident% = 250 THEN type$ = "PS/2 Model 30"
IF ident% = 249 THEN type$ = "PC Convertible"
IF ident% = 248 THEN type$ = "PS/2 Model 80"
' Get ROM creation date
DEF SEG = &HFFFF
dat$ = ""
FOR location% = 12 TO 5 STEP -1
  dat$ = CHR$(PEEK(location%)) + dat$
NEXT location%
' Get installed equipment list from RAM
DEF SEG = &H0
equlo% = PEEK(&H410)
equhi% = PEEK(&H411)
' Get usable memory
memlo% = PEEK(&H413)
memhi% = PEEK(&H414)
' Get keyboard status
kbdlo% = PEEK(&H417)
kbdhi% = PEEK(&H418)
' Get disk status
disks% = PEEK(&H441)
' Get video mode
vmode% = PEEK(&H449)
' Get column width
column% = PEEK(&H44A)
```

```
' Determine number of floppy drives present
ndriv% = 1 + ((equlo% AND 192) / 64)
' Determine number of serial ports present
nserp% = (equhi% AND 6) / 2
' Determine number of printers present
nprin% = ((equhi% AND 192) / 64)
' Determine whether a games adapter is present
IF (equhi% AND 16) THEN gam$ = "Yes" ELSE gam$ = "No"
' Determine whether a DMA controller is present
IF (equhi% AND 1) THEN dma$ = "No" ELSE dma$ = "Yes"
' Determine whether a maths coprocessor is present
IF (equlo% AND 2) THEN cop$ = "Yes" ELSE cop$ = "No"
' Determine whether a serial printer is present
IF (equhi% AND 32) THEN ser$ = "Yes" ELSE ser$ = "No"
' Display the information
LOCATE 9, 2: PRINT "System type:        "; type$
LOCATE 10, 2: PRINT "System ID:         "; HEX$(ident%)
LOCATE 11, 2: PRINT "Video mode:        "; vmode%
LOCATE 13, 2: PRINT "Screen columns:    "; colum%
LOCATE 13, 2: PRINT "Conventional RAM: "; 256 * memhi% + memlo%; "kbytes
LOCATE 14, 2: PRINT "Floppy drives:     "; ndriv%
LOCATE 15, 2: PRINT "Serial ports:      "; nserp%
LOCATE 16, 2: PRINT "Printers:          "; nprin%
LOCATE 17, 2: PRINT "PC games adapter:  "; gam$
LOCATE 18, 2: PRINT "DMA controller:    "; dma$
LOCATE 19, 2: PRINT "Maths coprocessor: "; cop$
LOCATE 20, 2: PRINT "Internal modem:    "; ser$
LOCATE 21, 2: PRINT "ROM creation date: "; dat$
GOSUB waitkey
RETURN
'
waitkey:
PRINT ul$
PRINT " Press any key to continue...
GOSUB keywait
RETURN
'
keywait:
DO
  r$ = INKEY$
LOOP UNTIL r$ <> ""
RETURN
'
warning:
PRINT ul$
PRINT " An error has occured!"
GOSUB waitkey
RESUME main
```

# Index

# MIDWIVES ON-CALL

Welcome to Melbourne Victoria Hospital—
and to the exceptional midwives
who make up the Melbourne Maternity Unit!

These midwives in a million work miracles
on a daily basis, delivering tiny bundles of joy
into the arms of their brand-new mums!

Amidst the drama and emotion of babies
arriving at all hours of the day and night, when
the shifts are over, somehow there's still time
for some sizzling out-of-hours romance…

Whilst these caring professionals might come
face-to-face with a whole lot of love in their
line of work, now it's their turn to find a
happy-ever-after of their own!

### *Midwives On-Call*

*Midwives, mothers and babies—
lives changing for ever…!*

**Dear Reader,**

A number of years ago my mother and I visited Australia. It was a beautiful and amazing country and I fell in love with it. I often speak of my visit to this day. When I was asked to join a group of world-class authors in writing the *Midwives On-Call* continuity, which was to be set in Australia, I jumped at the chance.

Ryan and Phoebe's story is set in Melbourne—one of the many places I had the pleasure of visiting. While in the area, my mother and I drove to the coast. On our way we visited a farm with a café much as Ryan and Phoebe do. We also went to see the Little Penguins come home. It's one of the most memorable things I've ever done. Like my characters, I had a lesson on what even the smallest of animals will do to take care of their young.

I'd be remiss if I didn't thank Fiona Lowe, one of my sister authors, who helped me—along with making me laugh—to work out the differences between the way the Aussies and the Americans speak. She was also wonderful in answering my questions about the area around Melbourne.

I hope you enjoy reading Ryan and Phoebe's love story. I like to hear from my readers. You can reach me at SusanCarlisle.com

*Susan*

# HIS
# BEST FRIEND'S
# BABY

BY
SUSAN CARLISLE

First published in Great Britain 2015
by Mills & Boon, an imprint of Harlequin (UK) Limited,
Eton House, 18-24 Paradise Road, Richmond, Surrey, TW9 1SR

© 2015 Harlequin Books S.A.

Special thanks and acknowledgement are given to Susan Carlisle
for her contribution to the *Midwives On-Call* series

ISBN: 978-0-263-25821-9

Harlequin (UK) Limited's policy is to use papers that are natural,
renewable and recyclable products and made from wood grown in
sustainable forests. The logging and manufacturing processes conform
to the legal environmental regulations of the country of origin.

Printed and bound in Great Britain
by CPI Antony Rowe, Chippenham, Wiltshire

**Susan Carlisle**'s love affair with books began when she made a bad grade in maths in the sixth grade. Not allowed to watch TV until she'd brought the grade up, she filled her time with books and became a voracious romance reader. She still has 'keepers' on the shelf to prove it. Because she loved the genre so much she decided to try her hand at creating her own romantic worlds. She still loves a good happily-ever-after story.

When not writing Susan doubles as a high school substitute teacher, which she has been doing for sixteen years. Susan lives in Georgia with her husband of twenty-eight years and has four grown children. She loves castles, travelling, cross-stitching, hats, James Bond and hearing from her readers.

### Books by Susan Carlisle

### Mills & Boon® Medical Romance™

#### *Heart of Mississippi*

*The Maverick Who Ruled Her Heart*
*The Doctor Who Made Her Love Again*

*The Doctor's Redemption*
*Snowbound with Dr Delectable*
*NYC Angels: The Wallflower's Secret*
*Hot-Shot Doc Comes to Town*
*The Nurse He Shouldn't Notice*
*Heart Surgeon, Hero...Husband?*

**Visit the author profile page at millsandboon.co.uk for more titles**

Joseph.
Thanks for being a great tool.

# MIDWIVES ON-CALL

*Midwives, mothers and babies—*
*lives changing for ever...!*

**Over the next four months enter the magical world**
**of the Melbourne Maternity Unit and the exceptional midwives there,**
**delivering tiny bundles of joy on a daily basis.**
**Now it's time to find a happy-ever-after of their own...**

**In April**, gorgeous Greek doctor Alessi Manos is determined to charm the
beautiful yet frosty Isla Delamere... but can he melt this ice queen's heart?
*Just One Night?* by Carol Marinelli

And when Dr Oliver Evans's estranged wife, Emily, crashes back into his life,
old passions are re-ignited. But brilliant Dr Evans is in for a surprise...
Emily has two foster-children!
*Meant-to-Be Family* by Marion Lennox

**In May**, midwife Sophia Toulson and hard-working paramedic Aiden Harrison
share an explosive attraction... but will they overcome their tragic pasts
and take a chance on love?
*Always the Midwife* by Alison Roberts

And hot-shot surgeon Tristan Hamilton's passionate night
with pretty student midwife Flick has unexpected consequences!
*Midwife's Baby Bump* by Susanne Hampton

**In June**, free-spirited locum midwife Ally Parker
meets top GP and gorgeous single dad Flynn Reynolds.
Is she finally ready to settle down with a family of her own?
*Midwife... to Mum!* by Sue MacKay

And when beautiful redhead Phoebe Taylor turns up on ex-army medic
Ryan Matthews's doorstep there's only one thing keeping them apart:
she's his best friend's widow... and eight months pregnant!
*His Best Friend's Baby* by Susan Carlisle

Finally, join us **in July**, when brooding city surgeon Noah Jackson
meets compassionate Outback midwife Lilia Cartwright.
Could Lilia be the key to Noah's locked-away heart?
*Unlocking Her Surgeon's Heart* by Fiona Lowe

And renowned English obstetrician Darcie Green
might think playboy Lucas Elliot is nothing but trouble—
but is there more to this gorgeous doc than meets the eye?
*Her Playboy's Secret* by Tina Beckett

**Experience heartwarming emotion and pulse-racing drama in**
*Midwives On-Call*
**this sensational eight-book continuity**
**from Mills & Boon® Medical Romance™**

**These books are also available in eBook format**
**from millsandboon.co.uk**

# CHAPTER ONE

*WHAT AM I doing here?* Phoebe Taylor asked herself for the hundredth time, pulling her light coat closer. She could no longer get it to meet in the middle. Bowing her head against a gust of Melbourne, Australia, wind, she walked on. It would rain soon.

She looked at the name on the street sign. Morris Lane. This was the correct place. Phoebe didn't even have to check the paper in her hand that was shoved into her pocket. She had it memorized. She'd read it often during the past few weeks.

When had she turned into such a pathetic and needy person?

It had happened slowly, over the last eight months as her middle had expanded. She'd always heard that a baby changed you. She'd had no idea how true those words were until it had happened to her. She was even more fearful of the changes she faced in the weeks ahead. The fact she'd be handling them all on her own, had no one to rely on, frightened her.

She started down the cobblestone street lined with town houses. Joshua had written that if she needed anything she could contact Ryan Matthews. But who was she to him? An old army buddy's wife. People said those types of things all the time but few meant them. But she had no one else to turn to. There were teachers she worked with, but they all had their own lives, husbands and children. They didn't have time to hold her hand. There were plenty of acquaintances but none that she would call on. She'd take this chance because Joshua had said to. And this was Joshua's baby.

But would this guy Ryan help her? Be there for her during the delivery afterwards? Take Joshua's place at the birthing suite? *Yeah, right.* She didn't see any man agreeing to that job. Who took on someone else's widow and unborn child? She could never ask that of him. Would she want to? She didn't know this man outside of Joshua saying he was an upstanding mate.

When the walls of reality had started closing in on her and panic had arrived, she'd been unable to think of where to turn. Joshua's letter had called to her. Seemed to offer her salvation. Phoebe inhaled and released a breath. She'd come this far. She wouldn't turn back now. What was the worst Ryan Matthews could do? Send her away? Act like he'd never heard of her?

What she was sure of was she didn't want to feel alone anymore. She wanted someone to lean on. Be near a person who had a connection to Joshua. Hear a story or two that she could tell her son or daughter about their father. Joshua and Ryan had been brothers in arms. Been there for each other. Joshua had assured her in his last letter seven months ago that if she needed anything, *anything*, Ryan was the person to find. Desperate, she was going to his house to see if that was true.

Phoebe located the house number. It was painted above the door in black against the white frame of the Victorian house. The car traveling down the street drew her attention for a second. She pulled the paper out and looked at the address again, then at the entrance once more. Studying the steps to the door, she hesitated. Now she was stalling.

What was she going to say to this guy?

She'd been rehearsing her speech for days and still didn't know if she could get it out. On the tram coming across town she'd practiced again but couldn't seem to get it right. Everything she'd planned made her sound crazy. Maybe she was. But she had to say something, give some explanation as to why she'd turned up on his doorstep.

*Hi, I'm Phoebe Taylor. You were a friend of my husband's. He said if I ever needed anything to come see you. So here I am.*

That should get his attention. She placed a hand on her protruding middle and chuckled dryly. *His first thought will probably be I'm here to accuse him of being the father.*

The wind gusted again as she mounted the steps. There were no potted plants lining them, like most of the other houses. Holding the handrail, she all but pulled her way up to the stoop. Could she get any bigger? Her midwife Sophia had assured her she could, and would.

After catching her breath, Phoebe knocked on the door. She waited. Thankfully, the small alcove afforded her some shelter from the wind.

When there was no answer, she rapped again. Seconds went by and still no one came. She refused to go back home without speaking to Ryan. It had taken her months to muster the courage to come in the first place. It was getting late, surely he'd be home soon.

To the right side of the door was a small wooden bench. She'd just wait for a while to see if he showed up. Bracing a hand against the wall, she eased herself down. She chuckled humorously at the picture she must make. Like a beach ball sitting on top of a flowerpot.

She needed to rest anyway. Everything fatigued her

these days. Trying to keep up with twenty grade fivers wore her out but she loved her job. At least her students kept her mind off the fact that she was having a baby soon. Alone.

Phoebe never made a habit of feeling sorry for herself, had prided herself on being strong, facing life head-on. She'd always managed to sound encouraging and supportive when Joshua had prepared to leave on tour again and again. When they'd married, she'd been aware of what she was getting into. So why was the idea of having this baby alone making her come emotionally undone?

Pulling her coat tighter and leaning her head into the corner of the veranda, she closed her eyes. She'd just rest a few minutes.

It was just after dark when Ryan Matthews pulled his sporty compact car into his usual parking spot along the street. It had been drizzling during his entire drive from the hospital. Street lamps lit the area. The trees cast shadows along the sidewalk and even across the steps leading to homes.

He'd had a long day that had involved more than one baby delivery and one of those a tough one. Nothing had seemed to go as planned. Not one but two of the babies had been breech. Regardless, the babies had joined the world kicking and screaming. He was grateful. All the other difficulties seemed to disappear the second he heard a healthy cry. He'd take welcoming a life over dealing with death any day.

Stepping out of the car, he reached behind the driver's seat and grabbed his duffel bag stuffed with his street clothes. Too exhausted to change, he still wore his hospital uniform. As much as he loved his job, thirty-six hours straight was plenty. He was looking forward to a hot shower, bed and the next day off. It would be his first chance in over two weeks to spend time in his workshop. A half-finished chair, along with a table he'd promised to repair for a friend, waited. He wanted to think of nothing and just enjoy the process of creating something with his hands.

Duffel in hand, a wad of dirty uniforms under his arm, he climbed the steps. The light remained on over his door as he'd left it. Halfway up the steps he halted. There was an obviously pregnant woman asleep on his porch. He saw pregnant women regularly in his job as a midwife at Melbourne Victoria Hospital's maternity unit. Today more than he'd wanted to. As if he didn't have a full load at the hospital, they were now showing up on his doorstep.

By the blue tint of the woman's lips and the way she was huddled into a ball, she'd been there for some time. Why was she out in the cold? She should be taking better care of herself, especially at this stage in her pregnancy. Her arms rested on her protruding middle. She wore a fashionable knit cap that covered the top of her head. Strawberry-blond hair twisted around her face and across her shoulders. With the rain and the temperature dropping, she must be uncomfortable.

Taking a resigned breath, Ryan moved farther up the steps. As he reached the top the mysterious woman roused and her eyes popped open. They were large and a dark sable brown with flecks of gold. He'd never seen more mesmerizing or sad ones in his life.

His first instinct was to protect her. He faltered. That wasn't a feeling he experienced often. He made it his practice not to become involved with anyone. Not to care too deeply. He tamped the feeling down. Being tired was all there was to it. "Can I help you?"

The woman slowly straightened. She tugged the not-heavy-enough-for-the-weather coat closer as she stared at him.

When she didn't answer right away he asked in a weary voice, "Do you need help?"

"Are you Ryan Matthews?" Her soft Aussie accent carried in the evening air.

His eyes widened and he stepped back half a pace, stopping before tumbling. Did he know her? She was such a tiny thing she couldn't be more than a girl. Something about her looked familiar. Could he have seen her in the waiting room sometime?

Ryan glanced at her middle again. He'd always made it a practice to use birth control. Plus, this female was far too young for him. She must be seeking medical help.

"Yes."

"I'm Phoebe Taylor."

Was that supposed to mean something to him? He squinted, studying her face in the dim light. "Have we met before?"

"I should go." She reached out to touch the wall as if she planned to use it as support in order to stand. When she did, a slip of paper fluttered to the stoop.

Ryan picked it up. In blue pen was written his name, address and phone number. Had she been given it at the clinic?

He glared at her. "Where did you get this?"

"I think I had better go." She made a movement toward the steps. "I'm sorry. I shouldn't have come. I'll go."

"I'm afraid I don't understand."

"I don't know for sure what I wanted. I need to go." Her words came out high-pitched and shaky.

He put out a hand as if she were a skittish animal he was trying to reassure. "Think of the baby." That must be what this was all about.

Her eyes widened, taking on a hysterical look. She jerked away from him. "I've done nothing but think of this baby. I have to go. I'm sorry I shouldn't have come." She sniffled. "I don't know…" another louder sniffle "…what I was thinking. You don't know me." Her head went into her hands and she started to cry in earnest. "I'll go. This is…" she sucked in air "…too embarrassing. You must think I'm mad."

He began to think she was. Who acted this way?

She struggled to stand. Ryan took her elbow and helped her.

"I've never done anything…like this before. I need to go."

Ryan could only make out a few of her garbled words through her weeping. He glanced around. If she continued to carry on like this his neighbors would be calling the law.

She shivered. What had she said her name was? Phoebe?

"You need to calm down. Being so upset isn't good for the baby. It's getting cold out and dark. Come in. Let your jacket dry." He needed to get her off the street so he could figure out what this was all about. This wasn't what he had planned for his evening.

"No, I've already embarrassed myself enough. I think I'd better go."

Thankfully the crying had stopped but it had left her eyes large and luminous.

She looked up at him with those eyes laced with something close to pain, and said in a low voice, "You knew my husband."

"Your husband?"

"Joshua Taylor."

Ryan cringed. Air quit moving to his lungs. JT was part of his past. The piece of his life he had put behind him. Ryan hadn't heard JT's name in seven months. Not since he'd had word that he had been killed when his convoy had been bombed.

Why was his wife here? Ryan didn't want to think of the war, or JT. He'd moved on.

They had been buddies while they'd been in Iraq. Ryan had been devastated when he'd heard JT had been killed. He'd been one more in a long list of men Ryan had cared about, shared his life with, had considered family. Now that was gone, all gone. He wasn't going to let himself feel that pain ever again. When he'd left the service he'd promised himself never to let anyone matter that much. He wasn't dragging those ugly memories up for anyone's wife, not even JT's.

Ryan had known there was a wife, had even seen her picture fixed to Joshua's CHU or containerized housing unit room. That had been over five years ago, before he'd left the service. This was his friend's widow?

He studied her. Yes, she did bear a resemblance to the young, bright-faced girl in the pictures. Except that spark of life that had fascinated him back then had left her eyes.

"You need to come in and get warm, then I'll see you get home." He used his midwife-telling-the-mother-to-push voice.

She made a couple of soft sniffling sounds but said no more.

Ryan unlocked the door. Pushing it back, he offered her space to enter before him. She accepted the invitation. She stopped in the middle of the room as if unsure what to do next. He turned on the light and dropped his bag and dirty clothes in the usual spot on top of all the other dirty clothes lying next to the door.

For the first time, he noted what sparse living conditions he maintained. He had a sofa, a chair, a TV that sat on a wooden crate and was rarely turned on. Not a single picture hung on the walls. He didn't care about any of that. It wasn't important. All he was interested in was bringing babies safely into the world and the saws in his workshop.

"Have a seat. I'll get you some tea," he said in a gruff voice.

Bracing on the arm of the sofa, she lowered herself to the cushion. She pulled the knit cap from her head and her hair fell around her shoulders.

Ryan watched, stunned by the sight. The urge to touch those glowing tresses caught him by surprise. His fingers tingled to test the texture, to see if it was as soft and silky as it looked.

Her gaze lifted, meeting his. Her cheekbones were high and a touch of pink from the cold made the fairness of her skin more noticeable. Her chin trembled. The sudden fear that she might start crying again went through him. He cleared his throat. "I'll get you that tea."

Phoebe watched as the rather stoic American man walked out of the room. Why had he looked at her that way? Where was all that compassion and caring that Joshua had written about in his letter? Ryan obviously wanted her gone as soon as possible. He wasn't at all what she'd expected. Nothing like Joshua had described him. She shivered, the cold and damp seeping through her jacket. What had she been thinking? This wasn't the warm and welcoming guy that Joshua had said he would be. He hadn't even reacted to her mentioning Joshua.

He was tall, extremely tall. He ducked slightly to go through the doorway. Joshua had been five feet eleven. Ryan Matthews was far taller, with shoulders that went with that height.

Though he was an attractive man with high cheekbones and a straight nose, his eyes held a melancholy gaze. As if he'd seen things and had had to do things he never wanted to remember, much less talk about.

A few minutes later Ryan handed her a mug with a tea-bag string hanging over the side. He hadn't even bothered to ask her what she wanted to drink. Did he treat everybody he met with such disinterest?

"I'm a coffee drinker myself. An associate left the tea here or I wouldn't have had it."

She bet it was a female friend. He struck her as the type of man who had women around him all the time. "You are an American."

"Yes."

"Joshua never said that you weren't Australian."

He took a seat in the lone chair in the room. "I guess he didn't notice after a while."

She looked around. Whatever women he brought here didn't stay around long. His place showed nothing of the feminine touch. In fact, it was only just a step above un-livable. If she had to guess, there was nothing but a bed and a carton for a table in the bedroom.

Phoebe watched him drink the coffee, the smell of which wafted her way as she took a sip of her tea.

Quiet minutes later he asked, "How long were you on my doorstep?"

"I don't know. I left home around four."

"It's after seven now." His tone was incredulous. "You've been waiting that long?"

"I fell asleep."

The tension left his face. "That's pretty easy to do in your condition."

"I can't seem to make it without a nap after teaching all day."

"Teaching?"

"I teach at Fillmore Primary School. Grade Five."

He seemed as if he was trying to remember something. "That's right. JT said you were going to school to be a teacher."

At the mention of Joshua they both looked away.

He spoke more to his coffee cup than to her. "I was sorry to hear about Joshua."

"Me, too." He and Joshua were supposed to have been best buddies and that was all he had to say. This guy was so distant he acted as if he'd barely known Joshua. She wouldn't be getting any help or friendship from him.

He looked at her then as if he was unsure about what he might have heard. "Is there something you need from me?"

Phoebe flinched at his directness. Not anymore. She needed to look elsewhere. She wasn't sure what she'd expected from him but this wasn't it. Joshua's letter had assured her that Ryan Matthews would do anything to help her but this man's attitude indicated he wasn't interested in getting involved.

"To tell you the truth, I'm not sure. You were a friend of Joshua's and I just thought…"

"And what did you think? Do you need money?"

"Mr. Matthews, I don't need your money. I have a good job and Joshua's widow and orphans' pension."

"Then I can't imagine what I can do for you, unless you need someone to deliver your baby?"

"Why would I come to you for that?"

"Because I'm a midwife."

"I thought he said you were a medic."

"I was in the army but now I work as a midwife. I still don't understand why you're here. If you need someone to deliver your baby you need to come to the Prenatal Clinic during office hours."

"I already have one. Sophia Toulson."

His brows drew together. "She's leaving soon. Did she send you here?"

She lowered her head.

Had he heard her say, "I just needed a friend, I guess." *A friend?*

He couldn't believe that statement. What kind of person showed up at a stranger's house, asking them to be their friend? Surely she had family and friends in town. Why would she come looking for him now? After all this time. She said she didn't need money so what did she want from him?

"Where's the father of the baby?"

Phoebe sat straighter and looked him directly in the eyes. "Joshua is the father of the baby."

"When...?"

"When he was last home on leave. I wrote to him about the baby but he was..." she swallowed hard "...gone by then." She placed the cup in the crack between the cushions, unable to bend down far enough to put it on the floor. Pushing herself to a standing position, she said, "I think I'd better go."

He glanced out the window. The rain had picked up and the wind was blowing stronger. He huffed as he unfolded from the chair. "I'll drive you home."

"That's not necessary. I can catch the tram."

"Yeah, but you'll get wet getting there and from it to your house. I'll drive you. Where's home?"

Despite his tough exterior, she liked his voice. It was slow, deep and rich. Maybe a Texan or Georgian drawl. "I live in Box Hill."

"That's out toward Ferntree Gully, isn't it?"

"Yes."

"Okay. Let's go."

He sounded resigned to driving her instead of being

helpful. This Ryan Matthews didn't seem to care one way or another. Had Joshua gotten him wrong or had Ryan changed?

"If you insist."

"I do." He was already heading toward the door.

"Then thank you."

This trip to see Ryan had been a mistake on a number of levels. But she had learned one thing. She was definitely alone in the world.

Forty-five minutes later, Ryan pulled onto a tree-lined street with California bungalow-style houses. The lights glowing in the homes screamed warmth, caring and permanency, all the things that he didn't have in his life, didn't want or deserve.

Since they'd left his place Phoebe hadn't tried to make conversation. She'd only spoken when giving him directions. He was no closer than he'd been earlier to knowing what she wanted.

"Next left," she said in a monotone.

He turned there she indicated.

"Last house on the right. The one with the veranda light on."

Ryan pulled his car to the curb. He looked at her house. It appeared well cared-for. A rosebush grew abundantly in the front yard. An archway indicated the main door. The only light shining was the one over it.

"Is anyone expecting you?"

"No."

"You live by yourself?"

"Yes. Did you think I lived with my parents?"

"I just thought since Joshua was gone and you were having a baby, someone would be nearby. Especially as close as you're obviously getting to the due date."

"No, there's no one. My parents were killed in an auto accident the year before I married. My only brother had moved to England two years before that. We were never really close. There is a pretty large age difference between us." The words were matter-of-fact but she sounded lost.

"Surely someone from Joshua's family is planning to help out?"

"No."

"Really? Why not?"

"If you must know, they didn't want him to marry me. They had someone else picked out. Now that he's gone, they want nothing more to do with me."

"That must have been hard to hear."

"Yeah. It hurt." Her tone said she still was having a hard time dealing with that knowledge. He couldn't imagine someone not wanting to have anything to do with their grandchild.

"Not even the baby?"

She placed her hand on her belly. "Not even the baby. They told me it would be too hard to look at him or her and know Joshua wasn't here."

"You've got to be kidding!" Ryan's hands tightened on the steering wheel.

"No. That isn't something that I would kid about."

"I'm sorry."

"So am I. But I just think of it as their loss. If that's the way they feel, then it wouldn't ever be healthy for the baby to be around them. We'll be better off without them."

Ryan looked at the house one more time. By its appearance, the baby would be well cared for and loved. "I'll see you to the door."

"That's not necessary." She opened the car door.

He climbed out and hurried around the automobile. She'd started to her feet. He held out a hand. After a second she accepted it. His larger one swallowed her smaller one. Hers was soft and smooth, very feminine. So very different from his. A few seconds later she seemed to gather strength. She removed her hand from his and stood taller.

"Come on, I'll see you to the door." Even to his own ears it sounded as if he was ready to get rid of her.

"I'll be fine. You've already helped enough by driving me home." She started up the walk lined with flowers and stopped, then looked back at him. "I'm sorry to have bothered you."

Ryan waited to see if she would turn around again, but she didn't. When the light went out on the porch he pulled away from the curb.

Phoebe closed the door behind her with a soft click. Through the small window she saw the lights of Ryan's car as he drove off.

What had she expected? That he would immediately say, "I'll take care of you, I'll be there for you"? She moved through the house without turning any lights on. She knew where every piece of furniture and every lamp was located. With the exception of the few times that Joshua had been home during their marriage, no one had lived with her. Nothing was ever moved unless she did it.

Their marriage had consisted mostly of them living apart. They had met when she was eighteen and fresh out of school. The tall, dark man dressed in a uniform had taken her breath away. Joshua had made it clear what it would be like, being married to a serviceman, and she had been willing to take on that life. She was strong and could deal with it.

It hurt terribly that his parents had said they wouldn't be around to help her with the baby. He or she needed grandparents in their life. With her parents gone they were the only ones. She'd been devastated when she'd received the letter stating they would not be coming around. They had sent some money. Phoebe had thought about returning it but had decided to start a fund at the bank for the baby instead. Not knowing their grandchild would be their loss.

For her the baby was about having a small part of Joshua still in her life. Her hope was that Joshua's parents might change their minds. Either way, right now she was on her own. Not a feeling she enjoyed. In a moment of weakness she'd gone to Ryan's house, but she didn't plan to let him know how bone deep the hurt was that Joshua's parents wanted nothing to do with her. How lonely she was for someone who'd known and loved Joshua.

She turned on the lamp beside her bed and glanced at the picture of her and Joshua smiling. They'd been married eight years but had spent maybe a year together in total. That had been a week or two here, or a month there. They had always laughed that their marriage was like being on vacation instead of the day in, day out experience of living together. Even their jobs had been vastly different. Joshua had found his place in the service more than with her. She'd found contentment in teaching. It had given her the normalcy and stability that being married to a husband who popped in and out hadn't.

Each time Joshua had come home it had been like the first heart-pounding, whirlwind and all-consuming first love that had soon died out and become the regular thud of everyday life. They'd had to relearn each other and getting in the groove had seemed harder to achieve. As they'd grown older they'd both seemed to pull away. She'd had her set life and routine and Joshua had invaded it when he'd returned.

Removing her clothes, she laid them over a chair and pulled her pj's out of the chest of drawers. She groaned.

The large T-shirt reminded her of a tent that she and Joshua had camped in just after they'd married. The shirt was huge and still she almost filled it.

Pulling it over her head, she rubbed her belly. The baby had been a complete surprise. She'd given up on ever having children. She and Joshua had decided not to have them since he hadn't been home often enough. She wasn't sure whether or not she'd cared when they'd married or if she'd believed he would leave the army and come home to stay. The idea of having a family had been pushed far into the future. It had become easier just not to consider it. So when she'd come up pregnant it had been a shock.

Her fingers went to her middle, then to her eye, pushing the moisture away. She'd grown up with the dream of having a family one day. Now she was starting a family but with half of it missing.

She pulled the covers back on the bed and climbed in between the cool sheets. Bringing the blanket up around her, she turned on her side, stuffing an extra pillow between the mattress and her tummy. The baby kicked. She laid her hand over the area, feeling the tiny heel that pushed against her side.

The last time Joshua had been home they'd even talked of separating. They'd spent so little time together she'd felt like she hadn't even known her husband anymore. She not only carried Joshua's baby but the guilt that he'd died believing she no longer cared. Friendship had been there but not the intense love that she should have had for a husband.

# CHAPTER TWO

THE NEXT MORNING Ryan flipped on the light switch that lit the stairs that led down to his workshop. He'd picked out this town house because of this particular space. Because it was underground it helped block the noise of the saws from the neighbors. The area was also close to the hospital, which made it nice when he had to be there quickly.

Going down the stairs, he scanned the area. A band saw filled one corner, while stationed in the center of the room was a table saw. The area Ryan was most interested in right now was the workbench against the far wall. There lay the half-made chair that he had every intention of finishing today. He would still have to spend another few days staining it.

Picking up a square piece of sandpaper, he began running it up and down one of the curved rockers. He'd made a couple of rockers when the nursery of the hospital had needed new ones. A number of the nurses had been so impressed they'd wanted one of their own. Since then he'd been busy filling orders in his spare time.

Outside the moments when a baby was born and offered its first spirited view of the new world with a shout, being in his shop was the place he was the most happy. Far better than his life in the military.

When he could stand it no longer, he'd resigned his commission. He'd had enough of torn bodies. He ran his hand along the expanse of the wood. It was level but not quite smooth enough. Now he was doing something he loved. But thoughts of Phoebe kept intruding.

He couldn't believe that had been Joshua's wife at his home the night before. Ryan had been living in Melbourne for five years. Joshua had always let him know when he was home, but in all that time he'd never met his wife. It had seemed like his friend's visits had come at the busiest times, and even though the two of them had managed to have a drink together, Ryan had never seen her. Now all of a sudden she had turned up on his doorstep.

Even after he'd gotten her calmed down he hadn't been sure what she'd wanted. It didn't matter. Still, he owed Joshua. He should check on her. But first he'd see what Sophia could tell him.

The next morning, at the clinic, Ryan flipped through his schedule for the day. He had a number of patients to see but none had babies due any time soon. Maybe he would get a few days' reprieve before things got wild again.

"You look deep in thought."

He recognized Sophia's voice and looked up. "Not that deep. You're just the person I wanted to talk to."

The slim woman took one of the functional office chairs in front of his desk. "What can I do for you?"

"I was just wondering what you know about Phoebe Taylor."

"Trying to steal my patients now?" Her eyes twinkled as she asked.

Ryan gave her a dubious look.

She grinned. "She's due in about five weeks. What's happened?"

"She was waiting for me when I got home yesterday. At first I thought she'd gotten my name and address from

you. That you were sending her to me because you would
be on your honeymoon when it was time to deliver."

Sophia shook her dark-haired head. "Oh, no, it wasn't
me. But I remember she mentioned you at one of her ap-
pointments and said she had your address."

"I thought maybe she was looking for a midwife. She
later told me she was the wife of an army buddy of mine."

"Yes, she told me that you were good friends with her
husband. Did she seem okay?"

"Not really. It was all rather confusing and she was
quite emotional. I let her get warm, gave her something
to drink and took her home."

"She's usually steady as a rock. I'll find out what's
going on at her next appointment."

"Thanks, Sophia. I owe her husband."

"I understand. You are coming to my wedding, aren't
you?"

Sophia was marrying Aiden Harrison in a few weeks
and she wanted everyone there for the event. Ryan wasn't
into weddings. He'd never been so close to someone he'd
felt like marrying them. After his years in the military
he was well aware of how short life could be. Too young
to really understand that kind of love when he'd entered
the army, he'd soon realized he didn't want to put someone through what Phoebe Taylor had been experiencing.

He didn't understand that type of love. Knew how fleet-
ing it could be. His parents sure hadn't known how to show
love. His foster-parents had been poor examples of that
also. They had taken care of his physical needs but he'd
always been aware that they hadn't really cared about him.
The army had given him purpose that had filled that void,
for a while. That had lasted for years until the hundreds of
faces of death had become heavier with every day. He well
understood that losses lasted a lifetime. Even delivering

babies and seeing the happiness on families' faces didn't change that. Those men he'd served with were gone. Yet, like JT, they were always with him.

He smiled at Sophia. "I plan to be there. I'll even dust off my suit for the occasion."

"That's great. See you later."

Ryan had seen his last patient for the day and was headed out the glass doors of the Prenatal Clinic in the hospital. A woman was coming in. He stopped to hold the door for her, then glanced up. It was Phoebe Taylor.

"Ah, hey."

"Hello." Her gaze flicked up at him and then away.

Phoebe must have been coming here for months. How many times had he passed her without having any idea who she was? She looked far less disheveled than she had two days ago. Her hair lay along her shoulders. Dressed in a brown, tan and blue dotted top over brown slacks and low-heeled shoes, she looked professional, classy and fragile.

"Are you looking for me?" Ryan asked.

"I'm here for my appointment with Sophia."

Another mother-to-be came up behind Phoebe. She moved back and out of the way, allowing the woman to go past her. Ryan held the door wide, moving out into the hall. He said to Phoebe, "May I speak to you for a minute?"

A terrified look flicked in her eyes before she gave him a resigned nod. He had the impression that if she could forget they had already met, she'd gladly do so.

Before he could say anything she started, "About the other evening. I'm sorry. I shouldn't have put you on the spot. I had no right to do that."

Here she was the one apologizing and he was the one who should be. "Not a problem. I should have visited you after Joshua died."

Her look was earnest. "That's all right. I understand. Well, I have to get to my appointment."

Apparently whatever she'd needed had been resolved.

"It was nice to meet you, Phoebe."

"You, too." She walked by him, opened the door and went through it. With a soft swish it closed behind her.

Why did he feel as if he needed to say or do more?

Ryan made it as far as his car before curiosity and a nagging guilt caused him to return to the clinic. He waited until Phoebe was finished with her appointment. Phoebe might not agree to him taking her to dinner, but he was going to try. He needed to know why she'd come to see him and even more if there was some way he could help her.

Now that she had contacted him he felt like he owed Joshua that.

On the way to his office he passed a nurse and asked that she let him know when Mrs. Taylor was finished.

Thirty minutes later the nurse popped her head in the door and said Phoebe was on her way out.

Ryan hurried to the waiting room and spotted her as she reached the door. When he called her name she stopped and turned. Her eyes widened in astonishment, then filled with wariness.

"I thought you had left." Phoebe sounded as if she had hoped not to see him again. After his behavior the other night he shouldn't be surprised.

"I came back. I wanted to ask you something."

She raised her brows.

Phoebe wasn't opening the door wide for him. She wouldn't be making this easy.

Thankfully this late in the day the waiting room was empty. "I wondered if I could buy you dinner?"

Phoebe turned her head slightly, as if both studying and judging him. He must have really put her off the other eve-

ning. He prided himself on his rapport with people, especially pregnant women and their families. He had let this
one down. The guilt he'd felt doubled in size.

"Please. I'd like to make up for how I acted the other
night."

"You don't owe me any apologies. I'm the one who
showed up on your doorstep unannounced."

"Why don't we both stop taking blame and agree to
start again?"

Her eyes became less unsure. "I guess we could do
that."

"Then why don't we start by having a burger together?"

"Okay." She agreed with less enthusiasm than he would
have liked.

"I know a place just down the street that serves good
food. Andrew's Burgers."

"I've heard of it but never been there."

"Great. Do you mind walking?"

"No, I haven't had my exercise today."

Ryan looked at her. If it hadn't been for the baby, she
would have been a slim woman. With her coloring she was
an eye-catcher, pregnant or not. Her soft, lilting voice was
what really caught his attention.

"If you'll wait I'd like to lock up my office."

She nodded. When he returned she was sitting in one
of the reclining chairs in the waiting room with her hands
resting on the baby.

"I'm ready."

Phoebe looked at him. She pushed against the chair
arm to support herself as she stood. "I think this baby is
going to be a giant."

"Every mother-to-be that I see thinks that about this
time."

As they made their way down the hall to the elevators, Ryan asked, "So how're you and the baby doing?"

A soft smile came to her lips. "Sophia says we're both doing great. I'll have to start coming to clinic every week soon. I just hate that I'm losing her as my midwife. I've become very attached."

"You are getting close."

"I am."

There was depression in her tone that he didn't understand. He knew little about her, but she struck him as someone who would be ecstatic about holding a new life in her hands and caring for someone. Yet he sensed a need in her that he couldn't put a finger on.

They went down the six floors to the lobby of the art deco building and out into the sunlight. The restaurant was a few blocks from the hospital.

"Let's cross the street. I know a shortcut through the park."

She followed him without question. A few minutes later they exited the park and were once again walking along the sidewalk. A couple of times they had to work themselves around other people walking briskly in the opposite direction. Ryan matched his stride to her shorter one and ran interference when someone looked as if they might bump into her.

"I can walk without help, you know."

He glanced at her. She was small but she gave off an air of confidence. It was in complete contrast to her actions that night at his house. Something was going on with her. "I know, but I wouldn't want you to accidentally fall and Sophia would have my head for it."

"I think they gave up chopping off heads in Australia a long time ago," she said in a dry tone.

"Still, I'm kind of scared of Sophia. I don't know if I could face her if I let you get hurt."

That got a smile out of her. "Here we are," Ryan said as he pulled the glass door of the restaurant open and allowed Phoebe to enter ahead of him.

She wasn't sure sharing a meal with Ryan was such a good idea. He'd asked nicely enough and she hadn't eaten out in so long she hadn't had the heart to say no. She suspected either his curiosity or some kind of obligation he felt toward Joshua had made him ask. No way had he changed overnight into being the emotional support she'd naively hoped he might be. A nice meal shared with someone was all she expected to get out of the next hour.

When Ryan was asked if they wanted a booth or table he glanced at her middle and grinned. He had a wide smile and nice even teeth. "I guess we'd better go for a table."

They were directed to one. The restaurant was decorated in a 1950s diner style, all chrome, red-covered chairs and white tile on the floor. Lighting hung over each booth and table. It was still early for the dinner crowd so it wasn't noisy. Phoebe wasn't sure if she considered that good or bad.

She took a seat. Ryan sat in the chair across the table from her.

"So I need to order a hamburger, I'm thinking." Phoebe took the menu out of the metal rack on the table.

"They have good ones. But there are also other things just as good."

The waitress arrived and took their drink order. Phoebe opened a menu but Ryan didn't. When the waitress returned with their glasses, she asked what they would like to order. Phoebe decided on the burger without onions and Ryan ordered his with everything.

The waitress left and Ryan asked, "No onions?"

"They don't agree with me."

"That's typical. I know a mother who said she couldn't cook bacon the entire first three months of her pregnancy."

"Smells used to bother me but that has become better."

Ryan crossed his arms and leaned on the table. "So do you know if it's a boy or a girl?"

"I don't know."

"Really?"

Phoebe almost laughed at his look of shock. "Don't want to know. I like surprises."

"That's pretty amazing in this day and age where everyone is wanting to know the sex and you don't. I wouldn't want to know, either. One of my favorite moments during a delivery is the look on the parents' faces when they discover the sex."

Phoebe got the impression that she'd gone up a notch in his estimation.

"You know, I don't know any other male midwife."

"There are only a few of us around. More in Australia than in the US."

"So why did you become one?"

"I wanted to do something that made me smile." He picked up his drink. "I was tired of watching people's lives being destroyed or lost when I was in the service. I wanted to do something that involved medicine but had a happy ending. What's better than bringing a life into the world?"

He was right. What was better than that?

The waitress brought their meals. They didn't speak for a while.

It fascinated Phoebe that they were virtual strangers but seem to be content sharing a meal together. This evening stood in sharp contrast to when they had met. Being around this Ryan put her at ease for some reason. After their first meeting she would have sworn that couldn't be possible.

She ate half her burger and chips before pushing them aside.

"You're eating for two, you know," Ryan said with a raised brow.

"The problem is that when this baby comes I don't want to look like I ate for three." She wiped her mouth with her napkin and placed it on the table.

"How's your weight gain?"

Phoebe leaned back in her chair. "That's certainly a personal question."

"I'm a midwife. I ask that question all the time."

"Yes, but you aren't my midwife."

He pushed his empty plate away. "I'll concede that. But I'm only asking out of concern."

"If it'll make you feel better my weight is just fine. I'm within the guidelines."

"Good. You look like you're taking care of yourself."

"I try to eat right and get some exercise every day." She looked pointedly at her plate. "Not that this burger was on the healthy chart."

He shrugged. "No, it probably isn't, but every once in a while it's okay."

They lapsed into silence again as the waitress refilled their glasses and took away their plates.

A few minutes later Phoebe said, "I know this might be tough but I was wondering if you might be willing to tell me some stories about Joshua. Something I could tell the baby. Something about him outside of just what I remember."

Ryan's lips tightened and he didn't meet her gaze.

"You don't have to if you don't want to."

After a moment he met her look. "What would you like to know?"

"I guess anything. I feel like you knew him better than me. You spent far more time together than we did. I was wondering how you met?"

Ryan's gray eyes took on a faraway look. "The Aussie and the US troops didn't always hit it off, but JT and I did. We didn't usually work together, but I was asked to go out on patrol with his platoon. Their medic was on leave and the replacement hadn't made it in yet. My commander agreed. It was supposed to be an easy in and out of a village under our control. All went well until we were headed out, then all hell broke loose. The Iraqis had us pinned down and we couldn't expect help until the next morning.

"A couple of JT's men were seriously injured. While we spent long hours hunkered down together we got to know each other pretty well. He told me about you, and I told him about growing up in Texas.

"When I told him that I was tired of having to patch up people that another human had destroyed, he encouraged me to do something different. Even suggested I move to Australia for a new start. He joked that if he ever left the army he'd use his skills to become a police officer."

Phoebe had never heard Joshua say anything about wanting to do that. He had told Ryan things he either hadn't wanted to share with her or couldn't. It made her sad and angry at the same time. She and Joshua had just not been as close as a married couple should have been.

"After that kind of night you know each other pretty well. We started getting together for drinks whenever we had leave at the same time." His eyes didn't meet hers. "JT found out that I didn't get much mail so he shared his letters with me."

For seconds Phoebe panicked, trying to remember what

she had said in her letters. Misery overtook the panic. During the last few years of their marriage her letters had been less about them personally and more about what was happening with her students, how Melbourne was changing, what she was doing at the house. It had been as if she'd been writing to a friend instead of her husband.

"I always looked forward to your letters. They were full of news and I liked to hear about your class. The letters your students wrote were the best. There was something about them that helped make all the ugliness disappear for a while."

"I'm glad they helped. My students liked writing them. Thank you for telling me about Joshua. I guess I just wanted to talk about him. This is his baby and he isn't around. Just hearing about him makes him seem a little closer. But it's time for me to go." She needed to think about what Ryan had told her. The fact that someone had known her husband better than she had made her feel heartsick.

Ryan stood and Phoebe did also. She led the way to the door. Outside Ryan turned in the direction of the hospital.

"I need to go this way to catch the tram. Thanks for dinner." She turned toward the left.

"I'll give you a ride home," Ryan said.

"I don't want you to drive all the way out to my house."

"I don't mind and you don't need to be so late getting home. Don't you own a car?"

"No, I can take the tram to almost anything I need."

"But you're making two-hour round trips to see Sophia. In America we can't live without a car. There isn't public transportation everywhere."

"Yes, but that's only once a month and it's worth it to have Sophia as my midwife. I wish she was going to be there for the delivery."

"I realize that I live in Australia, but I can't get used to prenatal care being called antenatal. It took me forever to tell the mothers I saw that they needed to come to the antenatal clinic. I just think prenatal."

"The ideas and ways we grow up with are hard to change."

"Yes, once an idea gets fixed in my head it's hard to make me budge. And with that thought, not to make you feel bad, but you look like you could use some rest. I'm driving you home."

"I am tired and I know now that you won't change your mind. I'm going to accept the ride."

"Good."

Ryan escorted Phoebe back to the hospital and to his car. The sidewalk wasn't near as busy as it had been earlier. It had been a long time since he'd done something as simple as stroll through a park with a woman. He couldn't remember ever doing so with one who was expecting. People smiled and greeted Phoebe. She returned them. A number of times they turned to him and offered their congratulations. The first time he began to explain but soon realized it was a waste of time. Instead, he nodded noncommittally.

"I'm sorry," Phoebe said after the first incident.

"Not your fault. You can't help what they think."

He had hardly pulled out of the parking area before Phoebe had closed her eyes. She was tired.

Ryan got a number of reactions when he told someone he was a midwife. He'd gotten used to it. But the one thing he couldn't get used to was not being able to understand all the nuances of the female body when a baby was growing inside it. The sudden ability to go to sleep anywhere and in any position was one of those. It must be like being in the army. He had learned to sleep anywhere at any time.

* * *

Phoebe blinked with the small jolt of the car stopping. She'd fallen asleep again. It was getting embarrassing.

"I'm sorry. I didn't mean to go to sleep."

"Not a problem. You're not the first woman I've put to sleep."

Phoebe gave him a questioning look. She bet she wasn't. What had her thinking of Ryan in that suggestive way?

"I'm the one sorry this time. I didn't mean it like that."

"Like what?" She gave him her best innocent look.

"You know, like…"

Phoebe enjoyed his flustered expression and the pinkness that began to work its way up his neck.

She rested her hands on each side of her belly. "I'm well aware of the facts of life and how a man can satisfy a woman."

He grinned. "You're laughing at me now."

Phoebe chuckled. "I guess I am." She opened her car door. "Thanks for the burger and the ride. Also thanks for telling me about Joshua. You have no idea how much it means to me."

"Hey, wait a minute."

Before she could get completely out of the car Ryan had come round and was standing on the path, reaching to help her. His hand went to her elbow and he supported her as she stood. He pushed the door closed behind her and it made a thud.

"Listen, if there's anything that I can do for you…"

He sounded sincere. "I appreciate it… Uh, there is one thing I could use some help with."

"What's that?"

His voice held an eager tone as if he was looking for a chance to atone for his earlier behavior. She hated to ask him but couldn't think of another way to get it done before the baby came. "I had a bed for the baby delivered but it needs to be put together. I would pay you."

Ryan looked as if she had slapped him. "You will not. How about I come by Saturday afternoon? If I have to work I'll call and let you know, otherwise I'll be here on Saturday."

"Thank you, that would be wonderful." And she meant it. She'd spent more than one night worrying over how she was going to get that baby bed assembled.

"Not a problem. Do you have tools or do I need to bring mine?"

"You might want to bring yours. I have a few but only necessities like a hammer and screwdriver."

"Then it's a plan. Why don't you give me your number?" Ryan took out his cellphone and punched in the numbers she told him.

"I'll be here after lunch on Saturday, unless you hear differently from me."

"Thank you."

"No worries. Furniture I can do."

Something about Ryan made her believe that he had many talents if he was just willing to show them.

"Come on. I'll walk you to your door."

Phoebe didn't argue this time.

"See you Saturday." With that he turned and left her to enter her home.

She was putting her key in the lock when she noticed the curtain of her neighbor's house flutter. Mrs. Rosenheim had been watching. She would no doubt be over the next afternoon to get all the particulars about who Ryan was and how Phoebe knew him.

Ryan was as good as his word. He was there on Saturday just after lunchtime with a tool bag in his hand. Mrs.

Rosenheim was sitting at Phoebe's kitchen table when the knock came at the door.

"I won't stay but I am going to check this boy out before I go."

Phoebe would have argued but it wouldn't have done her any good. Despite the fact that Mrs. Rosenheim was probably older than Phoebe's grandmother would be, she was a commanding presence and was only concerned for Phoebe's welfare. They had started taking care of each other two years ago when Phoebe had moved in.

Joshua had only been home once since she'd been living there. He'd not been impressed with Mrs. Rosenheim, calling her the "old busybody bird." Phoebe had learned to appreciate her concern. If nothing else, she knew someone would miss her if she didn't come home.

She opened the door for Ryan. "Come in."

"How're you doing?"

The question sounded like he was making pleasant conversation, but he was also looking at her with a trained eye. He smelled of sawdust with a hint of citrus. It made her want to step closer. Take a deeper breath.

"I'm feeling fine." She smiled and he nodded.

"Good. I told Sophia that I would check."

Mrs. Rosenheim shuffled into the room.

Ryan looked from her to Phoebe. "Ryan, this is my neighbor, Mrs. Rosenheim."

He sat his tool bag on the floor at his feet and extended a hand. "Nice to meet you."

"You're American."

"Yes, ma'am. Texan."

Mrs. Rosenheim made a noncommittal sound low in her throat. Ryan gave Phoebe a questioning look. She shrugged her shoulders.

"So you knew Mr. Taylor."

A guarded look came over Ryan's face. "Yes, JT and I served in Iraq together."

"Bad thing, leaving Phoebe here all by herself all the time. A man should want to be at home with his wife. She needs someone to watch over her. Help her."

Phoebe didn't miss the color wash out of Ryan's face.

"It was his job. The army," Phoebe said quietly.

"I know, sweetie. But a woman not only wants a man to help put a roof over her head but to be around when the times are hard." She directed the last few words at Ryan.

"Uh, Mrs. Rosenheim, I think we need to let Ryan get started on the bed. I'm sure he has other places he needs to go today." Phoebe shook her head at him when she started to say something.

"I'm next door if you need me." Mrs. Rosenheim made her way out with a last glance at Ryan.

"Formidable lady," Ryan said with a grin.

"Yes. She and Joshua didn't like each other on sight, but she's been good to me. She was with the men who came from the military department to tell me about Joshua. I don't know what I would have done without her shoulder to cry on. She's also the one who realized I was pregnant when I started being sick."

Phoebe suddenly needed to focus on something else. She shook away the memories. Ryan was the first male to have come into her home in over a year. He seemed to take up the entire space. "Anyway, let me show you where the bed is."

Ryan followed Phoebe down a hallway that had four doors leading off of it. She stopped at the next to last one and nudged the door open.

Against one wall was a large brown box that Ryan

guessed was the baby bed. That didn't surprise him. What did were the piles of books stacked around the room and the desk painted in a folk art style with a chair of the same kind sitting in one corner. The walls were painted a dark gray. Two cans of paint sat in another corner. He fully expected to see a room decorated in all the frills and with toys waiting for a baby. He'd listened to enough mothers talk about what they had done in the baby's room or were going to do to know that Phoebe was far behind in her preparations.

She placed her hand on the box. "This is the bed."

"Great. I'll get it put together."

Walking to the door, she looked back at him. "You didn't have to agree to this, but I really appreciate you doing it."

"Not a problem."

He'd been working for an hour when Phoebe returned to stand in the doorway. His back was to her but he felt her presence.

"I brought you something to drink." She moved to the desk and placed the drink on it.

Ryan stood from where he'd been tightening a screw on the back of the bed. He picked up the glass, took a long swallow of water and put it back on the desk again.

Phoebe had an odd look on her face that quickly disappeared.

Ryan said, "I guess I'm doing pretty well. I don't think I'm going to have but two screws and one thingamajig left over."

She laughed.

Had he ever heard anything more beautiful? It was almost musical. He vowed then to give her a reason to laugh often.

"My father always said that if you didn't have parts left over then you didn't put it together correctly."

"Where did you grow up?"

"In a small town about fifty miles from here."

"Is that where you met JT?"

"Yeah. We had a military base nearby. I worked at a local restaurant and Joshua and some of his mates came in for dinner one night and sat at my table."

"And, as they say, the rest was history."

"Yes, it was. I was wondering if…uh, you might like to stay for dinner? I do most of my cooking on the weekends so that I don't have to stand up any more than necessary during the week. How do grilled lamb chops with three vegetables sound?"

When had been the last time he'd eaten a home-cooked meal? Ryan couldn't remember. He grabbed what he did eat from the hospital cafeteria or from a fast-food place. The thought of sitting down to a real meal was more than he could resist. "That sounds great."

"Good. Then I'll go finish up."

She'd already moved to leave when he said, "Phoebe, I couldn't help but notice that you don't have this room set up for a baby."

Making a slow turn, she faced him. "I don't need you to make me feel ashamed. I bet you think I sank so far into feeling sorry for myself that I didn't pay attention to getting ready for the baby. I was still in shock over Joshua when I found out I was pregnant. I just couldn't bring myself to do anything for a while. Anyway, it has been pushed back. Maybe I'll have time to do something after the baby comes."

That wasn't going to happen. Ryan had also heard the new mothers talking about how they never got anything done any more. "I didn't mean to make you feel ashamed or defensive. I was thinking I could help. I see you have paint. How about letting me do the walls for you? I could also move this desk and chair to where you want it and the books."

"I hate to have you do all that."

"I don't mind. All you'd have to do is tell me where to put everything."

She rested her hand on her middle. A wistful look came to her eyes. "It would be nice to have the room ready for the baby. I had planned to buy some stuff for the walls."

"We could do that together." It was the least he could do for Joshua. This was practical stuff that needed doing. He had a strong back and could take care of them. He couldn't fix the fact she was having this baby all by herself but he could help with the everyday aspects of adding a new person to her household.

"That sounds like I'm asking too much."

"You're not asking. I volunteered. I'd like to do it. If JT were here, he'd be doing it. This will be my way of helping him out, like he did me."

Her eyes darkened for a second and then she nodded. "Then thanks. I'll gladly accept your help, but I'm going to warn you that you may wish you hadn't."

"How's that?"

"I have so many ideas for this room you'll get tired of me telling you what to do."

"We'll see. I'll be through here in about ten minutes, then I'd like to get started on the painting. Do you have any paint supplies?"

"They're in the shed in the backyard. When you get done, come to the kitchen and I'll take you out and show you where they are."

"Will do."

He watched her leave. Even with the bulk she carried

she had a graceful stride. What had possessed him to get this caught up in doing a baby's room? He made a practice of not getting involved.

Guilt, pure and simple.

# CHAPTER THREE

PHOEBE HAD SPENT so much time without a man or his help it made her nervous to have Ryan in her house. While he'd been putting together the bed, she'd been in the kitchen, cooking. Still, she'd been aware of every clatter or thump that had come from the direction of the bedroom. On occasion she'd heard a swear word. She smiled. More than once her father had bloodied his knuckles, putting a toy together for her or her brother.

It was nice to have someone in the house. She'd considered getting a dog or cat a couple of times just so there would be a living, breathing thing around. She'd decided to wait because she didn't want the poor animal alone in the house all day.

Ryan came around the corner. "All done. Come see what you think."

She put the plate on the table and headed down the hall, well aware of him following her. He'd pushed the bed up against the wall across from the window. It looked like the perfect place for it. She ran her hand along the railing. "It looks wonderful."

"Do you have a mattress for it?"

"Yes, it's in the other bedroom."

"I'll get it."

He soon returned with a mattress covered in protective

plastic. Together they worked to remove it. Ryan lifted the bedding and dropped it into place.

"It almost makes it real," she said with a note of wonder.

"What?"

"A baby coming."

He chuckled. "I would think that large mound you're sporting out front would make it seem pretty real."

"It does but the bed is something tangible."

"What about a rocker or any other furniture?"

She shrugged. "I'll have to go buy something. I was hoping I could find some pieces at a garage sale that I could redo. I wanted to paint it bright and add animals and plants, that sort of thing."

"You mean like the other folk art you have in the living room?"

She looked at him with a brightness that said they were talking about a passion of hers. "You know about folk art?"

"Only what it is. I'm more a straight paint and stain kind of guy. Fancy painting isn't my thing. So, if you'll show me where you want these books, I'll start moving them."

"They go in my bedroom."

She went out the doorway and turned toward the end of the hall, then went through an open doorway. Ryan followed more slowly. Why did it bother him that he had just been invited into his buddy's wife's bedroom? She hadn't even thought about what she was saying. When she looked back he was standing in the doorway.

"They go on this bookshelf. If you'll bring them to me, I can shelve them."

Ryan returned with an armload of books. She'd taken a seat on the floor in front of the shelving while he'd been gone.

He stacked the books on the floor and she went to work, putting them in place.

* * *

Ryan looked down at Phoebe. He saw pregnant women day in and day out, but there was something almost angelic about the way her golden hair covered a portion of her face and her small hands put the books so neatly into their spots.

He shook his head and strode toward the door. Had he been spending too much time in his shop alone? The sawdust was filling his brain.

Fifteen minutes later he had all the books moved. Phoebe hadn't worked as fast as he so she was still shelving books. Not wanting to sit on her bed, he stood near the door until she was finished.

"Thanks for doing this. I've been dreading it for weeks. That's why it hasn't been done." She continued to work.

Ryan's cell phone rang and he pulled it out of his pocket. "I have to get this."

She nodded.

"Ryan Matthews."

"It's Julie Habershire. My waters just broke."

"Okay. No need to panic. We talked about what to do if this happens. I'll meet you at the hospital. Drive safe."

"Ryan, the baby will be all right, won't it? It's early."

"The baby should be fine. Not so early it shouldn't be perfect. See you soon."

He touched the phone to disconnect the call. Phoebe looked at him with a slight smile on her face. "Are you always that calm and reassuring with your patients?"

"I try to be."

"That's a special gift."

"I just know that people are scared when they have never experienced something before, especially if it has to do with their bodies. I learned a long time ago if I don't sound upset, then they're more likely not to get upset."

"You must be good at your job."

He slipped the phone back into his pocket. "I hope my patients think so. Anyway, I've got to go. I hate to miss out on that meal, but babies don't wait."

"I understand."

"Would it be all right if I come back tomorrow and get started on that painting? Maybe get in on leftovers?"

"That sounds fine to me. After lunch?"

"Then it's a plan. See you then." He turned to head out the door and stopped. Coming back, he offered her his hand. "If I don't help you up, I'm afraid you might still be on the floor when I return tomorrow."

"Are you implying that I'm so big that I can't get up off the floor by myself?" She accepted his hand. He helped her rise. She did it with grace.

With her on her feet, he put up his hands as if defending himself. "Hey, I work with pregnant women every day and I know better than to do that. Have to go. See you later."

Her soft laugh followed him down the hall. He went out the front door with a grin on his face, something he'd done more in the last few days than he had in years.

The next afternoon Phoebe wasn't sure what was happening but she was going to take Ryan's help while it was being offered. She'd sat around for too long with no direction. Well aware that she needed to be getting the baby's room together, she hadn't had the heart to do so. It was just too sad to work on it by herself. Having the bed assembled made her want to do more. It needed sheets, blankets. There should be other pieces of furniture, pictures on the walls.

Next weekend she'd go to some garage sales and see if she could find a few items. She smiled. For once she was feeling some excitement over the prospect of being a mother. For now she'd be satisfied with just having the room painted.

She'd hardly finished her lunch sandwich when there was a knock at the door. Ryan stood there. Dressed in cargo pants and a white T-shirt that hugged his well-defined physique, he was a fine-looking man. Mrs. Rosenheim had made a point to tell Phoebe the same thing that morning. Ryan proved that just because she was pregnant it didn't mean that she couldn't be affected by a man. It took her time to draw enough breath to say hello.

"Hey," he said in that drawl that left her feeling like she was sitting beside a cool stream on a hot summer day. "How about showing me the paint supplies? If I need anything I'll still have time to go to the store before it closes."

"Okay. It's this way." This was the first time he hadn't taken time to ask her how she was doing. He seemed focused on the project. She kind of liked the fact that he didn't see her as only a pregnant woman.

At the shed, she started to raise the roll-top door. Ryan stopped her by placing his hand over hers. His hand wasn't smooth, like she had expected for a midwife. Instead, it had a coarseness to it that spoke of a man who did more than wear gloves all the time.

"Hey, you don't need to be doing that. Let me get it."

What would have taken her great effort seemed as easy for him as lifting a blind.

"The paint stuff is stacked up over there." She pointed to the right and toward the back of the shed.

"I see it." He leaned over some gardening pots to gather the items, while at the same time presenting her with a nice view of his behind.

"Would you mind carrying a couple of things?"

It took her a second to answer. "No."

Ryan looked over his shoulder and gave her a speculative look. "Here." He handed her a few brushes and a package of rollers, then came out holding an armload of drop cloths and a paint tray. "I think this is everything I need."

They walked back to the house. Phoebe held the door open for him to enter. He was laying supplies on the floor of the baby's room by the time she entered. He took what she carried from her and added them to the pile.

Scanning the room, he said, "Is the desk staying in here?"

She looked at it. Ryan's drive to get things done was surpassing what she had thought through. "I had planned to put it in the living room. But I'll need to move a few things around so it'll have a place. Give me a minute and I'll see what I can do."

"You're not moving anything by yourself."

Phoebe faced him with her hands on her hips. "I appreciate your help. Really I do, but up until a few days ago I had no help. No one telling me what I should and shouldn't do. I am fully capable of moving a few things. If it's too large for me to do so, I'll call you."

Ryan's look met hers. He pursed his lips. She'd got his attention.

"I'm sorry. I stepped over the line, didn't I?"

She nodded. "Yes. Just a little bit."

"Then please let me know if and when you need help." He bowed slightly.

"Thank you. I will." She left the room with her head held high. She was grateful for Ryan's help but she wasn't needy, despite what her behavior at his house had implied.

In the living room, she began moving small items off an end table. Ryan's soft whistle drifted up the hall. It was nice to have someone around. Her smile grew. It would be nice to have a baby in the house.

She had reached to move the end table when behind her came, "I knew I couldn't trust you."

Jerking to a standing position, she looked around to find Ryan standing with his shoulder leaning against the wall.

"Are you checking up on me?"

"Do you need to be checked up on?"

"No." The word didn't come out as confidently as she would have liked.

He came toward her. "I think you might." He placed his hands on the table and looked at her. "Where do you want this?"

She pointed to the other end of the sofa, where she'd cleared a space by moving a floor lamp.

Ryan moved the table into the spot. He ran a finger over a painted swirl on it. "This type of artwork is interesting."

"Thank you."

He looked at her. "You did this?"

"Don't act so surprised."

"I didn't mean it like that." He looked around the room. "You did all of this?"

She stood straighter. "I did, even down to making the cushions and curtains."

"I'm impressed. I like it."

She chuckled dryly. "Now I'm surprised. Joshua hated this type of decorating. He said it made us look like we couldn't afford better. I put most of it away when he came home. Pulled it out again when he had gone again."

Ryan looked at her for a long moment. "Well, I like it. It's you."

She didn't think anyone had said anything nicer to her in a long time. "Thank you. I appreciate that."

"You're welcome. Now, if I go paint another wall, can I trust you to behave?"

Phoebe glared at him. "Yes, I'll put our supper on to warm. Will that make you happy?"

"Yes." With that, he went off whistling down the hall.

Half an hour later Phoebe went to check on Ryan's progress. He was getting ready to start on the last wall. The others were already a pale yellow. A cheerful and happy color.

The room was small but he seemed very efficient. She watched as he bent to apply paint to the roller in the tray. The muscles on his back rippled. He reached up and brought the roller down along the wall. His biceps flexed and released.

Phoebe shook her head. She had been without a man for far too long and yet was far too pregnant to consider having a relationship with one now. Still, she was alive...

Ryan turned. By the look in his eyes and the way he watched her like a cat after a bird, he knew what she'd been doing. She'd never been much of a blusher but she felt the heat rising to her face.

"So what do you think?"

Thankfully he hadn't made a comment about her staring. "It looks beautiful."

"The paint goes on great."

She stepped farther into the room. "This isn't your first time to do this."

"No. My foster-father was a painter. I started working with him when I was fourteen." He moved back to filling the roller again.

Phoebe wasn't sure she should ask but she was too curious not to. "You were a foster-child?"

"Yeah. I never knew my father and my mother was a drug addict. I was five when I was taken away from her."

Her heart hurt for that little boy. "Oh, Ryan."

He shrugged. "It was tough but it was a long time ago."

Something about his attitude told her it still affected him. His focus turned to refilling the roller again.

"So your foster-father let you go to work with him?"

"It was more like made me go. I was a difficult teen and he thought it would help keep me in line. Something about idle hands leaving room for trouble."

"And did it keep you in line?"

"Not really. I ended up going into the army the day after I graduated from high school. It made my foster-parents happy, and me, too."

"Even your foster-mother?"

He glanced back at her. "She didn't mind, either. She was so exhausted from dealing with the smaller kids and my behavior she was glad to see me go. I should be finished here in about thirty minutes. Any chance I could get something to eat?"

He was apparently through discussing his childhood. She would see to it that her child felt loved and wanted. "It'll be ready."

Ryan washed up in the hall bathroom. Splashing water on his face, he looked into the mirror. What was he doing? He could feel himself getting in too deep. He'd enjoyed the afternoon more than he would have ever imagined. He spent most of his off hours in his shop and he found he rather liked being out in the daylight, spending time with someone.

He entered the kitchen. There he found more of the same decor as the rest of the house. The table had four chairs, each painted a different color yet they seem to complement each other. The eclectic look seemed to suit Phoebe.

The table was set. When was the last time he'd eaten dinner off something other than a takeout plate?

"You may sit there." Phoebe pointed to the chair closest to him and turned back to the oven. She pulled out a casserole pan and placed it in the center of the table.

Ryan leaned in close and inhaled. "Smells wonderful."

He didn't miss her pleased smile. Phoebe would make a great mother. She found pleasure in doing for others.

She handed him a serving spoon. "Help yourself."

Ryan didn't need to be told twice. He scooped two large helpings onto his plate. Phoebe took one. When she picked up her fork, he did also.

"I see you were taught manners. Not eating until everyone else does."

"My foster-mother was a real stickler about them." He put a forkful into his mouth. It was the best thing he'd eaten in years. "This is good. Real good."

"Thank you. It's my grandmother's chicken casserole recipe."

He ate a plateful and one more before he sat back and looked at Phoebe. She had only eaten about half of what she'd put on her plate.

"You need to eat more."

She looked down at her middle. "I don't think I need to get any bigger."

"You look wonderful."

"You are feeding me compliments now."

Ryan chuckled. "That wasn't my intent. But I guess I am."

"I'll take them any way I can get them." It was nice to be noticed by a male on any level.

Ryan pushed his chair back. "I guess I'd better get the paint supplies cleaned up."

He left and she cleared the table. When done, she went to see if she could help Ryan. He was in the process of moving the desk.

"That's heavy. Let me help you."

Ryan jerked around. "You will not."

"There's no way you can move that desk by yourself."

"It's all in the technique." He gripped it by each side and began walking it from one corner to the other until he'd moved it to the doorway.

"Do you have an old towel I can use?" Ryan asked.

"Just a second." Phoebe went into the bathroom and brought back the largest one she could find. She handed it to Ryan.

"You stay out here." He moved the desk out into the hall. Taking the towel, he laid it on the floor in front of the desk. Lifting one end he asked, "Can you put the towel under the desk as far as possible?"

Glad she could be of some help she did as he requested.

He then lowered the desk. "Perfect." Gathering the corners of the towel into his hands he slowly pulled the desk over the wooden flooring and down the hall.

Phoebe stepped into the doorway, letting him pass. When he was by, she stepped out and began to push.

Coming to a stop, Ryan growled, "What're you doing?"

"Helping."

"You shouldn't—"

"Stop telling me what to do. I'm not really doing much."

A grunt of disbelief came from his direction but the desk started moving again. She continued to help maneuver it, seeing that it didn't nick the walls or hit any other furniture. When the desk quit moving, she looked over it. Her gaze met Ryan's. For a second his intense gray gaze held hers. Warmth washed over her. Could he see things she'd rather keep hidden?

"Why did you stop?"

His mouth quirked. "I don't know where you want this."

Phoebe tried to squeeze through the space between the desk and the wall.

"Hold on a sec and let me move it." Ryan grabbed the desk and shifted it so she could join him.

"I want it put over there." She pointed to the space she had cleared under a window.

"Okay." He began walking and shifting the desk until it was in place. "I'll go get the chair." He left.

The desk really needed to be centered under the window. Phoebe placed one hip against the side and pushed. It only moved a few centimeters.

"I can't leave you alone for a minute." Ryan's deep voice came from behind her.

"It needs to be centered under the window."

"Then why didn't you say something?"

He put his hands on her waist or what had once been her waist. Her breath caught. Ryan gently directed her out of the way, then quickly put space between them. "I'm sorry. I shouldn't have done that."

Ryan acted as if he'd been too personal with her. "It's okay," she said.

"Stand over there, out of the way, and tell me when I have it where you want it."

"You do know I'm just pregnant, not an invalid."

He gave her a pointed look. "I'm well aware of that but some things you shouldn't be doing, whether you're pregnant or not. This is one of them. Now, tell me where you want it."

Shifting the desk an inch, he looked at her for confirmation. It still wasn't where she wanted it. "Move it to the right just a little."

Had he muttered "Women" under his breath?

"That's it. Perfect. Thank you."

He stood and rubbed his lower back.

She stepped closer. "Did you hurt yourself?"

He grinned. "No. I was just afraid that you might ask me to move something else."

"Hey, you're the one who volunteered."

"That I did. I might ought to think about it before I do that again." He continued stretching.

"Might ought to?" She liked his accent.

"Ought to. Texas. Southern. Ought to go. Ought to get."

Phoebe laughed. "I'll have to remember that. Use it sometime."

"I think you ought not make fun of me."

"And I think you ought not be so sensitive."

They both laughed.

It was the first real laugh she'd shared with someone in a long time. It felt good.

"Well, I guess I had better go. It's getting late."

"I really appreciate all your work today. The baby's room looks wonderful. I can hardly wait to go to some garage sales and look for a chest of drawers."

"And how do you plan to get something like that home?"

"I'll worry about that if I find one. Some people are willing to deliver if I ask."

"I don't have any mothers due for a couple of weeks so why don't I go with you on Saturday?"

She like the idea but didn't want to take advantage of him. "I hate to take up another one of your weekends."

"I'd like to go. I've got a buddy who has a truck and lets me borrow it sometimes."

The truck was a plus and it would be nice to have company. "I won't turn that down."

"Great. I'll be here early Saturday to pick you up."

Ryan headed out the front door. "See you then."

"Bye." Phoebe watched from the veranda as Ryan drove away. She could get used to having him around. Seeing him on Saturday gave her something to look forward to. Of course she appreciated his help but more than that she liked him. There was an easy way about him that made life seem like fun. She was far too attracted to him already. Joshua had been right about him. Maybe she had found someone she could depend on.

Warmth lingered where Ryan had touched her. A ripple of awareness had gone up her spine. What was she thinking? Joshua had been dead for less than a year and she had a baby on the way, and here she was mooning over Ryan.

Still, Saturday couldn't come soon enough.

# CHAPTER FOUR

RYAN PULLED THE truck to the curb in front of Phoebe's house just as the sun became warm.

What was he doing? The question kept rotating through his mind like a revolving door. He was too interested in Phoebe. But it was hard not to be. Those large, vulnerable eyes drew him in. Still, he admired the way she had stood up to him when he'd stepped over the line to bossing her around. The brief moments he'd touched her waist had told him that he could want more than just to help her. That wasn't going to happen. Still, he'd looked forward to spending the day with her.

Phoebe met him halfway up the walk. She wore jeans and a simple white shirt. Her eyes sparkled and for a woman of her size she walked with a peppy step. A smile covered her face. She reminded him of springtime. A fresh start.

If he'd seen any woman look more alluring, he couldn't remember when. "Mornin'."

"Hi. You ready to go? We need to get going. You know the early bird gets the worm." She carried a newspaper and passed him on the way to the truck, leaving the smell of flowers swirling in the air. He was tempted to breathe deeply. Let his mind commit it to memory.

"Uh...yeah. I'm ready." Ryan wasn't able to keep the

astonishment out of his voice. He hurried to join her. Phoebe was a woman on a mission.

She had climbed into the passenger seat and closed the door before he reached the truck. He took his place behind the wheel. "So where's the fire?"

"What?" She looked up from the open paper.

"What's the hurry?"

"I think they have just what I need at a sale and I don't want it to get bought up before we get there."

"Why didn't you call me? I could have come earlier."

"I didn't know for sure until I phoned a few minutes ago. They wouldn't promise to hold it for me so we've got to go."

Ryan grinned as he pulled away from the curb. There was nothing like a woman looking for a deal. "So where are we headed?"

"South. It's about forty minutes away." Phoebe gave him directions.

"South it is."

They traveled in silence until they were out of the city and he was driving along a two-lane highway.

"Do you have an address for the place we're going?"

Phoebe read it to him out of the paper.

"I have no idea where that is." Ryan kept his eyes on the road as a delivery truck whizzed by them.

"It's another half hour down this road, then we have to turn off."

"Have you always redone furniture?" It was ironic that she enjoyed something that was so similar to his passion.

"I've been doing it for a few years. I found I needed to fill the time when Joshua was away."

"You were lonely, weren't you?"

Phoebe didn't immediately answer. "It wasn't so hard at first. But it got more so as time went on."

Her melancholy tone implied that something more than loneliness had pushed her toward finding a hobby.

"Joshua didn't care for my painting taking up my time when he was home so I always put things away then."

He remembered what she'd said before about putting away her painted furniture because Joshua hadn't like it. That had surprised him. It didn't sound like the Joshua he'd known. Maybe he had changed since they'd known each other in the service. Ryan needed to find a safer subject. "Looks like it's going to be a pretty day."

"Yes, it does. I'm glad. I don't want anything I buy to get wet."

"I brought a covering in case we need it."

She gave him a smile of admiration.

The feeling of being a conquering hero went through him. What was happening to him? He smiled back. "Glad I could be of help."

"You're going to need to take a left turn in a couple of miles."

"You know this area well."

"This isn't the first time I've been down this way to garage sales."

They lapsed into silence until Phoebe began giving him directions regularly. They turned off the main road onto a dirt road that led up to a farmhouse with a steep metal roof and a porch circling it on three sides. A large barn with its doors opened wide stood off to the side. Two other cars were parked nearby.

"They keep the stuff they're selling in the barn," Phoebe said, with the door already open.

She hurried to the barn and Ryan joined her halfway there. They entered the dim interior. In an unused stall tables had been set up that contained all types of bottles, kitchen utensils, purses and other small items. On the other side were the larger items. Phoebe headed to them. She studied a cabinet that came up to his chest. It was much too high for her to make good use of it.

Phoebe pulled the drawers out and pushed them back in. "Would you mind tipping it forward so I can look at the back's construction?"

He had to give her credit for being knowledgeable and thorough. Ryan did as she requested.

She knocked against the wood and made a sound in her throat. Her hair curtained her face so he couldn't see what she was thinking. Running a hand over the edge and back again, she made another sound. Whether it was positive or negative he couldn't tell. It didn't matter. He was enthralled just watching her.

"You can let it down now."

Ryan lowered it to the ground.

She stepped back and studied it. "I think it'll do."

"May I make a suggestion?"

She looked at him as if she'd almost forgotten he was there. He didn't like that idea. That he could that easily disappear from her thoughts. Raising her chin and cocking her head, she gave him a questioning look. "Yes?"

"I think this chest is too tall for you. You can't even see over it."

Her eyes widened. She turned to face the chest. "You know, I can't. I hadn't thought about that."

"You need one where you can use all the space. You couldn't even find the baby powder if it got pushed to the back on this one."

"You're right. I guess now that I'm in the baby mood I'm getting in a panic to buy, afraid that time is running out. That I won't get it all done."

"We have all day. You have more places on your list, don't you?"

"Yes."

"Then let's go see what they have. Maybe we can find just the right one."

He offered his hand.

She looked at it for a moment and then placed hers in his. Her fingers were soft and cool. He closed his around them. It was as if they had chosen to face a problem together and see it overcome. Somehow this relationship had gone from less about getting a piece of furniture to having an emotional attachment. He didn't release her hand when she gave his a nudge.

Together, side by side this time, they walked back to the truck.

They visited two more places and didn't find what Phoebe was looking for.

"I don't know about you but I need something to eat," Ryan said, when he saw a sign for a café and ice-cream parlor.

"I am, too, but we might miss out on my chest."

"Then there'll be another one."

"Okay," Phoebe said, but her heart didn't sound like it was in it.

He pulled into a drive much like the one at the first house they had visited. As he came to the end of it he found a house with a restaurant attached to the back. "Come on. We'll have a sandwich, maybe some ice cream and plan our attack. Bring the paper and the map."

She didn't argue and had them in her hand when he came around the truck to meet her.

Ryan held the door for her to enter the café, then directed her to one of the small square tables in the room. Phoebe took a seat in one of the wooden chairs. He sat beside her.

She looked around the space. "I like this. It's my style."

"It does look like your type of decor."

The tables were covered in floral-print cloths. The chairs were mismatched, like hers.

A young man brought them a menu. He and Phoebe studied it for a moment.

"What're you going to have?" Ryan laid the menu on the table.

"A ham sandwich and lemonade."

"I think I'll have the same."

The waiter returned and Ryan gave him their order. When they were alone again, Ryan said, "Hand me that map, then read out the places you want to visit."

Phoebe did as he asked and he circled the places on the map. "Okay, is that it?"

"Yes."

"All right. Show me on the map your first and second, then third choice."

Phoebe pointed them out. He drew a line from one to the other to the other. "This is our game plan. We'll visit these. If we don't find what you want today, then we'll try again next weekend or whenever we can. Agreed?"

"Agreed."

The waiter brought their meals.

"Now let's eat. I'm starved."

She smiled. "You're always hungry."

Her soft chuckle made his heart catch. He was becoming hungry for more time with her.

Phoebe had always enjoyed junking but never as much as she had today. It turned out that Ryan was not only efficient but also a fun person to have around. She hadn't smiled or laughed as much as she had in the last few weeks. She'd almost forgotten what it was like to have a companion or to just appreciate male company.

Even so, there seemed to be a part of Ryan that he kept to himself. Something locked up that he wouldn't or couldn't share with the world or her.

After they had finished their lunch they climbed back into the truck and headed down the road. This time Ryan was not only driving but navigating as well. It didn't take them long to reach their first stop.

"It looks like they have a lot of furniture," Ryan said as they walked toward a shed.

"Maybe they'll have just the right thing."

A man met them at the shed door but let them wander around and look in peace.

Phoebe had been studying a chest. She turned to speak to Ryan but found he was in another area, looking at a rocker. "What have you found?"

She joined him and watched as he lovingly ran a hand down the arm of the chair. Now that she was closer she could tell it sat lopsided. There was a rocker missing.

"There was a woman who lived next to my foster-family who had a rocker like this. She and only she sat in it. She said it was the best seat in the house."

"She was nice to you."

"Yeah. Her house was where I would go if things got too hard for me at the Henrys'." She could only imagine the little boy who had needed someone on his side. "It's beautiful. I like that high-back style. Gives you someplace to lean your head."

Ryan moved another chair and a small table so that he could pull the rocker out. When he had plenty of space he tipped it over.

Phoebe admired the careful way he took in handling it. Despite his size, he was a gentle man.

"I think I can fix this. The structure is sound. All that's

missing is the one rocker. Would you like to have it for the baby's room? I can fix it. You can paint it or I'll stain it."

"You don't need to buy me anything."

He looked at her. "I wasn't buying you anything. I was getting something for the baby."

Before she could argue that it was the same thing, he walked away and had soon agreed a price with the owner.

She didn't find a chest of drawers there but they left with the rocker tied down in the back of the truck. At the next place she found nothing she liked.

As Ryan drove away she looked out the window. "I don't think we're going to find what I need today."

"Don't give up yet. We still have one more place on our list."

She studied his strong profile for a minute. He had a long jaw that spoke of determination but there were small laugh lines around his eyes. His forehead was high and a lock of hair had fallen across it as if to rebel against control. Much like the man himself.

"Do you always approach everything you do with such determination?"

"I guess old habits die hard. Being in the service will do that to you."

"Tell me what it was like being in the service. Joshua would never talk about it. He always said he didn't want me to worry."

This was the last subject Ryan wished to discuss. He wanted those days long gone and forgotten. Without his heart in it, he asked, "What do you want to know?"

"Was it as bad as the news makes it out to be?"

"Worse."

"I'm sorry."

"It's war. Few people understand. War is never pretty.

It's all death and destruction. Until you have looked into someone's eyes and watched life leave them, no one can ever grasp that."

"That happened to you?"

His glance held disbelief. "Yeah, more than once."

At her gasp he couldn't decide if he was pleased he'd shocked her or disgusted with himself for doing so. "I'm sorry. I shouldn't have said it like that."

"Yes, you should have. You have experienced horrible, unspeakable things while I've been here safe in my home." A second later she asked, "How did you deal with it?"

Ryan gripped the steering wheel and kept his eyes on the road. He wasn't sure he had or was. "I did what I had to and tried not to think about how lives were being shattered."

She laid a hand on his shoulder. Even that small gesture eased the flames of painful memories. Suddenly he wanted her to understand. "There was this one guy in my unit who had lost half his face. He cried and he kept repeating 'I'm going to scare my kids, I'm going to scare my kids.' How do you reassure someone in that kind of shape that he won't?"

As if a dam had broken he couldn't stop talking. "There was another guy who had tried to kill himself because he'd received a Dear John letter. We were in a war zone and we had our own guys trying to kill themselves."

"That had to be hard to deal with."

"Yeah, more than anyone should have to deal with. We lived in metal shipping containers that had been divided into two small rooms by thin wooden walls. We showered in bath houses, ate in the same mess hall. It's hard not to get involved in each other's lives."

"I imagine you do."

"Even though we had R and R time, you never truly

got away from it. We could go to the rec building, call our families or use the internet, but the minute we stepped out of the building the fence and sentries told us we weren't at home."

He'd confessed more than he'd ever told anyone about his time in the service. Had he terrified her? He glanced her direction. A single tear rested on her cheek.

His hand found hers. "I'm sorry. I shouldn't have told you all that."

"I'm glad you did. This baby deserves to know about his daddy and what he did. What life was like for him before he died. Thank you for telling me."

Ryan went back to looking at the road. "Joshua was a strong leader. I saw more than one man panic in the kind of situation we were in in that village. He held it together. Because of him I'm alive and so are a lot of other men. You can tell the baby that his father was a good soldier and a hero."

It was a relief to see the turnoff to their next stop. The conversation had gone in a direction he'd not expected or really wanted to continue. He made the turn into the road leading to the farmhouse. He released Phoebe's hand. The feeling of loss was immediate. "I have a good feeling about this place."

"I hope you're right."

Phoebe's voice held a sad note that he'd like to have disappear. He hadn't intended to bring what had been a nice day to a standstill. Even so, he had to admit it was a relief to get some of what he felt about the war off his chest. He'd carried that heaviness too long. It was strange that Phoebe, the wife of an army buddy, was the one person he had felt comfortable enough with to do so. He had never even told his coworkers as much as he'd just told Phoebe.

The house they were looking for came into view. He pulled to a stop in the drive.

"Doesn't look like we're at the right place. Let me double-check the address." Phoebe opened the newspaper.

A woman came around the corner of the house.

Ryan stepped out of the truck. "Excuse me, ma'am, but is this the place where the yard sale is?" he asked.

"Yes, but it has been over for an hour. We've put everything away."

Phoebe joined them. "Do you still have any furniture? I'm looking for a chest of drawers for my baby's room."

"I'm sorry but we had very little furniture and what we did have is all gone."

Ryan looked at Phoebe. He hated seeing that defeated look on her face. "We'll just have to try again on another weekend."

They were on their way back to the truck when the woman called, "Hey, I do have a chest of drawers out in the old smoke house that my husband says has to go. It was my mother's. It's missing a leg and a drawer, though."

Ryan looked at Phoebe. "I could fix those things. It wouldn't hurt to look."

Phoebe shrugged. "I guess so."

She didn't sound too confident. He gave her an encouraging smile. "Come on. You might be in for a surprise."

He certainly knew about them. Phoebe had been one of those in his life.

"It's back this way." The woman headed around the house. She led them to a wooden building that looked ready to fall down and opened a door.

Ryan looked into the dark space. All types of farming equipment, big and small, was crammed into it.

"You're gonna have to move some of that stuff around if you want to get to it," the woman said from behind him.

Glancing back over the woman's shoulder to where Phoebe stood, he saw her look of anticipation. Not wanting to disappoint her, he didn't have any choice but to start moving rakes, hoes, carts and even larger gardening implements. He definitely didn't want her to do that.

Picking up things and shifting them aside to make a narrow path, he could see a chest leaning against a wall. In the dim light provided by the slits in the boards it looked the right height. His heart beat faster. It might be just what Phoebe was looking for.

He made his way to it by squeezing between a stack of boxes and a tall piece of farming equipment that he couldn't put a name to. Pulling the chest away from the wall, he leaned it forward to look at the back.

"Doesn't it look perfect? It's just right."

His head jerked toward the voice. "Phoebe! What're you doing back here?" He shouldn't have been surprised. She managed to dumbfound him regularly.

"I wanted to see."

"You should have waited until I brought it out."

"What if you had done all that work and I wasn't interested? I didn't have any problem getting back here, except for between the boxes and that piece of equipment. I'm certainly no larger than you."

He eased the cabinet back against the wall. "What's that supposed to mean?"

"You're no little guy, with your broad shoulders and height."

He wasn't and he liked that she had noticed.

She circled around him, as if wanting to get a closer look at the chest. She pulled each drawer out and examined the slot where the missing drawer went. "What do you think?"

"What?" Ryan was so absorbed with watching her he'd missed her question.

"What do you think?" she asked in an impatient tone. "Can it be fixed?"

"Yes. It has sturdy construction. With a new drawer and a leg you would be in business."

She looked at him and grinned. Had he just been punched in the stomach?

"In business?"

"What kind of business would that be?"

"The baby business," he quipped back.

"I think I'll like that kind of business." Her smile was of pure happiness.

He returned it. "And I think you'll be good at it. So do you want the chest?"

"Yes, I do."

For a second there he wanted her to say that about him. He shook the thought away. Those were not ones he should be having. He and Phoebe were just friends. That was all they could be or should be.

"If you'll slide your way back out, then I'll bring this."

"I could help—"

Ryan leaned down until his nose almost touched hers. "No. You. Will. Not."

She giggled. "I thought that's what you might say." She gave him a quick kiss on the cheek and started for the path. "Thanks. You've been wonderful."

All he could do was stand there with a silly grin on his face. What was he, ten again?

With a groan, he began manipulating the chest through the maze. With less muscle than patience, he managed to get it outside. Before he could hardly stand the cabinet against the side of the building, Phoebe began studying it with a critical eye. She pulled each of the drawers out and pushed them in again.

"What do you want for it?" Phoebe glanced at the lady.

Heck, now that he'd worked to bring it into the light of day it didn't matter what the woman wanted. He'd pay her price just to not have to put it back.

"One hundred dollars," the woman stated.

"It has a leg and a drawer missing. How about thirty?" Phoebe came back with.

"Make it eighty, then."

Ryan watched, his look going from one woman to the other like at a tennis match.

"I don't think so. There's too much work to be done. Thanks anyway." Phoebe started toward the truck.

Ryan stood there in disbelief. She was going to leave after all the looking they had done today and the trouble he'd gone to get the chest out of the cluttered building? After she'd found what she wanted?

He gave her a pointed look. She winked. He was so stunned he couldn't say anything.

"How about we make it fifty?" the woman called after her.

Phoebe made almost a ballerina turn and had a smile on her face when she faced the woman. "Deal." Phoebe opened up her purse and handed the woman some bills.

He had to give Phoebe credit, she was an excellent bargainer.

She looked at him and grinned in pure satisfaction. What would it be like to have her look at him that way because of something he'd done? Heaven.

Clearing his head, he asked, "Ma'am, do you mind if I pull the truck closer to load this up?"

"Sure, that's fine."

Twenty minutes later, Phoebe was waving bye to the woman like they were long-lost friends.

"That was some dickering you did back there."

"Dickering?"

"Bargaining."

"Thanks."

"The next time I have to buy a car I'm taking you with me."

Phoebe smiled.

"Where did you learn to do that?"

"I don't know. I just know that it usually works. And it's always worth a try."

"There for a few minutes I was afraid that I was going to have to wrestle that chest back into that building."

"I wouldn't have let that happen. I wanted it too badly. I would have paid the hundred."

"Well, I'm glad to know that."

A few minutes later he pulled out onto the main highway that would take them to the larger road leading to Melbourne.

"Oh, the little penguins. I haven't seen them since I was young," Phoebe remarked as they passed a billboard.

"Penguins?"

"You don't know about the penguins? At Phillip Island?"

"No."

"They come in every night. It's amazing to watch. They go out every morning and hunt for food and bring it back for their babies. They're about a foot tall."

"How far away is this?"

"On the coast. About thirty minutes from here."

"Do you want to go?"

"They don't come in until the sun is going down. It would be late when we got home."

She sounded so wistful that he didn't have the heart to say no.

"Tell me which way to go."

"Surely you have something to do tonight. A date?"

"Why, Phoebe, are you fishing to find out about my love life?"

She rewarded him with a blush. "No."

"I have no plans. I'd like to see these tuxedo-wearing birds."

"Then you need to turn around and head the other direction."

"Yes, ma'am."

# CHAPTER FIVE

PHOEBE HADN'T BEEN to Phillip Island in years. She still had the picture her father had taken of her standing next to the penguin mascot. The area had changed. The building had been expanded and more parking added.

Ryan found a space and pulled into it. "I'm glad we ate when we did. I haven't seen any place to do so in miles."

"I was hungry, too."

Inside the welcome center they were directed outside. In another hour it would be dark. They followed the paved path that zigged and zagged down toward the beach. Other people mingled along the way.

"What's that noise?" Ryan asked.

"That's the baby chicks."

He looked around. "Where are they?"

Phoebe placed a hand on his arm. She pointed with the other at a hole in the grass embankment. "They're in there. Watch for a second and you'll catch a glimpse of them."

A grin came to Ryan's lips. "I see one."

"The penguin's mother and father leave the nest in the morning and spend all day hunting food. They return each night to feed the young and do it all over again the next day. Fifty kilometers or farther."

"Every day?" Ryan asked in an incredulous tone.

"Yes. The ocean is overfished so they have to go farther and farther. It's pretty amazing what parents will do for their children."

Ryan looked at her. "Are you scared?"

"Some. At first I was shocked, frightened, mad, then protective. It has been better here lately." She left off *because of you*.

"So it takes both parents to find enough food?"

"They are partners for life."

Ryan looked off toward the ocean and didn't say anything.

Had she made him nervous? Made it sound like she expected something from him? "I think I'm most scared that I won't be enough for the baby. That I can't be both mother and father."

"I think you'll do just fine. Your baby will grow up happy and loved. Let's head on down."

Phoebe didn't immediately move. Did he think she expected him to offer to help? That she thought he'd be around when the baby came? Would take Joshua's place? She wouldn't force commitment on any man. She was looking for someone who wanted to spend time with her. Who would put her first, over everything. Someone that would willingly be there for her and her baby.

She started walking but at a slower pace.

They walked in silence around a couple of turns before Ryan said, "Whew, the smell is something."

"There are thousands of small chicks living in this bank."

"Really?" Ryan leaned over the rail and peered down. "I don't see them."

"Most are asleep right now. When they wake up you can see their heads stick out. There is one small nest after another."

"Everywhere."

Phoebe chuckled. It was fun to be around when Ryan experienced something new. He seemed to get such enjoyment and wonderment from it. It made her see it the same way. "Yes, they are everywhere."

"If you had told me about this I wouldn't have believed it."

"You haven't seen the best yet. Come on, let's get a good seat."

"Seat for what?"

"To watch mum and dad come home." She took his hand and pulled him along the walk.

When she tried to let his hand go he hung on tighter. She relaxed and reveled in the feeling of having someone close. Ryan seemed to like having contact with her.

"What do you mean?"

"We have to go down to the beach. There are grandstands."

"Like bleachers?"

"Come on, I'll show you."

As they continued on Ryan pulled her to a halt every once in a while to peer into the bank. "I can't believe all these little birds here."

She just smiled. They finally made it down to the sand. She was glad to have Ryan's help as she crossed it and they found a seat on an aluminum bench.

Ryan looked around. "This many people will be here?"

"Yes, the three sets of bleachers will be full and there will be people standing along the rails."

"I wonder why I've never heard about this."

"I don't know but I do think it's the best-kept secret about Australia."

The bleachers filled as the sun began to set. Minutes later the crowd around them quieted.

"Look," Phoebe whispered and pointed out toward the water. "Here they come."

Emerging from the surf was a small penguin, and behind it another until there was a group of ten to twelve. They hurried up the beach and into the grassy areas.

A loud chirping rose as their chicks realized dinner had arrived. Soon after the first group, another one came out of the water. Then another. Occasionally the group would be as many as twenty.

Ryan leaned close. There was a smell to him that was all Ryan with a hint of the sea. Phoebe liked the combination.

"Why do they come out in groups?"

"For protection from predators. If they all come at once, then they all could be killed. They come out in groups and in waves. That way there will be someone left to take care of the chicks if something happens to them."

Who would take care of her child if something happened to her? She wasn't going to think about that. Glancing at Ryan, she saw that he was looking out at the water. Was he thinking about what she'd said?

As they watched the penguins, the sun went down and floodlights came on. Phoebe shivered as a breeze came off the water. Ryan put an arm around her and pulled her in close. She didn't resist his warmth. Instead, she snuggled into his side.

As they watched, a cluster came out of the water and quickly returned.

"See, that group was frightened by something. Watch for a minute and they will try it again."

Out of the water they came. Ryan gave her a little squeeze.

"You know, I expected the penguins to have black coats but they are really a dark navy."

"That was my biggest surprise the first time I saw them. Aren't they cute?"

"I have to admit they are."

They watched for the next hour. As they did so the penguins continued to come out in waves and the noise from the nests rose to almost a point to where Ryan and Phoebe couldn't hear each other.

Finally they sat there for another ten minutes and no more birds arrived. The crowd started moving toward the walkway.

"Is that it?" Ryan sounded disappointed.

"That's it for tonight."

"Amazing."

When they passed a park ranger, Ryan asked, "How many penguins are there?"

"Two thousand two hundred and fifty-one tonight."

"How do you know that?"

"We count them. There are rangers stationed in sections along the beach."

Ryan's arm supported her as they climbed the hill on the way back to the welcome center. He didn't remove it as they walked to the truck.

As they left the car park he said, "Thanks for bringing me. I'll be doing this again."

"I'm glad you had a good time."

"I did. I bet you are beat." He grinned. "You didn't even fall asleep on me today."

"I'm sorry. I can't help it."

"I'm just teasing you."

They talked about their day for a few minutes. It was the best one she'd had in a long time. Even before Joshua had died. Ryan had proved he could be fun and willing to try new things. She had more than enjoyed his company. Unfortunately, she feared she might crave it. Her eyelids became heavy and a strong arm pulled her against a firm cushion.

\* \* \*

Ryan hated to wake Phoebe but they were in front of her house. He had given thought to just sitting in the truck and holding her all night.

Visiting the penguins had been wonderful. He'd especially enjoyed the look on Phoebe's face when the first bird had waddled out of the water. It was pure pleasure. He'd like the chance to put a look on her face like that.

That was a place he shouldn't go. He'd been more than uncomfortable when the discussion had turned to how parents protected their young. He couldn't be that person in Phoebe's life and the baby's. That devotion those tiny birds had to their young wasn't in him. He couldn't let Phoebe start believing that it was. He wouldn't be around for the long haul. That required a level of emotion that he wasn't willing to give.

Still, she felt right in his arms. Too right.

He pushed those thoughts away and settled for practicality and what was best for Phoebe. She would be sore from sleeping in the truck and he would ache for other reasons. He smirked. Plus he was liable to end up in jail when her neighbor called the police.

"Phoebe." He shook her gently. "Phoebe. We're home."

Her eyes fluttered open. "Mmm…?"

"We're at your house."

"Oh." She tried to sit up but it wasn't happening quickly.

"I'm sorry, I didn't mean to fall asleep on you, literally and figuratively."

"Not a problem." And it hadn't been.

Ryan opened his door and got out before helping her out. He walked her to the door.

"What about my chest of drawers?"

"I need to fix the leg and build a drawer before you can do much with it anyway. I'll just take it home with me. You could come to my house and work on it. I'll do the paint stripping anyway. You don't need to be around those fumes."

"You've already done so much."

Ryan put a hand under her chin and lifted it. "Hey, today was no hardship for me."

She smiled. "I enjoyed it, too."

With reluctance he stepped back. "You need to get to bed."

"And you still have a drive ahead."

"I do. I'll see you in clinic Wednesday afternoon. Plan to come to my place afterward. I should have the leg on and the drawer done by then."

"Okay."

He liked the fact that she readily agreed.

"See you then."

Phoebe made her way into the hospital and up to the clinic waiting room. She hadn't been this nervous since her first visit. Her name was called and she was directed to an examination room. She was told to remove her trousers, sit on the exam table and place the sheet over her. Soon Sophia entered. "Well, have you made a decision on who you want to replace me?"

"Not yet. I hate to lose you. Are you sure you can't put off the wedding until after this baby is born?"

"I don't think Aiden will agree to that. You're going to have to make a decision soon."

"I know."

"I'm sorry that I can't be there to deliver." Sophia's smile grew. "But love doesn't wait."

"I understand. I wish you the best."

"So how's it going between you and Ryan? I know your first meeting was a little rocky."

Phoebe smiled. "That would be an understatement. It turns out he's a great guy. He's been helping me get the baby's room together. I asked him to put the baby bed together and he volunteered to paint the room."

"I'm not surprised. He's the kind of person who keeps to himself and quietly goes about helping people."

A few minutes later Sophia had left and Phoebe had just finished dressing when there was a knock on the door. "Come in."

Ryan entered. "Hey."

"Hi." She sounded shy even to herself. She'd never been timid in her life.

"So how're you feeling?"

"Fine."

"Great. No aches or pains after our adventure on Saturday?"

She appreciated his friendly manner. "I was tired but no more than I'm sure you were."

"I have to admit it was a long day. You mind waiting on me in the waiting room? I have one more patient to see."

"Sure."

She hadn't been waiting long when he came out of the office area.

"You ready?"

She stood. "Ryan, I have to work tomorrow. I can't be out late. Maybe I should just come by this weekend."

"Don't you want to see what I've done with the chest?"

Ryan sounded like a kid wanting to show off his new toy. He opened the door leading to the main hall. She went out and he followed.

"Sure I do, but I also have to get to bed at a decent hour."

"I'll drive you home."

"I don't want you to have to do that."

He looked at her. Worry darkened his eyes to a granite color. "Is something wrong? Did I do something wrong?"

"No, of course not."

"Then stop arguing and come on. I'll get you home for your regular bedtime. We'll go to my place and then walk down to a café for dinner. Then I'll take you home."

"Okay. If you insist."

"I do."

Twenty minutes later Ryan unlocked the front door to his home. She followed him in. The place looked no different than it had the last time she had been there yet everything had changed. She felt welcomed where she hadn't before.

Ryan dropped his clothes in a pile next to the door just as he had done before. "Are you thirsty?" he called from the kitchen area.

"No, but I would like to use the bathroom."

"That's right. Pregnant women and their bladders. You'll find it off my bedroom. Sorry it isn't cleaner."

"I'll try not to look."

Phoebe walked to the only doorway she'd never been through. She stopped in shock. The most perfect bedroom suite she'd ever seen filled the room. The furnishing here was nothing like what was in the rest of the house. There was such a contrast it was like being in two different worlds. She went to the sleigh-style bed and ran her hand along the footboard, then turned to study the large dresser. The workmanship was old world with a twist of the modern. She'd never seen any like it. She'd give anything to have furniture like this.

"Hey, Phoebe—" Ryan walked into the room.

"These are beautiful pieces. Where did you get them?" She walked around the end of the bed to the bedside table. She couldn't stop herself from touching it.

"I made it."

She pivoted. "You did? It's amazing. If you ever give up being a midwife, you could become a millionaire, making furniture. It's just beautiful."

A hint of redness crept up his throat.

"Thank you. I don't think it's that good. But I'm glad you like it. You ready to go downstairs?"

"Downstairs?"

"That's where my workshop is."

"I haven't made it to the bathroom yet."

"You go. The door to the basement is in the kitchen. I'll leave it open."

A few minutes later Phoebe gingerly descended the stairs. She was half way down when Ryan rushed over.

"Give me your hand and I'll help you. I forget how steep the steps are."

"I think I've got it." She took the last three steps, then looked around. The area was immaculate. There was equipment spaced around the room that she couldn't put a name to but there wasn't a speck of sawdust on the floor. It was in marked contrast to his living area upstairs. He obviously loved and spent a lot of time down here.

Her cabinet stood near a wooden workbench. Ryan walked over to it. There was a look of anticipation on his face. As if it really mattered to him what she thought. He moved from one foot to the other. The man was worried about her reaction.

"So what do you think?"

"About what?"

"The chest."

"I know what you're talking about, silly. I'm just teasing you. It looks wonderful."

As if he'd been awarded a prize, his chest puffed out.

She would have never thought that this self-assured man would be that concerned about her opinion.

"I couldn't find a leg that matched the others so I bought four new ones that were as close to the original as I could find."

"They look great. The drawer looks like it was made with it. I'm not surprised after I saw your bedroom furniture. Thank you, Ryan. It's perfect."

"I managed to strip some of the paint but it still needs more work. I was going to do some of it tonight but I promised to get you home."

"You know I'd rather have that finished so I can work on it than go out for a meal. Why don't I go down to the café and get takeout—?"

"While I work?" Ryan finished with a grin. "I think you could be a slave driver for a little bit."

"You're the one that said I shouldn't be stripping it. I would have put it out in the backyard where there was plenty of ventilation."

He propped his hands on his hips. "And just how were you planning to move it out of the weather?"

"I would have found a way. Ms. Rosenheim could help me."

"That would have been a sight worth watching."

She glared at him. "You don't think we could do it?"

He threw up his hands. "I don't think I would put anything past you two."

"Good. You need to remember that. Now, I'm going to get us something to eat and you'd better get busy."

"Yes, ma'am."

His chuckle followed her up the stairs.

Ryan was aware of Phoebe returning. Her soft footfalls crossed overhead. As she moved around in the kitchen, something about the sound made him feel good inside. When her eyes lit up at the sight of the chest of drawers he felt like he could carry the world on his shoulders. For so long he'd only seen the look in eyes of those in pain or life slipping away. He could do nothing to change it but this time he'd been able to help someone and see pure joy. It was the same feeling he had when he delivered a baby.

Taking the can of paint stripper off the bench, he poured it into an empty food can. Using a brush, he applied it to the wood of the chest.

He liked too many things about Phoebe. The way her hair hid her face like a curtain and then when it was drawn away discovering she'd hidden a smile from him. The way she insisted on helping. Phoebe was no shrinking violet. She was a survivor. JT's baby was lucky. JT's baby!

What was happening to him? Phoebe was JT's wife. *Was.* It didn't matter how attracted to her he was, she would always belong to JT. There was the bro code. You don't take your best friend's girl.

Ryan picked up the putty knife and began to scrape the paint off in thin sheets.

*No matter how much you might want to.*

A board creaked above him.

It didn't matter. Phoebe didn't feel that way about him. She'd been alone during a hard time in her life and she was searching for a connection to JT. All *he* meant to her was someone who had known the father of her baby. He would be her friend and nothing more.

Still, it was as if he saw the world as a better place when he was around her. Like his wounds were finally closing. That life could be good. Not black-and-white. Living or dying. But happy, healthy and hopeful.

"Hey, down there, your dinner is served." There was a

cheerful tone to her voice, like someone calling another they cared about.

Ryan's heart thumped hard against his chest. Wouldn't it be nice to be called to every meal that way? Even those little things improved life.

Phoebe was filling their glasses when Ryan's footsteps drew her attention to the door of the basement. It had been over a year since she had called someone to dinner and here she was doing it twice in less than two weeks. She liked it. There was something about it that made her feel like all was as it should be in her world.

"Smells good."

"You do know that all I did was pick it up, don't you?" she said, putting the pitcher back on the corner.

"Yes, but you did a good job with that."

He looked at the table. She had set their places with what little she could find in Ryan's woefully low-stocked kitchen. Passing a shop, she'd impulsively bought a handful of flowers. She hoped he didn't think she was suggesting that this was more than a friendly meal.

He nodded toward them. "Nice touch."

She smiled. "I like fresh flowers. I couldn't resist them."

"I'll have to remember that. Let me wash my hands."

Ryan went to the sink. With his back to her she had a chance for a good look. What would it be like to run her hands across these wide shoulders? To cup what must be a firm butt?

She didn't need to be thinking like that. But she was pregnant, not dead.

"What's wrong? You feeling okay? You have an odd look on your face."

She'd been caught ogling him. "No, no, I feel fine."

A slow smile stole over his face and his eyes twinkled, pushing the worry away. "Okay, let's eat. I'm hungry."

Had he figured out what she'd been thinking?

They each took one of the two chairs at the table.

"I didn't know what you liked so I got two kinds of soups and two sandwiches, hoping you liked at least one of each."

"It all looks good."

"I didn't move your mail off the table. I thought you might not be able to find it if I did." She pushed it toward him. Ryan's hand brushed hers when he reached for it.

The flutter in her middle had nothing to do with the baby moving. She jerked her hand back.

"Is that a valid comment on my housekeeping skills?"

"Not really, but now that you mention it I've not really seen any of those skills outside your shop."

He laughed. "I deserve that. I'm not here much and when I am I go downstairs. As for my mail, I usually let it stack up and then open anything that isn't bills when I get around to it." He glanced through the pile and pulled an envelope out, tearing it open. Slipping a card out, he studied it a moment, then laid it on the table. "It's an invitation to Sophia's wedding next weekend."

"You weren't kidding. That had to have come weeks ago."

He gave her a sheepish look. "I'm sure it did."

"I'm happy for her but I hate it she isn't going to be there to deliver this baby. I've become attached to her. It's hard to give her up. I don't want just anyone to deliver. But I've got to make a choice soon."

There was a long pause before Ryan leaned forward and said, "I'd like to do it."

Phoebe sucked in a breath. "You want to do what?"

"Be your midwife. Would you let me take over from Sophia?"

She wasn't sure it was a good idea but she didn't want to hurt his feelings by saying no immediately. She'd been looking for emotional support, not medical help. Ryan being her midwife sounded far too personal. "Ooh, I don't know if I'm comfortable with that."

"You need a midwife and I'm one."

"Yes, but isn't there something about not delivering people you know?"

His gaze held hers. "I don't see it as being a problem. And I'd rather be the one there if there's a complication than wishing I had been."

She nodded.

"Phoebe, I'd like to be a part of bringing Joshua's baby into the world."

Wasn't this what she'd been looking for? Someone to support her? Be there for her? She loved Sophia but she wasn't available. Why shouldn't Ryan be the one? Because she had feelings for him that had nothing to do with the baby.

He shifted forward in his chair. "I didn't mean to put you on the spot."

"No, no. It's okay. I'm just not sure what to say. Let me think about it."

"Take all the time you need."

She didn't have much time. He had proved more than once he was the guy Joshua had said he was. What she knew was that she didn't feel as alone as she had only a few weeks ago. Ryan had been tender and caring with her so why wouldn't he be a good midwife? Right now what she needed to do was change the subject. "Where's Sophia getting married?"

"I forget women are always interested in a wedding."
He slid the card toward her.

Phoebe picked it up. It was a classic embossed invitation. "They're getting married at Overnewton. It'll be a
beautiful wedding. That's an amazing place."

Ryan gazed at her over his soup spoon.

"What wedding doesn't a woman think is beautiful?"

"Mine wasn't. We got married at the registry office."

"Oh?"

"It was time for Joshua to ship out and we decided to
just do it. I wore my best dress and he his dress uniform.
And we did it."

"Do you wish you'd had a fancier wedding?"

"Sometimes. But that was us back then. Fast in love,
fast to the altar. It seemed exciting. My parents were gone.
My brother showed up and one of Joshua's friends from
school was there. We all went out to eat lunch afterward.
The next day Joshua was gone."

"No honeymoon?"

"We took a trip into the mountains, camping, when he
came home nine months later. Those were good times."

It was nice to talk about Joshua. People were hesitant
to ask about him. They were always afraid it would make
her cry. What they didn't understand was that she wanted
to talk about the husband she'd lost. Wanted to remember.
She and Joshua had had some fun times. It was a shame
they had grown apart there at the end. She'd wanted better for him. For him to think of her positively.

She picked up her sandwich. "How about you? Ever
been married?"

"No."

"Not even close?"

"Nope. Never found the right one."

"I bet there have been women who thought you were the right one."

He shrugged.

"So you've been a 'love them and leave them' guy?"

Ryan looked at her. "I wouldn't say that. It's more like it's better not to get involved unless your heart is fully in it. Mine never has been."

His eyes held a dark look, despite the effortlessness of the words. There was more to it than that but she didn't know him well enough to probe further. "I guess that's fair."

"You know, Joshua used to talk about you all the time. It was Phoebe this and Phoebe that."

"Really?" She'd always thought she'd been more like a toy that he'd come home to play with and then left behind to pick up again during the next holiday. Would things have been different between them if Joshua had not been gone so much?

"He talked about how you liked to camp and hike. What a good sport you were. I liked to hear stories about places you went, things you did."

Guilt washed through her. And the last time Joshua had been home they'd done nothing special. Instead, they'd talked about getting a divorce. How had their relationship deteriorated so much? Would anyone ever love her like she needed to be loved? Want to come home to her every night? Have a family? She put down her half-eaten sandwich and pushed back her chair. "I need to get this cleaned up and get home. It's getting late."

"Do you mind if I finish my sandwich before we go?"

"I'm sorry. I didn't mean to be rude." She settled in her chair again.

"It's okay."

Phoebe watched as Ryan finished his meal. As soon as he had she started removing their plates and glasses.

"I need to put a cover over a few things before we leave." Ryan went down the stairs.

Ten minutes later she called through the door to the basement, "I'm ready to go when you are."

"I'll be right up."

Coming from Ryan, she could depend on it happening.

# CHAPTER SIX

JUST UNDER AN hour later Ryan joined Phoebe on the sidewalk in front of her house.

"Thanks for the ride home."

"When are you planning to come to my house and work on the cabinet? This weekend? I'll have it ready for you by then."

"I hadn't thought about that. I guess I need to get busy. I'll bring my paints and be there early on Saturday morning."

"I can come get you—"

"No, I'll take the tram." She started up the walk.

"I don't mind."

She looked at him. "Ryan, please."

"Okay, okay. Have it your way. Come on, you're tired." He took her elbow and they started toward the door.

Phoebe stopped walking.

Ryan jerked to a stop. "What—?"

She kicked off her shoes and picked them up by two fingers. "My feet are killing me."

They continued to the door. Phoebe unlocked it, pushing it open.

"If you soak and massage your feet it would help," Ryan said behind her.

"I don't do feet." She dropped her shoes inside the door.

Ryan followed her in and closed the door behind him. "That's all right, because I do. You get a bath and come back here. Bring a bottle of your favorite lotion with you. I'll be waiting."

"It's late. We've both had a long day."

"It won't take long and I promise you'll like it. So stop complaining and go on."

Phoebe gave him a dubious look but went off toward her bedroom.

While she was gone Ryan found a cook pot and put water on to heat. Looking under the sink, he pulled out a wash pan. He added a little dish soap to it. He searched the cabinets for a container of salt and, finding it, he added a generous amount to the soap. When the water started to steam he poured it into the pan.

Going to the bathroom in the hallway, he pulled a towel off the rack. Returning to the living room, he placed the towel on the floor in front of the most comfortable-looking chair. He then went for the pan of water.

"What's all this?" Phoebe asked. She wore a gown and a housecoat that covered her breasts but not her belly. Her hair flowed around her shoulders and her cheeks were rosy. Ryan had never seen a more captivating sight.

Gathering his wits and settling his male libido, he took her hand and led her toward the chair. "I'm going to help make those feet feel better. You sit here."

She lowered herself into the chair.

"Now, slowly put your feet into the water. It may be too hot."

"This feels wonderful." She sighed, lowering her feet into the water.

He left her to get a chair from the kitchen, returned and placed it in front of her.

"What're you planning now?"

Taking a seat, he faced her. "I'm going to massage your feet."

"I'm not letting you do that!"

"Why not? You ticklish?"

Phoebe didn't look at him. "No."

"I think you're lying to me. Did you bring the lotion?"

She shifted to her right and put her hand in her house-coat pocket. She pulled out a bottle and handed it to him. Without even opening the bottle he recognized the scent he thought of as hers. He reached down, his hand wrapping her calf and lifting it to rest on his thigh.

"I'm getting you wet." She tried to pull her foot away.

He held it in place. "If it isn't bothering me, then don't let it bother you. Lean back and relax. Close your eyes."

He squirted a liberal amount of lotion into his palm and began rubbing Phoebe's foot. At the first touch she flinched and her eyes popped open. Their gazes met as he began to massage her skin. Seconds later, her eyes closed and she relaxed. As he worked the tissue on the bottom of her foot she let out a soft moan.

"Where did you learn this?" she asked almost with a sigh.

"In the army. The men in the hospital always seemed to respond and became calmer if they had a massage of some kind."

"I can understand that."

His hands moved to her ankle and then along her calf, kneading the muscles.

"I'm sorry if I put you in a difficult position when I asked to be your midwife." He squeezed more lotion into his hand and started at her toes again and pushed upward.

"It was sweet of you to ask."

He wasn't sure that Phoebe thinking of him as sweet was to his liking.

"Well, something that was said seemed to upset you." He gently pulled on one of her toes.

"It wasn't what you said as much as something I remembered."

"I guess it wasn't a good one." His fingers continued to work her toes.

"No. When Joshua was home the last time, we talked about separating."

"That's tough." He moved up to her knee and started down again.

"We had grown apart. I had my life and he had his. We just didn't make sense anymore." A tone of pain surrounded every word.

"I'm sorry to hear that. It must really have been difficult to deal with when you realized you were pregnant."

"That would be an understatement. How about an ocean of guilt?"

Ryan could more than understand that feeling. He placed her foot back into the pan and picked up the other one. He gave the second one the same attention as he had the first.

Phoebe leaned back and neither one of them spoke for the next few minutes. Ryan was content to watch the expression of pleasure on her face.

"You sure know the way to a woman's heart."

His hands faltered on her calf. He didn't want her heart. Having someone's heart meant they expected some emotion in return. He didn't get that involved with anyone.

Her eyes opened and met his look. There was a realization in them of what she'd said. Regardless of what his mind told him, his body recognized and reacted to the longing in her eyes. His hands moved to massage her knee and above, just as he had done before, but this time the movements requested more. Unable to resist, his fingers brushed the tender tissue of her inner thigh.

Phoebe was no longer thinking about her feet. This gorgeous, intelligent hunk of man in front of her wanted her. She couldn't remember the last time she'd felt desired. If it had ever felt this compelling.

Ryan's gaze captured hers. His eyes were storm-cloud gray. He held her leg with one hand and slowly trailed a finger upward past her knee to tease her thigh again before bring it down. It was no longer a massaging motion but a caress. With what looked like regret in his eyes, he lowered her foot into the water.

With his gaze still fixed on her, he offered both of his hands.

She took them. He gently pulled her closer and closer until she was in an upright position. Leaning forward, his mouth drew near. "I may be making a huge mistake but I can't help myself."

Ryan's lips were firm, full and sure as they rested on hers. He pressed deeper.

Phoebe wanted more but wasn't sure what that was or if she should want it. This was the first kiss she'd had since Joshua's parting one. She pulled away, their lips losing contact. Her eyes lifted and her look met Ryan's. He didn't hold it. Without a word, he scooped her up into his arms. She wrapped her hands around his neck.

"What?"

"Just be quiet." The words were a low growl. He carried her down the hall to her bedroom and stood her on her feet next to her bed. "Get in."

His tone was gruff. She didn't question, instead doing as he asked. He tucked the extra pillow under her middle and pulled the covers over her shoulders before he turned off the light and left the room. "Good night, Phoebe."

Had he been as affected by the kiss as she had? She still trembled inside. Ryan's lips meeting hers had been wonderful and shocking at the same time. He had surprised her. Everything had remained on a friendly level until his hand had moved up her leg. She'd wanted his kiss but hadn't been sure what to do when she'd got it.

Those days of schoolgirl insecurity had returned. She was soon going to be a mother. Did he feel sorry for her because of the baby? Joshua? Or just because he thought she needed the attention at the moment? The doubts had made her pull away. Now she regretted doing so. Her body longed for him. But it couldn't be. She wouldn't have Ryan feel obligated to her because of her situation. She'd put him on the spot when she'd shown up at his house and she had no intention of doing that to him again. It was best for them just to remain friends.

A few minutes later the front door was opened and closed. Ryan had gone. She didn't have to wonder if the pan and chair had been put away or the front door secured. Ryan would have taken care of that just like she knew she could rely on him to be there for her.

Ryan couldn't sleep and any time he couldn't do that he went to his workshop. What had he been thinking when he'd kissed Phoebe? That was the problem. He hadn't been thinking but feeling. Something he couldn't remember doing in a long time. The need to do more than touch her had pulled at him to the point he'd been unable to stand it any longer. When she'd raised those large questioning eyes…

How could he have done it? He had kissed his dead best friend's wife. Someone who had trusted him. Could there be a greater betrayal? He'd stepped over the line. Way over. Both personally and professionally. It wouldn't happen again. He could put his personal feelings aside and concentrate on the professional. That was enough of those thoughts.

He had the chest of drawers to finish and sand, and there was also the rocking chair to repair. Phoebe would be here in two days ready to work on them. Soon that baby's room would be complete and the baby here. Then he could back out of Phoebe's life. He would have done then what he could do to honor JT. Phoebe would no longer need him.

Had he seen a cradle at Phoebe's? She would need a cradle for the first few months to keep the newborn close. He'd been given some pink silkwood by an associate who was moving out of town. It had been stored away for a special project. This was it.

Would he have time to get it done before the baby came? If he worked on it every chance he had, he might make it. He'd finish the chest and then start on the cradle. If he worked on the rocker while Phoebe was busy painting, he could keep the cradle a surprise.

He had plenty to do so there wouldn't be time to think about Phoebe. The feel of her lips. The desire in her eyes. The need that was growing in him. With his mind and hands busy he wouldn't be tempted to kiss her again. He had to get control of his emotions. In Iraq he'd been the king of control. He needed to summon some of that now. Compartmentalize when he was around Phoebe. Keep that door she was pushing open firmly closed.

On Saturday morning Ryan came home as the sun was coming up. He'd been gone all night, delivering a baby. Phoebe would be there in a few hours. He wanted to get some sleep before she arrived. Taking a quick bath, he crawled into bed.

He woke with a start. Something wasn't right. The room was too bright. He groaned. He'd slept longer than he'd planned. But something else was off.

*Music.* His workshop. He had a radio there. Had he left it on?

Wearing only his boxer shorts, he headed for the kitchen. The music grew louder. The basement door stood wide open and a humming mixed with the song playing drifted up the stairs. He moved slowly down the steps, being careful not to make a noise. Halfway down, he bent over to see who was there.

*Phoebe.* She sat on a stool with her back to him, painting a side of the chest. She'd been smart enough to open the outside door to let out any fumes. Ryan trod on the next step hard enough that she would hear it. He didn't want to scare her by calling her name.

She twisted around. "Hey."

There was a tentative sound to her voice. Was she thinking about what had happened the last time they had seen each other? Was she worried he might try to kiss her again? He needed to put her at ease. "Hey, yourself. You're not afraid of being hurt when you come into someone's house while they're sleeping?"

"I knocked and knocked. I tried the front door and it was open. I came in and saw you were sleeping. I figured you'd had a late night and had left it open for me."

He nodded. Some of that was true, except he had planned to be up when she arrived. "I had a delivery early this morning."

"How's the mother and baby?"

He moved down the stairs going to stand beside her. "Great. Beautiful girl named Margaret."

"Nice. What do you think?" She indicated the work she'd been doing.

Phoebe had left the wood a natural color and was paint-ing a vine with flowers down the side. "Looks great. What're your plans for the rest of it?"

"I'm going to paint the drawers different colors and paint the other side like this one."

"Sounds nice. Well, I'm going up and see if I can find some breakfast. Then I'll be back down."

He was headed up the stairs when Phoebe said in a bright voice, "Hey, Ryan. I like those boxers. Very sexy."

There was the straightforward Phoebe he'd come to ap-preciate. Ryan glanced down and shook his head. He'd for-gotten all about what he was wearing. "Thanks. I do try."

Phoebe laughed. Ryan did have a good sense of humor. She liked that about him. In fact, she liked too much. He was sexy man and a good kisser, as well. He hadn't men-tion the kiss or even acted as if he would try again. She couldn't let that happen. Her life was already too compli-cated. She wouldn't add another emotional turn to it. If he didn't say something, she would have to.

A harsh word filled the air.

She heaved herself off the stool and walked to the door. Another harsh word and pounding on the floor filled the air. She climbed the stairs.

Ryan stood at the sink with the water running.

She moved to his side. "What happened?"

"I burned my finger."

Phoebe smirked at his whiny tone. She went to the re-frigerator and opened the freezer compartment. Taking out an ice cube, she handed it to him. "Here, hold this over it."

With a chagrined twist to his mouth he took it. Phoebe looked around the kitchen, found a napkin from a fast-food restaurant and handed that to him, as well. He placed the ice in it and put it on his finger.

"Nothing like the big strong medic needing a medic."

"Hey, taking care of someone hurt is different than being hurt yourself."

She grinned. "Or cooking. Looks like you were having eggs and bacon."

Phoebe pulled the pan that looked as if it had been hastily pushed to the back burner forward and turned on the stove. The bacon was half-cooked.

"I didn't mean for you to come up and cook for me. I'm interrupting your painting."

"It can wait."

She picked up the two eggs sitting on the counter. Cracking them, she let them drop into the pan. There was a *ding*. The toast popped up.

Ryan pulled the slices out and placed them on a plate. "See, I can make toast without hurting myself."

"You get a gold star for that."

"Is that what you give your students when they're good?"

"Fifth years are too old for that sort of thing. Mostly they are happy to get to be first in line to lunch."

He stood nearer than she was comfortable with, but there was nowhere for her to go and still see what she was cooking. It made her body hum just to have him close. This was not what she'd told herself should happen.

"JT was very proud of the fact you're a teacher."

"Really? I always felt like he resented me having to go to work when he was home." Phoebe lifted the bacon, then the two fried eggs out of the pan, placing them beside the toast. She put the frying pan on the back burner and turned off the stove.

Ryan took the plate and sat down at the table. "Maybe that was because he wanted to spend as much normal time with you as possible. Nothing was normal where we were. People thought differently, ate differently, dressed differently. Everything was different. When I had leave I just wanted as much normalcy as I could get."

She slid into the chair across from him. "Then why did he always look forward to going back?"

"I don't know if I can really answer that question. Because it was his job. Because you feel like you're doing something bigger than yourself, something important. You're helping people who can't help themselves. Then there's the excitement. The adrenaline rush can be addictive.

"What I do know is that JT was good at his job. He was good to his men, protected them at any cost, even to himself."

She nodded. Some of the ache over their last words left her. "Thanks for telling me. Now I better understand why he always seemed so eager to return. Sometimes I worried it was more to get away from me. If you think you can finish up your breakfast without injuring yourself, I'll go and work on the chest."

Half an hour later Ryan went down the stairs. "I'm just going to work over here, out of your way."

"You're not going to be in my way."

Over the next hour they said little to each other as they both concentrated on their own projects. Every once in a while she glanced at Ryan. It appeared as if he was drawing off a pattern onto a plank of wood once when she looked. Another time he looked like he was studying a pattern he had spread across the workbench. There was something easy and comfortable about the two of them doing their own things together. It was the companionship she had been missing in her marriage.

Phoebe rubbed her hand over the baby as she looked at the painting she'd just completed. The world would be a good place for him or her. She felt more confident about that now. Glancing at Ryan, she found him with his butt leaning against the bench looking at her.

"Is something wrong?"

"No, I was just enjoying watching you."

Warmth flooded her. She had to stop this now or their new-found friendship might be damaged. She needed it too much to let that happen. "Uh, Ryan, about the other night…"

Ryan tensed slightly, as if he was unsure what she was going to say next.

"Why did you kiss me?"

"Because I wanted to." His eyes never wavered. Ryan was being just as direct.

She shifted on the stool. "That's nice but it can't happen again."

"Why not? We're both adults. I'm attracted to you. I believe you like me. So why not?"

"Because I don't think I can handle any more emotional baggage right now. I've lost a husband who died thinking I no longer loved him. Finding out I was expecting his baby was a shock of a lifetime. Realizing I'm going to have to raise a baby on my own is all I can handle right now. I can't take on more upheaval. I just think it would be easier if we remain friends and friends only."

He nodded. "I understand." Then he turned back to his work at the bench.

Phoebe believed he did. But she hadn't missed that he'd made no promises. She pressed her lips together. Did she really want him to?

Ryan opened the door to the examination room at the clinic the next Wednesday afternoon. To his shock, Phoebe was his next patient. He hadn't seen her since Saturday around noon when he'd had to leave her to deliver a baby. He'd told her she could stay as long as she wished and just to close up before she left as he doubted he'd be home before she was ready to leave.

Hours later he'd arrived home to a neat and tidy house. His bed had been made and his kitchen spotless. Even his pile of dirty clothes had gone. They were neatly folded on his bed. He'd had to admit it was nice to be cared for. It would be easy to get used to.

He'd been astonished at how much he'd missed Phoebe in the next few days and how much he was looking forward to seeing her again. After her statement about nothing more happening between them he didn't want to push her further away. Still, the thought of kissing her kept running through his mind. He'd be tempted when he saw her, but instead he would put on his professional hat and control himself.

"Hi, Phoebe," he said, as he stepped into the room and to the end of the table she was sitting on so he could face her. "This is a surprise."

She smiled. "Hey."

"Thanks for cleaning my house. You shouldn't have but I'm glad you did."

"It was nothing. It gave me something to do while I waited for the paint to dry. I saw the rocker. It looks great. You have a real talent."

"Thanks. Did you ask to see me for some reason?"

"I did. I'd like you to deliver my baby."

She had his complete attention.

"That is, if you still want to."

Ryan did. He owed it to JT. For not only his life when they had been pinned down, but because he had made a new start because of him. He had left the army, become a midwife and moved to Australia. Death was no longer a daily event. Ryan had been afraid that if he'd continued to be a medic that he would have never seen another side of life. Would have gone deeper into depression. He'd needed a change and JT had helped him see that.

That was what it had been about when he'd first asked but now, if he was truthful with himself, he wanted to be there for Phoebe and baby. They had started to matter more than he would have ever believed. "I'd be honored."

"I can't think of anyone I'd rather have."

"Thanks. So for your first official visit with me I'm going to listen to the baby's heartbeat, check your blood pressure, measure the size of the baby and check the position by feeling your belly."

"I understand." She said this more to the floor than him.

"Hey, Phoebe." She met his gaze. "Are you sure you're good with me taking over?"

"I do want you to do the delivery, it's just that this exam stuff the first time is a little…awkward."

"For both of us. So what do you say that we get it over with and go have some dinner? Why don't you lie down on the table and tell me what else you have planned for the baby's room?"

Ryan enjoyed her nervous chatter. He didn't blame her. More than once he reminded his hands not to tremble as he placed his hand on her skin and felt for the baby's position. "Well, you and the baby are doing great. You get dressed and we'll get that dinner."

"Do you invite all your patients out to eat?" she asked in a saucy tone.

"No, I do not. I save that for very special ones."

Less than half an hour later they were ordering their dinner at a café a few blocks from the hospital.

"I would have been glad to cook."

"You've done enough of that for me."

"As compared to all you have done for me?" Phoebe glared at him.

"Okay, let's not fight over who has done more." Ryan grinned back at her. "So how have you been?"

"I'm feeling fine. Just ready for this baby to get here and tired of people treating me like I can't do anything for myself. I was moving a box across the floor in my classroom the other day. It wasn't heavy but the janitor rushed to help me. On the tram on the way in a woman offered to hold my schoolbag. She said, 'Honey, isn't that too heavy for you?' I know she was just being nice but I'd like to go somewhere and enjoy being me instead of a pregnant woman."

"People are just naturally helpful when someone is carrying a baby."

The waiter brought their dinner.

"I know. But besides the baby, there's also Phoebe Taylor in here." She pointed to her chest.

He knew that too well. The sweet taste of her kiss still lingered in his memory like the fragrance of fresh-cut wood. Still, he shouldn't have stepped over that line. He owed her an apology but he couldn't bring himself to utter the words. Nothing in him regretted kissing her, not even for a second. Maybe he could show her he'd honor her decision in another way. He would show her he could be a gentleman. That she had nothing to fear on that level from him.

"Sophia really wants me at her wedding Friday evening. Would you like to go with me? We could dance the night away. I'll promise not to treat you like a pregnant woman." That was a promise he already knew he would break. He was far too attracted to her. The pregnancy hadn't even entered his mind when he'd kissed her. Still he would work not to go beyond that barrier Phoebe had erected.

At her skeptical look, he said, "No touching outside of dancing. Just friends."

"I don't know."

"Come on, Phoebe, you know you want to. Dinner and dancing. You don't want me to show up dateless, now, do you?"

She smiled at that. "I don't think you would have any trouble getting a date if you wanted one."

"It seems I'm having to work pretty hard right now to get one."

Phoebe smirked. "Okay, but only because you sound so pitiful. My dancing may be more like swaying."

"I don't mind. We'll just go and enjoy ourselves."

"All right. It may be a long time before I get to do something like that again."

"Well, every man wants to hear that kind of enthusiasm when he asks someone out."

"I didn't mean for it to sound like that. Thanks for inviting me."

The waiter stopped by the table and refilled their glasses.

"That was much better. Why don't I bring the chest of drawers and the rocker out when I come to pick you up? That's if you don't mind me dressing at your place."

"That sounds fine. I can hardly wait to see what they look like in the baby's room."

The wedding suddenly didn't seem like the drudgery that Ryan had thought it would be.

They finishing their meal talking about movies they'd enjoyed and places they would one day like to visit.

On Friday, Phoebe wasn't sure which she was looking forward to more, seeing the furniture installed in the baby's room or the evening of dancing with Ryan. Thankfully it was a school holiday so she didn't have to lose any of her leave time by being off that day.

Ryan had said she was special. She liked being special to someone and especially to him. But it wasn't something she was going to let go any further.

Ryan had taken over her care. As odd as it was, it seemed right to let him be there when the baby was born. In the last couple of weeks he had more than proved himself the compassionate and understanding person Joshua had promised he would be. She couldn't have asked for better help. And it had been cheerfully given. She liked Ryan too much. Appreciated his support. She could use all those attributes when she delivered.

He was as good as his word. Which she had learned Ryan always was. He pulled up in front of her house at three o'clock.

She stepped out onto the veranda when she saw a sports car followed by a red truck she recognized pull to the curb. Ryan stepped out of the car and waved. She strolled down the path toward him. A man almost as tall as Ryan climbed out of the truck.

"Phoebe, this is Mike. He came along to help me move the chest in."

"Hi, Mike, thanks for going out of your way to do this."

"Nice to meet you. No worries. Ryan has given me a hand a few times."

She looked at Ryan but he gave no explanation. Knowing him, he'd gone out of his way more than once to help people, yet he had no one special in his life. It was as if he was all about deeds but not about becoming emotionally involved. Did he feel the same way about her?

"Let's get these in. Phoebe and I have a wedding to attend," he said to Mike.

The two men undid the straps securing the chest and rocker in the truck bed. They carried the chest into the house.

"Show us where you want it," Ryan said to her. She followed them down the hall and into the baby's room.

She had them place it against the wall opposite the bed. "Perfect."

Ryan grinned. "I'll get the rocker."

"Thank you for your help," Phoebe told Ryan's friend as he followed Ryan out the door.

He waved an arm. "No problem, mate."

She waited there for Ryan to return.

Doing a back-and-forth maneuver, he brought the rocker through the doorway. "Where do you want it?"

"Next to the bed, I think."

He placed it where she'd suggested.

She gave the top of the chair a nudge and watched it rock.

"Aren't you going to try it?"

"Yes, I am." She promptly took a seat, placing her hands on the ends of the arms. Moving back and forth a couple of times, she looked up at him and said in a reverent tone, "It's wonderful. Just wonderful."

"I'm glad you like it."

"I do." She continued to rock and rub the arms with her hands.

"I hate to mention this but we need to get a move on or we'll be late to Sophia's wedding."

"I know. All I need to do is slip on my dress. It shouldn't take long." She pushed out of the chair with obvious reluctance.

"My suit is in the car. Mind if I change in the other bedroom?"

"Make yourself at home," Phoebe said, as she walked out of the room. She stopped and faced him. "Ryan, it's really nice to have you around. You have been a good friend the last few weeks. I really needed one."

* * *

A lump came to Ryan's throat he couldn't clear. His heart thumped in his chest. All he could do was look at her. Before he could speak she was gone. With those few words from her he received the same high he did when he delivered a baby. That the world could be a good and kind place. Her happiness was starting to matter too much.

What had he gotten himself into? As hard as he'd worked to keep their relationship centered on helping her get ready for the baby, he'd still grown to care for the fascinating and fabulous woman that was the mother. If he wasn't careful he could become far too involved with Phoebe. Start to care too much. Did he have that in him?

He'd dressed and was waiting in the living room for Phoebe when she entered, carrying her shoes. She wore a modest sleeveless pale blue dress that had pleats in front. Her hair was down but she had pulled one side of it away from her face. It was held in place with a sparkling clasp. She was beautiful in her simplicity.

"I hate to ask this but could you help me buckle my shoes? I've been working for five minutes to figure out how to do it around this baby and it's just not working."

Ryan smiled. "Have a seat and I'll give it a try."

She sat on the sofa and Ryan went down on one knee.

"You look like Prince Charming, dressed in your suit."

"More like a shoe salesman."

They both laughed.

She handed him a shoe and he lifted her foot and put it on.

Working with the small buckle, he said, "No wonder you were having such a hard time. This would be difficult for an aerospace engineer."

"Yes, but they look good."

Ryan rolled his eyes.

"Let's get the other one on. Man went to the moon with less effort than I'm putting into this."

She gave his shoulder a playful slap. "Remind me not to ask you for help again."

He gave her a pointed look. "And your plan for getting these off is?"

She smiled. "You are now acting like a shoe salesman and not Prince Charming."

He finished the task and stood. "Just so you'll recognize it, this is the part where I am Prince Charming." He reached out both hands.

Phoebe put hers in his and he pulled her up until she stood. Ryan continued to hold her hands as he stepped back and studied her. "You look beautiful."

She blinked and a dreamy smile spread across her face. "Thank you. That was very Prince Charming-ish. You look very dashing yourself."

He chuckled. A ripple of pride went through him at her praise. "I do try."

She removed her hands from his and went across the room to where a shawl and purse lay in the chair nearest the front door. "We should go."

"Yes, we should. It's an hour's drive and I've not been there before."

"I know how to get there. I've been by Overnewton Castle many times. I've always wanted to go there for afternoon tea but never have been in."

"Well, princess, this is your chance." Ryan opened the door.

As she went out onto the veranda she said, "Yeah, like I look like a princess. More like a duck."

*Not to me.*

## CHAPTER SEVEN

PHOEBE HAD HEARD that Overnewton Castle was gorgeous but she'd never imagined it was anything like this magnificent. As Ryan drove up the tree-lined drive, the Victorian Tudor-style house came into view. It resembled a castle with its textured masonry, steep roofs and turrets. The multiple stories of corners and angles covered in ivy made it look even more impressive. The expanse of rolling hills and river below created a view that was breathtaking. It was a fairy-tale spot to hold a wedding or a princess for the evening.

"Wow, what a place," Ryan said, as he pulled into the car park that was secluded by trees. "After getting engaged in a hot-air balloon, I shouldn't be surprised that Sophia and Aiden would pick a place like this to marry."

"You don't like it?"

"Sure. It's just a little over the top for me."

"I love it." She did rather feel like a princess, being out with Ryan with the beautiful house as a backdrop.

He came around and helped her out. "I'm more like a beside-the-creek kind of guy but I have to admit this is a nice place."

"Getting married beside a creek, with the water washing over the rock, does sound nice." She pulled the shawl closer around her. When she had trouble adjusting it Ryan removed it, untwisted it and placed it across her shoulders once more. His hands lingered warm and heavy on her shoulders for a second. She missed his touch the instant it was gone.

"I think it's more about making a commitment and less about having a wedding."

Worry entered her voice. "You don't think Sophia and Aiden will last?"

"I'm not saying that. I think they'll do fine. It's just that I was in the service with too many guys whose wives had to have these big weddings and the marriages didn't last two years." He took her arm and placed it through his, putting his other hand over hers. She felt protected. Something that had been missing in her life for too long. They walked in the direction of the house.

"I had no idea you were such a cynic."

Ryan shrugged. "Maybe I am, but I just know what I've seen."

Her foot faltered on the stone path and he steadied her by pulling her against him. They continued down the path until it opened into a grassy area where white chairs had been arranged for the ceremony. Surrounding the area were trees, green foliage and brightly blooming flowers. It was a cozy place for a garden wedding.

"This must be the place." Ryan led her through the hedge opening.

Men and women stood in small groups between the house and the ceremony area. Phoebe recognized a few staff members from the hospital. An unsure feeling washed over her. Should she be here?

"Something wrong?" Ryan asked, as they made their way across the garden.

He always seemed to know when she was disturbed. She pulled away from him. "Are you sure you should have brought me? These are the people you work with and I'm not one of them."

"Look at me, Phoebe." She did. His gaze was intense. "I wanted you here with me." He took her hand. "I want to introduce you to some people I work with."

With Ryan beside her she was capable of facing anything. Phoebe had no doubt that he would remain beside her. She could rely on him. What it all came back to was that she could trust him. He would be there for her. This was the kind of relationship she'd been looking for, dreamed of. A man who would stand beside her. She glanced at his profile, and smiled.

Phoebe recognized a number of the guests from their pictures on the wall of the clinic but there was no reason that they would know her. She had only been a patient of Sophia, and now Ryan. Still, were they surprised to see him show up with a pregnant date?

She pulled on Ryan's hand, bringing him to a stop. "In that case, we both need to look our best. Let me straighten your tie."

"What's wrong with my tie?"

"It just needs an adjustment." Phoebe stepped so close that the baby brushed against him as she reached up to move his tie a centimeter to the left. "Now it's perfect."

Their gazes met.

"No, *you're* perfect." She blinked. His low raspy voice sent a ripple of awareness through her.

"Thank you," she said softly, "and thanks for this evening. It's already been wonderful." She meant that with all her heart.

His brow arched. "We haven't done anything yet."

"I know, but it was nice just to be invited out." *And to be treated as someone special.*

The group opened up as they approached to include

them. Ryan went around the circle, introducing everyone. His hand came to rest on the curve of her back. "And this is my friend, Phoebe Taylor."

She noticed that Ryan had presented her as a friend when he'd only introduced the people he worked with as his colleagues. It seemed as if he didn't have many people he considered friends. Yet he and she had formed what she would call a friendship. Why didn't he have more of them?

Ryan was acting nothing like he had the day she had met him. Was he hiding from the world for some reason? What had happened?

She smiled and listened to the conversation and banter between the members of the group. Ryan wasn't left out. He was obviously liked so why didn't he consider any of them his friends?

A few minutes later the notes from a harp sounded to announce it was time for the ceremony to begin. People started taking their seats.

"Sophia has pulled out all the stops for this wedding. I don't believe I've ever been to one with someone playing the harp," Ryan whispered. His breath brushed her neck as they stood in line, waiting for the usher to seat them.

Shivers ran down her spine. Thankfully her reaction went unnoticed because a tuxedo-wearing groomsman approached. He offered his arm and escorted her down the aisle, with Ryan following.

As they took their seats Ryan spoke to a couple of women sitting behind them. One he introduced as Isla, the head midwife in the maternity unit, and her husband, Dr. Alessandro Manos, who was one of the doctors there. Phoebe recognized Isla from visits to the clinic. A number of times Phoebe had seen her in the hallway. She was also very familiar with the prominent Delamere name. It appeared often in the society pages. She and Isla had something in common. Isla was pregnant as well but not as far along as she was. The other woman was Dr. Darcie Green. Phoebe was told she was a visiting obstetrician from London but she didn't catch her date's name.

After they were settled in their chairs she glanced at Ryan. He wore a stoic look. She leaned toward him. "This really isn't your favorite thing to do, is it?"

His shoulder touched hers. They must have looked like two lovers whispering. What would it be like to be loved by Ryan? Amazing would be her guess. She'd sworn to herself she wouldn't cross the line, had made Ryan pledge the same, but she wasn't sure she wanted it that way any longer.

"Do you know a man that enjoys this?"

She paused. "No, I guess not. We don't have to stay."

"I promised dinner and dancing and I don't plan to disappoint you." Ryan moved closer, putting his mouth to her ear. The intimacy made her grow warm. "*Men* do like food and holding women."

Was he looking forward to dancing with her as much as she was look forward to spending time in his arms? Thankfully, a woman stood in front and began to sing a hymn, leaving Phoebe no more time to contemplate the anticipation of having Ryan hold her. She wasn't sure she could have commented if she'd had a chance. Minutes later the parents of the bride and groom were seated. The harpist played again. The groom and groomsmen stepped to the altar, which was defined by a white metal arch.

Phoebe straightened her back as far as she could to see over the heads of those sitting in front of them. The men wore black tuxedos, making them look not only dashing but sophisticated. She glanced at Ryan and imagined what he would look like in a tux. Very handsome, no doubt. She could only see the top of the best man's head. He was in a wheelchair.

Ryan put his arm across the back of her chair and whispered, "That's Aiden's brother, Nathan, in the chair."

Phoebe nodded.

The harpist continued to play as the bridesmaids came down the aisle. They were dressed in bright yellow knee-length dresses of various styles. Each carried a bouquet of white daisies. As they joined the men, they made a striking combination against the backdrop of trees and plants.

A breeze picked up and Phoebe pulled her wrap closer. She felt Ryan adjusting the wrap to cover her right arm completely. His hand rested on her shoulder. There was something reassuring about the possessive way he touched her.

She looked at him and smiled.

It was time for Sophia to come down the aisle. At the first note of the traditional wedding march everyone stood. Phoebe went up on her toes to catch a glimpse of the bride going by.

"Move so I can see." She nudged Ryan back a step so she could peer around him.

He gave her an indulgent smile and complied.

What little she could observe of Sophia looked beautiful. When she reached Aiden all the guests sat.

Ryan's hand came to rest on her shoulder again. He nudged her close. "You really do like this stuff."

"Shush," Phoebe hissed.

He chuckled softly.

It wasn't long until Sophia and Aiden were coming back down the aisle as man and wife.

Ryan took Phoebe's hand as they filed out of their row. He continued to hold it while they walked across the garden toward the house where the reception would be held.

They entered the main hall through glass doors. Cocktails and hors d'oeuvres were being served there. Phoebe gasped at the beauty of the majestic circular staircase before them. It and the dark wood paneling were all the decoration required.

"Come over here," Ryan said, placing his hand on her waist. "If you plan to dance the night away, I think you need to get off your feet and rest while you can."

For once she accepted his concern and consideration. She'd gone so many years doing everything for herself that having someone think of her was fabulous. This evening she was going to enjoy being pampered. Having it done by Ryan would be even nicer.

There were high-backed chairs sitting along the wall and she took one of them. Ryan stood beside her. When the waiter carrying drinks came by they both requested something nonalcoholic, she because she was pregnant and he because he said he would be driving. She liked it that he was acting responsibly. Now that she was having a baby it seemed she thought about that more.

A number of people stopped and spoke to Ryan. While he talked to them, his fingers lightly rested against the top of her shoulder. It would be clear to everyone that she was with him. He never failed to introduce her. A few people gave her belly a searching look and then grinned at them. They must have thought they were a couple.

"Why, hello, Ryan. I never took you for a wedding kind of guy. I've never even seen you at a Christmas party." The words were delivered in a teasing tone by a woman who joined them.

Phoebe looked up at Ryan and he seemed to take the comment in stride.

"Hello, Vera. It's nice to see you, too. Sophia twisted my arm on this one. Couldn't get out of it. I'd like you to meet Phoebe Taylor." He directed the next statement to Phoebe. "Vera is the hospital's chief anesthetist."

"Hi." Phoebe smiled at Vera.

"Nice to meet you." Vera's attention went back to Ryan. "I had no idea you were expecting a baby."

"It's not mine."

"Oh." She made the word carry a mountain of suggestions and questions.

"Phoebe was a wife of a friend of mine in the service. He was killed eight months ago."

Vera looked down at Phoebe. "I'm sorry."

"Thank you." Somehow the pain of Joshua not being there had eased over the last few weeks.

"So when's the baby due?"

"In just a few weeks," Phoebe said.

"You're being followed at Victoria antenatal?" Vera showed true interest.

"You mean prenatal," Ryan quipped.

She glared at him. "I wished you'd get away from calling it that. I have to think twice when you do."

"And I have to think when you called it antenatal. Old habits die hard."

"I guess they do. Well, I'd better mingle. Nice to meet you, Phoebe."

"Bye." Once again Ryan had proved that he was well liked and respected. So why didn't he socialize with his colleagues?

A few minutes later the guests were called to dinner. On a table outside the room was a place card with Ryan's name on it and a table number. He picked it up and led the way.

The room was stunning. Round tables with white tablecloths covering them to the floor filled it. Chairs were also covered in white with matching bows on the back. At the front of the room, facing the guests, was one long table for the bridal party.

By the time they arrived at their table, Isla and Darcie, the two women who had sat behind them during the ceremony, were already there. Ryan took the chair next to Darcie, and Phoebe sat on his other side. Another couple who knew Isla joined them and took the last seats. Everyone introduced themselves. Most of Phoebe's time was spent talking to the woman beside her. Occasionally, someone across the table would ask a question but hearing was difficult with the amount of chatter in the room.

The bridal party was introduced and Sophia and Aiden took their places before the meal was served. The noise dropped as people ate.

"So, Phoebe," Isla asked from directly across the table, "when's your baby due?"

That was the most popular question of the evening. "In a couple of weeks."

"Are you being seen in the MMU?"

"I am. Sophia was my midwife but she thought falling in love was more important." Phoebe smiled.

"That does happen. Who's following you now?"

"That would be me," Ryan announced. There was a note of pride in his voice.

A hush came over the table. Phoebe didn't miss the looks of shock on the two women's faces. Was something wrong? She glanced at Ryan. It wasn't a secret. Why should it be?

"Phoebe needed someone and I volunteered," Ryan offered, as he picked up his water glass and took a sip.

Both women looked from him, then back to her and back again. Ryan didn't seem fazed by their reaction.

Finally Isla said, "Ryan's one of the best. You'll be happy with his care."

After they had eaten their meal, Ryan watched Phoebe make her way to the restroom. His attention was drawn away from her when Isla sat down in Phoebe's place.

Isla leaned close and hissed, "Just what do you think you're doing?"

He sat back, surprised by her aggression. "Doing?"

Darcie moved in from the other side, sandwiching him in. "You're dating a patient!"

"I am not."

"What do you call it when you bring the woman you're going to deliver for to a wedding as your date?" Isla asked.

"I call it dating," Darcie quipped.

"Look, Phoebe is the widow of a service buddy of mine. All I'm trying to do is be her friend. She doesn't have anyone else."

"That wasn't a friendly arm around her at the ceremony. Or a friendly look just a second ago when she walked away," Isla stated, as if she were giving a lecture to a first-year student.

"Or when you were looking at her as she fixed your tie," Darcie added.

"You saw that?" Ryan was amazed. They had seen what he'd believed he'd been covering well—his attraction to Phoebe.

"Yes, we…" Darcie indicated her date "…went past you and you didn't even see us, you were so engrossed."

"I was not."

"You can deny it all you want but I'm telling you what I saw. The point here is that you shouldn't be dating a patient. It's bad form and if someone wanted to make a big deal of it you might lose your job." Isla looked around as if she was checking to see if anyone was listening.

Ryan chuckled. "You're overreacting to two friends spending an evening together."

"I still say you better be careful. You're stepping over the line with this one," Isla said.

Darcie nodded her agreement.

He leaned back and looked at one then the other. "Well, are either one of you going to report me?"

The two women looked at each other. Both shook their heads.

"Thank you. I asked Phoebe to come with me because she's had a rough year, finding out her husband was killed and then that she was pregnant. This was her big night out before the baby comes. In any case, all of that about me delivering the baby will be a moot point in a few weeks. So, ladies, I appreciate your concern but I'm going to show Phoebe a pleasant evening and if that looks bad to you I'm sorry."

They grinned at each other.

"You were right, Isla. He does care about her." Darcie smirked.

Isla patted him on the shoulder. "Good luck."

Ryan wasn't sure what that meant but it was better than being reprimanded for something he didn't believe was a problem.

Phoebe returned, and Isla moved back to her chair and kissed her husband on the cheek as she sat down. She smiled at Phoebe.

After Phoebe sat she leaned over and whispered, "Is everything all right?"

He took her hand beneath the table, gave it a squeeze and held it. "Everything is great."

Dessert had been served by the time the bride and groom started around the room, greeting their guests. When they reached Phoebe and Ryan's table Sophia hugged each person in turn until she worked her way to Ryan.

"Well, I'm glad to see you. I wasn't sure you'd be here."

Ryan hugged Sophia in return. "O ye of little faith."

She laughed and turned to Phoebe. For a second there was a look of astonishment on Sophia's face when she saw her but it soon disappeared. "Phoebe, I'm so glad to see you. I'd like you to meet my husband, Aiden."

While Phoebe spoke to Aiden, Ryan didn't miss the look that passed between Sophia, Isla and Darcie.

Did his feelings for Phoebe really show that much? They must if they were that obvious to the three women. How had he let it happen? He glanced at Phoebe. The devil of it was, he hadn't. All it took was just being around Phoebe to make him care. And that he did far too much.

She giggled at something Sophia said. He wanted her too much. There was little that was professional about his feelings. How would she take it when he told her that he could no longer be her midwife?

The strains of an orchestra tuning up came from somewhere in the house.

Sophia's father asked everyone to join them for dancing and a toast to the bride and groom in the solarium. Ryan took her hand as they made their way there. It was as if he didn't want to break the contact with her. She didn't want to, either.

Phoebe had been sure that what she'd already seen of the castle couldn't be surpassed, but she'd been wrong. Two-thirds of the solarium consisted of glass walls and glass ceiling. It had turned dark and small lights above created a magical place.

Ryan directed her to one of the café-size tables stationed around the room. They sat and watched the bride and groom dance their first dance. The staff saw to it that everyone had a glass of champagne to toast the couple. Ryan smiled as he tapped her glass. Phoebe took the smallest sip and set the glass down. His joined hers on the table. The orchestra began to play again.

Ryan stood and offered his hand. "It's time I made good on my promise. Would you care to dance?"

"Why, sir, I think I would." Phoebe smiled at him and placed her hand in his.

"I'll have to tell you that I'm not a very good dancer," Ryan said, as he led her out on to the floor.

She laughed. "Have you looked at me lately? I'm not very graceful so I don't think it'll matter if you're a good dancer or not."

"Then I guess we're the perfect match."

Were they really?

Ryan took her into his arms, holding her close as they moved around the floor. He'd touched her before but had never put his arms completely around her. It was lovely to have him so close. He smelled like a warm forest after a spring rain. She leaned in and inhaled. Wonderful.

The overhead lights were turned low and the tiny ones became more brilliant. They slowly swayed to the music. Did fairy tales really come true? Phoebe had no idea if they were with the beat or not. It didn't matter. The next song was a faster one and they separated. She felt the loss of Ryan's warmth immediately and her body waited impatiently to have it returned. Not allowing her to completely lose contact, he continued to hold one of her hands. As soon as the faster dance was over, he brought her back into his embrace. Her fingers rested on his shoulders and his found her waist. As they moved slowly, they looked into each other's eyes. Something was occurring here that she'd never planned, never thought would happen. She was falling in love.

"Does dancing with me make you think of that game you might have played in gym class where you had to keep a ball between you and your partner without using your hands?"

He stopped moving. "How's that?"

"Dancing with the baby between us."

Ryan laughed. "I had skill at that game. Always won." He pulled her closer. "You're the best partner I've ever had."

Her hand cupped his face. "You're a nice guy."

Ryan's eyes grew intense and he cleared his throat. "It's warm in here. Why don't we go outside for a few minutes?"

She nodded. He led her through a half-hidden glass door that looked like part of the wall, onto a brick patio.

"It feels good out here." Phoebe breathed in the cold evening air. The music from inside drifted around them. It was painfully romantic. Was Ryan feeling the same need?

"It does." Ryan stood a couple of steps away, just out of touching distance.

She wanted his touch. Wanted to feel desired. It had been too long. Even with Joshua the last time she hadn't felt desire. Sex had become more of an obligation, expectation than anything else. There should be more than that in a relationship. There was with Ryan. Would he think she was too forward if she reached for him?

A wide set of steps led to a pond below. Surrounding it was an extensive grassy area. The lights of the solarium reflected off the water, making the view even more dream-like. Phoebe started down the steps.

"Where're you going?" Ryan asked.

"I thought I'd stand in the garden and admire the so-larium." She was already watching the others dance when Ryan joined her.

"It reminds me of a carousel music box I once had as a child. As it played, horses with people riding them went by in shadow. It was like watching something magical. I could look at it for hours. I loved it," she whispered, as much to herself as to him.

"You are a romantic." He now stood close enough that his arm brushed hers as their fingers intertwined.

"Because I think there can be fairy tales?"

He didn't say anything for a while. "I haven't believed in fairy tales for a long time, but somehow when I'm around you they do seem possible."

"I know you've lived through some horrible things you can't seem to leave behind, but you need to know there's good in life, too. Happy times that can replace the bad. Like this baby. Joshua is gone, yet in a way he's bringing new life into the world. Something good for me."

"Good can be hard to find."

His fingers tightened. Phoebe glanced at him. He stood rigid, as if the discussion was painful for him. His gaze met hers and she said, "It can be. And it can come from unexpected places, too."

"Like you?"

"I like to think so but I wasn't talking about me so much as from friends and family. Finding people that matter to you. Letting them know they are important to you."

"I can't do that."

She stepped closer, her body touching his. "I think you can. In fact, I know you can. You've been a friend to me these last few weeks."

They continued to stand there, not saying a word. It wasn't until the doors were opened wide by the Overnewton staff members that the spell was broken and they broke apart. The crowd poured out of the solarium and began lining up along the steps.

"I guess it's time for Sophia and Aiden to leave," Phoebe murmured.

"We should join everyone." Ryan didn't sound like he

really wanted to. Had their conversation put a dampener on the evening? She would hate that to happen. Had she ever enjoyed a wedding more?

As they stood at the bottom of the steps, a gust of wind caught her shawl. She shivered and pulled it closer.

"You're cold." Ryan removed his jacket and placed it over her shoulders. It still held his body heat. His scent. She pulled it tighter around her.

Someone near passed them each a small container of bird seed. As Sophia and Aiden descended the steps they were showered with the seed for good luck. When they reached Phoebe and Ryan, Aiden whisked Sophia into his arms and carried her to a waiting car.

Phoebe looked down at her expanded middle. "I'd like to see someone whisk me up like that."

Suddenly her feet were in the air and she was being held against a hard chest. "Oh."

Her arms went around Ryan's neck. He swung her around a few times. She giggled.

Ryan put her on her feet again. "I didn't see it as a problem."

As he smiled down at her, a tingle grew low within her from the warmth she saw in his eyes. She glanced around. Some of the crowd was watching them. She didn't care. What she wanted was to help make Ryan see that fairy tales could come true. He had the biggest heart of anyone she knew, loyal, caring and generous. With a wicked sense of humor that only made her love him more. That's what she felt. Love for him. She'd fallen under his spell. He wasn't going to leave her. More than once he'd proved he'd be there when she needed him. She could depend on him.

Phoebe's hands remained about his neck. She looked up into his eyes and smiled. "That was fun."

"I think it's time for us to go." He looked down at her, his voice coming out soft and raspy.

Ryan walked Phoebe to her door. She'd been quiet on their drive home. Had she been thinking about those moments when they had looked into each other's eyes? He'd known then there was no going back. He wanted her and she wanted him. It had been there in her crystal clear look of assurance.

As he'd pulled out onto the main road, he'd taken her hand and rested it on his thigh. She hadn't resisted. For once she hadn't fallen asleep during the drive. Had she been as keyed up as he'd been? He wanted her but he couldn't lead her on. Have her believe there was more than just a physical attraction between them.

Her hand had remained in his the entire way back to Box Hill. She had asked for his help with her shoes when they'd arrived at his car. He had obliged. When they'd arrived at her house she'd stepped out of the car carrying them by two fingers.

They walked to her front porch. "It was a perfect evening, Ryan. Thank you so much for inviting me."

"I'm glad you had a good time. Mine wouldn't have been near as nice if you'd not gone with me."

She fumbled with her purse.

"Hand those to me." Ryan indicated the shoes. She found her keys and unlocked the door, pushing it open. Ryan followed her in.

"Would you like some coffee?" Phoebe dropped her shoes beside the door.

"I thought you didn't drink coffee."

She turned to look at him. "I don't. I bought it for you."

"Then, yes, I would." It had been a long time since someone had bought anything especially for him. It meant she thought about him even when he wasn't around. That idea he liked far too much.

He followed her to the kitchen. He leaned against the door frame and watched as Phoebe put a kettle of water on a burner. He was fascinated by the combination of her in a beautiful dress with bare feet, preparing coffee. There was something so domestic about the picture that it made him want to run as far away from there as he could get while at the same time it pulled him in, making him wish for more, had him longing for someone special in his life.

Phoebe stood on her toes to reach the bag of coffee. Her dress rose enough that he had a view of the backs of her knees and thighs. An impulse to run a hand along all that skin and under her dress made his pants tighten. Heaven help him, he wanted her so badly. Right here, right now. The entire evening had been leading up to this moment. From the time he'd was on his knee, helping her put her shoes on, until now he'd known he had to have her.

He should walk away. Go out the door without a word said. The gentleman in him, the professional, screamed for him to leave. But he wouldn't. The temptation to kiss her was too great. Unable to resist, he closed the small distance between them. Pushing her hair away, he kissed her neck. He pressed his front to her back, letting his desire be known. "I know what I agreed to, but I can't stop myself. I want you."

Before he could say more, she pushed back against him, gaining enough room to face him. She wrapped her hands around his waist and lifted her face. Her eyes were clear and confident. The quiver of her lips gave him a hint of what this boldness was costing her. Still, she was offering.

Slowly his mouth met hers.

A flood of disappointment went through him when she

pulled away seconds later but quickly turned into a storm of longing as Phoebe's lips met his again. They were soft and mobile. Small cushions of bliss. This was better than he remembered. He wanted more.

Ryan reached around her and turned off the burner, then pulled her closer. He brought his lips more fully against hers.

Phoebe's hands moved to grip his biceps. She shifted, pressing her breasts to his chest.

The arousal he felt at the first touch of her lips grew, lengthened. Hardened. His mouth released hers and moved across her cheek. He left a trail of butterfly kisses on his way to the sweet spot behind her ear. Phoebe moaned, then tilted her head so that he could better reach her neck. She snuggled against him.

The desire to have her made his muscles draw tight. He wanted her here. Now. His hands caressed her back and settled low on her hips. He gathered her dress in his hands and pulled her against his throbbing need.

"Phoebe, you'll have to stop us because I can't," he murmured as his mouth pressed down on hers, begging her for entrance.

Her hands went to the nape of his neck in an eager movement, pulling his lips more firmly to hers. She opened her mouth, and his tongue didn't hesitate to gain entrance. Hers met his to tease and tantalize. It was a duel of pleasure that he didn't want to win.

His body hummed with a need that only Phoebe could ease.

She pulled her mouth away.

"Aw. What's wrong?"

"The baby kicked."

*Damn.* He'd forgotten all about the baby. How could he? Because he was so focused on his hunger for Phoebe.

He stepped back far enough that he was no longer touching her.

"I'm sorry. I didn't mean to hurt you."

"Silly, you weren't hurting me." She took a predatory step toward him. "Babies kick."

"I shouldn't, we shouldn't…"

"Come on, Ryan. We're adults. I'm certainly aware of the facts of life, and I'm sure you are, too. So we both know that what we were doing wouldn't hurt the baby. I want this. I want you. From what I could tell, you wanted me."

*That would be an understatement.*

"I'm going to my bedroom. I hope you join me. If not, please lock up on your way out."

She went up on the tips of her toes, kissed him and left the kitchen. Ryan stood there with his manhood aching and the choice of a lifetime to make.

How like Phoebe to be so direct. If he joined her, could he remain emotionally detached? He already cared more than he should and certainly more than he was comfortable with. But if he didn't, he would never know the heaven of being with Phoebe. There was no decision. A beautiful, desirable woman that he wanted was offering him the world. There was no question of whether or not to accept.

# CHAPTER EIGHT

PHOEBE SAT ON the edge of the bed in her room. A lone lamp burned on her bedside table. She'd never been so brazen in her life. But how else was she going to get through to Ryan? She wanted him desperately. Needed his calm caring, his reliability and assurance in her life. It was so quiet in the house that she feared he'd slipped out and gone home. Seconds later her heart thumped against her ribs at the sound of footfalls in the hallway.

He'd stayed.

Ryan hesitated at the door. Their gazes met, held. He removed his tie and jacket and dropped them over the chair, then he stalked across the floor and pulled her to her feet and into his arms.

This was where she belonged.

His mouth met hers. She opened for him. Their tongues mated in a frenzied battle of touch and retreat. Heat flowed through her, strong and sure, pooling low in her. Ryan's lips left hers and he buried his face in her neck. He nipped at her skin. The desire that flickered in her blazed.

He gathered her dress along one leg, sliding a hand under the fabric. She hissed as his fingers touched her skin. His hand glided around her leg until it found the inside of her thigh and squeezed lightly. She shivered.

Ryan removed his hand. He met her gaze. Placing his hands on her shoulders, he turned her around.

"What...?"

"Shush," he all but growled. He gathered her hair, running his fingers through it. "Beautiful," he murmured, before placing it over a shoulder.

There was a tug at the top of her dress. He opened the zipper. The tug ended and his lips found the skin between her shoulder blades. A shudder traveled down her spine. His mouth skimmed over each vertebra to her waist. There he spent some time kissing and touching with the tip of his tongue the curve of her back.

She began to move but he said, "Not yet."

Ryan's fingertip followed the same path upward, then his palms until he brushed her dress off her shoulders. She crossed her arms, preventing the dress from falling away from her breasts.

He kissed the length of the ridge between her neck and arm. "So silky."

Phoebe sighed. This was too wonderful. "Let me turn off the lamp."

He guided her to face him. "Phoebe, look at me."

Her eyes rose to meet his gaze.

"You're beautiful." He placed his hands on either side of the baby. "That's a new life you're carrying. There's nothing more amazing or natural than that. Please don't hide it from me."

If she could have melted she would have. "You're sure?"

"Honey, I'm more than sure." Ryan moved closer to bring his taught length against her belly, leaving her in no doubt of his desire.

It was an empowering thought to know that was all for her.

Stepping back, he took both her hands and opened

her arms. The dress fell away, leaving her breasts visible, cupped in a lacy pink bra. Her dress gathered on her belly. Ryan gave it a gentle tug at the seams and the dress pooled around her feet on the floor.

His gaze fixed on her breasts. He sucked in a breath and she crossed her arms again.

"Please, don't. You're amazing. I want to admire you."

"They're so large." She couldn't look at him.

Ryan lifted her chin with a finger until her gaze met his. "I don't know a man in the world who doesn't love large breasts. Especially if they are his to admire."

The heat building in her grew. Ryan knew how to make her feel beautiful.

He removed her arms. Using a finger, he followed the cleft of her cleavage. Her nipples pushed against her bra as they swelled. A tingle zipped through her breasts. His finger traced the line of her bra first over one mound and then the other. She swayed and Ryan slipped an arm around her.

With a deft movement of his fingers he unclipped her bra. He slipped it off one arm. His tongue followed the same path as his finger. On the return trip, he veered off. At the same time his free hand lifted her right breast, his mouth captured her nipple.

Her womb contracted. "Ryan…" she muttered. She wasn't sure if she was begging for him to stop or to continue.

Ryan supported her as she leaned back, offering herself completely to him. Her hands went to his shoulders in the hope she could steady her body and her emotions. His mouth slid to the other nipple. Her fingertips bit into his shoulders.

Ryan's hand traced the line of her undies until he reached her center. It brushed her mound and retreated. Her center throbbed with the need for him to return. Using the arm around her waist, he pulled her toward him until she was no longer leaning back. His hand swept the other strap of her bra off and down her arm, letting the undergarment drop to the floor.

She looked at him. Ryan's gaze was fixed on her breasts. His hand reached up and stopped millimeters from her nipple. It had the slightest tremor to it. She would have missed it if she hadn't been watching. They both understood the facts of life well and still these moments of passion were overwhelming. He touched the tip of her nipple with the end of his finger.

Something similar to lightning shot through her.

"So responsive," Ryan murmured in a note of satisfaction as he ran a finger gently over her skin. It was as if a breeze had come through. He did the same to the other breast.

Phoebe quaked all over. There was something erotic about watching Ryan touch her. Her nerve endings tingled. She had to touch him. See his reaction.

He moved back and lifted both her breasts, kissing each one in turn. Taking a nipple in his mouth, he traced it with his tongue and tugged. She bucked against him.

"Clothes." The word came out as a strangled sound. "I want to see you."

A noise came low in his throat. Leaving a kiss on the curve of her breast, he stepped back. Undoing his tie, he jerked it from his collar and began unbuttoning his shirt.

While he did that she released his belt. She ran the back of her hand down the bulge of his manhood. His body's reaction to hers was stimulating. It gave her a boldness she'd never had before. She backed away until her legs found the side of the bed and she sat. Looking up at Ryan, she caught his gaze. "Come here. It's my turn."

His shirt fluttered to the floor. He stepped close enough

for her to touch him. Finding his zipper, she slowly lowered it. Her hand moved to touch him but he stopped her by capturing her hand and bringing it to his lips. "Don't." The word sounded harsh with tension. "I don't think I can control myself if you do."

Phoebe pulled her hand from his. Sliding her hands between the waist of his pants and his hips, she pushed. His trousers fell to the floor. He wore red plaid boxers that didn't disguise his size. Ryan was no small man anywhere.

He kicked off his shoes, then finished removing his slacks. Leaning over, he jerked off his socks.

Phoebe reached out and ran her hand through his hair. Her fingers itched to gather the mass and pull him to her. Had she ever been this turned on? She wanted Ryan beside her, on her and in her like she'd never wanted before. Her hands slowly slipped from his hair and Ryan looked at her. He nudged her back on the bed and came down beside her.

"I want to touch you like you did me." Phoebe rolled to her side.

He faced her.

Her heart leaped at his unspoken agreement. The lovemaking between Joshua and her had always been fast and desperate, never slow and passionate, as she was experiencing now.

Ryan wasn't sure he could stand much more of Phoebe's administering. As it was, he gritted his teeth to control his need to dive into her.

Her index finger traced the line of his lips. He captured the end and drew it into his mouth and sucked. Her eyes darkened. She slowly removed her finger. His manhood flinched. Did she have any idea how erotic she was?

Phoebe's small hand ran down the side of his neck in a gentle motion. It glided over his shoulder. She placed a kiss there. Her hair hid her face as it flowed over his skin like silk. He couldn't resist touching it, watching it move through his fingers. Pushing it away from her face, he cupped her cheek and brought her lips to his. She eagerly accepted. Her hands fluttered across his chest, moving up to the nape of his neck.

When he leaned over to take the kiss deeper, Phoebe pushed against his shoulders, breaking the connection. One hand at his neck dropped lower to run across his chest. She took an infinite amount of time tracing each of his ribs. As if she was trying to commit each curve, dip and rise of him to memory. His muscles quivered from the attention.

Her hand went lower, a finger dipping into his belly button. At his sharp inhalation she giggled. He loved the sound. Her hand moved to his side and rubbed up and down it to return to his stomach. She smoothed her fingers over his hip. The tips slipped under the elastic band of his boxers and retreated just as quickly.

Phoebe rose enough to accommodate the baby and kissed the center of his chest. At the same time her fingers went deeper under his boxers than before, touching the tip of his manhood.

Only with a force of control he hadn't known he possessed did he manage not to lose it.

Pulling her back, he gathered her to him and kissed her with a depth of need he was afraid to examine. She clung to him as if she never wanted to let him go.

"Phoebe, I need you now."

"I'm here."

Ryan scooted off the bed and removed his boxers. Phoebe's intake of breath made his manhood rise. He held out his hand and she took it, standing. His hands found the waistband of her undies and slipped them down her legs. She stepped out of them. He flipped the covers back to the end of the bed. Phoebe climbed in and seconds later he had her in his arms again.

"I don't want to hurt you. Or the baby."

She met his direct look with one of her own. "You would never do that."

The confidence she had in him shook him to the core. This wouldn't just be a physical joining but an emotional one, as well. He'd never intended to care but he did.

Ryan shifted to the center of the bed, then brought her over him until she straddled his waist. On her knees above him, her beautiful full breasts hung down like juicy melons, tempting him to feast. He wasted no time in doing so. As he savored all that was offered, Phoebe shifted so that her entrance teased his length. It ached in anticipation of finding home.

Phoebe kissed him as he lifted her hips and positioned her on him. He slid into her and they became one. He held his breath. It wasn't he but she who moved first. He joined her. Using his hands, he helped control their movements. At her frustrated sound he eased his grip and she settled farther down on him.

His hands remained lightly on her as he guided her up and down again and again. She was a beauty with her golden hair hanging down, her eyes closed and her head thrown back. With a shudder and a hiss of pleasure, she looked at him and gave him a dreamy smile.

*Yes, he was the king of the world.*

He kissed her deeply and flexed his hips against hers. After two powerful thrusts he found his own bliss.

Phoebe rolled off Ryan. Her head came to rest on his arm, a hand on his chest, her baby between them. She wished it would always be this way. She loved Ryan. He cared for her. She had no doubt of that. His lovemaking proved it.

But would he ever admit it to himself or her that he might want something lasting? It didn't matter, it wouldn't change how she felt.

She yawned. "I'm tired."

Ryan grinned. "Me, too. For a pregnant lady you sure can be rough on a man."

"So what you're saying is that you're not man enough for me."

Ryan pulled her to him for a kiss that curled her toes. His already growing manhood pushed against her leg.

"You need me to prove I'm man enough?"

"No, I think you did that just fine a few minutes ago. Right now, I need to rest. Too much dining, dancing and man." Her eyes closed to the feel of Ryan's hand rubbing her back.


Phoebe woke to the sun streaming through the bedroom window. She was alone. Panic filled her. Had Ryan left?

A clang came from the direction of the kitchen. She'd woken once during the night. Her back had been against his solid chest and his hand had cupped her right breast. It had been a perfect night. She wanted more of them.

He'd said nothing about how he felt. He had been an attentive and caring lover. She had never felt more de-sired. Still, she might be reading more into his actions than there was.

"Hey, I was hoping you were still asleep." Ryan walked into the room with a smile on his face and carrying a tray.

Phoebe pulled the sheet up to cover her chest. "Good morning to you, too. What do you have there?"

"It's supposed to be your breakfast in bed."

She'd never had anyone feed her in bed. Sitting up, she peered at the tray. "Really? That sounds nice."

He didn't seem to feel any morning-after awkwardness. She would be happy to follow his lead. Her biggest fear the night before had been that she would be a disappointment because of her size. The second fear had been that there would be unease between them this morning. Ryan had made it clear he wasn't turned off by her body. By his actions so far this morning, he was the same Ryan he had been last night.

He sat the tray at the end of the bed. She recognized it as one off the table in her living room. On it was sliced apples, two bowls of cereal and two glasses of orange juice.

"Lean forward."

Phoebe did as he asked. Ryan stuffed pillows behind her and she settled back. He joined her on the bed.

"No bacon and eggs?" She added a mock pout. "Afraid you'd burn yourself?

"You're so funny. I did what I was capable of doing. We can have something more substantial later."

"This looks wonderful to me."

She kissed him on the cheek.

"That wasn't much of a thank-you kiss. I think you can do better." His lips found hers. Seconds later Phoebe wanted to forget about their breakfast and concentrate on nothing but Ryan. Her arms went around his neck and she pulled him closer.

Ryan broke the kiss. "We need to be careful or we'll have juice and cereal everywhere. As much as I'd like to go on kissing you, I know you need nutrition."

"That sounded very midwife-ish."

He lowered his chin and gave her a serious look. "Well, that's what I am."

"And you are mine."

*He was hers.* Ryan liked the sound of that but he could never be what she needed. He couldn't commit to being hers, like she deserved. He wasn't who she thought he was. She should have someone who could love her whole-heartedly, holding nothing back. He had to see to it that their relationship remained light and easy. But after what had happened between them last night, that might be impossible.

"As your medical professional, I say eat."

"Can I put something on first?"

"I don't mind you the way you are." He grinned.

"That's sweet of you to say but I think I'd be less self-conscious with my gown on. After all, you have your underwear on."

Ryan stood. "Okay, if it'll get you to eat something, tell me where your gowns are."

She pointed to a chest. "Second drawer."

He didn't make a habit of going through a woman's personal things and found it almost too much like they were in a lifelong relationship to do so in Phoebe's. As quickly as he could, he pulled out a light blue gown. Returning to her, he helped her slip it over her head. Sitting on the edge of the bed, he asked, "Satisfied now?"

"Yes, I'm not used to breakfast in bed and I'm sure not used to sharing it with someone when I have no clothes on."

"I like you naked."

"Even with this beach ball of a belly?" She touched her middle.

He kissed her. "Women are at their prettiest when they are expecting. You glow."

She gathered her hair and pulled it over one shoulder. Her chin went up and she batted her eyelashes. "I glow? I like that."

"Yes, you glow but you would be brighter if you'd eat

something." Ryan pulled the tray closer and handed her a glass of juice.

They spent the next few minutes discussing the wedding, the weather and what other plans she had for the baby's room.

When they had finished eating Ryan stood, took the tray and was on his way out the door when Phoebe's squeak stopped him. He wheeled to look at her. Concern washed over him. Was something wrong? Should he take her to the hospital? "Are you okay?"

"Yes, just the baby making its presence known." She grinned. "I did have a little more activity last night than I normally do."

Relief flooded him. He needed to calm down, not overreact. Being a midwife, he should know better, but this was Phoebe. He cared for his patients but on no level did that came close to what he felt for Phoebe. How was he going to remain professional when he delivered the baby? Maybe it would be better if someone else did. "I'm sorry."

"I should hope not! Because I'm sure not."

"Thanks. My ego would have been damaged otherwise."

"I wouldn't want that to happen." She winced and shifted in the bed. "This baby is getting his morning exercise."

Ryan grinned. "I have an idea to help with those aches and pains. You stay there while I take this to the kitchen. I'll be right back. Don't move."

The anticipation of being in Ryan's arms again was enough to have Phoebe's blood humming. He soon returned with the bottle of lotion in his hand he had used the other night during her foot massage.

"Oh, I'm going to get another foot massage." She couldn't keep the eagerness out of her voice and started moving toward the edge of the bed.

"No. Stay where you are. Just move forward some." He put the lotion on the bedside table.

Her brow wrinkled but she did as he asked. What did he have planned this time?

Ryan climbed in bed behind her, putting a leg on each side of her hips so that she now sat between his.

"What're you doing?"

There was all kind of movement behind her until Ryan's arms came around her and pulled her back against his chest. "I was having a hard time getting the pillows to stay in place. Pull your gown up."

"What is this? Some special pregnant woman's sex position?"

He chuckled behind her. "Is that all you think about? Sex?"

"When you're around, yes."

He kissed her neck. "Thank you for the nice compliment but right now I have something else in mind. Now pull your gown up."

She did as he said until it was gathered under her breasts then adjusted the sheet over her thighs, giving her some modesty.

Ryan reached around her neck.

"Hey, is this a fancy way of choking me?"

"You sure are making it hard for me to be nice to you."

Cold hit her bare middle, making her jerk. "Ooh."

"That'll teach you not to have such a smart mouth," Ryan said in a teasing tone. His hands began to glide over her middle. "You're all tense. Lie back and enjoy."

She did, settling against his chest and closing her eyes. Ryan's hands made slow circles over her middle.

"This is wonderful. Did you learn to do this in the service, too?"

"No. But I did deliver my first baby there."

"Will you tell me about it?"

Ryan's body tensed behind her. He was quiet so long she wasn't sure he would say anything more.

"One weekend we were invited to a local celebration. I'm still not sure what it was for, but anyway some of the unit went along. We ate the food. Played with the kids.

"You know, kids are the same wherever you go. All they want is their parents there for them and to play and be happy. Every child deserves that." Ryan's hands drifted to the sides of her belly. His palms pressed lightly against her. "Especially this one."

Phoebe placed her hand over one of his. "He or she will have that. I promise."

It would be wonderful if Ryan would be a part of helping her make that come true. But he said nothing that indicated he wanted that kind of involvement in their lives.

"After the celebration we were going back to the base but had to stop because there was mechanical trouble with one of the trucks. There happened to be three or four huts that locals lived in nearby. There was a loud scream from that direction. A couple of the men went to investigate. It turned out that there was a woman having a baby. She was in trouble. They returned for me.

"I don't think I've even been in a house that had less. It was made of mud bricks, with a grass roof and dirt floor. Water was drawn from a barely running creek half a mile away. The kitchen consisted of a pot over a fire. In this horrible war-torn country, in this nothing shelter was a woman trying to give birth. The only people around were a couple of children about the ages of six and eight."

His hands stopped moving but continued to rest on her.

"I had the interpreter ask her if she would like me to help. Her culture dictated that she shouldn't agree but she

was in so much pain she wouldn't tell me no. I had seen a
baby delivered once. I'm not sure who was more scared,
me or her. I sent everyone out but the interpreter. It took
some explaining on the interpreter's part to get her to understand I needed to examine her. Finally she relented.
The baby's shoulder was hung. I was thankful it wasn't
breech, which was what I'd expected. It was work but I
managed to help bring the baby into the world. It was
exhilarating. The baby had a healthy cry and the mother
a smile on her face when I left. Imagine living like that
and still smiling. I knew then that it was far better than
patching up men who had been shot or torn apart by land-
mines. As soon as I returned to camp I put in my papers
to get out of the army."

"Did you ever see the baby again?"

"No. I never wanted to. I was afraid of what I might
find. Children have a hard life in Iraq. You know, this conversation has suddenly taken a negative turn. Not what I
intended. How about you tell me what you have planned
for this week."

His fingers started moving over her skin again.

"I think I forgot to tell you that some of the teachers at
school are giving me a shower on Monday after classes. I
hope now I'll have some baby clothes to fill the drawers of
the chest. I also hope to buy a few pictures for the walls.
If I do, would you hang them for me?"

"As long as someone doesn't go into labor, I don't see
why not."

She twisted to look at him. "Could you come out to
dinner one night?"

Ryan's fingertips fluttered over her middle. "Sounds
great to me. Sit up. I want to massage your lower back."

She did so and he pushed her gown up to her shoulders. He put more lotion in his hands and began to rub her lower back firmly.

"For a little bit you could get a permanent job doing that."

Ryan's hands faltered a second, then started moving again. Had she said the wrong thing?

"Well, I've done all I can to make you comfortable."

"It was wonderful. Feel free to stop by and do that anytime. If I got a foot massage and body rub on the same day, I might melt away."

"I wouldn't want you to do that. I like knowing you're around." Ryan moved out from behind her. "As much as I would enjoy staying in bed with you all day, I promised to cover for Sophia this afternoon and tomorrow until the new midwife takes over on Monday."

She hated to see this time with Ryan end.

"Mind if I get a quick shower?" he asked.

"Of course not," she said, pulling her gown back into place.

"Why don't you stay in bed, take it easy today?" Ryan suggested, as he picked up his clothes off the floor.

"Are you afraid you were too rough on me last night?"

His grin was devilish. "Are you kidding? It was more like you being rough on me. I had no idea a pregnant woman could be so aggressive."

She threw a pillow at him. "I'll show you aggressive."

Ryan's deep laughter filled the room even after he'd closed the bathroom door behind him.

Phoebe was in the kitchen when he came in to say goodbye. His shirtsleeves were rolled halfway up his forearms. He had his jacket over his arm and his tie in his hand. A couple of damp locks of hair fell over his forehead. She had never seen anyone look more desirable.

She resisted the urge to grab his hand and beg him not to

leave. When he went out the door she was afraid that fragile fairy-tale bubble they had been living in since yesterday afternoon would burst. Could she ever get it back again?

Phoebe stood with her back to the counter. "I'll be in town on Thursday for my next checkup."

"I'll see you then if not before. I have to go."

"I know. There are babies to deliver."

He grinned. "And they don't wait."

"I sure hope not. I'm ready now for this one to come." She looked at a picture on the wall instead of him, scared he might see her sadness. There had never been this type of emotion when Joshua had left and she'd known she wouldn't see him for months. She had it bad for Ryan.

Phoebe walked with him out to the veranda. At the steps he wrapped her in his arms and pulled her tightly against him, giving her a kiss. Letting her go, he hurried down the steps.

"A little overdressed for a Saturday morning, aren't you, dear?"

Phoebe smiled as Ryan threw up a hand and continued down the path. "Good morning, Mrs. Rosenheim. Beautiful day, isn't it?"

Phoebe waved as he pulled away.

"I see you found a young man who'll be around for you." Mrs. Rosenheim's voice carried across the gardens.

Phoebe waved and called, "I hope I have."

Ryan pulled up in front of his house, turned off the engine and banged his head against the steering wheel a couple of times.

What had he done? He knew the answer and didn't like it one bit. He'd spent the night with his best friend's wife. Crossed the professional line and, worse, he'd started to think of Phoebe as more than a friend. She was his lover. How low could he go?

He'd even spent most of the morning playing house with her. He had nothing emotionally to offer Phoebe. She needed someone to rely on, to love her and the baby. He wasn't that guy. He didn't commit to anybody. There wasn't even a cat or a dog in his life.

He had no intention of pledging himself to a woman with a child. Or to any woman, for that matter. He wouldn't be any good at it. Worse, didn't even want to try. He wouldn't take the chance on heartache. Fun while it lasted was all he'd ever wanted. He'd had all the pain he was willing to live with. He'd see to the practical things, like getting the baby's room ready and even delivering the baby, but then he was backing out.

Some other man would take his place. Phoebe was an attractive woman. No, that wasn't strong enough. She was beautiful and smart, funny, with a quick wit, and someone far better than him would come along. He was afraid he would hurt her, but over time she would get over it. Someone would enter her life and give her what she deserved. Maybe in time she'd forgive him.

He sat up and stared out the window. His hands tightened on the wheel. Someone else would share her bed. The thought made him sick. But it was the way things should be. For her sake and the baby's.

Ryan opened the door of the car and climbed out. There was a light mist, just as there had been the evening he'd found Phoebe on his doorstep. Would he always think of her when it rained? No, he couldn't let things go any further, but he worried they had already gone too far. He'd enjoyed her body too much, liked having someone to laugh with, eat with, to look forward to seeing. He'd never had trouble keeping himself shut off but now he couldn't seem to get past his feelings for Phoebe.

He needed to get into his shop, work. Push her out of his mind. He groaned. The project he was working on was the cradle. He wasn't even safe from her in his only sanctuary. How had she invaded his life so completely in such a short time? Why had he let her? Because he'd fallen for her. Cared about her more than he had anyone since JT. How ironic was that?

Disgusted with himself, he climbed out of his car and slammed the door before heading for his front door.

Maybe when he finished the cradle and Phoebe delivered, he would be able to get her out of his mind. A nagging voice kept telling him that wasn't going to happen.

# CHAPTER NINE

PHOEBE WALKED THROUGH the archway entrance of the hospital on Thursday afternoon on her way to her appointment. Her soft-soled shoes made squeaking sounds as she crossed the tiles on the floor of the lobby. At the lift, she pushed the button for the sixth floor. She could hardly contain her excitement over seeing Ryan.

Despite their plans, she'd not seen him since he'd left her house on Saturday morning. She'd only heard from him once. That had been a quick phone call to say that he couldn't make it to dinner. It was a full moon and he'd been busy. He needed to remain near the hospital.

She understood. When it was her turn to deliver she would want to know he was close. He had asked how she was doing but otherwise the call had been short and to the point. Still, she had to remember that he worked odd hours and had no control over when those would be.

The doors to the lift whooshed open and she entered. Would he kiss her? Probably not. That would be very unprofessional during an antenatal visit. Maybe he would take her out to eat or, better yet, home. She had missed his touch but more than that she missed talking and laughing with him.

She was acting like a silly schoolgirl with her first crush. Here she was almost a mother and giddy over a man.

The lift doors opened again and Phoebe stepped out and walked toward the clinic. Inside, she signed in at the window. She took a chair and looked at the pictures of the medical staff lining the wall. They included Ryan. He looked handsome but far too serious in his picture. Nothing like the man with the good sense of humor that she knew. Besides him there were a number of people she'd met or recognized from the wedding.

"Phoebe."

It was Ryan's voice. She would have known it anywhere. Every night she heard it in her dreams. Her head jerked up and their gazes met. There was a flicker of delight in his before it turned guarded. Wasn't he glad to see her?

Phoebe smiled. "Hi."

He cleared his throat and said, "Hello. Are you ready to come back?"

She moved to stand. It took her a second more than she would have liked but Ryan hadn't moved from his position at the door. A few days ago he would have hurried to offer her help. "Yes, I'm ready."

"Come this way."

What was going on? Maybe he didn't want anyone to see him touch her or overhear them. Still, this was a little much. She'd always spoken in a friendly manner to Sophia. That was part of the appeal of having a midwife— it was more like having a friend there to help deliver her.

"Follow me," he said, and led her down the hallway to an exam room. Once she'd entered he closed the door.

She sat on the exam table.

"So how have you been?" Ryan asked, as if speaking to someone he'd just met.

Phoebe gave him a questioning look. Ryan couldn't see it because his focus was on the computer. Other than those few seconds when their eyes had met after he'd called her name he hadn't looked at her again.

"Any pains?"

Just in her heart all of a sudden. "No."

"Well, it won't be long now."

Why was he talking to her like that? As if he didn't really know her? Was he afraid someone might walk in on them? "No, it won't. Next week is my due date."

He finally looked up but his focus was over her right shoulder. "You know that the chance of a baby coming on a due date is slim. A first baby is almost always late."

"I know." This all business attitude was getting old. "How are you, Ryan? I've missed you this week."

He went back to studying the computer screen. "I've been busy. Sophia being out makes things a little complicated."

Apparently their relationship was included in that.

"Any chance we could get something to eat this evening?"

"I have a mother in labor on her way in. I'm going to the unit as soon as I'm finished here."

Phoebe had never received the brush-off before but she recognized it when she heard it. *I won't cry, I won't cry.* She clenched her teeth.

Ryan was acting as if they'd never been intimate. But they were at the clinic and he should act professionally. But he was overdoing it.

He left without giving her another look.

What had happened between now and Saturday morning that had made him so distant? He was acting like the guy she'd met that first night. When he returned she was going to find out what was going on.

She was prepared and waiting on the table when he returned. He wasn't by himself. A woman in her midtwenties followed him into the room.

"Phoebe, this is Stacy. She's the new midwife who has joined our group. Would you be willing to let her do the exam?"

She looked at him in disbelief. He wouldn't meet her gaze. Now he didn't even want to touch her.

"All right." Phoebe drew the words out.

Stacy stepped to the table. "Phoebe, may I check the position of the baby? I promise I have gentle hands."

Phoebe said nothing. She knew gentle hands and those belonged to Ryan.

As Stacy's hand moved over her expanded middle, she rattled off some numbers while Ryan typed on the computer.

"Well, you're doing fine. Everything is as it should be. I don't see why you won't have an uneventful delivery," Stacy gushed. "I look forward to being there."

*"What?"* Phoebe looked at Ryan. Nothing was as it should be.

He looked over her head as he spoke. "Stacy is going to step in for me. My, uh, caseload is heavy and she's taking some of my patients."

Stacy was all smiles when she said, "I'll see you here next week for your appointment or at the delivery, whichever comes first. Do you have any questions for us?"

*Yes, she had a pile of questions but none that she could ask in front of Stacy.*

"No" came out sounding weak.

"Okay, then. I'll see you next week," Stacy said, without seeming to notice the tension between her and Ryan.

He opened the door and left without even looking at her. Stacy followed.

Phoebe sat in silence. Stunned. Never had she felt so

used. She'd shared her body with Ryan. Opened her heart. Believed that she meant something to him. Now he was treating her like she was nothing. What a jerk. He didn't even have the backbone to tell her that he no longer wanted to help deliver the baby.

She climbed off the table and dressed. Had she ever felt more humiliated? Discarded?

Ryan was there four hours later when a new life entered the world. This time he missed the amazement he usually felt. All he could think about was Phoebe's large sad eyes when he'd left the exam room. What must she think of him? Probably the same as he was thinking of himself.

He had called to check on her a few days earlier, using all his self-control to wait as long as he had before he'd picked up the phone. Justifying the call, he'd told himself he was after all her midwife. But that hadn't been the real reason he'd done it. He'd been desperate to hear her voice. He'd done some difficult things in his life but acting as if he didn't care about Phoebe in front of her had been the hardest. It had been even more challenging not to touch her. She'd looked so dejected when he'd walked out of the room. The devil of it all was that he cared about Phoebe more than anyone else in the world.

The irony was that he had treated her the way he had because he couldn't deal with the depth of his feelings for her and his inability to handle the mountain of guilt for how he had treated someone who had been important to JT. He was so messed up he had no business being involved with anyone. Until Phoebe, he had managed to keep everyone at bay, but she had slipped past his defenses.

The dark of the night mirrored his emotions as he drove home hours later. For once in his life he wished someone was there to come home to. He let himself into his house and dropped his clothes on the floor. That was a habit that he and Phoebe shared. They both dropped things as soon as they came in the door. He his clothes and she her shoes.

Going to his bedroom, he flipped on the light. When he looked at his bed all he could see was the way Phoebe had lovingly admired his work. He'd never shared his workshop with anyone before. Even the few times female company had stayed over he'd never taken them down there. It had taken one sunny day of driving Phoebe around to garage sales to open it to her.

How quickly she had found a way into his home, his shop and his heart. But none of that mattered. He would never be able to be there for her as she needed. She deserved someone who could open his heart completely. Hold nothing back. Be there for her for the long haul. He wouldn't invest in people that way after he had he'd lost so many of them. He couldn't take the chance of going there again. It was better to let her go now.

Ryan turned off the light, removed his clothes but didn't bother to pull the covers back before he lay on the bed. He squeezed his eyes shut and put his arm over his eyes. All he could see was the confusion, then disappointment and pain in Phoebe's eyes.

Had he ever been happier than he had been in the last few weeks? When had he last thought about even being happy? It certainly hadn't been for a long time. He could remember that emotion. A few times when he'd been a kid. But he'd recognized happiness when Phoebe had kissed him on the cheek. Or when they had watched the little penguins waddle out of the water to take care of their chicks, or the look on Phoebe's face when she'd looked down at him as they'd become one. Because of her he'd known true happiness.

He hadn't realized how he'd shut out the world until she

had shown up on his doorstep, leaving him no choice but to rejoin it again. He'd carried the pain of war, the agony of trying to help men and women whose lives would never be the same, bottled up until Phoebe had started asking questions. He'd talked more about his time in the war in the last few weeks than he'd done in the last ten years. The more he'd told her the easier it had become to talk about those times. Now it felt like a weight had been lifted off his chest. After he'd returned from a difficult mission, he'd been required to talk to the shrink. He'd never thought it useful. Thanks to Phoebe, he was starting to see a value in not holding those memories in.

All this didn't matter anyway. He'd hurt Phoebe so badly today that even if he tried to have a relationship with her she would close the door in his face. No, it was better this way.


Phoebe leaned her head against the glass window of the tram. The clack of the cars made a rhythm that would have lulled her to sleep if her emotions hadn't been jumping like balls in a pinball machine. She fluctuated between disbelief and anger.

How had she let Ryan matter so much? Worse, how had she been misled by him?

He had made her believe he cared. It hadn't only been his lovemaking but the way he'd thought of little things to help her. Painting the baby's room, going with her to garage sales, massaging her feet. Her back. In just a few weeks he had done more for her and with her than Joshua had done during their entire marriage.

So what had happened to make Ryan do such an about-face?

Had she pushed too hard? Assumed things she shouldn't?

Had making plans for them to eat together, see each other scared him off?

When she heard her stop called she prepared to get off. She still had a few blocks to walk before she made it home. She was tired. Didn't even plan to eat anything before going to bed. If Ryan knew he would scold her. Maybe not, after what she'd experienced today.

Slipping her key into the lock a few minutes later, she opened the door. She entered and turned on the light. How different this homecoming had been from the one she had imagined. She'd hoped that Ryan would bring her home and stay the night. That bubble had been completely popped.

Phoebe kicked her shoes off. She chuckled dryly. The action made her think of Ryan dropping his clothes inside his door. Making her way to her bedroom, she turned on her bedside lamp, then undressed. She slid between the sheets and leaned over to turn the light off. The picture of her and Joshua caught her attention.

Had the fact that she was carrying Joshua's baby been the reason Ryan had suddenly slammed the door between them? Was the baby too much of a reminder that she would always be tied to Joshua? Or was it that they represented the painful loss of Joshua? Or the other men that Ryan had seen die. In some way they must be part of the past he worked so hard to shut out or forget.

Sliding the drawer out of the bedside table, Phoebe pulled out the crumpled letter Joshua had sent her. Opening it, she smoothed it out on the bed before reading it. Had Joshua known he wasn't coming home when he had written it? Had he known he was leaving on a dangerous patrol like Ryan had described? Even after they had discussed separating, had he wanted her to be happy, to find someone else? Had he thought Ryan might be that person?

Whatever it was, she'd done as Joshua had said and gone to Ryan. Joshua had been right. There she'd found the piece of her life that had been missing all these years. Moisture filled her eyes. But Ryan didn't want her. Once again she was on her own. Would she ever find a real partner in life?

Turning off the light, she curled around her baby. At least this little one would be someone to love who would return it.

Sunday afternoon there was a knock at the door.

Her heart leaped. Was it Ryan?

Phoebe answered it to find Mrs. Rosenheim waiting on the veranda. Phoebe's spirits dropped like a person falling off a bridge. Had she really expected it to be Ryan?

"Hello, dear. I was just checking on you. I've not seen you all weekend. Didn't want you to have that baby and me not know about it."

"I'm right here. No baby yet." She didn't want any company. How could she get rid of her neighbor gracefully?

"From the sound and look of you, something else is going on." Mrs. Rosenheim brushed past Phoebe into the living room.

Phoebe really didn't feel up to dealing with the older woman. She wanted to wallow in her misery alone.

"I haven't seen that nice young man around."

That was all it took for Phoebe to burst into tears.

"My goodness, it's all that bad?" Mrs. Rosenheim patted her on the arm. "Why don't you fix us some tea and tell me all about it?"

Phoebe swiped at her cheek, then nodded. Maybe it would be good to tell someone about what had happened.

As she put the kettle on and prepared the cups, Phoebe told Mrs. Rosenheim about how she'd met Ryan.

"Well, at least that absent husband of yours did one thing to show he cared," Mrs. Rosenheim murmured.

"Joshua cared—"

Mrs. Rosenheim waved her hand. "Let's not argue about that. So, what put you in this tizzy about Ryan?"

Phoebe placed a teacup in front of Mrs. Rosenheim and one in front of the chair across from her. She wouldn't sit in Ryan's chair. How quickly he had become a central part of her life.

Phoebe told her about how Ryan had acted during her clinic visit. During the entire explanation Mrs. Rosenheim sipped her tea and nodded.

"Sounds scared to me. So what do you plan to do?"

"Do? What can I do?"

"Yes, do. You're getting ready to have a baby. Do you want to bring a baby into the world feeling that kind of discord? Go and make Ryan explain himself. Tell him how you feel."

Phoebe sighed. "You're right. I need to talk him. Get the air cleared. I was so shocked and hurt by his actions that I've not been able to think."

"Then I suggest that you make yourself presentable and give that man a piece of your mind."

Ryan already had her heart, he might as well get part of her mind. If things stayed the way they were, she would lose him. To move on she needed answers, and those could only come from Ryan.

Phoebe bowed her head against the wind that was picking up as she walked along Ryan's street. Like the first time she had visited him, she had practiced what she was going to say on the tram ride there. She was going to demand answers. More than that, she was going to get answers.

Would Ryan be home? She'd thought of calling first but had been afraid that he would make some excuse as to why she couldn't see him. She would have none of that.

She had accepted Joshua's decisions. Knowing what he did was important hadn't disguised the fact he'd been more interested in fighting wars than being with her. She wouldn't let Ryan put her to the side. She'd stay at his place until she knew what was going on.

Phoebe walked past Ryan's car. He was home. She climbed the steps to his door and groaned. Her back was killing her. The baby had grown so large.

She hesitated. Would Ryan answer if he realized it was her? It didn't matter. She was staying until she found out what his problem was, even if she had to sleep on his veranda all night. That wouldn't happen. No matter how hard Ryan was trying to push her out of his life, he was too kind and tenderhearted to leave her out in the elements.

To come all this way and not knock was ridiculous. She was no longer the woman she'd been when she'd shown up on his doorstep last month. With or without him, she would have this baby and the two of them would make it. It would be wonderful to have Ryan in their lives, but if not, she and the baby would still survive. That much she did know.

Lifting her hand, she boldly knocked on the door. Seconds went by with no answer. There was no sound from inside. Again she knocked. Nothing. Maybe Ryan was in the basement and couldn't hear her. She turned to descend the steps and search for a way around back when the door opened.

Ryan looked as if he hadn't slept in days. There were dark circles under his eyes. His hair stood on end. He was still wearing his hospital uniform and it was rumpled, as if he'd been too distracted to change. Her heart went out to him for a second and then she reminded herself of why she was there. Life hadn't been kind to her since last Thursday, either.

# CHAPTER TEN

*PHOEBE.*

Ryan's heart skidded to a halt then picked up the pace double-time. What was she doing here?

How like her to show up unannounced on his doorstep. Was that how they had started out?

She looked wonderful, irritated and determined all at the same time. He had missed her. There had never been another time in his life when he'd longed for someone like he had for Phoebe.

"What're are you doing here?"

"We need to talk." She stepped forward, leaving him no choice but to move and let her in.

"Talk?"

She whirled to face him with surprising agility. "You mean after your performance the other day you don't think we need to talk?"

Ryan closed the door. He really didn't want to do this. "Performance?"

"Really, Ryan? You don't think you owe me an explanation for your behavior at the clinic?"

"I did my job."

"Job? Was it your job to take pity on the poor widow woman and go to bed with her?"

Ryan flinched. That hurt. Yes, she was hitting below the belt but he deserved it.

"What I don't understand is why I let you get away with acting like there was nothing between us. Or why I've given you so many days to explain yourself. I didn't expect a public display at the clinic but I did expect you to act as if I had some importance."

"Stacy was there—"

"That's your excuse for going AWOL on me and not hearing from you? You know, I would never have taken you for a coward."

Ryan winced. That's what he had been. If he ran, then he wouldn't have to face what he'd done and how he felt about Phoebe. He sat in his chair. Phoebe's glare bore down on him. "Look, you don't understand."

"Oh, I understand. This is all about you hiding from the world, the things you saw in Iraq and your feelings. If you don't let someone in, then you don't have to worry about them dying, like your friends did. Like Joshua.

"You live mechanically. You just go through the days. Look at this place." She swung her arm around, indicating the room. "You just exist here. No pictures, no rugs, a sofa and a chair. Your bedroom is a step better only because of your woodwork. It shows some warmth. The one place where you actually look like you're living is ironically in your shop, and it's underground. You come up and do what you have to do and then disappear again like a mole that's afraid of the light, but in your case you're afraid of feeling anything for someone. You care more about that furniture downstairs than you do people. In fact, those inanimate objects in your bedroom have received more love than you show the rest of the people in your life."

She was right. There was nothing he could say to defend himself.

"You're afraid that if you care too much you'll lose part of yourself. But you'll never be happy that way. You have to let people in. Let them see the person I see. The warm and caring person. The fun and humorous one. The person who gives despite any pain to himself."

Ryan raised a hand with his index finger up. "Hey, don't be putting me on a pedestal. I'm not one of your fairy-tale knights on a white horse, riding in to save the day."

Phoebe looked at him. Was he right? Had she tried to make more of their relationship than there was? Had she been so desperate that she had clung to Ryan? Needed anyone to rely on? To fill the void of loneliness?

"I haven't." Her remark sounded weak even to her own ears.

"Haven't what? Become self-contained, built your own perfect little world where Joshua came home as the hero, loved you and left to return again? Where you were willing to accept a small piece of his life just so you could have someone to share that perfect life? Except it wasn't all that perfect, was it? You wanted more. A family, but you couldn't or wouldn't tell him that it was time to think of you."

She cringed. Was that what she had been doing? "You're wrong."

"Really? Did you ever once ask JT to take an assignment that would bring him home for longer than three months? Did you ever ask him to choose you over the army?"

She hadn't.

"I can see you didn't. What were you afraid of? That he would leave you all together? As strong as you act on the outside, you're a marshmallow of self-doubt on the inside. You don't understand why you weren't good enough to make JT want to stay at home. You feel sorry for yourself but cover it with acting as if you can handle everything on your own. No matter how hard I might try, I could never fix those for you. That's something you have to recognize and do for yourself."

All Ryan's accusations hit home. A number of them she didn't want to face.

"Phoebe, I can't be someone that I'm not. Seeing what humans can do to each other makes you stop and think before you get involved. I cared then and what did it get me? All I wanted was out." He spoke to the floor, then looked at her.

"That's understandable. But look at you now." She lowered her voice. "You help bring life into the world. You sure picked a funny occupation to not care about anyone."

"That was part of the appeal of being a midwife. I'm only involved in a patient's life for a short time. After the baby comes I'm done."

"How sad. You know you brought warmth and joy into my world. I came to your doorstep lonely, sad and afraid. For heaven's sake, I was weeks away from having a baby and I didn't even have a room ready. I was going through the motions, just like you, until we met. It was far past time for us both to start living our lives again."

"I have lived like that. I've had friends. Joshua was a friend and look what happened to him. You say that I'm afraid but you are afraid of something, too, and that is being alone. You've lost your parents, you brother is no-where around, Joshua is gone, his parents are jerks and now you're clinging to me. People leave and die, it's a part of life."

Phoebe stepped forward. "I'm well aware of that. The question is, are you? People die. Do you think I don't understand that? He was my husband. My parents are gone. Even my brother is halfway across the world from me."

Ryan jumped up. Phoebe stepped backward. He move forward and glared at her. With his hands balled at his sides, he barked, "And I'm the man who slept with his best friend's wife."

Phoebe blinked and stumbled backwards. She quickly righted herself. That was what all of this was about? Some male idea of solidarity to his best friend. Ryan thought he'd betrayed Joshua.

He made a sound of disgust and turned away. His shoulders were tense. She wanted to reach out and touch him. Reassure him that he'd done nothing wrong. If she did, she feared he'd reject her forever. She had to reason with him, get through to him. Reaching into her pocket, she pulled out Joshua's letter. Maybe with Joshua's help she could.

"Ryan, Joshua is dead."

He jerked slightly.

"We're alive." She kept her voice low. "He doesn't stand between us. He's gone. You did nothing wrong. In fact, it was very right. Here, I think you should read this." She stepped around him and handed him the letter. "I'm going to leave you to read it."

Walking to the bedroom, she went into the bathroom. Her back was aching. Maybe the baby was just pressing against something it shouldn't. Would Joshua's letter help Ryan let go or would it only make things worse? She hoped with all her heart it made him see the truth.

Ryan opened the crumpled pages. Why had Phoebe given him something to read? He scanned the page and saw JT's name at the end. Guilt churned in his stomach. With his heart bumping against his chest wall and his hands shaking, he let his focus move to the top of the page.

*Phoebe—*

*I know I've not always written like I should. For that I'm sorry. Especially when you have been so good about it. I know now that when we married you didn't bargain on us spending so much time apart. For that I'm sorry also. When we parted a few weeks ago I knew things had changed between us. We have spent too much time living separate lives to the point where our relationship has slipped into one of friendship instead of one that we both wish it could be. I have done you an injustice. You have such a large capacity to love that it was never fair of me to deny you that.*

*I wish for you a happy life. If you ever need anything and don't know where to turn I want you to find my friend, Ryan Matthews. He will help you. We are buddies from his army days. I trust him with my life and you can with yours. He lives in Melbourne. He will take care of you. Believe in him, he won't let you down. I think you will like him. I hope you do.*

*Take care, Phoebe. Have a good life.*

*Joshua*

JT had sent Phoebe to him. As if he'd known they would needed each other. Had it been JT's way of giving his blessing to their relationship? He looked at the letter. How long had Phoebe had this? Why hadn't she said something sooner?

Ryan went into his room. Phoebe must have purposely taken her time in the bathroom because she was coming toward him. She stopped and stared at the cradle sitting in a corner. She must have missed it on her way to the bathroom because the closet door stood open, obscuring it.

It was his finest piece of work to date. He didn't know

if he would ever do better. It was as if his heart and soul had been emptied into it. It sat low to the floor with a high front and sides that wrapped around slightly. It looked like one that would be handed down in a wealthy family. It was as much like one he'd seen in a history museum back home as he could make it.

Going over to the cradle, Phoebe ran her hand along the smooth lip of one side. She pushed it and watched the slow movement back and forth.

"It's for the baby." The emotion in his voice made it come out as a croak.

She glanced at him. "It's the most beautiful thing I've ever seen."

He raised his hand with Joshua's letter in it. "This is why you came here that first night."

She nodded.

"Why didn't you tell me?"

"At first because you acted all cold and unwelcoming and I wasn't sure Joshua had been right about you."

His lips formed a tight line. "I wasn't at my best. I'm sorry. So why not later?"

She shrugged. "I started to trust you. You agreed to deliver the baby. I wanted you to and the letter didn't matter anymore. I had started to care about you. I had hoped you cared about me. Thought you did until I saw you on Thursday."

"I'm sorry I hurt you. I hated doing so but I didn't know how else to handle it. The night we made love was the most wonderful of my life but on my way home I thought of Joshua, of how I was not the best man for you. I knew we couldn't continue." He looked at the letter. "But after reading his letter, I wonder…"

"If it was Joshua's way of telling us both to move on? That we would need each other? I don't know if he thought this…" she pointed to him and then herself "…would happen, but I think he knew we could help each other. We were the two people he knew best in the world. I don't think what's between us is wrong. I think we honor him by caring about each other and living well. I love you, Ryan, and want you in my and this baby's life. By the way, you could have talked to me on Thursday, just like you are doing now."

His chest tightened. He'd rather die than not be the person Phoebe needed him to be. "I don't know if I can give what you and the baby should have."

Her look met his. "I don't think either one of us knows that for sure. Yes, there're risks but that's what love is all about. Think with your heart, not your head. I know you care." She touched her chest. "I feel it here. That was part of the reason I came." She grinned. "And because I was so mad. But everything you do proves you care. For example…" she touched the cradle "…you messed up with this. It shows your true feelings. You care. There's no doubt that you do, you're just scared of doing so.

"I've been waiting most of my life to have someone love me, really love me, want to be with me. I thought it was Joshua but I soon learned we didn't want the same things. I wanted the rocker on the veranda and watching the sunset and he wanted to always be going off somewhere. Don't get me wrong, what he was doing was important but that didn't bring me any closer to my dreams.

"I love you, Ryan. I don't want you doing anything for me out of obligation to Joshua any more. I want you to care about me for me."

Could he be a part of that? He wasn't sure. But he had been for the last six weeks. He'd never been happier. Had he found the place he belonged? The place where all the ugliness in life disappeared? When had the last time been he'd thought of the war? He'd already realized that talking to Phoebe had eased the past. Now, could he grasp what she was offering and hang on to it?

There was a silence between them. The air between them was heavy with tension.

"I guess I should be going."

She sounded defeated.

"I've said what I came to say. Found out what I needed to know." She moved past him and headed for the door.

Fear flooded him that surpassed any he'd ever felt before. Even when bullets had been flying over his head. If he let her go out the door he might lose her forever. He couldn't let that happen. His fingers wrapped around her forearm, stopping her.

Her gaze came up to meet his. There was a question there, along with hope.

"I don't want you to leave."

Her hand came up to cup his cheek. "I don't want to go."

The band around his chest popped, letting all the love he'd held back flow. He gathered her to him and brought his mouth to hers. Phoebe melted against him. Deep kisses, small sweet ones, filled his world until they broke apart.

"Can you stay the night?" Ryan looked down at her.

"Yes. My maternity leave starts tomorrow. No due babies?"

"Only this one." Ryan placed his hand on her belly. "And I intend to keep a close eye on him or her. Not let the mother out of my sight or out of my arms."

Phoebe smiled, one that reached her eyes. "That sounds perfect to me. I promise to be willing to accept life isn't about fairy tales if you're willing to believe they are a possibility."

"Agreed." Ryan kissed her again.

She broke away. "Augh." She reached behind her and rubbed her lower back.

"What's wrong?"

"My back aches."

He gave her an intense look. "When did it start?"

"On my way here."

He grinned. "You may be in labor."

"Really?" Her hands went to her belly and a dreamy look covered her face.

"We'll see what happens in the next few hours. It still might be Braxton-Hicks contractions or, in other words, false labor pains. Come with me. I have something we can do to keep your mind off them." He took her hand and led her toward the bath.

"Can we do that if I'm in labor?"

Ryan chuckled. "No, but there are plenty of other things that we can do that are almost as satisfying."

"Like a foot massage?"

"That could be arranged. But I have some new ideas in mind. Like starting with a nice warm shower."

Inside the bathroom, he reached in the tub area. Turning the water on, seconds later the shower sprayed water. Ryan turned back to her and began removing her clothes.

"I can do that."

"But I want to." He carefully worked each button out of its hole. Soon she was naked. He didn't touch her but he took his time looking.

"You're embarrassing me."

"Because I enjoy admiring you? I think you're the most amazing woman I know." With a look of regret he pulled the curtain back and offered her his hand. "Be careful. We don't need you slipping."

Phoebe took it and stepped under the steaming water. A few minutes later the curtain was pulled back and Ryan joined her. His manhood stood tall between them. He was dazzling. "Oh, I wasn't expecting you."

"I need a bath, too. Saves water to share. Turn around and let me massage your back."

Phoebe did as he instructed. He made slow circles with the pads of his thumbs pressing but not too hard.

"That feels great."

Ryan continued to ease the ache for a few more minutes before his hands moved around to make wide circular motions over her belly. He pulled her back against him. His length pressed against her butt. He didn't move but said close to her ear, "Hand me the soap."

She took it out of the holder and placed it in his hand. He stepped back and began to run the soap across her shoulders, then down her back. "Turn around."

Phoebe did. His hands traveled to her breasts. She watched the tension grow in his face. A muscle jumped in his jaw. He continued his ministrations. Her nipples grew and tingled. His hand moved on to her belly and down to do her legs. As he stood he kissed the baby.

Her breath caught and her lips quivered. She put her hands on both sides of Ryan's face and brought his mouth to hers. He returned her kiss, then set her away.

"You need to get out before the water turns cold."

"What about you?"

"I think I'll stay for a while."

Phoebe stepped out of the shower with a smile on her face. It was nice, being desired. She dried off. "Ryan, I don't have any more clothes. Do you have a large shirt I can wear?"

"You don't need any clothes. Just climb into bed. Is your back still hurting?"

"A little. It comes and goes."

A few minutes later Ryan came out of the bathroom in

all his naked glory. He was all man. Leaving the room, he returned with a fat candle and a pack of matches. He set the candle on the bedside table and lit it before he turned off the overhead light.

"Move over." He climbed in next to her. "Face me, Phoebe."

She rolled to her side and he did also. Ryan's hand started rubbing her belly and moving around to her back and forward again. He looked into her eyes.

A few minutes later he cleared his throat. "I loved the aggressive way you pushed your way in here tonight and made me see reason. JT and I could have used you on patrol with us a couple of times."

She snickered. "I actually learned that maneuver from Mrs. Rosenheim. She's been using it on me for a few years now. In fact, she did so this afternoon. She's the one who encouraged me to come and see you."

"Well, remind me to give her a kiss when I see her again."

Phoebe placed her hand on his chest. "You might not want to do that because she could expect it every time you see her."

"I think it'll be worth taking the chance." He captured her hand and held it against him.

"Ryan, I want you to know that I'm not going to push you for more than you can give or do. Ooh…" Phoebe tensed.

He looked at her closely. "Stronger?"

"A little."

"Why don't you try to get some sleep? You may need it later. I'll be right here." Ryan rolled to his back and pulled her closer. His length lay firm against her hip. Regardless of his obvious need, he made no move to do anything but care for her. She drifted off to sleep knowing she and the baby were in good hands. A sharp pain radiating around her waist woke her. The candle had burned low.

"How're you doing?"

"That pain was stronger."

Ryan set up in bed. "Then we need to start timing them. Let me know when you feel the next one."

She lifted one corner of her mouth and gave him a look. "I don't think you'll have to be told. I'm a wimp when it comes to pain. You'll hear me."

He chuckled. "I'll keep that in mind as this goes on. Do I need to call in someone else so they can lose their hearing?"

"You've already done that with Stacy."

Ryan had the good grace to look repentant. "I'm sorry about that. I'll try to make up for that by doing what I can to help make you comfortable. Do you need anything? Need more support on your back?"

"I'm fine right now but I do love to have my back rubbed."

"Then a back rub is what you'll get." He climbed out of bed.

"Where're you going?"

"I'm just going around to the other side."

"But I liked you here." She watched him walk by the end of the bed. Even in labor he turned her on.

"I appreciate the compliment but I can do a better job over here. Less distractions." His hands moved across her back.

"Like what?"

"Your beautiful face. When your pains get to twenty minutes apart we'll need to call Stacy and go to the hospital."

"Do we have to? I want you to deliver," she said in a melancholy tone.

"No, I guess we don't have to. Do you want to deliver at your house? If you do, we need to get moving."

"I'd like to have the baby here. In this beautiful bed. Just you and me."

Did he realize that if he agreed it would be a sign of commitment? He was giving her and the baby permission to enter his personal space. To share his home and bed for a significant event.

Ryan's hands stopped moving for a second then started again. "I would like that."

She smiled, then winced.

"I take it that was another pain. Try to breathe through them. It'll make it easier. Remember your lessons."

"Is this the moment that you morph into a midwife?"

"It's time. I'm going to get my bag and put on some pants. You stay put."

"You're going to put on clothes when I'm not wearing any?"

"It's a long shot that something might go wrong. If I have to call for help I don't want to get caught with my pants down, so to speak."

Phoebe laughed.

He gave her a reprimanding look. "You go on and make fun but it would be hard for me to live that one down."

She enjoyed the sight of Ryan's backside as he search a drawer. He pulled out some boxers and stepped into them. Going to the wardrobe, he came out wearing a pair of athletic shorts. He then left the room and returned with a backpack. Ryan flipped the bedside lamp on and blew out the candle.

"I liked it better the other way." Phoebe rolled toward him.

"I did, too, but I need to see." Ryan unzipped the back-pack and removed a stethoscope. He placed it on her belly, then listened to her chest and back. Finished, he put the stethoscope on the table. "Sounds good."

"I'm scared" slipped out before she knew it.

Ryan pushed her hair away from her forehead and kissed her. "There's nothing to be afraid of. I'll be right here with you all the way. This is a natural process."

"That's coming from a man who never had a baby."

"That's true, but I've been there when a lot of them have been born. I'll give you an example of how natural it is. My great-great-grandmother had twelve babies. They all lived. While she was in labor she would fix breakfast for the family and get everyone off to the fields. They were farmers in north Alabama. She would lie on the floor and have the baby, then tie the cord off with a thread from a flour sack because it was thin enough to cut the cord. She would clean herself and the baby up, then get into bed. At the end of the day when everyone came in from the field there would be a new baby to greet."

"Are you expecting me to do that?" Her voice rose.

Ryan took her hand and squeezed it. "No, I'm not. What I'm trying to say is that if my grandmother can do it by herself twelve times, then the two of us can certainly do it together once without any problem."

"I think I can do anything as long as I have you to help me."

Ryan leaned over and gave her a leisurely kiss. "I feel the same way, honey."

Another pain gripped her. She clutched Ryan's hand.

When it had passed he said, "Why don't you walk around some? It would help with the pain and get the labor moving along."

"I'm not going to walk around your place with no clothes on, in labor or not."

"Okay, let me see if I can find something comfortable

for you to wear." Ryan went to his wardrobe. The sound of
hangers being pushed across a rod came out of the space.
"This should do it."

He returned to the bed with a button-up shirt in his
hand. "Swing your feet over the side and I'll help you get
this on."

She did and he held the shirt while she slipped her arms
into it. The sleeves fell well past her hands. Ryan buttoned
it for her, then rolled the sleeves up to the middle of her
forearms.

He reached out and wiggled his fingers. "Let me help
you stand."

Phoebe took them and let him pull her to her feet.

Ryan stepped back and looked at her. "Cute. I do believe I like you wearing my shirt."

Phoebe pushed at her hair, trying to bring it to some
kind of order. "Thanks. I just hope I don't mess it up."

"Not a problem. It'll be for a good cause.

"Okay, let's do some walking. There isn't as much space
here as there is at the hospital but we'll just make do."

Ryan stayed by her side as they made a pass round the
living room through the kitchen and back to the bedroom.
"Let's do it again," he encouraged as she looked wistfully
at the bed. With each contraction Ryan checked his watch,
which he had slipped on his wrist before they'd started out
of his bedroom.

"They're getting closer."

After one particularly lengthy pain he said, "Tell me
about your shower at school."

It was his sly way of keeping her mind off what was
going on with her body. She was grateful for his efforts. "It
was wonderful. I received all kinds of cute baby things."

He touched her arm to encourage her to keep walking.
"Did you get some baby clothes, like you were hoping?"

"I did. I filled a drawer and have some hanging in the wardrobe."

"You must have had a lot of people there."

They continued the slow pace around the house.

"I was surprised. Most of the teachers came. Those who didn't sent presents by others. Everyone was very generous."

"Why were you surprised? Haven't you been working there for some time?"

"I have but they have all seemed to be a little standoff-ish since Joshua was killed. It became worse when I told them I was pregnant. It was as if they didn't know what to say or do so they did nothing."

"I'm sorry you were so alone for so long. You should have come to me sooner."

She stopped and looked at him.

He put up a hand. "I know, I know. I wasn't very ap-proachable at first. For that I'm sorry."

She smiled. "But you came around very nicely, so I'm happy." But he hadn't said anything about loving her. Even when she had confessed her love for him. She could wait. Ryan showed he cared in so many other ways. He was someone she could count on. Even if she couldn't, she had learned she could depend on herself. "Oh."

"Breathe. Don't hold your breath." Ryan showed her how.

They made small swooshing sounds together.

"I think it's time to get you settled in. I also need to check and see where that baby is."

Ryan led her toward the bedroom.

"How much longer?" As she went by the footboard, she let her fingers trail over the surface of the wood.

"Let me examine you, then I'll have an idea."

She sat on the edge of the bed while he prepared it.

"You're not going to make me lie on the floor like your great-great-grandmother did?"

"I hadn't planned to, but I can." He shook out a blanket as if getting ready to place it on the floor.

"I was kidding."

He smiled. "I'm glad to hear that. I was worried about my back hurting when I bent over to help deliver."

"What kind of midwife are you? Being more worried about your comfort than mine?"

Ryan put a hand down on the mattress on each side of her. His face was inches away from hers. "Honey, I care too much about you to let you be uncomfortable." Ryan kissed her deeply and moved away. He helped her settle into the center of the bed and then he did the exam.

"You're well on your way. Dilated five centimeters. When you get to ten you'll be ready to have a baby."

Another pain cramped her back and radiated around to her sides. She grabbed Ryan's hand. He rode it out with her, all the time whispering sweet encouragement.

Ryan had seen countless husbands in the delivery suite when their wives had been giving birth. Some handled the process with aplomb while others were just a step above worthless. Ryan knew what was going to happen and still waves the size of a tsunami rolled through his stomach because this time it was Phoebe having the baby and he was that significant other helping. He felt more like that guy who was useless.

She had taken over his life, captured his heart and made him a ball of nerves in a situation where he usually had all the confidence. Even with all his reassurances, he worried that something might not go right during the birth. If she died or the baby did, he didn't know what he would do.

He'd survived other deaths but he didn't think he could live without Phoebe.

"You look worried all of a sudden. Is something wrong?" Phoebe asked.

"No, everything is fine. You're doing wonderfully. Keep up the good work."

"I need to go to the bathroom?"

"Sure." Ryan stood and helped her up. "I'll leave the door open. If you need me I'll be right out here."

While Phoebe was in the bathroom Ryan pulled out his cellphone and called the hospital to let them know that he was in the process of delivering Phoebe's baby. He wanted them aware so that if there was a problem someone could be here to help in minutes.

"Ryan!"

"Yes?" He hurried toward the bathroom.

"My waters just broke."

"Well, this baby is getting ready to make a showing. Stay put and I'll help you get cleaned up. I'll find you something dry to wear."

He left to search for another shirt. This time he went to the chest of drawers and found a T-shirt. It might not fit over all of her middle but at least it would cover her lovely breasts so that he could concentrate on delivering the baby. He went back to Phoebe.

"You're going to run out of clothes." She pushed a button through a hole.

"If I do, I won't mind. I like you better naked anyway."

Moisture filled her eyes and she gave him a wry smile. "Thanks. You really are being wonderful."

"Not a problem." A delivery had always been a matter-of-fact event for him. A job with a happy ending most of the time. But with Phoebe it was much more. This was an event to cherish.

He helped her pull the T-shirt over her head.

"This doesn't cover much," she complained.

"I need to see your belly and you can pull the sheet up to cover yourself if you must. I don't know why you're being so modest. I've seen all of you and there isn't anything or anyone more stunning. Now, come on and get into bed. We have a baby to welcome into the world."

Another pain shot through her.

"Let's get you settled and I'm going to have another look." He help her move to the center of the bed.

"I'm feeling pressure."

"Good, then you're almost ready. Bend your legs."

Ryan placed her feet in the correct spot so he could see. He put on plastic gloves and checked her. "You're almost there."

"Here comes another one." Phoebe gritted her teeth.

"Look at me," Ryan demanded.

She did.

"Now, let's breathe together."

Phoebe followed his lead.

With the contraction over, Ryan lightly trailed his fingers over her middle until the tension left her and she lay back.

"I need to get a few things out of the bathroom and find something soft to swaddle the baby in. You should have let me know you were planning this tonight and I could have been better prepared."

"You're a funny man, Ryan Matthews."

"I thought you could use some humor right about now." He found the things he needed and placed them at the foot of the bed within arm's length.

Another pain took Phoebe and she met his look. They went through it together. This was one time he didn't mind looking into the pain in someone's eyes.

"I feel pressure. I need to push."

"Hold on just a second."

"This baby isn't waiting for you," she growled.

Ryan examined her. "The head has crowned." He moved to the end of the bed and leaned over the foot-board. "Phoebe—" his voice was low "—I want you to look at me. On the next contraction I want you to push."

Her gaze met his between her knees. They didn't have to wait long. "Push."

Ryan reached for the baby's head and supported it. His look went to Phoebe again. "You're doing beautifully."

Another contraction hit. His gaze held hers. He wished he could hold her hand and comfort her but he couldn't be at two places at once. "Push, honey."

Ryan glanced down. The baby's shoulders slid out and the rest of the tiny human followed. He saw birth all the time but none had been more amazing.

Exhausted, Phoebe fall back on the bed.

"It's a boy," Ryan announced. He tied off the umbilical cord before cutting it and laid the baby on Phoebe's stomach.

She reached a hand up to touch the tiny head.

At the baby's squeaking sound, Ryan came around to the bedside table and reached for the suction bubble. He cleaned the air passages and mouth. Grabbing a clean towel, he wiped the newborn.

The sight before him was more beautiful than any he'd ever witnessed. His heart swelled. For once he could understand the feeling new parents had when their child was born.

"He's perfect, Phoebe." Ryan couldn't keep the reverence out of his voice.

She looked at him with a tired smile. "He is, isn't he?"

Ryan leaned down and kissed her on the forehead. "No

more perfect than you. I'm going to lay him beside you and go get a washcloth and finish washing him up. You and I still have some work to do." He took a towel from the end of the bed. Wrapping the baby in it, he placed him beside her.

Phoebe secured him with her arm.

"Don't move." Quickly he went to the bathroom and prepared a warm washcloth. Returning to Phoebe, he cleaned the baby boy, swaddled him in a sheet and placed him in the cradle.

Going to the end of the bed, Ryan said, "Okay, Phoebe, I need a couple of big pushes and we'll be done here. Then you can rest."

Half an hour later Ryan had Phoebe settled with the baby at her breast. He stood at the end of the bed and watched them. He was so full of emotion all he could do was stare. It had been an honor to be a part of such a special event. Phoebe's eyelids lifted.

They were full of love that extended to him.

"What's your middle name?"

"James."

Phoebe looked down at the baby. "Joshua James Taylor." She looked back at Ryan. "We'll call him JJ."

Ryan's eyes watered.

"Why don't you join us and get to know your namesake?"

Ryan didn't hesitate to join them on the bed. Phoebe lifted her head and he slipped an arm under her neck. JJ mewed as if he wished the two adults would stop interrupting his sleep. He soon quieted. Ryan ran his palm over JJ's silky head. Despite having delivered hundreds of babies, Ryan had never spent any time enjoying the touch and feel of a newborn. He picked up the tiny hand and JJ wrapped it around Ryan's finger. His heart was captured.

Ryan had spent so much of his life alone and now he wanted more. He would never go back to living closed off from people. His world was right here in his arms and he was going to hold on to it tight.

He looked at Phoebe. Her eyes were clear and confident. "We are yours. All you have to do is accept us."

"I love you, Phoebe. And I love JJ. I want to be a part of your lives if you will let me."

"And we love you. We are family now."

Ryan kissed her tenderly on the lips. When he lifted his mouth from hers Phoebe's eyelids had already closed. He shut his, releasing a sigh of contentment. He'd gone from being a man alone and caring nothing about the future to a man who had everything he could hope for, including a bright future. Life was worth living.

* * * * *

*Don't miss the next story in the fabulous*
MIDWIVES ON-CALL *series*
*UNLOCKING HER SURGEON'S HEART*
*by Fiona Lowe*
*Available in July 2015!*

# MILLS & BOON®
## Hardback – June 2015

## ROMANCE

| | |
|---|---|
| **The Bride Fonseca Needs** | Abby Green |
| **Sheikh's Forbidden Conquest** | Chantelle Shaw |
| **Protecting the Desert Heir** | Caitlin Crews |
| **Seduced into the Greek's World** | Dani Collins |
| **Tempted by Her Billionaire Boss** | Jennifer Hayward |
| **Married for the Prince's Convenience** | Maya Blake |
| **The Sicilian's Surprise Wife** | Tara Pammi |
| **Russian's Ruthless Demand** | Michelle Conder |
| **His Unexpected Baby Bombshell** | Soraya Lane |
| **Falling for the Bridesmaid** | Sophie Pembroke |
| **A Millionaire for Cinderella** | Barbara Wallace |
| **From Paradise...to Pregnant!** | Kandy Shepherd |
| **Midwife...to Mum!** | Sue MacKay |
| **His Best Friend's Baby** | Susan Carlisle |
| **Italian Surgeon to the Stars** | Melanie Milburne |
| **Her Greek Doctor's Proposal** | Robin Gianna |
| **New York Doc to Blushing Bride** | Janice Lynn |
| **Still Married to Her Ex!** | Lucy Clark |
| **The Sheikh's Secret Heir** | Kristi Gold |
| **Carrying A King's Child** | Katherine Garbera |

# MILLS & BOON®
## Large Print – June 2015

## ROMANCE

| | |
|---|---|
| **The Redemption of Darius Sterne** | Carole Mortimer |
| **The Sultan's Harem Bride** | Annie West |
| **Playing by the Greek's Rules** | Sarah Morgan |
| **Innocent in His Diamonds** | Maya Blake |
| **To Wear His Ring Again** | Chantelle Shaw |
| **The Man to Be Reckoned With** | Tara Pammi |
| **Claimed by the Sheikh** | Rachael Thomas |
| **Her Brooding Italian Boss** | Susan Meier |
| **The Heiress's Secret Baby** | Jessica Gilmore |
| **A Pregnancy, a Party & a Proposal** | Teresa Carpenter |
| **Best Friend to Wife and Mother?** | Caroline Anderson |

## HISTORICAL

| | |
|---|---|
| **The Lost Gentleman** | Margaret McPhee |
| **Breaking the Rake's Rules** | Bronwyn Scott |
| **Secrets Behind Locked Doors** | Laura Martin |
| **Taming His Viking Woman** | Michelle Styles |
| **The Knight's Broken Promise** | Nicole Locke |

## MEDICAL

| | |
|---|---|
| **Midwife's Christmas Proposal** | Fiona McArthur |
| **Midwife's Mistletoe Baby** | Fiona McArthur |
| **A Baby on Her Christmas List** | Louisa George |
| **A Family This Christmas** | Sue MacKay |
| **Falling for Dr December** | Susanne Hampton |
| **Snowbound with the Surgeon** | Annie Claydon |

# MILLS & BOON®
## Hardback – July 2015

## ROMANCE

| | |
|---|---|
| **The Ruthless Greek's Return** | Sharon Kendrick |
| **Bound by the Billionaire's Baby** | Cathy Williams |
| **Married for Amari's Heir** | Maisey Yates |
| **A Taste of Sin** | Maggie Cox |
| **Sicilian's Shock Proposal** | Carol Marinelli |
| **Vows Made in Secret** | Louise Fuller |
| **The Sheikh's Wedding Contract** | Andie Brock |
| **Tycoon's Delicious Debt** | Susanna Carr |
| **A Bride for the Italian Boss** | Susan Meier |
| **The Millionaire's True Worth** | Rebecca Winters |
| **The Earl's Convenient Wife** | Marion Lennox |
| **Vettori's Damsel in Distress** | Liz Fielding |
| **Unlocking Her Surgeon's Heart** | Fiona Lowe |
| **Her Playboy's Secret** | Tina Beckett |
| **The Doctor She Left Behind** | Scarlet Wilson |
| **Taming Her Navy Doc** | Amy Ruttan |
| **A Promise...to a Proposal?** | Kate Hardy |
| **Her Family for Keeps** | Molly Evans |
| **Seduced by the Spare Heir** | Andrea Laurence |
| **A Royal Amnesia Scandal** | Jules Bennett |

# MILLS & BOON®
## Large Print – July 2015

## ROMANCE

| | |
|---|---|
| The Taming of Xander Sterne | Carole Mortimer |
| In the Brazilian's Debt | Susan Stephens |
| At the Count's Bidding | Caitlin Crews |
| The Sheikh's Sinful Seduction | Dani Collins |
| The Real Romero | Cathy Williams |
| His Defiant Desert Queen | Jane Porter |
| Prince Nadir's Secret Heir | Michelle Conder |
| The Renegade Billionaire | Rebecca Winters |
| The Playboy of Rome | Jennifer Faye |
| Reunited with Her Italian Ex | Lucy Gordon |
| Her Knight in the Outback | Nikki Logan |

## HISTORICAL

| | |
|---|---|
| The Soldier's Dark Secret | Marguerite Kaye |
| Reunited with the Major | Anne Herries |
| The Rake to Rescue Her | Julia Justiss |
| Lord Gawain's Forbidden Mistress | Carol Townend |
| A Debt Paid in Marriage | Georgie Lee |

## MEDICAL

| | |
|---|---|
| How to Find a Man in Five Dates | Tina Beckett |
| Breaking Her No-Dating Rule | Amalie Berlin |
| It Happened One Night Shift | Amy Andrews |
| Tamed by Her Army Doc's Touch | Lucy Ryder |
| A Child to Bind Them | Lucy Clark |
| The Baby That Changed Her Life | Louisa Heaton |